Lecture Notes in Computer Science 15703

Founding Editors

Gerhard Goos
Juris Hartmanis

Editorial Board Members

Elisa Bertino, *Purdue University, West Lafayette, IN, USA*
Wen Gao, *Peking University, Beijing, China*
Bernhard Steffen , *TU Dortmund University, Dortmund, Germany*
Moti Yung , *Columbia University, New York, NY, USA*

The series Lecture Notes in Computer Science (LNCS), including its subseries Lecture Notes in Artificial Intelligence (LNAI) and Lecture Notes in Bioinformatics (LNBI), has established itself as a medium for the publication of new developments in computer science and information technology research, teaching, and education.

LNCS enjoys close cooperation with the computer science R & D community, the series counts many renowned academics among its volume editors and paper authors, and collaborates with prestigious societies. Its mission is to serve this international community by providing an invaluable service, mainly focused on the publication of conference and workshop proceedings and postproceedings. LNCS commenced publication in 1973.

Samir Chatterjee · Jan vom Brocke ·
Ricardo Anderson
Editors

Local Solutions for Global Challenges

20th International Conference on Design Science Research in
Information Systems and Technology, DESRIST 2025
Montego Bay, Jamaica, June 2–4, 2025
Proceedings, Part I

Editors
Samir Chatterjee
Claremont Graduate University
Claremont, CA, USA

Jan vom Brocke
University of Münster
Münster, Germany

Ricardo Anderson
The University of the West Indies
Mona, Jamaica

ISSN 0302-9743   ISSN 1611-3349 (electronic)
Lecture Notes in Computer Science
ISBN 978-3-031-93975-4   ISBN 978-3-031-93976-1 (eBook)
https://doi.org/10.1007/978-3-031-93976-1

© The Editor(s) (if applicable) and The Author(s), under exclusive license
to Springer Nature Switzerland AG 2025
Chapter "Designing Grammar-Guided LLM Outputs for Open Data Integration – A DSR Approach to IoT Data Platforms" is licensed under the terms of the Creative Commons Attribution 4.0 International License (http://creativecommons.org/licenses/by/4.0/). For further details see license information in the chapter.

This work is subject to copyright. All rights are solely and exclusively licensed by the Publisher, whether the whole or part of the material is concerned, specifically the rights of translation, reprinting, reuse of illustrations, recitation, broadcasting, reproduction on microfilms or in any other physical way, and transmission or information storage and retrieval, electronic adaptation, computer software, or by similar or dissimilar methodology now known or hereafter developed.
The use of general descriptive names, registered names, trademarks, service marks, etc. in this publication does not imply, even in the absence of a specific statement, that such names are exempt from the relevant protective laws and regulations and therefore free for general use.
The publisher, the authors and the editors are safe to assume that the advice and information in this book are believed to be true and accurate at the date of publication. Neither the publisher nor the authors or the editors give a warranty, expressed or implied, with respect to the material contained herein or for any errors or omissions that may have been made. The publisher remains neutral with regard to jurisdictional claims in published maps and institutional affiliations.

This Springer imprint is published by the registered company Springer Nature Switzerland AG
The registered company address is: Gewerbestrasse 11, 6330 Cham, Switzerland

If disposing of this product, please recycle the paper.

Preface

Design science research in Information Systems is gaining exciting momentum, and the DESRIST conference series has been at the heart of this evolution—sparking curiosity, shaping discourse, and laying a strong intellectual foundation for scholars and innovators in the field. This volume contains full papers that were presented at DESRIST 2025 – the 20th International Conference on Design Science Research in Information Systems & Technology – held from June 2–4, 2025, at Montego Bay, Jamaica.

Over the years, DESRIST has brought together researchers and practitioners engaged in all aspects of design science research. As in previous years, scholars and design practitioners from various areas, such as information systems, business and operations research, entrepreneurship, computer science, and interaction design came together to discuss the challenges and opportunities ahead. This year's conference was somewhat unique in the sense that for the first time DESRIST was held in the Caribbean, in particular at Montego Bay, Jamaica, one of the rapidly growing economies embracing AI and technology. It built on a long legacy of 19 years of successful DESRIST conferences.

This year's conference theme was "Contextual Design Science Research: Local Solutions for Global Challenges". In an increasingly interconnected world, global challenges such as climate change, public health crises, and socio-economic disparities require both broad strategies and localized interventions. This theme encouraged the exploration of how grassroots efforts, regional innovations, and community-based approaches can contribute to solving worldwide problems. That way we encouraged authors to report on grassroots journeys of design science research towards greater societal value contribution.

The conference was organized around several main themes and tracks: Emerging DSR Methods and Novel Applications, Data-Driven Design Science, DSR Education, Healthcare Systems, Ageing and Wellbeing, Responsible Artificial Intelligence Design, Cybersecurity Privacy and Ethics, Innovation and Entrepreneurship, and Sustainable Development and Environmental Solutions. Each track was headed by distinguished track chairs who managed the review of papers that were submitted in their respective tracks. In total, we received 111 submissions (102 papers, and 9 prototypes). Each research paper was reviewed double-blind by a minimum of two referees. This Springer volume contains 38 research papers with an acceptance rate of 37%. About 23 papers were assigned as posters that were presented to attendees.

We would like to thank all the authors who submitted papers to the DESRIST 2025 conference. We hope the readers will find the papers as interesting and informative as we did. We would like to thank all the track chairs, program committee members, and reviewers for their invaluable service. We would also like to thank the other members of the Organizing Committee, as well as volunteers, whose dedication and effort helped bring about a successful DESRIST 2025 conference. Our special thanks go to Alton Bodley for managing the submission system and for his tireless service as a web master. We would also like to thank Gunjan Mansingh and Lila Rao at The University of the West

Indies and all the sponsors for their support. Our deepest gratitude to Gregor Kipping of the University of Münster for handling the Springer Proceedings. Special thanks to Charlette Donalds and Ricardo Anderson for working out all the local arrangements details at the Ocean Coral Spring Resort in Montego Bay. We believe the papers in these proceedings provide many interesting and valuable insights into theory and practice of DSR. They open up new and exciting possibilities for future research in the discipline.

June 2025

Samir Chatterjee
Jan vom Brocke
Ricardo Anderson

Organization

Conference Chairs

Gunjan Mansingh — University of the West Indies, Jamaica
Lila Rao — University of the West Indies, Jamaica

Program Chairs

Samir Chatterjee — Claremont Graduate University, USA
Jan vom Brocke — University of Münster, Germany
Ricardo Anderson — University of the West Indies, Jamaica

Doctoral Consortium Chairs

Kaushik Dutta — University of South Florida, USA
Srikar Velichety — University of Memphis, USA
Amir Haj-Bolouri — University West, Sweden

Prototype Chairs

Chinazunwa Uwaoma — Claremont Graduate University, USA
Clinton Daniel — University of South Florida, USA

Industry Workshop Chairs

Brian Donnellan — Maynooth University, Ireland
Maurice McNaughton — University of the West Indies, Jamaica

Local Arrangements Chair

Charlette Donalds — University of the West Indies, Jamaica

Website/Submissions Chair

Alton Bodley — University of the West Indies, Jamaica

Springer Proceedings Chair

Gregor Kipping — University of Münster, Germany

Publicity/Marketing Chair

Sanjoy Moulik — University of California, Riverside, USA

General Chairs

Munir Mandviwalla — Temple University, USA
Alan Hevner — University of South Florida, USA
Jeffrey Parsons — Memorial University of Newfoundland, Canada

Track Chairs

Emerging DSR Methods and Novel DSR Applications

Leona Chandra Kruse — University of Agder, Norway
Robert Winter — University of St. Gallen, Switzerland
Sofie Wass — University of Agder, Norway

Data-Driven Design Science

Debra VanderMeer — Florida International University, USA
Wallace Chipdza — Claremont Graduate University, USA

DSR Education

Asif Gill	University of Technology Sydney, Australia
Mahdi Fahmideh	University of Southern Queensland, Australia
Sandeep Purao	Bentley University, USA

Healthcare Systems, Ageing and Wellbeing

Monica C. Trembley	William & Mary, USA
Heiko Gewald	Neu-Ulm University of Applied Sciences, Germany

Responsible Artificial Intelligence Design

Arin Brahma	Loyola Marymount University, USA
Benjamin van Giffen	University of Liechtenstein, Liechtenstein

Cybersecurity, Privacy and Ethics

Curtis Busby-Earle	University of the West Indies, Jamaica
Jonna Järveläinen	University of Jyväskylä, Finland

Innovation and Entrepreneurship

Christoph Seckler	ESCP Business School, Germany
Hannes Rothe	University of Duisburg-Essen, Germany

Sustainable Development and Environmental Solutions

Roya Gholami	University of Illinois Springfield, USA
Kenan Degirmenci	Queensland University of Technology, Australia

Reviewers

Lavlin Agrawal
Sultana Lubna Alam
Abdullah Albizri
Ahmad Aljanaideh
Abdullateef Almuhrij
Bo Andersson
Giovanni Apruzzese
Arnold F. Arz von Straussenburg
Aycan Aslan
Erkko Autio
Madhushi Bandara
Anol Bhattacherjee
Ivo Blohm
Timo Phillip Böttcher
Michael Breitner
Philipp Brune
Lorenzo Matthias Burcheri
Hanna Buyssens
Claudia Caceres
Karina Cagarman
Marcel Cahenzli
Vanessa Casillas
Arturo Castellanos
Alfred Castillo
Curtis Charles
Friedrich Chasin
Alexander Chung
Katja Crusius
Christian Daase
Jishnu Das
Kenan Degirmenci
Maria Diaz
Barbara Dinter
Polina Durneva
Edona Elshan
Nafis Erfan
Ali Eshraghi
Erwin Fielt
Mark Frydenberg
Michael Gau
Leonhard Gebhardt
Arman Ghafoori
Mona Ghazi

Anna-Lena Glatzel
Wayne Goodridge
Maximilian Greiner
Maike Greve
Samrat Gupta
Tobias Hackl
Amir Haj-Bolouri
Maximilian Haug
Laura Hefer
Andreas Hein
Pascal Henninger
Savindu Herath
Paniz Herrera
Alan Hevner
Özgün Imre
Florence Jacob
Jenny Jakobs
Christian Janiesch
Andreas Janson
Asli Kalayci
Varun Karamshetty
Jesse Katende
Tobias Kautz
Christina Keller
Koffka Khan
Bijan Khosrawi-Rad
Gregor Kipping
Maria Assumpta Komugabe
Björn Konopka
Marc-Fabian Körner
Whitney Kotlewski
Marek Kowalkiewicz
Marc Emmanuel Kratz
Aneesh Krishna
Jayan Chirayath Kurian
Erdelina Kurti
Joakim Laine
Ulrike Lechner
Mahei Manhai Li
Hongxiu Li
Yafang Li
Benedict Lösser
Roman Lukyanenko

Johan Magnusson
Bettina Maisch
Munir Mandviwalla
Osama Mansour
Anna Margolis
Rahel Sophie Martjan
René Mauer
Stephen McCarthy
Tahereh Miari
Patrick Mikalef
Sean Miller
Tala Mirzaei
Anik Mukherjee
Pavankumar Mulgund
Matthew Mullarkey
Nicole Namyslo
Sonali Narbariya
The Hong Hanh Nguyen
Andreas Nilsson
Rohit Nishant
Shawn Ogunseye
Anselm Ohme
Harri Oinas-Kukkonen
Tero Päivärinta
Dragana Paparova
Jeffrey Parsons
Liz Paushter
Jose Pineda
Oliver Posegga
Jan Pries-Heje
Lea Püchel
Mohammed Qelhas
Minna Rantanen
Konstantin Remke
Peggy Richter
Mirka Saarela
Stefan Schmager
Simon Schmid
Melanie Schmidt
Kevin Schmitt
Sofia Schöbel
Thorsten Schoormann
Christoph Seckler

Avijit Sengupta
Ramy Shenouda
Vivek Singh
Atish Sinha
Matthias Söllner
Paolo Spagnoletti
Pauline Speckmann
Philipp Spleth
Kilian Sprenkamp
Philip Stahmann
Philipp Staudt
Veda Storey
Lisa Straub
Timo Strohmann
Simon Sturm
Tea Tavanxhiu
Say Yen Teoh
Llewellyn Thomas
Babu Veeresh Thummadi
Matthias Tuczek
Karthikeyan Umapathy
Victoria Uren
Alexander van der Staay
Joachim Vandaele
Srikar Velichety
Altus Viljoen
Ace Vo
Jörn von Lucke
Hendrik Wache
Heinz-Theo Wagner
Michael Weber
Sascha Weimar
Oliver Werth
Lauri Wessel
Manuel Wiesche
Maria A. Wimmer
Axel Winkelmann
Anna Wolters
Tobias Wuttke
Eva-Maria Zahn
Christian Zeiß
Markus Zimmer
Philipp zur Heiden

Contents – Part I

Emerging DSR Methods and Novel DSR Applications

Reframing the Problem Space: A Layered Model for Coevolving Problems
and Solutions 3
   Hanna Buyssens and Stijn Viaene

AI-Based Design Science Research: An Exploratory Framework
for Leveraging Artificial Intelligence in Design Science Research 18
   Michael Gau, Felix Kretzer, Alexander Maedche, and Jan vom Brocke

Exploring Action Design Research as a Reflective Practice
for Sense-Giving and Sense-Making of Meaning: A Phenomenological
Approach 32
   Amir Haj-Bolouri, Hanna Buyssens, and Stijn Viaene

On the Role of Vision in Design Science Research 57
   *Bijan Khosrawi-Rad, Susanne Robra-Bissantz, Timo Strohmann,
   and Jan vom Brocke*

Enacting Creativity Rigorously in Design Science Research: Towards
a Typology of Creativity Strategies 68
   Marc E. Kratz, Christoph Seckler, and Jan vom Brocke

GALEA – Leveraging Generative Agents in Artifact Evaluation 83
   Nicolas Prat, John P. Lalor, and Ahmed Abbasi

Past Lessons, Future Directions: An Author-Informed Review of Design
Science Research in Information Systems 99
   Sebastian Reiners, Gregor Kipping, Fabian Tingelhoff, and Michael Gau

The Relevance of Design Features: From Abstract Knowledge to Practical
Implementation 116
   Timo Strohmann and Bijan Khosrawi-Rad

Data-Driven Design Science

Designing Geospatial Tools to Address Maternal and Infant Health
Disparities: Analyzing Low Birth Weight Patterns 137
   *Katja Crusius, Maria Assumpta-Komugabe, Paniz Herrera,
   and Samir Chatterjee*

LLM-Augmentation for Idea Evaluation: Developing a Reference Model
for Evaluation Pipelines 151
  Philipp Gordetzki

A Design of Sensible Generative Artificial Intelligence System
to Understand User Intent 164
  Yanjing Ren, Tengteng Ma, Shivendu Shivendu, and Alan Hevner

Designing Grammar-Guided LLM Outputs for Open Data
Integration – A DSR Approach to IoT Data Platforms 178
  *Dennis M. Riehle, Arnold F. Arz von Straussenburg,
  and Timon T. Aldenhoff*

DSR Education

Artifact Validity in Design Science Research (DSR): A Comparative
Analysis of Three Influential Frameworks 199
  Sylvana Kroop

Designing Knowledge for Conversational AI Applications: A Bloom's
Taxonomy Perspective 216
  Tim Christopher Lange and Ricarda Schlimbach

Designing a Large Language Model Based Conversational Agent
for Language Acquisition 232
  *Nicolas Neis, Philipp Spleth, Cecilie Kudlek, Rüdiger Zarnekow,
  and Axel Winkelmann*

Designing Digital Infrastructures for Trans-situated Learning 248
  Jonas Sjöström and Hannes Göbel

Healthcare Systems, Ageing and Wellbeing

Towards Digital Pause: A Framework for Promoting Well-Being in Adults
Through Conscious Unplugging 265
  Tahereh Miari, Zelal Kutby, Javier Aguilar, and Samir Chatterjee

From Stress to Success: Designing a Diagnosis and Intervention Platform
for Knowledge Workers 281
  Falco Korn, Erik Karger, Frederik Ahlemann, and Alexandar Schkolski

Designing for Trust: Integrating Self-referencing in Large Language
Model-Based Health Coaching 296
  Sophia Meywirth, Andreas Janson, and Matthias Söllner

Author Index 311

Contents – Part II

Responsible Artificial Intelligence Design

Enabling Responsible LLM-Based Grading in Higher Education – Design
Guidelines and a Reproducible Data Preparation Pipeline 3
   *Arnold F. Arz von Straussenburg, Anna Wolters, Timon T. Aldenhoff,
and Dennis M. Riehle*

GenAI-CoP: A Reusable Co-creation Process for Identifying Generative
AI Agents 21
   *Philipp Reinhard, Mahei Manhai Li, Sarah Oeste-Reiß,
and Ulrich Bretschneider*

The EU AI Act: Implications for Ethical AI in Education 36
   Mirka Saarela, Sachini Gunasekara, and Ayaz Karimov

Interactive Explainable Intelligent Systems: Requirements, Design
Principles, and Prototypical Implementation 50
   Pauline Speckmann, Mario Nadj, and Christian Janiesch

Reflective Design Theorizing with User Interviews: A Case Study for AI
Energy Labels 65
   *Alexander van der Staay, Raphael Fischer, Magdalena Wischnewski,
Katharina Poitz, and Christian Janiesch*

Toward Procedural AI Governance: Designing a Phase Model for AI
Development Projects 80
   *Michael Weber, Martin Biller, Timo Phillip Böttcher, Andreas Hein,
and Helmut Krcmar*

Cybersecurity, Privacy, and Ethics

Designing a Cybersecurity Compliance Index Framework to Identify
and Evaluate Trends and Strategies that Support Organizational
Decision-Making 97
   Juanita Dawson and Chinazunwa Uwaoma

Innovation and Entrepreneurship

Sustainability in Supermodernity: Design Principles for Innovating
Non-places 115
   Leonhard Gebhardt and Konstantin Remke

Designing an Effective Augmented Reality Interaction Technique
to Develop AR Instructions 131
   Kay Hönemann, Björn Konopka, and Manuel Wiesche

Venture Design Research: Description and Illustration 146
   Andreas Nilsson, Johan Magnusson, and Tero Päivärinta

A Successful Finance-Sector Case of Digital Transformation: Eliciting
Four Design Principles 162
   Jan Pries-Heje and Ann-Dorte F. Nielsen

Structured Creativity: Enhancing Business Model Innovation
with Generative AI 178
   Christoph Scheiber, Timo Phillip Böttcher, Erwin Fielt,
   Marek Kowalkiewicz, Michael Weber, and Helmut Krcmar

Empowering SMEs Through a Co-opetition Platform: A Design Science
Research Approach to Hyperautomation and Resilience 193
   Lisa Straub, Christian Zeiß, Maximilian Greiner, Axel Winkelmann,
   and Ulrike Lechner

A Process for Corporates to Launch New Ventures Under Uncertainty:
An Echeloned DSR Approach 208
   Joachim Vandaele, Christoph Seckler, and René Mauer

Dare to Prepare: Designing a Negotiation Preparation Card Deck 223
   Eva-Maria Zahn, Ernestine Dickhaut, and Matthias Söllner

Sustainable Development and Environmental Solutions

Emergency Management: Designing Mobile Applications to Support
Citizens During Storm Floods 241
   Marten Borchers, Enrico Milutzki, Alexander Bode, Valeria Magdych,
   Martin Semmann, and Eva Bittner

Anchoring Collaboration: Design Principles for Stakeholder Management
in Ports 256
   Tim Brée, Frederik Ahlemann, Fabian Lohmar, Klaus Krumme,
   Jan-Hendrik Kamlage, Marius Rogall, and Erik Karger

Ensuring Usefulness: Socio-Technical Design Principles for Digital
Product Passports 271
   Kim Krüger, Wenxuan Li, Timo Phillip Böttcher, and Helmut Krcmar

Towards a Persuasive Decision Support Interface for the Sustainable Use
of Dynamic Electricity Tariffs 286
   *Lorenzo Matthias Burcheri, Gilbert Fridgen, Hanna Marxen,
   and Jyoti Kumari*

Author Index 297

Emerging DSR Methods and Novel DSR Applications

Reframing the Problem Space: A Layered Model for Coevolving Problems and Solutions

Hanna Buyssens[1,2](✉) and Stijn Viaene[1,2]

[1] Vlerick Business School, Ghent, Belgium
{hanna.buyssens,Stijn.viaene}@vlerick.com
[2] KU Leuven, Leuven, Belgium

Abstract. This paper advances the Design Science Research (DSR) paradigm by addressing the fundamental challenge of coevolving problems and solutions in dynamic, uncertain, and iterative environments. Although DSR frameworks excel in structured problem-solving, they lack mechanisms to conceptualize problem spaces under high uncertainty. A robust understanding of such spaces remains critical for DSR's practical relevance. This study introduces an extended conceptualization of the problem space building upon the model proposed by Maedche et al. [1]. We extend the problem conceptualization as a fluid, iterative process in which problems and solutions continuously shape each other through stakeholder-artifact interactions. By integrating theoretical concepts of effectuation and affordances, our model empowers researchers and practitioners to navigate complex, rapidly evolving problem spaces while providing a structured yet flexible approach for iterative problem and solution refinement. We demonstrate the model's practical application in a real-world DSR project, showcasing its ability to enhance problem-solving in socially and technologically intricate domains. This approach ensures that DSR remains adaptive, responsive, and effective in uncertain contexts.

Keywords: Design science research · problem space · affordances · effectuation · problem-solution coevolution

1 Introduction

Design Science Research (DSR) has steadily gained prominence for its capacity to address real-world challenges and generate knowledge through the design of innovative artifacts. Rooted in structured, means-ends processes [2, 3], it emphasizes the importance of clearly understanding the problem from the outset, ensuring that the research remains focused, purposeful, and aligned with stakeholder needs [4–6].

As DSR continues to evolve, it is increasingly applied to "wicked problems"—complex, dynamic challenges marked by shifting boundaries and the coevolution of problems and solutions [7, 8]. While iterative processes in DSR implicitly acknowledge this coevolution [3, 9], existing frameworks rarely explain how problem definitions adapt to emerging solutions or contextual insights. This makes it challenging to maintain the necessary flexibility and responsiveness required to effectively address evolving challenges [10].

Consequently, while iterative processes are integral to DSR, the interplay between the evolving problem and solution spaces often remains underexplored. For example, Maedche et al. [1] have proposed a conceptualization of the problem space that explains the key concepts and interrelationships of these concepts; however, their conceptualization, while useful, does not fully capture situations in which problems and solutions may coevolve. In DSR projects dealing with uncertainty, problems are often not merely preconditions to solutions but rather, in part, redefined through the design of artifacts and the insights gained during the design process [10]. This coevolutionary perspective highlights the need for a better understanding of the integrated and context-sensitive approach to tackling complex challenges, where problems and solutions are treated as interdependent and continuously evolving constructs.

In short, while DSR frameworks have been effective in addressing well-defined problems, there is a lack of clear guidelines on how problem definitions evolve alongside solutions in environments of uncertainty and change. As such, we pose the following research question:

How can DSR conceptualize and support the coevolution of problems and solutions in uncertain environments?

This paper proposes a dynamic conceptualization of the problem space that emphasizes iteration and creativity in situations where problems and solutions coevolve. This conceptualization offers researchers and practitioners a more flexible model to navigate uncertainty and rapidly changing environments, supporting the iterative redefinition of problems as new insights and opportunities emerge. Building on the foundational work of Maedche et al. [1], we extend their conceptual model by integrating affordance theory and effectuation. This extension broadens the focus from causation-driven and goal-oriented design to more opportunity-driven and emergent design practices, emphasizing iteration and creative problem-solving.

Effectuation, a decision-making logic rooted in entrepreneurial theory, offers a way to navigate complex and uncertain environments by focusing on what can be achieved with available resources rather than relying on pre-defined outcomes [11]. When combined with affordance theory, which examines how artifacts enable context-dependent actions [12, 13], this perspective fosters a dynamic and iterative coevolution of problem and solution space. Artifacts and their evolving affordances stimulate new insights, which in turn reshape problem understanding, creating cycles of adaptive innovation [14, 15].

Our model explicitly links iterative problem redefinition to artifact design, emphasizing how user-artifact interactions uncover latent affordances and opportunities. By framing problems and solutions as mutually constitutive, the approach provides structured guidance for navigating coevolution in complex, uncertain contexts.

The remainder of the paper is structured as follows: we begin by describing the problem space in the context of DSR, elaborating on the inherent challenges of dealing with ambiguity, uncertainty, and coevolution. We then discuss the theories informing our approach, i.e., effectuation and affordance theory, providing the foundation for our extended conceptualization. Next, we present our model, as well as a real-world application of the model. We end the paper with a discussion and concluding remarks.

2 Background

2.1 The Problem Space in DSR

DSR is a well-established methodology originating from software design [16, 17]. The method focuses on the creation and evaluation of artifacts—whether technological, organizational, or procedural—to solve real-world problems. Essentially, a DSR project aims to develop design knowledge that describes a means-ends relation between a "problem space" and a "solution space" [18]. Defining the problem space is a foundational step in DSR, as it sets the stage for the entire research process, ensuring all subsequent efforts are aligned, purposeful, and contextually relevant [1, 19].

Hevner et al. [3] highlight the critical importance of identifying and understanding organizational problems. They argue that the development of purposeful artifacts must be grounded in real-world needs, ensuring alignment between the design process and the requirements of the organizational context. This alignment, in turn, enables meaningful and impactful outcomes. Similarly, problem identification is integral to the widely adopted stage-gate model for DSR proposed by Peffers et al. [20]. Their framework outlines six key stages: (1) problem identification and motivation, (2) defining objectives for a solution, (3) designing and developing the artifact, (4) demonstrating the artifact's effectiveness, (5) evaluating the artifact, and (6) communicating the results.

Furthermore, the significance of problem identification is reinforced in the Action Design Research (ADR) methodology proposed by Sein et al. [9], a variant of DSR that emphasizes the interplay between artifacts and the organizational context. According to Sein et al. [9], defining the problem is not merely a procedural step but a process of inspiration, shaping the research agenda and offering opportunities for scholarly knowledge creation (p. 40).

From the above, it is evident that a clear and context-sensitive understanding of the problem space is a critical success factor for any DSR or ADR project. This was also argued by Maedche et al. [1], who offer a conceptual framework for structuring the problem space. The authors emphasize the importance of thoroughly analyzing and articulating the problem space to avoid addressing the "wrong problem" with the "right method." Their model is designed to ground, situate, diagnose, and resolve the problem while ensuring all aspects are comprehensively addressed. The framework centres on four interrelated concepts: stakeholders, needs, goals, and requirements (see Fig. 1). Together, these components provide a structured approach for systematically exploring the problem space and ensuring that the design process is grounded in a nuanced understanding of the problem context. A key strength of their model is the clear distinction between "goals" and "requirements," which prevents premature specification of requirements. Additionally, by explicitly incorporating stakeholders, their conceptualization ensures diverse perspectives are accounted for, minimizing the risk of pseudo-problems and enhancing the relevance and applicability of design solutions.

2.2 The Problem of the Problem

A well-defined problem is undeniably a critical element in any research project. However, in real-world contexts, defining the problem can be inherently challenging, particularly

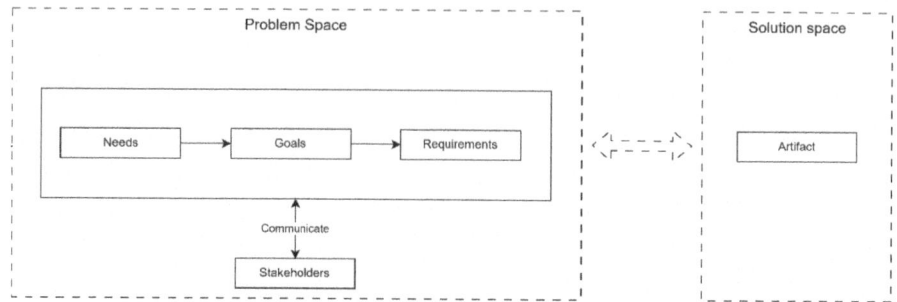

Fig. 1: Conceptualization of the problem space from Maedche et al. [1]

when the problem is engrained with significant uncertainty and conflicting stakeholder perspectives [18]. Some DSR projects are characterized by complexity, uncertainty, and ambiguity—traits often associated with "wicked problems" [21]. Wicked problems lack clear boundaries and well-defined solutions, requiring a flexible and adaptive approach to problem-solving. These problem spaces are ill-defined or difficult to deal with and oftentimes require researchers to manage the coevolving nature of the problem and the solution [10]. In such situations, researchers must embrace a flexible and adaptive approach to problem-solving, one that allows for iterative refinement and the integration of diverse perspectives [22].

Herbert Simon [23], in *"The Sciences of the Artificial"*, addressed the inherent difficulties of problem definition by conceptualizing design as a "search process." According to Simon, real-world problem-solving rarely begins with clearly defined goals. Instead, it is often driven by exploration, discovery, and iterative engagement. This perspective emphasizes that goals and problem definitions evolve as understanding deepens, with the design process focusing on uncovering opportunities and possibilities rather than pursuing pre-defined solutions (pp. 106–109).

While the search process is acknowledged in the methodologies proposed by many DSR scholars [3, 9, 20], the approaches often implicitly assume that the problem is clearly defined in an early phase. They briefly suggest that unknowns can be resolved through iteration but offer little detail on how this process unfolds. For example, Sein et al. [9] mention that *"once identified, articulated, and scoped, the problem serves as inspiration for research efforts and presents the opportunity for scholarly knowledge creation"* (p. 40). However, they do not go in-depth as to how problem articulation evolves over time or how iterative cycles influence the ongoing refinement of the problem definition.

Arguably, in many DSR projects, problem definition is an early-phase activity, with insufficient guidance on how it informs or transforms the conceptualization of the problem space throughout the design process, especially in cases where the problem and solution coevolve.

Recent scholarship has stressed the need for more iteration in problem definition. For example, Tuunanen et al. [18] have noted that DSR projects are often embedded with significant complexity (wickedness) and, therefore, require iterative approaches to problem understanding and objective formulation (p.428). They propose a methodology that divides the research process into multiple "design echelons" – distinct layers of inquiry that iteratively refine both the problem definition and the emerging solution. However, the specific mechanisms driving this iterative coevolution have not been thoroughly explored. Maedche et al. [1] also recognized the potential for problems and solutions to coevolve and incorporate this interplay into their framework through a bidirectional relationship between the problem and solution spaces (see arrow between problem and solution space in Fig. 1). However, while their model recognizes this interplay, it could be further enriched by detailing the mechanisms that facilitate this coevolution.

Building on these foundations, this work extends Maedche et al.'s [1] conceptualization to better address contexts where initial problems are not easily defined and where problems and solutions coevolve. In such situations, it is essential to establish a flexible reference scope for the problem space that can be iteratively refined throughout the project as new insights emerge.

2.3 Theoretical Foundation

To address the challenge of coevolving problems and solutions in uncertain contexts, we propose effectuation and affordance theory as complementary kernel theories for problem definition in DSR. These frameworks diverge from traditional cause-effect logic, offering dynamic, relational lenses to navigate ambiguity and iterative problem-solution dynamics.

Effectuation, introduced by Sarasvathy [11] in entrepreneurial research, challenges traditional causation-based decision-making by proposing a logic designed to thrive under uncertainty. Unlike causation, which begins with a specific goal and identifies the means to achieve it, effectuation starts with the available means and allows goals to emerge through iterative exploration. At its core, effectuation prioritizes learning, experimentation, and a pragmatic approach to control. It embraces a dynamic interplay between means and ends, shaped by the decision-makers or designers' vision and their ability to tolerate uncertainty.

While DSR methodologies traditionally rely on cause-effect thinking with well-defined goals, some scholars argue that effectuation offers a more suitable alternative for navigating uncertain and rapidly evolving problem spaces [24, 25]. Both DSR and effectuation are grounded in pragmatic philosophy, emphasizing the co-creation of knowledge and solutions, which suggests significant potential for synergy [26]. In the context of DSR, effectuation shifts the focus from solving static, pre-defined problems to dynamically co-creating solutions through iterative engagement with stakeholders.

Rather than designing artifacts for predetermined outcomes, researchers can leverage these artifacts, resources, constraints, and stakeholder inputs to discover novel possibilities, fostering creativity and resilience [22, 25]. Additionally, effectuation reframes the role of artifacts in DSR, positioning them not as static solutions to pre-defined problems but as dynamic enablers of emergent opportunities [11]. By adopting an effectual mindset, DSR researchers and practitioners can better accommodate uncertainty, foster innovation, and create artifacts that evolve alongside their contexts.

Affordance theory complements this perspective by grounding artifact-user interactions in relational dynamics. Affordance theory, introduced by Gibson [27] and later elaborated by Norman [28], emphasizes the potential actions that an object or environment enables for its users. In the context of DSR, affordances refer to the interaction possibilities that emerge when users engage with an artifact. This perspective highlights how design decisions influence user behaviors and social interactions [12, 29]. By focusing on affordances, researchers can design artifacts that meet not only existing needs but also reveal new opportunities for user engagement and innovation. For example, Pan et al. [30] employed affordance theory in the design of a wildlife management analytics system to investigate how monitoring systems shape interactions between human and non-human actors. They utilized affordance-based design (ABD) by Maier, Fadel [15] to explore the non-deterministic nature of design, emphasizing how artifacts and their outcomes evolve throughout the process.

Affordances and ABD diverge from traditional, function-driven design by emphasizing the dynamic relationship between users and artifacts. Instead of viewing artifacts as static solutions to pre-defined problems, ABD treats them as evolving enablers of action, capable of adapting to changing contexts and user behavior. Central to this perspective is the relational nature of affordances, which emerges from the interactions between a user, an artifact, and the surrounding environment. This relational view underscores that affordances are not inherent properties of an artifact but are co-constructed through the engagement and context-specific needs of the user [15, 30]. By recognizing this interplay, researchers can design systems that are better attuned to the shifting dynamics of real-world usage.

This approach aligns naturally with the iterative, experimental nature of DSR, allowing researchers to refine artifacts based on real-world feedback continuously. In this research, affordance theory complements effectual logic by emphasizing adaptability, exploration, and iterative refinement in response to uncertainty. It provides a lens to examine how features of the environment and technology shape and constrain actions, enabling researchers to better understand the dynamic interplay between user behaviors and system design, as well as providing a lens to conceptualize coevolution between problems and solutions [13].

3 Formulation of the Problem Space

In this section, we present our extension to the conceptualized model described by Maedche et al. [1], with reference to the original in Fig. 1. We first briefly elaborate on the original model before presenting the extension. The original model is grounded in four foundational concepts: needs, goals, requirements, and stakeholders. **Needs** represent the essence of the problem, encapsulating what is desired or required to address a particular situation or unlock potential opportunities. They are central to the problem space and often reflect challenges or aspirations that drive the design process. **Goals** provide direction and intent by outlining the desired outcomes or states that align with these needs, serving as a bridge between abstract aspirations and concrete design efforts. **Requirements** operationalize goals by specifying detailed, actionable criteria that the designed artifact must meet to address the identified needs effectively. These requirements ensure that the artifact remains purposeful and aligned with overarching objectives. Finally, **stakeholders** are the individuals, groups, or entities that have an interest in, influence over or are impacted by the design project. They play a critical role in contextualizing the needs, goals, and requirements, often bringing diverse and sometimes conflicting perspectives. Resolving these conflicts and integrating stakeholder input is essential for clarifying and focusing the problem space [1].

Maedche et al.'s [1] model separates "requirements" from "goals," ensuring that requirements are not prematurely specified. Additionally, they explicitly incorporate stakeholders to account for diverse perspectives, preventing the formulation of pseudo-problems.

The original conceptualization is inherently more causal and grounded in a Heideggerian understanding of *causa finalis* (the final cause or purpose of an artifact) [31]. Heidegger's concept of *causa finalis* focuses on an arifact's intrinsic purpose or end goal, which, in traditional problem-solving frameworks, would remain relatively static. The artifact is seen as being created for a specific purpose, and its design and use are framed within this pre-defined intent [32]. However, in wicked problem contexts, the end goal or purpose of an artifact may shift as new opportunities, constraints, and interactions emerge; the space, therefore, may converge within the scope (sometimes referred to as exaptive, which means repurposing existing artifacts, processes, or ideas for uses beyond their original design or intent) [33]. The *causa finalis* in our extended model is, therefore, not a fixed destination but rather an evolving point of reference and reflection that adapts in response to the emergent affordances discovered through stakeholder-artifact interactions. This more fluid interpretation of purpose is aligned with the dynamic nature of effectuation, which encourages iterative exploration and the coevolution of problems and solutions.

We build on Maedche et al.'s [1] foundation by introducing an additional layer to the model that incorporates a dynamic, means-driven perspective, which we refer to as the effectual layer. While the original model provides a structured referential scope for defining the problem space—which we refer to as the referential layer—we propose complementing it with an effectual layer that emphasizes the iterative and emergent coevolution of problems and solutions. This layer leverages the evolving solution artifact as a catalyst for discovering new affordances through stakeholder interaction. Arguably, both layers play a crucial role in the problem definition: the referential layer offers a solid foundation for initial problem scoping, ensuring clarity and direction (convergence), while the effectuation layer accounts for the fluid nature of goals and requirements, allowing them to emerge and adapt as the project progresses (divergence). This layered approach enhances the model's capacity to navigate dynamic problem spaces, fostering innovation and responsiveness in rapidly changing environments. We present the dual-layered perspective extending the conceptualization in Fig. 2 and describe the two layers as follows:

1. **Referential Layer:** Retains the original structure of stakeholders, needs, goals, and requirements, ensuring clarity and a referential scope of the project. This creates convergence in the project.
2. **Effectual Layer:** Incorporates affordances and effectuation to enable iterative exploration and adaptation, fostering the coevolution of problems and solutions and presenting more guidance. This creates divergence within the scope of the problem space.

The referential layer aligns with Maedche et al.'s [1] original model, providing a structured foundation for problem scoping. In contrast, the effectual layer introduces affordances, emergent goals (opportunities), and adaptive requirements. Here, affordances arise dynamically from interactions among users, artifacts, and contexts. The affordances are, therefore, not fixed characteristics of the artifact but are co-constructed through the dynamic interplay between the artifact's design features, the user's capabilities, and the specific environment of interaction [15, 34]. Affordances gradually emerge as stakeholders engage with the artifact, generating new perceived action potentials. These interactions explain how problems and solutions can coevolve: as new features are introduced into the artifact, stakeholders may perceive and enact new affordances, uncovering additional opportunities within the scope determined by the referential layer. By enabling iterative experimentation and fostering the discovery of novel uses and interactions, affordances support the dynamic exploration of possibilities. This process emphasizes exploration over prediction, allowing for the continuous redefinition of goals and requirements as the design process unfolds in a non-deterministic manner [13, 30]. This perspective aligns with effectuation by focusing on the iterative exploration of available means (e.g., the artifact's affordances) to uncover new opportunities and refine the problem space dynamically [11].

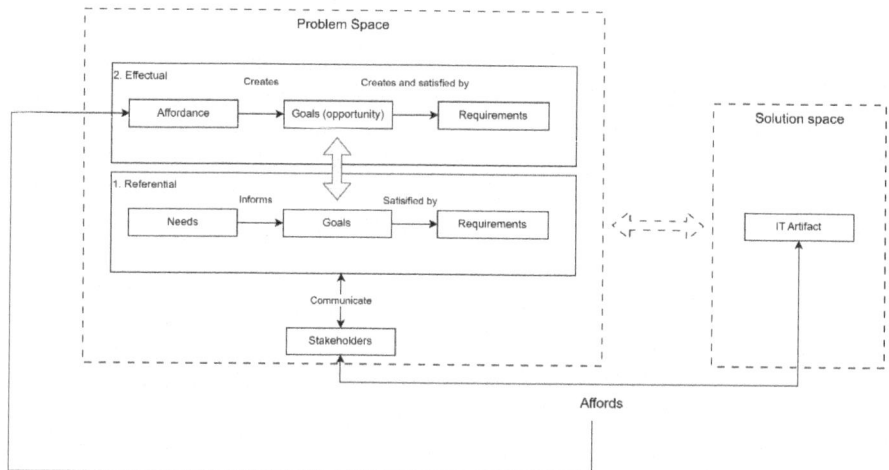

Fig. 2: Layered conceptualization of problem space adapted from Maedche et al. [1]

Goals (opportunities) in the effectual layer extend beyond the goals in the referential layer by accommodating the emergent opportunities (affordances) as the problem and solution coevolve. Unlike pre-defined goals that are tied to specific needs, these goals are iterative and responsive, arising through the affordances and interaction of stakeholders with the artifact. This perspective emphasizes that goals are adaptable as new opportunities are discovered during the design process and as artifacts are put into use [24]. These goals emerge in addition to the initial goals defined in the referential layer.

Finally, the **requirements** in the effectual layer reflect the operationalization of emergent goals but differ from their static counterparts by remaining flexible and adaptive as well. They are refined iteratively based on stakeholder feedback and the evolving problem context, ensuring alignment with both the artifact's affordances and the dynamic goals. Effectual requirements also account for behaviors and capabilities that arise from the interaction between users, artifacts, and their environment, highlighting how they cannot be fulfilled by an artifact in isolation. By focusing on emergent behaviors and iterative adaptation, the framework supports a more nuanced and flexible approach to defining and satisfying requirements, ensuring they remain responsive to both the artifact's evolving affordances and the complex realities of stakeholder engagement.

Stakeholders remain the same in both layers. However, in the effectual layer, they play an even more critical role in contextualizing the needs, goals, and requirements as the relational dynamic between stakeholders and the artifact becomes even more central. This relational element is pivotal in the emergence of affordances, as it is through the active engagement of stakeholders with the artifact that new action potentials are revealed.

We argue that in the context of wicked problems, we need both layers, as they serve as an ambidextrous guideline for exploring and exploiting [22]. The relationship between both layers is represented by the bidirectional arrow between the two and can be explained as follows: the referential layer will provide the initial scope of the project, thereby diverging the initial problem space. However, in the next step, when the initial artifact is being developed and the solution maturity grows, there may be new opportunities that emerge, which can be relevant to the problem space but were not initially identified. As such, an act of convergence may appear within the project's scope. By focusing on the affordances that are relevant to the initial problem scope, researchers can iteratively refine the artifact and uncover emergent opportunities that may not have been evident during the initial problem-scoping phase. This dual-layered approach ensures that the research process remains grounded in a well-defined starting point while also allowing for the necessary flexibility to adapt and respond as new insights arise.

4 Application of the Conceptualization

We will briefly illustrate the application of the proposed conceptualization through a previously conducted research project involving two industry partners and one research partner. Details of the project can be found in [35]. We illustrate the conceptualization in Fig. 3.

The project focused on designing a blockchain-based platform to facilitate sustainable water trade. One of the participating companies, a water provider, sought to create an exchange platform that would enable the transparent trading and donation of potable water while emphasizing sustainability. Sustainability was a central element of the project, as the company's strategic goals were aligned with Sustainable Development Goal (SDG) 6, which aims to ensure the availability and sustainable management of water and sanitation for all [36]. By adhering to this objective, the company aimed to contribute to global efforts to promote water conservation, improve access to clean water, and foster responsible water usage. The blockchain-based platform was designed

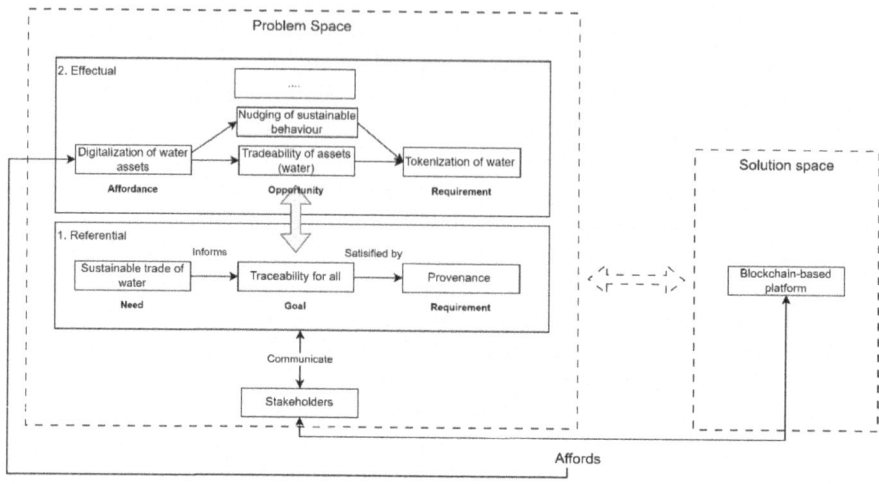

Fig. 3: Example of reconceptualized problem space

to support these objectives by enabling transparent, traceable, and ethical trade practices, ensuring that the exchange and donation of water resources occurred in a manner consistent with the principles of sustainability and social responsibility.

At the start of the project, the solution space was already somewhat defined, as the decision to use blockchain as foundational technology was made upfront. The stakeholders included a range of actors, such as the company implementing the platform, as well as customers, philanthropic organizations, and regulators, each contributing diverse perspectives on the project's objectives.

The **referential layer** represents the initial outline of the project, centered on the **need** for a water exchange that is transparent and sustainable. This need was translated into clear **goals**, one of which entailed ensuring traceability for all water transactions, building trust, and enabling sustainability. Provenance, identified as a critical **requirement**, operationalized this goal and informed the design and integration of a blockchain-based platform. By adhering to the structured approach of the static layer, the company articulated its initial aspirations and laid the groundwork for the artifact's development. The formulations in this layer were crucial as they provided a clear and referential scope for the project. The objective was to establish an exchange for trading water while ensuring traceability and sustainability, aligned with the goals of SDG 6.

As the project progressed, the complexities of addressing sustainability challenges led to the incorporation of the **effectual layer**. The effectual layer allowed for flexibility and creativity as stakeholders interacted with the technology and each other, uncovering new opportunities and refining the project's direction. One of the key emergent opportunities was the realization that blockchain's assetization mechanism could be used to represent water as a digital asset. This idea was not pre-defined at the start but emerged through iterative experimentation and stakeholder engagement. It allowed the company to create a secondary marketplace for offsetting water waste through a credit system, similar to carbon credits, while still ensuring transparency of all water transactions.

The **affordances** of blockchain technology, such as its assetization mechanism, became a central driver of innovation. These affordances were discovered as stakeholders experimented with the technology and explored its potential applications. For example, while the initial problem statement focused on the trading of physical water, the blockchain's ability to digitize water assets led to the creation of mechanisms like digital water tokens, which could incentivize sustainable water use. This affordance emerged through the use of technology and improved communication between the company and the developers.

As new affordances were discovered, **goals (opportunities)** were iteratively refined. The creation of a secondary marketplace for water offsetting became a new goal that was not initially envisioned, as well as the creation of a nudging mechanism to offset water. Moreover, the goals in the initial layer dictated that there needed to be traceability; this could also be further facilitated through this mechanism and, therefore, remained within the scope of the problem.

Additionally, these opportunities translated into new project **requirements** to support the trade of digital water assets and incentivize sustainable behaviors, ensuring that the technology could effectively support the newly discovered goals.

The application of our extended conceptualization to the blockchain-based water trade project illustrates how the integration of referential and effectual layers supports both structured problem formulation and iterative innovation. By leveraging emergent affordances like blockchain's assetization mechanism, the project adapted to new opportunities, evolving goals, and dynamic requirements, ensuring a flexible and responsive approach to the challenges at hand while remaining grounded in the referential scope of the problem.

5 Discussion

This paper contributes to the ongoing evolution of the DSR paradigm by addressing the challenges associated with dynamic, uncertain contexts and coevolving problems and solutions. While traditional DSR approaches are well-suited for tackling clearly defined, stable problems [3, 9, 20], they often lack guidance when applied to contexts where problem boundaries, stakeholder needs, and technological affordances are fluid, and problems and solutions coevolve. By proposing an extension to the conceptualization of the problem space by Maedche et al. [1], this study aims to accommodate DSR researchers and practitioners to better navigate uncertainty and align solutions with emergent stakeholder needs and affordances.

A key contribution of this work lies in the layered model—comprising both referential and effectual layers—extending the conceptualization proposed by Maedche et al. [1]. While the original model provides a structured, referential foundation for understanding the problem space through stakeholders, needs, goals, and requirements, providing a reference for the problem scope, our adaptation introduces an additional iterative dimension that explicitly accounts for coevolving problems and solutions. The referential layer provides a stable, structured starting point for scoping and defining the problem space, offering clarity and focus during the early stages of design. The effectual layer adds flexibility and adaptability, enabling iterative exploration and coevolution as new affordances, opportunities, and requirements emerge during the design process. By accommodating the emergence of affordances through stakeholder-artifact interactions and enabling iterative goal and requirement refinement [14, 15], the model aligns DSR more closely with the realities of coevolving problems and solutions.

We argue that this approach can help DSR researchers better navigate emergent opportunities by shifting focus from rigid problem definitions to the discovery of new possibilities as they arise. This iterative perspective supports the identification of unforeseen affordances, allowing researchers to explore innovative solutions that might otherwise remain unconsidered [22].

For designers, this model encourages an open mindset by emphasizing iterative learning and adaptation, aligning well with principles of divergent and convergent thinking. While this adaptive approach enables researchers to navigate complex and evolving problem spaces, it also introduces the risk of scope creep—the unintentional expansion of a project's boundaries, objectives, or deliverables [37]. Scope creep can occur when the iterative discovery of affordances and emergent opportunities leads to a continuous redefinition of goals, potentially diverting resources and diluting focus. As such, an initial convergent scope based on the initial referential layer is necessary to create a reference for the remainder of the project. While these boundaries can be somewhat fluid, they provide an anchoring, ensuring that the iterative process remains purposeful and focused on addressing the core challenges.

6 Future Research

We applied the model to a single case, and its broader validity remains to be tested through empirical application across diverse real-world contexts. To assess its utility, scalability, and adaptability, the proposed layered model requires practical implementation across various domains. Future research could further explore its applicability to DSR projects facing similar challenges in different settings. Specifically, studies could investigate the conditions under which the dynamic, effectual layer provides added value versus when traditional DSR approaches might be more effective. For instance, in well-defined, stable problem spaces, future research could examine whether the structured efficiency of traditional methodologies outweighs the complexity introduced by a coevolutionary approach. Additionally, further research could evaluate scenarios where incorporating the effectual layer leads to unnecessary iterations or resource expenditures, helping refine guidelines for selecting the most appropriate approach based on the specific characteristics of a given problem space.

A key aspect of this discussion is the evolving nature of both the problem and solution spaces. While our study, similar to Maedche et al. [1], centered on the problem space, we abstracted the solution space to a relatively static "IT artifact". In reality, this space consists of many more elements (design principles, user behavior, etc.) and is anything but static. We used affordances as interaction-driven potentials to capture how artifacts and their contexts coevolve (e.g., blockchain's tokenization feature enabling unforeseen sustainability mechanisms). Building on this foundation, future research could more explicitly model the evolution of the solution space and examine how these shifts reshape problem definitions over time. A deeper exploration of the solution space would not only refine the model's applicability but also provide clearer guidelines on when and how effectual and coevolutionary mechanisms offer the most value in different DSR contexts.

7 Conclusion

This paper builds on the existing DSR paradigm by addressing the evolving challenges associated with coevolving problem and solution spaces in uncertain contexts. While traditional DSR frameworks have been effective in addressing well-defined problems, they often have no clear guidelines on how to define the problem when it is embedded with fluidity, uncertainty, and the iterative nature of real-world design challenges, particularly in technologically and socially complex contexts. To address this gap, we extend the model proposed by Maedche et al. [1], incorporating a layered perspective that integrates referential elements with dynamic, effectuation-based processes. Central to this approach is the concept of affordances, which emphasizes the emergent possibilities enabled by interactions between artifacts, stakeholders, and environments. Our proposed model supports the coevolution of problem and solution spaces by highlighting iterative affordance discovery, adaptive goal formation, and emergent requirements, thereby enhancing DSR's capacity to tackle complex design challenges.

Acknowledgments. We would like to thank Shirley Gregor, Matti Rossi and Amir Haj-Bolouri, whose insights were invaluable in shaping this work. We would also like to thank Fujitsu Belgium for funding this research.

Disclosure of Interests. The authors have no competing interests to declare regarding this article.

References

1. Maedche, A., Gregor, S., Morana, S., Feine, J.: Conceptualization of the problem space in design science research. In: Design Science Research in Information Systems and Technology (DESRIST 2019), vol. 2019, pp. 18–31. Springer, Worcester, MA
2. Gregor, S., Jones, D.: The anatomy of a design theory. J. Assoc. Inf. Syst. **8**(5), 312–335 (2007). https://doi.org/10.17705/1jais.00129
3. Hevner, A.R., March, S.T., Park, J., Ram, S.: Design science in information systems research. MIS Q. **28**(1), 75–105 (2004). https://doi.org/10.2307/25148625
4. Van de Ven, A.H.: Engaged Scholarship: A Guide for Organizational and Social Research. Oxford University Press, Oxford (2007)
5. vom Brocke, J., Hevner, A., Maedche, A.: Introduction to design science research. In: vom Brocke, J., Hevner, A., Maedche, A. (eds.) Design Science Research: Cases, pp. 1–13. Springer (2020)
6. Vaishnavi, V.K.: Design Science Research Methods and Patterns: Innovating Information and Communication Technology. Auerbach Publications (2007)
7. Balint, P.J.: Wicked Environmental Problems: Managing Uncertainty and Conflict. Island Press (2011)
8. Buchanan, R.: Wicked problems in design thinking. Des. Issues. **8**(2), 5–21 (1992)
9. Sein, M.K., Henfridsson, O., Purao, S., Rossi, M., Lindgren, R.: Action design research. MIS Q. **35**, 37–56 (2011)

10. Strong, D.M., Tulu, B., Agu, E., Pedersen, P.C.: Search and evaluation of coevolving problem and solution spaces in a complex healthcare design science research project. IEEE Trans. Eng. Manag. **70**(3), 912–926 (2020)
11. Sarasvathy, S.D.: Causation and effectuation: toward a theoretical shift from economic inevitability to entrepreneurial contingency. Acad. Manag. Rev. **26**(2), 243–263 (2001)
12. Seidel, S., Chandra Kruse, L., Székely, N., Gau, M., Stieger, D.: Design principles for sensemaking support systems in environmental sustainability transformations. Eur. J. Inf. Syst. **27**(2), 221–247 (2018)
13. Fayard, A.-L., Weeks, J.: Affordances for practice. Inf. Organ. **24**(4), 236–249 (2014)
14. Leonardi, P.M.: When flexible routines meet flexible technologies: affordance, constraint, and the imbrication of human and material agencies. MIS Q. **147-67**, 147 (2011)
15. Maier, J.R., Fadel, G.M.: Affordance based design: a relational theory for design. Res. Eng. Des. **20**, 13–27 (2009)
16. Walls, J.G., Widmeyer, G.R., El Sawy, O.A.: Building an information system design theory for vigilant EIS. Inf. Syst. Res. **3**(1), 36–59 (1992)
17. Nunamaker, J.F., Chen, M., Purdin, T.D.: Systems development in information systems research. J. Manag. Inf. Syst. **7**(3), 89–106 (1991)
18. Tuunanen, T., Winter, R., Vom Brocke, J.: Dealing with complexity in design science research: a methodology using design echelons. MIS Q. **48**(2), 427–458 (2024)
19. Kuechler, W., Vaishnavi, V.: A framework for theory development in design science research: multiple perspectives. J. Assoc. Inf. Syst. **13**(6), 3 (2012)
20. Peffers, K., Tuunanen, T., Rothenberger, M.A., Chatterjee, S.: A design science research methodology for information systems research. J. Manag. Inf. Syst. **24**(3), 45–77 (2007)
21. Rittel, H.W., Webber, M.M.: Dilemmas in a general theory of planning. Pol. Sci. **4**(2), 155–169 (1973)
22. Hevner, A., Gregor, S.: Envisioning entrepreneurship and digital innovation through a design science research lens: a matrix approach. Inf. Manag. **59**(3), 103350 (2022)
23. Simon, H.A.: The Sciences of the Artificial, 3rd edn. MIT Press, Cambridge, MA (1996)
24. Drechsler, A., Hevner, A.: Effectuation and its implications for socio-technical design science research in information systems. In: Design Science Research in Information Systems and Technology (DESRIST 2015), pp. 77–84. DESRIST, Dublin (2015)
25. Hevner, A., Malgonde, O.: Effectual application development on digital platforms. Electron. Mark. **29**(3), 407–421 (2019)
26. Klenner, N.F., Gemser, G., Karpen, I.O.: Entrepreneurial ways of designing and designerly ways of entrepreneuring: exploring the relationship between design thinking and effectuation theory. J. Prod. Innov. Manag. **39**(1), 66–94 (2022)
27. Gibson, J.: The theory of affordances. In: Perceiving, acting and knowing: Towards an ecological psychology. Erlbaum (1977)
28. Norman, D.A.: The Psychology of Everyday Things. Basic Books (1988)
29. Krancher, O.J., Luther, P.: Software development in the cloud: exploring the affordances of platform-as-a-service. In: International Conference of Information Systems (ICIS 2015), Fort Worth, Texas (2015)
30. Pan, S.L., Li, M., Pee, L., Sandeep, M.: Sustainability design principles for a wildlife management analytics system: an action design research. Eur. J. Inf. Syst. **30**(4), 452–473 (2021)
31. Heidegger, M., Krell, D.F.: Martin Heidegger: Basic Writings, San Francisco (1993)
32. Gregor, S., Hevner, A.R.: Positioning and presenting design science research for maximum impact. MIS Q. **37**, 337–355 (2013)
33. Hevner, A., Vom Brocke, J., Maedche, A.: Roles of digital innovation in design science research. Bus. Inf. Syst. Eng. **61**, 3–8 (2019)

34. Strong, D.M., Volkoff, O., Johnson, S.A., Pelletier, L.R., Tulu, B., Bar-On, I., et al.: A theory of organization-EHR affordance actualization. J. Assoc. Inf. Syst. **15**(2), 2 (2014)
35. Buyssens, H., Viaene, S.: Design principles for a blockchain-based multi-sided platform for the sustainable trade of water: an affordance approach. J. Clean. Prod. **471**, 143212 (2024). https://doi.org/10.1016/j.jclepro.2024.143212
36. Affairs DoES (ed.): The Sustainable Development Goals: Report 2022. United Nations (2022)
37. Viaene, S.: Data scientists aren't domain experts. IT Prof. **15**(6), 12–17 (2013)

AI-Based Design Science Research: An Exploratory Framework for Leveraging Artificial Intelligence in Design Science Research

Michael Gau[1,2](✉) ⓘ, Felix Kretzer[2] ⓘ, Alexander Maedche[2] ⓘ, and Jan vom Brocke[1,3] ⓘ

[1] University of Liechtenstein, Vaduz, Liechtenstein
`michael.gau@uni.li, jan.vom.brocke@uni-muenster.de`
[2] Karlsruhe Institute of Technology (KIT), Karlsruhe, Germany
`{felix.kretzer,alexander.maedche}@kit.edu`
[3] University of Münster, Münster, Germany

Abstract. Design Science Research (DSR) has proven effective in generating knowledge on innovative solutions to real-world problems. DSR methodology has matured with DSR processes involving multiple design phases, each requiring distinct skills and resources. Previous work, however, has primarily considered humans to conduct DSR tasks. At the same time, in many areas of our modern lives, we increasingly see the use of artificial intelligence (AI) in value-adding human-AI collaborations. This research investigates the potential of AI to support and enhance DSR. Drawing from recent advancements in AI applications across various domains, we explore how AI technologies can be systematically integrated into different DSR tasks. We propose an exploratory framework that provides guidance for researchers and practitioners seeking to leverage AI in DSR. We examine the potential benefits of AI integration in each task. The research contributes to the advancement of DSR methodology by exploring AI integration in DSR, potentially increasing efficiency and effectiveness in design knowledge creation and reuse. Our findings suggest that while AI can significantly enhance DSR activities, success requires careful consideration of AI capabilities and limitations within each task. Our work addresses an important gap in current DSR literature by suggesting AI integration while maintaining the methodological rigor essential to design science research.

Keywords: Artificial Intelligence · Design Support · Research Methodology · AI-based Design · DSR

1 Introduction

Design Science Research (DSR) focuses on generating knowledge for solving real-world problems by developing and evaluating innovative solutions, including concepts, models, methods, and instantiations [28]. The DSR methodology has its roots in the field of engineering, with a particular focus on designing socio-technical systems to develop utility in specific real-world use contexts [58]. Real-world problems, or often so-called wicked problems, tend to be complex challenges, and the organization of such DSR projects is also challenging. While various contributions to the DSR methodology exist, a core element is to decompose DSR into distinct tasks focusing on different aspects and requirements of design, comprising problem analysis, objectives definition, solutions design, solution demonstration and evaluation [36, 47, 57, 61], and each phase posing specific requirements and demanding particular proficiencies [27].

The fast development of AI technologies and their application in various domains, ranging from using AI-based tools to design and craft scenes and landscapes in video games [8] to AI support to create and improve complex microchip design [23], provides new opportunities for DSR. Conducting DSR projects includes many different design activities where AI has a great potential to support design science researchers and practitioners. For instance, in the problem exploration phase, AI can help researchers identify and extract design knowledge from existing research [17, 20]. Moreover, applying such methods facilitates design knowledge reuse, fosters knowledge accumulation, and supports scientific progress [49]. AI-supported tools have proven to be effective within the phases of requirement definition and the design and development of artifacts (e.g., through automated checking of requirements fulfillment [33] optimizing based on interface-related metrics [37] or design heuristics [16]). In the evaluation phase, AI-powered tools have been utilized for software testing (e.g., as summarized in [66]) or freed researchers from performing repetitive tasks, such as coding qualitative interview results [12].

Applying AI in design processes can significantly speed up the design process and lead to remarkable design output. However, designers need to understand the capabilities and challenges of applying AI in design activities and adapt the way they do their design work [55]. For instance, researchers introduced the concept of delegation in AI-based human-computer interactions [2]. Moreover, there is a gap in providing structured guidance for design science researchers leveraging AI in design activities along the DSR process. In summary, it can be said that AI adoption in DSR is still at an early stage, and given the fast technological development, DSR needs to revisit the potential use of AI for DSR constantly. For that purpose, we intend to provide a conceptual framework to conduct such an assessment.

In this essay, we aim to investigate and explore the potential use of AI in DSR. To structure our investigation, we refer to the specific phases of a DSR process. We frame the broader discourse on how AI can be applied at each step of the DSR process and propose an exploratory framework that suggests various ways of applying AI in DSR. Furthermore, we illustrate the benefits and potential risks of leveraging AI in each process step and provide practical examples. The remainder of this paper is structured as follows. In the next section, we briefly account for the current state of research in DSR processes to establish a frame of reference. We then attend to AI-based design. Next, we integrate both fields by systematically discussing how to apply AI in each step of the DSR process. We give examples of contemporary tools, models, and algorithms, and, in the interest of dealing with fast technological development, we also abstract our findings further to get to types of AI solutions and affordances for DSR. We close with some concluding remarks.

2 Research Background

Our research is positioned at the interface of established DSR processes and tools and the rapidly developing field of AI-based design. Below, we provide a brief insight into both fields of design science research processes and tool support.

2.1 DSR Process

DSR enables the design of novel IS artifacts [28, 58] with different types of knowledge generation and contribution [24]. Researchers can use routine design to apply known solutions to known problems, use inventions to develop new solutions to new problems or follow an improvement approach to adapt mature solutions from another domain to create better solutions to known problems. In the field of IS, there exist many guidelines and reference processes that guide designers in conducting DSR projects. On the process level, for instance, Peffers et al. [47], Kuechler and Vaishnavi [36], Sein et al. [57], or Tuunanen et al. [61] provide guidance by proposing reference models describing the DSR process and its underlying activities for conducting DSR projects. On the tool level, tools such as BAUSTEIN [54], the DSR grid [7], or MyDesignProcess [6] provide support in structuring, organizing, and managing DSR projects.

Following the proposed reference processes, typical DSR projects require completing the following phases: problem analysis, objective and requirement definition, design and development, demonstration, evaluation, and communication [36, 47, 57, 61]. Additionally, each phase demands sub-activities and tasks to be conducted by design science researchers.

2.2 AI-Based Design

The vast development of AI and AI-based applications offers new possibilities for supporting design science researchers in conducting DSR projects. Especially generative AI's capabilities have increased in recent years. Its applications can be found in many different domains and design tasks. For instance, game designers use AI as co-designers, supporting them in repetitive design activities, such as crafting large landscapes in open-world games or designing realistic roads in rugged landscapes [56]. Another example of AI used in the design process is the field of microchip design. Chipmakers leverage AI to improve conceptual design, simulations, analysis, verification, and testing [23]. Generative AI, more specifically, large language models (LLM) and its applications, for instance, ChatGPT,[1] Claude.ai,[2] Gemini,[3] Copilot,[4] and many more, are advanced AI systems to understand, generate, and process human-like text. LLMs are large-scale generative models, typically powered by transformer architectures [62]. LLMs enable in-context learning, allowing the model to perform new tasks [15]. To contextualize LLMs

---

[1] https://chatgpt.com/.
[2] https://claude.ai/.
[3] https://gemini.google.com/.
[4] https://copilot.microsoft.com/.

for the use case at hand, LLMs can be fine-tuned and exhibit capabilities with zero-shot [48], few-shot, and Chain-of-Thought (CoT) prompting [31]. These capabilities have great potential to support designers in conducting DSR tasks, such as formulating requirements, generating code, or supporting in writing (see [21, 35, 44, 53]).

Franzoi et al. have presented research on applying LLMs to generate design knowledge in the space of process management [18]. They introduced using generative AI to allow for representation-agnostic process knowledge organization. They report on a DSR project with a multinational company; they developed and evaluated a digital agent to import process knowledge from various formats, e.g., text, video, and audio, and, in turn, provide process knowledge in various formats, such as text, video, or audio. Another example can be found in the chip design domain. Researchers demonstrated the potential use of AI in the design process of hardware chips as a powerful tool to create new chip designs and reduce human workload [41].

The use of AI tools in design projects can produce astonishing design outcomes, but new capabilities are required to apply these tools successfully in design processes. Designers need to be able to manage AI tools and understand the often surprising behaviors and novel usage strategies of tools as they generate design artifacts [55]. The aim of this research is to provide systemic guidance on leveraging AI in DSR processes.

3 An Exploratory Framework for AI-Based DSR

Design science research aims to generate design knowledge for solving real-world problems [28]. This knowledge is generated during various phases of the design process, and different types of knowledge can be generated in DSR projects [3]. Typically, each DSR endeavor includes a problem analysis, defines design objectives or design requirements, implements the artifact, demonstrates and evaluates, and finally communicates the findings (see [36, 47, 61].). In each phase of the design process, researchers conduct sub-activities that contribute knowledge to the specific phase. In the following, we illustrate the potential use of AI in each phase of the DSR and provide selected examples derived from the literature.

3.1 Problem Analysis

The problem analysis phase intends to explore the domain, context, and stakeholders' needs of the problem to get a profound understanding of the problem space [8]. AI offers significant potential to enhance research rigor and efficiency. AI technologies can support multiple aspects of problem exploration, particularly systematic literature analysis [65]. Especially through natural language processing, knowledge search and extraction can provide support in exploring the knowledge base [17]. Besides exploring scientific knowledge, AI may also be leveraged to perform automated reviews of existing software artifacts [22]. Additionally, AI can provide reading support, e.g., in the form of summary generation.

Another approach during the problem exploration phase is applying qualitative interviews with experts or stakeholders [46]. Interviews are time-consuming and do not scale. Chatbots can interact in a structured manner with potential users or experts on a large scale [19, 26, 50]. Analyzing and interpreting the data, sentiment analysis, theme extraction, and comprehensive problem space mapping have a high potential to support the descriptive synthesis [65]. Moreover, AI can facilitate data pattern recognition and context analysis, enabling researchers to identify and validate problems more effectively. However, most AI systems–especially deep learning systems–operate as backboxes, making it difficult for humans to interpret. It is crucial when using AI-based problem exploration that researchers need to preserve the ability to critically select, analyze, and interpret the sources [45]. Furthermore, conducting interviews with problem owners also contributes to building empathy in the problem analysis phase. Thus, we believe that the hybrid combination of human-based interviews with AI-based interviews represents a promising approach.

3.2 Objectives and Requirements Definition

In the objective and requirement definition phase, artificial intelligence offers the potential for generating explicit requirements from problem space descriptions. Generative AI techniques, particularly natural language processing, can systematically analyze complex textual descriptions of problem domains to extract and formulate structured requirements [35, 40]. Apart from providing support in generating requirements, LLMs can also leverage support in requirement quality assurance by evaluating the requirements against predefined characteristics, such as completeness, feasibility, correctness, and many more [39]. Additionally, AI-driven approaches can help researchers uncover hidden dependencies and potential conflicts that might be overlooked in traditional manual analysis [1].

The AI-generated requirements can serve as a robust foundation for subsequent design science research phases, enabling more systematic, comprehensive, and rigorous artifact development by providing a clear, scientifically derived articulation of the problem space's specific demands and constraints. By articulating requirements, the scoping of the problem space also takes place. This important and challenging task can be supported by AI, but the final decisions must remain in the hands of the designer.

3.3 Design and Development

During the design and development phase, AI has a huge potential to serve as a co-creator in design activities [59]. Although some recent work has focused on generating interfaces via image-based AI methods such as *Stable Diffusion* [68], LLMs are increasingly employed to support various design tasks. With LLMs, designers can easily search for interface examples using natural language and inspiring designs [32]. Additionally, AI can significantly enhance the prototyping process by rapidly generating multiple design variations based on specified requirements and user stories [33]. For example, AI can leverage historical user behavior data to recommend prototypes that align with established usability heuristics while maintaining consistency with brand guidelines [16]. Tools like GPT-4 can understand natural language descriptions of desired interfaces and generate corresponding wireframes [5, 11], accelerating the iterative prototyping process. Moreover, AI can convert rough sketches or mockups into working code for a graphical interface [51]. Advanced generative AI models can understand context, user requirements and constraints [9], and accessibility guidelines to create responsive and inclusive interfaces. The AI can also suggest interactive elements, animations, and micro-interactions that enhance user experience while ensuring compliance with design systems and technical constraints.

Code generation in the design and development phase of DSR has been revolutionized by AI technologies, particularly large language models. AI systems, such as GitHub Copilot,[5] Amazon Q Developer,[6] or Cursor,[7] an AI code editor, can efficiently translate high-level requirements into functional code across multiple programming languages while automatically generating necessary boilerplate code, test cases, and documentation [42]. By analyzing patterns in existing codebases, AI can suggest optimizations, identify potential bugs, and assist with code refactoring to improve maintainability and increase code understandability [44]. Although human verification remains essential to ensure the generated code meets specific project requirements and security standards, AI-powered code generation significantly accelerates the development process. It enables researchers to prototype and implement their design artifacts more rapidly compared to manual coding [53]. This capability allows DSR practitioners to focus more on innovative aspects of their research while reducing time spent on routine coding tasks.

3.4 Demonstration

The demonstration phase aims to use and apply the designed artifact to solve one or more instances of the problem. This can be done in experimentation, simulation, case study, or other appropriate proof [47]. For user interface demonstrations, AI-generated content can be used as interactive innovations to augment processes and enhance design outcomes. Virtual showcases can be used to interact with products and asses design elements before the actual release [29]. Natural language-based AI has also been used to style artifacts for users during the artifact's usage [30], offering personalization. Moreover, AI-based assistance has the capability to transform artifact descriptions into comprehensive podcasts. Tools such as NotebookML[8] learn from user-uploaded multimodal content and provide a comprehensive podcast, including virtual hosts discussing the provided material [14]. Generative AI, such as ChatGPT, also has the potential to analyze data collected in the demonstration phase. For instance, it can be applied in exploring qualitative data, having the power to disrupt the coding of data segments by generating descriptive themes [43].

3.5 Evaluation

The evaluation phase is crucial in evaluating the designed artifact and the design theory and ensuring the rigors of the research [63]. In this phase, AI offers sophisticated support for rigorous artifact assessment through advanced analytical capabilities. First, generative AI may be used to review and suggest improvements to evaluation designs. Furthermore, generative AI has great potential in simulating user data, creating realistic

---

[5] https://github.com/features/copilot
[6] https://aws.amazon.com/q/developer/
[7] https://www.cursor.com
[8] https://notebooklm.google.com/

experiments, and making specific quantitative studies feasible or safer with synthetic data [52]. For example, generative AI allows the creation of artificial users that can interact with the software artifact and, on this basis, provide evaluation data.

As another example, AI has been used to predict the perceived tappability of mobile UI components, guiding designers to improve interface understanding. Moreover, AI technologies enable comprehensive performance measurement by conducting automated usability testing and performing comparative analyses across multiple dimensions of design artifacts [4, 25]. Finally, large language models (LLMs) may support automated data analysis.

Especially in adopting LLMs in the evaluation phase of DSR projects, researchers' oversight remains critical to ensure contextual understanding and awareness of potential bias in the applied models [67]. Furthermore, a potential reproducibility risk of using LLMs as substitutes for human study participants and data analysis has recently been raised and discussed [34]. This issue becomes particularly critical if AI-based assistance inadvertently replaces authentic human input, for instance, when crowd-workers rely on AI despite clear instructions not to [64].

3.6 Communication

A critical phase of the DSR process is the communication phase. Due to the complex nature of DSR projects, it can be challenging to report the results and communicate the important aspects of DSR projects [10, 24]. The advances of LLMs have enabled many capabilities supporting researchers in the communication phase. For instance, LLMs can support summarizing, paraphrasing, rewriting in certain tones, or idea generation and inspiration tasks [21].

Another potential application of AI in the communication phase is supporting researchers by reviewing and providing feedback on paper drafts. Recent research illustrates that the feedback of LLMs, in this case OpenAI's GPT-4, is perceived as useful and beneficial, especially in the manuscript improvement process. However, there are also limitations, and LLMs struggle to provide feedback in certain aspects and often struggle to provide an in-depth critique, for example, feedback on the research method design [38].

The goal of this paper is to explore the potential use of AI along the above-described phases of a typical DSR project and open up the possible design space for designers to reuse and produce design knowledge using AI. Table 1 *provides an overview of our exploratory framework, including a summary of the potential use of AI along the discussed DSR phases and activities.*

4 Discussion and Implications

Following DSR reference processes, researchers need to conduct many different activities during the single phases of DSR projects [36, 47, 57, 61]. Managing and executing these activities can be challenging and requires different proficiencies [27]. The development of AI and its applications have rapidly increased in the past decades. The capabilities and illustration of the results of AI-based tools are promising to support design science

Table 1. Exploratory Framework: Overview of the potential use of AI along the DSR process.

DSR Activity	Potential AI Support
Problem Analysis	• Knowledge-based Search and Review • Interview Bots: Data Collection & Analysis • Reading Support Including Summary Generation
Objectives and Requirements Definition	• Generating Requirements Based on the Problem Space Description • Supporting Requirement Quality Assurance
Design & Development	• UI Prototyping • Generation of Code (Frontend and Backend)
Demonstration	• Generate Interactive Demonstrations • Systematically Collect and Analyze Demonstration Data
Evaluation	• Perform Evaluation Design Reviews and Suggest Improvements • Quantitative Evaluation with Artificial Users (Simulation) • Data Analysis Support
Communication	• Writing Support • Friendly Review Support

researchers in conducting DSR activities. They can be beneficial for the design process and increase the output performance of the designed artifact [55].

The successful integration of AI in DSR depends critically on data quality, proper alignment with existing DSR methodologies, and maintaining the balance between automated support and human interpretation. AI-based augmentation of the problem exploration phase has the potential to enhance the rigor and relevance of DSR outcomes while maintaining the essential human-centered approach that characterizes design science research. In the design and implementation phase, AI can serve as a co-designer, creating parts or event entire artifacts. LLM-based tools are capable of transferring text-based requirements into prototypical user interfaces or into functional code that can be executed [33, 59]. Leveraging such tools can speed up the prototyping or development phase and allow exploring the solution space on a large scale by testing multiple solutions.

However, there are also challenges in current AI-based tools applied in scientific research, such as hallucinations, misapplications, unreasonable expectations, interpretability, or bias issues [60]. Due to the black box characteristics of AI tools, these issues are difficult to identify. Critical reflection and thorough use of AI-generated output are needed when using such tools in scientific research [45]. Additionally, ethical issues need to be considered when applying AI in design processes that address both immediate and long-term societal impacts. As demonstrated by Dignum et al., the integration of ethical considerations must occur at the architectural level rather than as a post-development consideration [13]. Recent studies emphasize that bias in AI design systems can perpetuate societal inequalities, particularly in generative design applications [69]. To address this, designers need to be aware of the following aspects: (1) algorithmic fairness, including the detection of bias across multiple demographic dimensions through both supervised and unsupervised methods; (2) transparency mechanisms, which encompass the interpretability of results; and (3) the protection of privacy regarding the data provided to AI tools.

In this paper, we propose an exploratory framework for supporting design science researchers in leveraging AI in DSR activities along the DSR process. We explore the potential of leveraging AI-based tools and their applications to support researchers or practitioners in conducting DSR projects. This study comes along with some limitations. First, the proposed exploratory framework provides only suggestions based on existing research and practice of leveraging AI in design and lacks, therefore, the actual insights and needs of design science researchers. Future research could address this issue by conducting interviews or focus groups, collecting qualitative data, and deriving additional requirements from (experienced) design science researchers. Second, the proposed framework does not contain a complete list of AI-based tool support available in the field. We illustrate, using a limited set of AI-based tools, the potential of leveraging these tools in a selected set of DSR activities. Some DSR projects might require different DSR activities where different AI tools might provide better support. Finally, the proposed framework is not evaluated. This is ongoing research, and as a next step, we plan to evaluate the framework. We will demonstrate the proposed framework to design science researchers with different backgrounds and different levels of experience and evaluate its usefulness in conducting DSR projects. Moreover, we hope our exploratory framework for leveraging AI in DSR will advance DSR projects and their outcomes. Future research can also rely on our findings and provide practical tools by instantiating the proposed framework and implementing tangible AI-based support for researchers and practitioners.

5 Conclusion

Scholars in the DSR field and beyond are excited about the possibilities of using AI to support various research tasks. In this paper, we have explored how AI can benefit the DSR process, outlining the opportunities for leveraging AI along the DSR process. The proposed exploratory framework illustrates the potential of applying AI in the single phases and activities of DSR projects. Moreover, we demonstrate the potential challenges and pitfalls in each phase. With this paper, we hope to stimulate a discussion about the benefits and risks of applying AI in DSR and, on this basis, to drive the topic forward in the DSR community.

Disclosure of Interests. The authors have no competing interests to declare that are relevant to the content of this article.

References

1. Atas, M., Samer, R., & Felfernig, A.: Automated Identification of Type-Specific Dependencies between Requirements. Presented at the 2018 IEEE/WIC/ACM International Conference on Web Intelligence (WI) December 1 (2018). https://doi.org/10.1109/WI.2018.00-10
2. Baird, A., Maruping, L.: The next generation of research on IS use: a theoretical framework of delegation to and from agentic IS artifacts. Manag. Inf. Syst. Q. **45**(1), 315–341 (2021)
3. Baskerville, R.L., Kaul, M., Storey, V.C.: Genres of inquiry in design-science research: justification and evaluation of knowledge production. MIS Q. **39**(3), 541–564 (2015)
4. Bhatia, S., Gandhi, T., Kumar, D., Jalote, P.: Unit test generation using generative AI: a comparative performance analysis of autogeneration tools. In: Proceedings of the 1st International Workshop on Large Language Models for Code, pp. 54–61. Association for Computing Machinery, New York (2024). https://doi.org/10.1145/3643795.3648396
5. Brie, P., Burny, N., Sluÿters, A., Vanderdonckt, J.: Evaluating a large language model on searching for GUI layouts. Proc. ACM Hum.-Comput. Interact. **7** (2023). https://doi.org/10.1145/3593230
6. vom Brocke, J., et al.: Tool-Support for Design Science Research: Design Principles and Instantiation. Social Science Research Network, Rochester, NY (2017). https://doi.org/10.2139/ssrn.2972803
7. vom Brocke, J., Maedche, A.: The DSR grid: six core dimensions for effectively planning and communicating design science research projects. Electron. Mark. **29**, 379–385 (2019). https://doi.org/10.1007/s12525-019-00358-7
8. vom Brocke, J., Winter, R., Hevner, A., Maedche, A.: Accumulation and evolution of design knowledge in design science research—a journey through time and space. J. Assoc. Inf. Syst. **21**, 520–544 (2020). https://doi.org/10.17705/1jais.00611
9. Brückner, L., Leiva, L.A., Oulasvirta, A.: Learning GUI completions with user-defined constraints. ACM Trans. Interact. Intell. Syst. **12**, 1–40 (2022). https://doi.org/10.1145/3490034
10. Cahenzli, M., Winter, R.: Writing DSR articles for maximum impact. In: ECIS 2023 Research Papers (2023)
11. Cheng, C.-Y., Huang, F., Li, G., Li, Y.: PLay: parametrically conditioned layout generation using latent diffusion. In: Proceedings of the 40th International Conference on Machine Learning. JMLR.org, Honolulu, Hawaii (2023)
12. Choksi, M.Z., Aubin Le Quéré, M., Lloyd, T., Tao, R., Grimmelmann, J., Naaman, M.: Under the (neighbor)hood: hyperlocal surveillance on nextdoor. In: Proceedings of the 2024 CHI Conference on Human Factors in Computing Systems. Association for Computing Machinery, New York (2024). https://doi.org/10.1145/3613904.3641967
13. Dignum, V.: Responsible artificial intelligence: recommendations and lessons learned. In: Eke, D.O., Wakunuma, K., Akintoye, S. (eds.) Responsible AI in Africa: Challenges and Opportunities, pp. 195–214. Springer International Publishing, Cham (2023). https://doi.org/10.1007/978-3-031-08215-3_9

14. Dihan, Q.A., Nihalani, B.R., Tooley, A.A., Elhusseiny, A.M.: Eyes on Google's NotebookLM: using generative AI to create ophthalmology podcasts with a single click. Eye. **39**(2), 215–216 (2025). https://doi.org/10.1038/s41433-024-03481-8
15. Dong, Q., et al.: A survey on In-context learning. arXiv preprint arXiv:2301.00234 (2024)
16. Duan, P., Warner, J., Li, Y., Hartmann, B.: Generating automatic feedback on UI mockups with large language models. In: Proceedings of the 2024 CHI Conference on Human Factors in Computing Systems. Association for Computing Machinery, New York (2024). https://doi.org/10.1145/3613904.3642782
17. Folha, R., Carvalho, A.: Towards managing design science knowledge with large language models. In: AMCIS 2024 Proceedings (2024)
18. Franzoi, S., Delwaulle, M., Dyong, J., Schaffner, J., Burger, M., vom Brocke, J.: Using large language models to generate process Knowledge from Enterprise content. In: Lecture Notes in Business Information Processing (LNBIP). Springer, Krakow (2024)
19. Gau, M., Greif-Winzrieth, A., Maedche, A., Weinhardt, C., vom Brocke, J.: Engaging citizen scientists: designing an open research system for collaborative problem exploration. Electron Markets. **35**(1), 12 (2025). https://doi.org/10.1007/s12525-025-00757-z
20. Gau, M., Maedche, A., vom Brocke, J.: Accessing the design science knowledge base—a search engine for the accumulation of knowledge across decentrally organized publications. In: Design Science Research for a New Society: Society 5.0, pp. 266–278 (2023). https://doi.org/10.1007/978-3-031-32808-4_17
21. Gmeiner, F., Yildirim, N.: Dimensions for designing LLM-based writing support. In: In2Writing Workshop at CHI (2023)
22. Gnewuch, U., Maedche, A.: Toward a method for reviewing software artifacts from practice. In: Drechsler, A., Gerber, A., Hevner, A. (eds.) The Transdisciplinary Reach of Design Science Research, pp. 337–350. Springer International Publishing, Cham (2022). https://doi.org/10.1007/978-3-031-06516-3_25
23. Greengard, S.: AI reinvents chip design. Commun. ACM. **67**(9), 16–18 (2024). https://doi.org/10.1145/3673645
24. Gregor, S., Hevner, A.: Positioning and presenting design science research for maximum impact. MIS Q. **37**, 337–356 (2013). https://doi.org/10.25300/MISQ/2013/37.2.01
25. Guilherme, V., Vincenzi, A.: An initial investigation of ChatGPT unit test generation capability. In: Proceedings of the 8th Brazilian Symposium on Systematic and Automated Software Testing, pp. 15–24. Association for Computing Machinery, New York (2023). https://doi.org/10.1145/3624032.3624035
26. Hanschmann, L., Mokelke, M., Maedche, A.: LadderChat-an LLM-based conversational agent for laddering interviews. In: 8th International Workshop on Chatbots and Human-Centred AI. Springer LNCS, Thessaloniki (2024)
27. Hevner, A.R., vom Brocke, J.: A proficiency model for design science research education. J. Inf. Syst. Educ. **34**(3), 264–278 (2023)
28. Hevner, A.R., March, S.T., Park, J., Ram, S.: Design science in information systems research. MIS Q. **28**(1), 75–105 (2004). https://doi.org/10.2307/25148625
29. Jin, J., Yang, M., Hu, H., Guo, X., Luo, J., Liu, Y.: Empowering design innovation using AI-generated content. J. Eng. Des. **36**(1), 1–18 (2025). https://doi.org/10.1080/09544828.2024.2401751
30. Kim, T.S., Choi, D., Choi, Y., Kim, J.: Stylette: styling the web with natural language. In: Proceedings of the 2022 CHI Conference on Human Factors in Computing Systems. Association for Computing Machinery, New York (2022). https://doi.org/10.1145/3491102.3501931
31. Kojima, T., Gu, S.S., Reid, M., Matsuo, Y., Iwasawa, Y.: Large language models are zero-shot reasoners. In: Proceedings of the 36th International Conference on Neural Information Processing Systems. Curran Associates Inc., Red Hook (2022)

32. Kolthoff, K., Bartelt, C., Ponzetto, S.P.: Data-driven prototyping via natural-language-based GUI retrieval. Autom. Softw. Eng. **30, 1**, 13 (2023). https://doi.org/10.1007/s10515-023-00377-x
33. Kolthoff, K., Kretzer, F., Bartelt, C., Maedche, A., & Ponzetto, S.P.: Interlinking user stories and GUI prototyping: A semi-automatic LLM-based approach. arXiv preprint arXiv:2406.08120 (2024). https://doi.org/10.48550/arXiv.2406.08120
34. Kosch, T., Feger, S.: Risk or chance? Large language models and reproducibility in HCI research. Interactions. **31**(6), 44–49 (2024). https://doi.org/10.1145/3695765
35. Krishna, M., Gaur, B., Verma, A., & Jalote, P.: Using LLMs in software requirements specifications: an empirical evaluation. Presented at the 2024 IEEE 32nd International Requirements Engineering Conference (RE) June 1 (2024). https://doi.org/10.1109/RE59067.2024.00056
36. Kuechler, W., Vaishnavi, V.: On theory development in design science research: anatomy of a research project. EJIS. **17**(5), 489–504 (2008). https://doi.org/10.1057/ejis.2008.40
37. Lee, C., et al.: GUIComp: a GUI design assistant with real-time, multi-faceted feedback. In: Proceedings of the 2020 CHI Conference on Human Factors in Computing Systems, pp. 1–13. Association for Computing Machinery, New York (2020). https://doi.org/10.1145/3313831.3376327
38. Liang, W., et al.: Can large language models provide useful feedback on research papers? A large-scale empirical analysis. NEJM AI. **1**(8), AIoa2400196 (2024). https://doi.org/10.1056/AIoa2400196
39. Lubos, S.,et al.: Leveraging LLMs for the quality assurance of software requirements. Presented at the 2024 IEEE 32nd International Requirements Engineering Conference (RE) June 1 (2024). https://doi.org/10.1109/RE59067.2024.00046
40. Meth, H., Mueller, B., Maedche, A.: Designing a requirement mining system. J. Assoc. Inf. Syst. **16**(9) (2015). https://doi.org/10.17705/1jais.00408
41. Mirhoseini, A., et al.: A graph placement methodology for fast chip design. Nature. **594**(7862), 207–212 (2021). https://doi.org/10.1038/s41586-021-03544-w
42. Moradi Dakhel, A., Majdinasab, V., Nikanjam, A., Khomh, F., Desmarais, M.C., Jiang, Z.M.: GitHub copilot AI pair programmer: asset or liability? J. Syst. Softw. **203**, 111734 (2023). https://doi.org/10.1016/j.jss.2023.111734
43. Morgan, D.L.: Exploring the use of artificial intelligence for qualitative data analysis: the case of ChatGPT. Int J Qual Methods. **22**, 16094069231211248 (2023). https://doi.org/10.1177/16094069231211248
44. Nam, D., Macvean, A., Hellendoorn, V., Vasilescu, B., Myers, B.: Using an LLM to help with code understanding. In: Proceedings of the IEEE/ACM 46th International Conference on Software Engineering, pp. 1–13. Association for Computing Machinery, New York (2024). https://doi.org/10.1145/3597503.3639187
45. Ngwenyama, O., Rowe, F.: Should we collaborate with AI to conduct literature reviews? Changing epistemic values in a flattening world. J. Assoc. Inf. Syst. **25**(1), 122–136 (2024). https://doi.org/10.17705/1jais.00869
46. Nielsen, P.A.: Problematizing in IS design research. In: Hofmann, S., Müller, O., Rossi, M. (eds.) Designing for Digital Transformation. Co-Creating Services with Citizens and Industry, pp. 259–271. Springer International Publishing, Cham (2020). https://doi.org/10.1007/978-3-030-64823-7_24
47. Peffers, K., Tuunanen, T., Rothenberger, M.A., Chatterjee, S.: A design science research methodology for information systems research. J. Manag. Inf. Syst. **24**(3), 45–77 (2007). https://doi.org/10.2753/MIS0742-1222240302
48. Radford, A., Wu, J., Child, R., Luan, D., Amodei, D., Sutskever, I.: Language models are unsupervised multitask learners. OpenAI Blog. **1**, 8–9 (2019)

49. Reining, S., Ahlemann, F., Mueller, B., Thakurta, R.: Knowledge accumulation in design science research: ways to foster scientific progress. SIGMIS Database. **53**(1), 10–24 (2022). https://doi.org/10.1145/3514097.3514100
50. Rietz, T., Maedche, A.: Ladderbot - a conversational agent for human-like online laddering interviews. https://papers.ssrn.com/abstract=4062500 (2022). https://doi.org/10.2139/ssrn.4062500
51. Robinson, A.: Sketch2code: Generating a website from a paper mockup. arXiv preprint arXiv:1905.13750 (2019)
52. Rossi, S., Rossi, M., Mukkamala, R.R., Thatcher, J.B., Dwivedi, Y.K.: Augmenting research methods with foundation models and generative AI. Int. J. Inf. Manag., 102749 (2024). https://doi.org/10.1016/j.ijinfomgt.2023.102749
53. Sakib, F.A., Khan, S.H., Karim, A.H.M.R.: Extending the frontier of ChatGPT: code generation and debugging. In: 2024 International Conference on Electrical, Computer and Energy Technologies (ICECET), pp. 1–6 (2023)
54. Schoormann, T., Möller, F., Chandra Kruse, L., Otto, B.: BAUSTEIN—A design tool for configuring and representing design research. Inf. Syst. J. **34**(6), 1871–1901 (2024). https://doi.org/10.1111/isj.12516
55. Seidel, S., Berente, N., Lindberg, A., Lyytinen, K., Nickerson, J.V.: Autonomous tools and design: a triple-loop approach to human-machine learning. Commun. ACM. **62**(1), 50–57 (2019)
56. Seidel, S., Berente, N., Martinez, B., Lindberg, A., Lyytinen, K., Nickerson, J.V.: Autonomous tools in system design: reflective practice in Ubisofts ghost recon wildlands project. IEEE Comput. **51**(10), 16–23 (2018)
57. Sein, M.K., Henfridsson, O., Purao, S., Rossi, M., Lindgren, R.: Action design research. MIS Q. **35**(1), 37–56 (2011). https://doi.org/10.2307/23043488
58. Simon, H.A.: The Sciences of the Artificial. MIT Press, Cambridge, MA (1996)
59. Suh, S., Chen, M., Min, B., Li, T.J.-J., Xia, H.: Luminate: structured generation and exploration of design space with large language models for human-AI co-creation. In: Proceedings of the 2024 CHI Conference on Human Factors in Computing Systems, pp. 1–26. Association for Computing Machinery, New York (2024). https://doi.org/10.1145/3613904.3642400
60. Susarla, A., Gopal, R., Thatcher, J.B., Sarker, S.: The Janus effect of generative AI: charting the path for responsible conduct of scholarly activities in information systems. Inf. Syst. Res. **34**(2), 399–408 (2023). https://doi.org/10.1287/isre.2023.ed.v34.n2
61. Tuunanen, T., Winter, R., vom Brocke, J.: Dealing with complexity in design science research: a methodology using design echelons. MIS Q. **48**, 427–458 (2024). https://doi.org/10.25300/MISQ/2023/16700
62. Vaswani, A., et al.: Attention is all you need. arXiv preprint arXiv:1706.03762 (2023)
63. Venable, J., Pries-Heje, J., Baskerville, R.: FEDS: a framework for evaluation in design science research. Eur. J. Inf. Syst. **25**(1), 77–89 (2016). https://doi.org/10.1057/ejis.2014.36
64. Veselovsky, V., Ribeiro, M.H., Cozzolino, P., Gordon, A., Rothschild, D., & West, R.: Prevalence and prevention of large language model use in crowd work. arXiv preprint arXiv:2310.15683 (2023)
65. Wagner, G., Lukyanenko, R., Paré, G.: Artificial intelligence and the conduct of literature reviews. J. Inf. Technol. **37**(2), 209–226 (2022). https://doi.org/10.1177/02683962211048201
66. Wang, J., Huang, Y., Chen, C., Liu, Z., Wang, S., Wang, Q.: Software testing with large language models: survey, landscape, and vision. IEEE Trans. Softw. Eng. **50**(4), 911–936 (2024). https://doi.org/10.1109/TSE.2024.3368208
67. Wang, P., et al.: Large language models are not fair evaluators. arXiv preprint arXiv:2305.17926 (2023). https://doi.org/10.48550/arXiv.2305.17926

68. Wei, J., Courbis, A.-L., Lambolais, T., Xu, B., Bernard, P.L., Dray, G.: Boosting GUI prototyping with diffusion models. In: 2023 IEEE 31st International Requirements Engineering Conference (RE), pp. 275–280 (2023). https://doi.org/10.1109/RE57278.2023.00035
69. Wei, X., Kumar, N., Zhang, H.: Addressing bias in generative AI: challenges and research opportunities in information management. Inf. Manag. **104103** (2025). https://doi.org/10.1016/j.im.2025.104103

Exploring Action Design Research as a Reflective Practice for Sense-Giving and Sense-Making of Meaning: A Phenomenological Approach

Amir Haj-Bolouri[1](✉), Hanna Buyssens[2], and Stijn Viaene[2]

[1] School of Economics, Business, and IT, University West, Trollhättan, Sweden
amir.haj-bolouri@hv.se
[2] Vlerick Business School and KU Leuven, Brussel, Belgium
{hanna.buyssens,stijn.viaene}@vlerick.com

Abstract. Action Design Research (ADR) explicitly promotes reflection and learning as an important stage for supporting other ADR stages (e.g., building, intervention, and evaluation). Yet, very few ADR studies demonstrate a clear trajectory for how to reflect and learn, what varieties of reflection and learning do exist, and if there are any methods for supporting the reflection process. In response to the possibility of further evolving the reflection and learning stage, for this paper, we explore how ADR can be used as a reflective practice for sense-giving and sense-making of meaning. We do so by employing a phenomenological approach that serves an epistemology for a reflective practice together with concepts for conceptualizing variances of meaning, sense-giving, and sense-making. The results of our work propose three phenomenological themes for engaging with ADR as a reflective practice: (1) *Anticipatory Reflection and Learning*, (2) *Retrospective Reflection and Learning*, and (3) *Contemporaneous Reflection and Learning*. Consequently, the themes' utility is illustrated via two different ADR projects, and the implications of the themes for practice and theory are discussed as fruitful for future ADR, as well as Design Science Research (DSR), in Information Systems (IS).

Keywords: Action Design Research · Reflective Practice · Phenomenology · Meaning · Sense-Making · Sense-Giving

1 Introduction

Action Design Research (ADR) is a research approach in the field of Information Systems (IS) that reflects and incorporates a combination of ideas from both Design Science Research (DSR) (e.g., [1, 2]), and Action Research (AR) (e.g., [3, 4]). ADR emphasizes the collaboration among researchers and industry partners to identify and solve specific problems in organizational settings through development of design knowledge (e.g., design principles) that stem from the building, intervention, and evaluation of ensemble artifacts (e.g., socio-technical systems, IT-artifacts) [5]. Since the introduction of ADR in 2011 to the IS field in general, and the design science community in particular, the decade of applying ADR demonstrates its acceptance and use across different areas of IS research [6]. Working accordingly to the ADR approach does also generate certain challenges for researchers who want to balance developing viable solutions for solving organizational problems, with knowledge that formalizes learning outcomes into generalizable outputs [7]. One particular challenge is about how to meaningfully engage with third stage of *Reflection and Learning* [8].

Engaging with reflection and learning in an ADR project is important because it helps the researcher to transit conceptually from building a solution for a particular instance to applying that learning to a broader class of problems. According to ([5], p. 44), being able to consciously reflect on the problem framing, the theories chosen for an ADR project, and the emerging ensemble artifact, is critical to ensure that contributions to knowledge are identified. More specifically, ([5], p. 43) provide a set of tasks for an ADR researcher to facilitate reflection and learning: (1) reflect on the design and redesign during the project, (2) evaluate adherence to principles, and (3) analyze intervention results according to stated goals. Subsequently, the tasks are aligned with the principle of *Guided Emergence*, which emphasizes that the ensemble artifact will reflect not only the preliminary design created by an ADR team but also the ongoing shaping by organizational use, perspectives, and participants, as well as by outcomes of authentic and concurrent evaluation ([5], p. 44). Moreover, the principle emphasizes that the ADR team should be sensitive to signals that indicate an ongoing refinement of the ensemble artifact, which then feeds into formalized design principles.

However, even though the ADR approach has been applied by a large group of IS researchers over a decade, extended and further developed by a modest amount of IS researchers (e.g., [9, 10]), and critiqued by some IS researchers (e.g., [11]), very little—if any work—has been written about ADR and how to engage with reflection and learning throughout an ADR project. On the other hand, in other design research traditions that ADR draws inspiration from—e.g., Participatory Design (PD) [12]—design is considered as a reflective practice, which emphasizes Donald Schön's [13] notions of "reflective activity", "reflection-in-action", and "knowing-in-action". According to ([13], p. 62), when a practitioner or researcher reflects in and on his practice, the possible objects of his reflection are as varied as the kinds of phenomena before him and the systems of knowing-in-practice that he brings to them. This reasoning has been proposed by [14] for improving knowledge generation in DSR, whereas other design researchers have advocated the importance of reflection and learning regarding (i) tacit norms and appreciations that underly a judgement, (ii) the strategies and theories implicit in the design process, (iii) the feeling for a situation that has leads to adopt a particular course of design action helps researchers to give sense to, and (iv) make sense of, meaning in design [15]. Hence, based on such ideas, for this paper we take the opportunity to explore the following research question: *how can ADR be used as a reflective practice that engages scholars with sense-giving and sense-making of meaning?*

We approach the prompted research question via two ongoing ADR projects: one project that emphasizes reflection and learning of designing Immersive Virtual Reality (IVR) training for meaningful learning of conflict management, and one project that centers on creating meaningful technologies to tackle environmental sustainability challenges, also emphasizing reflection and learning. The first author of this paper is the principal researcher of the first project, whereas the second and third authors are focusing on the second project. Together, we explore the formulated research question by highlighting insights from our own reflective practice and elucidate how we have engaged with the third ADR stage of reflection and learning. As a way of engaging with ADR as a reflective practice, we reflect upon the activities that we engaged with for sense-giving and sense-making of meaning in each project. But because the ADR method is "agnostic" in the sense that it does not recommend any specific kinds of methods or theories for reflection and learning, we employed a phenomenological approach that allowed us to contemplate our lived experiences on how and why we experience ADR as a reflective practice. Phenomenology is nevertheless considered to be the underlying epistemology of a reflective practice [16, 17], where reflecting the lived experiences is a central task for understanding how a method, theory, or practice engages with sense-giving and sense-making of meaning [18].

Against this backdrop, this study engages with a phenomenological approach for understanding how ADR is used as a reflective practice within two different ADR projects. As a result, the study proposes a possible extension of the third ADR stage by introducing three overarching themes that explicate reflection and learning in ADR projects: (1) *Anticipatory Reflection and Learning*; (2) *Retrospective Reflection and Learning*; and (3) *Contemporaneous Reflection and Learning*. This extension was then incorporated with a phenomenological approach on what "meaning" means, how meaning structures emerge in a process of reflection and learning, and how ADR scholars can engage with sense-giving and sense-making of meaning across different abstraction levels. The main contribution of this paper is thus to help others in the design science community with guidance on how they can structure a narrative for thinking and writing about their reflection and learning processes, whereas a second contribution is to introduce a clear definition of "meaning" for the DSR community and demonstrate how sense-giving and sense-making of meaning makes the project experience not only "efficient", "sufficient", or "relevant", but also "meaningful". Finally, the study shows the viability of phenomenology as a form of meta-reflection that unveils how a process of reflection and learning becomes meaningful for IS researchers in the design science community.

2 Reflection and Learning in Action Design Research

ADR is, as far as we know, one of the few seminal variants of DSR methods that explicitly highlights a stage for reflection and learning, whereas other seminal DSR methods provide frameworks that highlight other aspects of a DSR project, such as: evaluation [19], framing and executing DSR projects with a focus on formulating problems, formulating solutions, design and evaluation of IT-artifacts, demonstration and communication of DSR outputs [2, 20], positioning of DSR outputs [1], and theory development [21]. When employing ADR, scholars are encouraged to work in cycles by following four stages as depicted in Fig. 1.

As shown in Fig. 1, the ADR framework highlights reflection and learning as an integrated stage with the stages of problem formulation, and building, intervention, and evaluation (BIE). Most ADR projects seek to accompany cycles of BIE with reflection

Exploring Action Design Research as a Reflective Practice   35

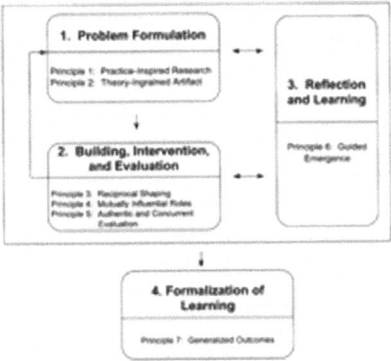

Fig. 1. Action Design Research: Stages and Principles [5]

and learning. For example, ([8], p. 2) describe their ADR project as *"[...] highly iterative... where each iteration concludes with a consideration of the artifact... [that] acts as the impetus for thorough reflection and learning, which then feeds back into the problem formulation."* It is through reflection and learning that ADR scholars challenge *"[...] 'organizational participants' existing ideas and assumptions about the artifact's specific use context in order to create and improve the design."* ([5], p. 42). This quality of ADR, highlighting the implications of reflection and learning, has subsequently been applied sufficiently in a wide array of research projects, and *"[...] because of its ever-expanding applications, the ADR concepts and process model continue to grow and evolve to meet the demands of new and challenging environments."* ([10], p. 6). It is thus no surprise that ADR is a powerful method for design-oriented research in IS field, but why is reflection and learning important for the ADR project? In 1988, ([22], p. 8) argued that it was *"[...] not sufficiently simply to have an experience in order to learn; without reflecting upon this experience, it may quickly be forgotten, or its learning potential lost. It is from the feelings and thoughts emerging from this reflection that generalizations or concepts can be generated."* After all, *"[...] we learn from reflection on experience. Reliving of an experience leads to making connections between information and feelings produced by the experience."* ([23], p. 9). Moreover, *"[...] reflection allows us to draw conclusions about our past experiences and develop new insights that we can apply to our future activities."* ([24], p. 11). The importance of reflection and learning as an intertwined unit of activities and experiences is, as can be seen from the shared citations so far, important for engaging with research as a reflective practice, something which [13, 25] interconnects with experimentation where practitioners constantly interpret situations by means of problem setting and problem solving, a process which can lead to a reframing of the situation.

In a similar way as Schön's notion of a reflective practice, we can see examples of ADR projects where scholars have generated insights about problems and solution spaces as if they were conducting a reflective practice [26, 27], or projects that emphasize reflection for generating implications for theory and principles [28, 29]. Most notably of how an ADR scholar has systematically engaged with a reflection and learning, can be seen in [8]'s study, where they provide vignettes for their process of reflection and learning based on [30]'s "What? Model of Reflection". The focus of [8]'s study is, however, not solely on reflection and learning, nor on the potentials of exploring ADR as a reflective practice, but on the importance of the problem formulation stage in ADR, which interplays with the stage of reflection and learning. We acknowledge the importance of both [8]'s and others' important work on why further ADR scholars should engage with the problem formulation stage. However, for this study, we wish to explore further how ADR can be considered as a reflective practice that engages with a sense-giving and sense-making process of meaning, which requires a further look into what "meaning" is and how a meta-reflection can further unveil a deeper understanding about the ADR stage of reflection and learning.

3 The Phenomenological Approach: Sense-Giving and Sense-Making of Meaning in a Reflective Practice

In design research circles, scholars generally refer to Schön as the philosopher and educator who, through his proposal of the reflective-practice concept, offered an alternative to the symbolic information processing (SIP) approach defended by [31] in his *Sciences of the Artificial*. In describing what a reflective practice is, Schön ([13], p. 54) has suggested that phrases such as "thinking on your feet" and "keeping your wits about you" suggests not only that "we can think about doing something but that we can think about something while doing it". In relation to characterizing a reflective practice, [13] introduced other interrelated notions such as "reflection-in-action" and "knowing-in-action", where the former notion is the reflective form of the latter notion [32]. It is Schön ([13], pp. 8–9)'s assumption that *"[...] competent practitioners usually know more than they can say. They exhibit a kind of knowing in practice, most of which is tacit... Indeed, practitioners themselves often reveal a capacity for reflection on their intuitive knowing in the midst of action and sometimes use this capacity to cope with the unique, uncertain, and conflicted situations of practice."* In other words, the reflection that lies behind actions, are to be found in practice, which in itself, according to the phenomenologist Van Manen [17], requires a form of epistemology of reflection. It is Van Manen's, as well as other scholars' [33, 34], convincing idea that phenomenology provides a epistemological grounding of the reflective practice, something that [35] also addresses as a constitutive part of a phenomenology of practice.

Phenomenology is known as arguably the first philosophy of consciousness founded by Edmund Husserl, and then later further developed by successors such as Martin Heidegger, Maurice Merleau-Ponty, Alfred Schütz, Dan Zahavi, and Max Van Manen. At its core, phenomenology provides a method for transcendental reflection that makes an effort to disclose the phenomena of the world as they appear in our lived experiences [18]. Phenomenology views the lived experience as a way of "being-in-the-world" of sense-giving and sense-making of meaning, where the "lived experience" is viewed from within the lifeworld, experiences and choices that a person has in each situation, and the knowledge that a person reflects in relation to a world of practices [36]. The lifeworld is in turn referred to as the world of immediate experiences common to all of us, not the private world of any individual, but rather the "self-evident", "pre-scientific", and "taken-for-granted" world that is the nexus between all people and is all that constitutes meaning in the social world [37]. These phenomenological ideas, as well as others, have been adopted by prior IS researchers to study artifacts [38], situated practices [39], the immersive virtual reality [40], embodiment [41], design research [42], and the cyberspace [43]. For this study, however, we want to emphasize how phenomenology can be used for sense-giving and sense-making of meaning.

3.1 Variances of Meaning in Phenomenology

The phenomenological inquiry helps a reflective practitioner to both (a) give-sense, and (b) make-sense, of meaning. In phenomenology, "meaning" is not reduced to semantics nor language per se—as it is in other traditions such as semiotics [44]. Moreover, the phenomenological view on meaning is also distinguished from psychological, sociological, ethnographic, biographic, and social and human science disciplines. As such, phenomenological meaning is found in the lived experience which announces the intent to explore directly the variances of meaning through reflection [45]. Phenomenology in its original sense aims thus at *retrospectively* bringing to our awareness some experience we lived through to be able to reflect phenomenologically on the living meaning of this lived experience [46]. Subsequently, Table 1 provides a synthesized overview of variances on what meaning is in phenomenology.

To approach meaning through phenomenology, is to reflect upon how a reflective practice can localize 'horizons' that open up for sense-giving and sense-making [54]; 'localize' here means finding out the intentionality (e.g., the direction of) of the lived experience, whereas a 'horizon' signifies a background that, from the outset, presents itself as stable with a structured feeling of objectivity, whereas in reality, the horizon stands still until it is disrupted through phenomenological sense-giving and sense-making of meaning [35].

3.2 Phenomenological Approach for Sense-Giving and Sense-Making

"Sense-giving" in phenomenology (also known as 'Noesis') refers to the process of developing means for familiarity, and is found through different types of sense-giving: *narrational* sense-giving that conceptualizes meaning structures in the lived experiences [18], *expressional* sense-giving that contextualizes meanings of things and experiences through cues, language, and relational content of events [45], and *spatial* sense-giving that attributes practical sense to meaning via codes, inscriptions, norms, and values in places/spaces. Sense-giving of meaning also happens on an intersubjective level through actions, signs, and expressions that take place between individuals, where one individual's status in society might influence the variant(s) of meaning that attributes human actions, signs, and expressions [55]. Sense-giving is thus, in a similar way that Gioia & Chittipeddi ([56], p. 442) describe, concerned with the process of attempting to influence sense-making and meaning construction of others toward a definition of a reality.

"Sense-making", on the other hand, refers in phenomenology (also known as "Noema") to the process of overcoming the subject-object split by encompassing a phenomenological ontology, which focuses different types of sense-making: *phenomenal*

Table 1. Categories of 'Meaning' in Phenomenology

Variances of Meaning	Description
Meaning as Cultural Signs, Materials, and Symbols	This category draws on Schütz's [37] idea of meaning as cultural signs, materials, and symbols, which together, are pivotal for making a world seemingly intelligible. In turn, technology is a mediator of meaning in that space, where examples of such include how digital technologies mediate sense-giving of 'digital attitudes' in digital experiences that occur through a taken-for-granted manner of sense-given meaning of avatars in virtual reality [47].
Meaning as Content of Intersubjective Expressions	This category draws on Van Manen's [36] idea of meaning as the content of expressions that emerge through actions, practices, and processes in the social world. Content refers to what is relatable to humans' intersubjectivity and include expressions that are for instance brought forth through technology in relation to a practice. This can be agreement on a shared definition, which for instance can is seen in research on sense-giving of meaning through a technology-mediated perspective-taking and perspective-making [48].
Meaning as Structure of Focal Things	This category draws on Heidegger's [49] idea of meaning as something that emerges when encountering 'focal things'. Focal things are defined as modern technologies that create a framework for a world in which relations and identities are formed [50]. This kind of 'en-framing' (Ge-stell) makes it possible for humans to create and share meaning within the structure of the framework, through an encountering with technology instances, such as sense-making of meaningful practices [51].
Meaning as Gripping a Horizon of Relations	This category draws on Merleau-Ponty's [52] idea of meaning as an act of gripping a horizon of relations. Gripping can be actual or potential but is an active event that transcends a specific world's perceived boundaries through chiasm/crossing of interworlds, such as when technology mediates co-extended spaces for sense-making of meaning [53].

sense-making "de-worlds" ([57], p. 317) a particular situation by transcending meaning structures from the outside [58]; *detached-deliberate* sense-making is cognitive-discursive and it involves engaged abstraction that generates conceptual sense of reviewing meaning from an intersubjective perspective; *involved-deliberate* sense-making emerges when habitual behaviours of the natural attitude to the world (e.g., taken-for-granted attitude to everyday life) is interrupted through a breakdown (e.g., an unexpected event) that leads to a contextual opening of meaning in action (e.g., what actions mean for that specific context); and *immanent* sense-making is implicated in individuals' skillful enactment and performance of routine activities and is achieved by sensorially grasping the meaning of a situation [59].

Moreover, the phenomenological approach for sense-giving and sense-making of meaning departs from the mainstream view in organizational research, which focuses on episodic interruptions of organizational activities, forcing individuals to deliberately search for how to restore the interrupted activity [60]. Instead, the phenomenological view emphasizes a relation between types of sense-giving and sense-making along three levels: *intersubjective level* (e.g., individuals interact to synthesize new meaning so that a merged subject emerges; *generic subjective level* (e.g., individuals become substitutable in filling in roles and following scripts); and *extrasubjective level* (e.g., individuals enact taken-for-granted institutional meaning) [61]. It is along these levels that different types of sense-giving and sense-making takes place phenomenologically through *sensibility* (e.g., conceptual, contextual, practical, or spectatorial), *embodiment* (e.g., meaning that is given or made sense of via/through the body), and *temporality* (e.g., sense-giving and sense-making of meaning in and over time).

4 Research Setting: Horizons for Phenomenological Examples

A phenomenological reflection of sense-giving and sense-making can only be done from a first-person perspective and is characterized by both an "opens up" (also known as "Epoché") and "closes down" (also known as "Reduction") ([35], p. 822) that aims to reflect the phenomenological question: "What is this experience like?". Consequently, in order to ask instances of that question, phenomenologists emphasize the importance of "examples", or as when Casey ([62], pp. 23–37) refers to Husserl when he says that *"[...] it is on the basis of examples, and of examples alone, that the phenomenologist is able to attain eidetic insights."* The "eidetic insights" refer here to the meaning structures that appear in the lived experience, where examples are experiential data of these insights that can be manifested as a study, investigation, probing, reflection, analysis, interrogation.

Phenomenological examples are usually cast in the practical format of lived experience descriptions, such as: anecdotes, stories, narratives, vignettes, or concrete accounts—without being treated as "illustrations" nor as empirical "samples" of factual data ([35], pp. 256–260). The following section aims to show how we, for this study, use the "method of examples" in pursuing phenomenological questions and insights that help us explore ADR as a reflective practice, and to give-sense to, and makes-sense of, meaning in two different ADR projects. In this section, we outline the horizons and then present the questions and rationale we used for conducting our phenomenological reflection.

4.1 Overview of the Horizons: ADR Projects

In presenting the research setting of this study, we stay true to the phenomenological approach that is used for conducting a reflection on how ADR can be used as a reflective practice that engages scholars with sense-giving and sense-making of meaning. The "horizons" that we aim to disrupt are thus located in each authors' ADR experiences, whereas the sense-giving and sense-making of meaning is something we will engage in through phenomenological questioning. The ADR projects are thus considered as the horizons for conducting a phenomenological questioning that demonstrates how ADR can be used as reflective practice. The projects are summarized in Table 2.

Table 2. ADR Projects: A Summary

ADR Project	Short Summary	Project Period & Conducted Cycles
1. Designing Immersive Learning Environments for Training Conflict Management	The aim of the project is to develop knowledge about how to design immersive learning environments in VR for preparing operators for conflict management onboard trains. An alpha prototype has been built in VR, and evaluated together with train operators as end-users. Subsequently, design knowledge has been developed and communicated in form of mid-range theories and design principles	Mid 2023-Mid 2026 2 ADR cycles
2. Designing Blockchain-Based Multi-Sided Platform for Smart Distribution of Water	The aim of the project is to develop knowledge about how to design blockchain-based multi-sided platforms for smart distribution of water that yields transparency, traceability, and resource equity for increased sustainability. Subsequently, design knowledge has been developed and communicated in form of design principles.	Aug 2022–Feb 2024 2 ADR cycles

The **first ADR project's** research setting consists of a shared world together with the partners SJ, Tenstar, and Hypr10; SJ is Sweden's train operating company and is the main stakeholder of the project in need of the immersive learning environment (as described in Table 2), whereas Tenstar and Hypr10 are involved partners in form of companies that develop immersive learning environments in VR. The cycles of reflection and learning have so far been conducted as integrated with the BIE cycles of: (1) design thinking workshops for developing a conceptual model with user journeys and narratives that conceptualize training scenarios of preparing train operators for conflict management in VR; (2) an alpha prototype for one of the training themes in IVR that deals with managing conflicting ticketing scenarios onboard trains. The aim of the reflection and learning has thus been to reflect upon results from the BIE cycles and to generate early version of design principles, and to continuously reflect upon developed knowledge that ingrains the alpha prototype within the large ADR team. Examples of the BIE-outputs are shown in Fig. 2.

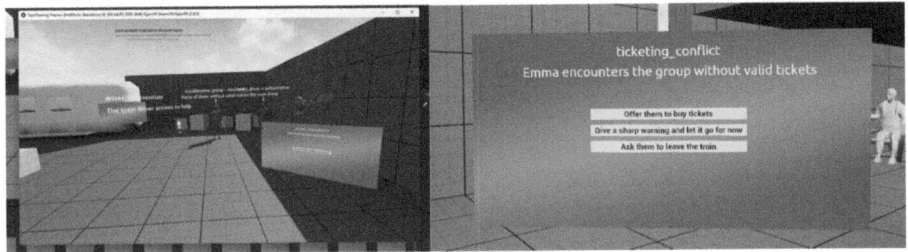

Fig. 2. ADR Project 1: Alpha Prototype and Immersive Learning Environment in VR

The **second ADR project's** research setting consisted of partners Botanical Water Technologies (BWT) and Fujitsu. BWT, an Australian start-up, aimed to develop a blockchain-based platform for tracking and verifying the sustainable sourcing and distribution of water. Fujitsu Belgium was responsible for designing and developing this platform to meet BWT's requirements. The primary objective of the blockchain platform was to embed sustainability into every aspect of its design. The ADR process in this project also followed iterative cycles of BIE, with reflection and learning as a continuous and central activity in every step of the BIE process. The BIE cycles resulted in two designated interventions in which reflection and learning was stimulated with all workshop participants. During these interventions, the Benefits Dependency Network (BDN) was employed as a tool to facilitate reflection and learning, serving as a shared language. The outcomes from these interventions resulted in: (1) an ends-driven formalization of the BDN framework, that focuses on obtaining sustainable outcomes through designated means, and (2) an affordance-means-driven framework, focusing on the blockchain's action potential and its emergent features. The trigger points for the interventions were initiated by mismatch between theoretical constructs and real-world observations, as the blockchain was both a tool and an enabler for sustainable decision making. This urged the researchers to reframe the project's scope and theoretical foundations. Results from the ADR project are illustrated in Fig. 3.

4.2 Phenomenological Questions

In coming up with phenomenological questions for reflection, we incorporate the phenomenological approach of giving-sense and making-sense of meaning from our ADR

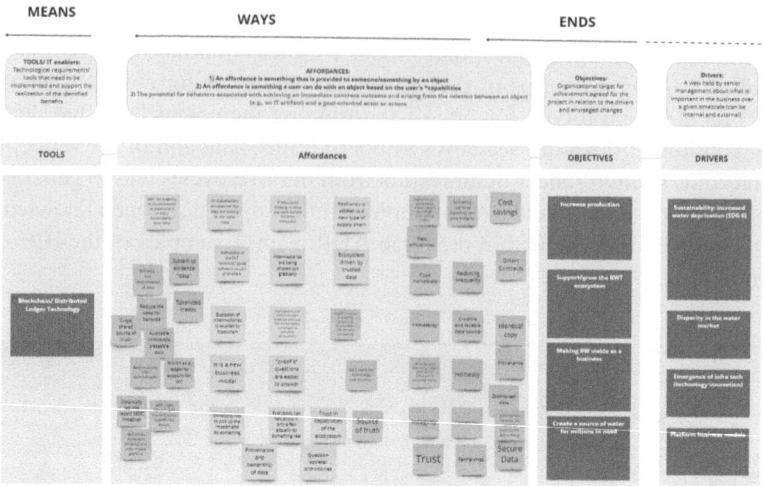

Fig. 3: ADR project 2: Affordance-based BDN

projects. More specifically, the phenomenological approach underpins the prompting of questions with the aim of generating eidetic insights that helps us making an understanding about a reflective practice more accessible, concrete, or intelligible [35]. Phenomenological questions are thus prompted to reflect on examples to express the variances of meaning, which are typically tacit until made knowable as a phenomenon in its singularity [36].

A "singularity" cannot be grasped through concepts because concepts are already generalized bits of language, and language universalizes. But phenomenological questions make the "singular" seen from within in retrospect ([63], p. 10), by focusing temporality of questions as: "What?" (a description of the phenomenon), "So What?" (a reflection about the phenomenon), and "Now What?" (eidetic insights following from understanding the phenomenon), all of which are contextualized within the experience from a particular setting (e.g., ADR project).

"What" questions are in phenomenological questioning supplemented with "When" questions that reflects temporality of events and happenings [35], whereas "Why" questions are added to unveil why an event is singular and provides eidetic insights for expressing exemplary aspects of meaning of a phenomenon (e.g., aspects of why reflection and learning is integrated with the design process of an ADR project). For this study, we combined these categories of questions and prompted the following phenomenological questions:

- *What was it like reflecting and learning before, during, and after, in the ADR project?*
- *What was it like engaging with the BIE cycles and reflection at the same time during the design process of the ADR project?*
- *What was it like working with theory/theories for reflection and learning in the ADR project?*
- *What was it like co-reflecting together with other members of the ADR team?*
- *What was it like not reflecting and learning in the ADR project?*

- *What was meaningful with the reflection and learning process of the ADR team?*
- *When was it meaningful to reflect during the ADR project?*
- *When did you not reflective and learn during the ADR project?*
- *When did co-reflection occur during the ADR project?*
- *When did the design activities help you reflect in the ADR project?*
- *Why do you think that reflecting and learning was important for the formalization of learning outcomes in your ADR project?*
- *Why do you think that reflection and learning needs to be integrated with the design process in your ADR project?*
- *Why do you think that the design process helps the ADR researcher to reflect, and the ADR team to co-reflect together?*
- *Why do you think that reflection and learning is meaningful for an ADR project?*

Together, the phenomenological questions above engaged the authors of this paper in a phenomenological reflection about the reflection and learning stage of each ADR project. The reflection and learning stage are focused because it is that specific stage that opens up for exploring eidetic insights that provide an understanding about how ADR can be used as a reflective practice.

5 Phenomenological Themes for Engaging with Action Design Research as a Reflective Practice

In this section, we present the eidetic insights from the phenomenological questioning in form of phenomenological themes (shown in Table 3) that depict examples of how ADR can be used as a reflective practice for engaging with sense-giving and sense-making of meaning. Providing eidetic insights via themes, is a common approach in phenomenology of practice for helping scholars to recognize the meaningfulness of certain human experiences and events [45]. The phenomenological themes are, in other words, an intermediate reflective tool for engaging other scholars and readers into reflections that induce them into a wondering engagement with certain phenomenological questions [35]. As such, the phenomenological themes opens up and closes down our eidetic insights about the reflection and learning cycles of each ADR project, which the authors flesh out via the themes in form of anecdotes, narratives, or vignettes. Subsequently, each theme connects to the phenomenological approach for sense-giving and sense-making of meaning to demonstrate each authors' concrete account of their reflective practice in the ADR projects.

Each theme in Table 3 brings forth how the reflection and learning stage of ADR can be understood in relation to temporality as a phenomenological factor. We will now discuss each theme in union with our phenomenological approach that unveils the authors' projects as examples of how ADR can be used as a reflective practice. Subsequently, quotes from each author will be provided to depict answers to the phenomenological questions. Here, we would like to emphasize that "Author 1" is working with the first depicted ADR project, whereas "Author 2" and "Author 3" are working with the second ADR project. Subsequently, "Author 2" is a junior researcher (doctoral student), whereas "Author 3" is a senior researcher, which also distinguishes their reflections from each other—e.g., the junior researcher's retrospective reflection and learning was sometimes

Table 3. Phenomenological Themes for Using ADR as a Reflective Practice

Theme	Description	Sense-Giving Examples	Sense-Making Examples
Anticipatory Reflection and Learning	Reflection and learning that concerns the future—e.g., future emerging events during BIE-cycles of an ADR project.	Narrating meaning for affecting future stakeholder perspectives Contextualizing shared meaning creation for developing future emerging design principles Attributing meaning for influencing the selection of design methods	Construction of meaning-making for future meta-requirements Envisioning of future design processes through intersubjective meaning
Retrospective Reflection and Learning	Reflection and learning that concerns past experiences of—e.g., past events that are reflected upon during the reflection and learning cycles of an ADR project	Inscribing anecdotal meanings from past problem formulations Value-setting shared meaning from past formalized learning outcomes Weaving new cultural meaning from past encounters with shaping the ensemble	Embodiment of meaning structures from past design of artifact Interpretation about the past structural meaning of intervention
Contemporaneous Reflection and Learning	Reflection and learning that concerns the "here and now"– e.g., a stop-and-think type of reflection about concurrent events of an ADR project	Distributing situated meaning for present ensemble interventions Framing meaning structures for present decision makings Re-defining meaning expressions for transformation of present problem spaces	Enacting intersubjective meaning-making from present breakdowns Re-viewing meaning of past problem spaces from present problem perspectives

of anticipatory nature for the senior researcher because of their different levels of project experience.

5.1 Anticipatory Reflection and Learning

How reflective is the anticipatory moment where the ADR scholar is mostly engaged with giving sense to future ADR activities, and what is it like reflecting and learning before future ADR activities have been evoked and executed? These questions are overarching questions of the first theme. By means of concrete experiential examples, the eidetic insights of the authors are for this theme distinguished into three forms of anticipatory reflection and learning: (a) *sense-giving the anticipation of something*, (b) *sense-giving the anticipation with something and the passing of time belonging to it*, and (c) *sense-making profound anticipations*. We now apply the phenomenological approach of sense-giving and sense-making, to explore how these forms of anticipatory reflection and learning can elaborate ADR as a reflective practice.

For example, when the authors reflected upon "What" questions, eidetic insights about sense-giving and sense-making of meaning through anticipatory reflection and learning, were mostly related to first form. Here, the phenomenological reflection concerned examples about the "selection of design methods", and "considerations of affecting the selection design methods and future stakeholder perspectives":

"What I remember is that the ADR team reflected early upon what design method to adopt for conducting the second ADR stage cyclically. This boiled down to anticipating what meaning we can attribute to the selection process by inferring from the competencies in members' prior experiences of using design thinking." (Author 1)

"Early on in the first design cycle, we observed and reflected on the mismatch between our theoretical assumptions and what was observed. We understood early on that our sense-making was affected by predefined theoretical constructs that did not match reality. As such we reflected on alternative theoretical framings, to implement in our next intervention." (Author 2)

"We had a lot of conversations about how we could do design research in a context characterized by uncertainty in the problem space, as we were engaging with the fuzzy, badly understood, high-level notion of sustainability, and the solution space, with blockchain being an emergent technology. This notion of wickedness made us anticipate a highly iterative, emergent, even 'surprising' design process, where we would have to be ready to improvise or pivot method and use of theory." (Author 3)

When reflecting upon "When" questions, the authors' reflection exemplified insights that were mostly related to the second and third forms of anticipatory reflection and learning, with respect to reflections concerning examples about the "development of future design principles", and "formulation of future meta-requirements":

"About less than 5 months through the project, we started thinking about what kind of design principles we need to develop, in what order of the project, and how to develop them to give sense to a class of problems. Now, we are anticipating to refine the principles in order for them to encapsulate newly developed design knowledge from new BIE cycles." (Author 1)

I understood early on in the project, that there was little stability throughout the project. As a young researcher, I've realized that making sense of the fuzziness of the process would be challenging and I needed to equip myself with the necessary tools to do so. To find some stability, I looked to the literature to help define the meta-requirements for our blockchain platform, seeking insights from how other projects in similar domains had approached this challenge. By reviewing these case studies, we were able to anticipate the kinds of principles that would guide our design process, particularly in ensuring that our platform could remain adaptable and sustainable." (Author 2)

"In wrapping our heads around the wicked design context we were engaging with, we spent time anticipating what meaning we could reasonably attribute to our design prescriptions. The notion of trying to cater to a desirable 'propositional' nature of design principles came out strong." (Author 3)

Finally, when reflecting upon "Why" questions, the authors' reflection exemplified insights that were mostly related to the third form of anticipatory reflection and learning, with respect to reflections about "alteration of understanding future solution spaces", and "envisioning future design processes":

"Some of the ADR members anticipated that we would shape our understanding about future solution spaces via learning outcomes from the design thinking process. The anticipation was based on experiences from prior design research projects, and thus gave sense to define a solution space that allows us to be flexible and less chained to isolating views on how we perceive future variants of solution spaces in the project." (Author 1)

"What made the project so interesting for me was learning how the notion of "sustainability by design" is rather fuzzy. Finding a partner company that was willing to explore that with us gave us the confidence that it was more than just a 'fuzzy concept'." (Author 2)

"One of the reasons I wanted to do this project, was that it allowed us to reflect in practice about a common perception or pre-conception of a negative relation between blockchain implementations and sustainability. We, thus, anticipated adding meaning to 'sustainability by design' with a 'controversial' case of blockchain technology in point; also anticipating potential meaningful generalization for similar perceptions related to other emergent technologies such as AI." (Author 3)

5.2 Retrospective Reflection and Learning

How reflective is the retrospective moment where the ADR scholar is engaged with making sense of past ADR activities, and what is it like reflecting and learning after ADR activities have been executed when the ADR team is still engaged with anticipating the future? These questions are overarching questions of the second theme. By means of concrete experiential examples, the eidetic insights of the authors are for this theme understood in relation to two different forms of retrospective reflection and learning: (a) *sense-making something from the past*, and (b) *sense-giving something emerging* by sense-making something similar from the past. We now apply the phenomenological approach for sense-giving and sense-making, to explore how these forms of retrospective reflection and learning can elaborate ADR as a reflective practice.

For example, when the authors reflected upon "What" and "When" questions, eidetic insights about sense-making of meaning through retrospective reflection and learning, were primarily related to first form. Here, the phenomenological reflection concerned examples about the "embodiment of meaning structures", "inscribing anecdotal meanings", and "value-setting shared meaning from past formalized learning outcomes":

> *"During the second cycle, we worked with reflecting on how we can embody ideas, impulses, and insights from the past design process, to make sense of what makes the design activities meaningful for our own reflection and learning as researchers."* (Author 1)

> *"In the second BIE cycle, we came to understand that our design activities were fundamentally a continuous process of sense-making. While our creative approach to the project appeared chaotic at times, it was, in fact, a deliberate and meaningful sequence of decisions shaped by deep reflective exercises throughout the process. This was mostly facilitated by the fact that the ADR research team consisted of a junior scholar, making sense of the environment, and a senior scholar providing guidance throughout the project, based on past experiences."* (Author 2)

> *"In retrospect, the work on this project challenged our meaning of ADR as a design process progressing 'in stages', at least for this problem class. The sense of design process linearity implied in the notion of 'stage' did not reflect well the experience of an interconnected system of design activities, with reflection and learning continuously engaging with other activities."* (Author 3)

When reflecting upon "Why" questions, the authors' reflection exemplified insights that were primarily related to the second form, with respect to reflections concerning examples about "weaving new cultural meaning from past encounters with shaping the ensemble", and "interpretation of past structural meanings of intervention":

> *"We can now, after 1 and a half year, see how our project has brought new cultural meaning to the stakeholders' organizational practices by letting them encounter the shaping process of the ensemble artifact cyclically. This is similar to weaving dots into a thread that gets larger and longer over time, to a degree where others also start seeing what the process and outcome of the weaving means to their lifeworld."* (Author 1)

> *"It was inspiring to see how our workshops on 'sustainability by design' had impact on the decision-making process of the company. From feedback with the company, we learned that they meaning of sustainability had changed over the course of the project. Mostly this was due to the fact that throughout the project I was making sense their operations and how I could match that with the notion of 'sustainability', triggering multiple questions, that (coincidentally) challenged the way they viewed the concept."* (Author 2)

"Through this project of making sense of and giving sense to 'sustainability by design', the company has demonstrated that its commitment to sustainability goes beyond offering a sustainability product to the market. It extends to how they build and operate their business, making their claims of dedication to a sustainable world far more credible for internal and external stakeholders." (Author 3)

5.3 Contemporaneous Reflection and Learning

How reflective is the contemporaneous moment where the ADR scholar is engaged with giving sense to, and making sense of, on-going ADR activities? And what signifies this kind of reflection that takes place here and now, as opposed to in the past or for the future? These questions are overarching questions of the third and final theme. By means of concrete experiential examples, the eidetic insights of the authors are for this theme understood in relation to three different forms of contemporaneous reflection and learning: (a) *sense-giving and sense-making something here and now*, (b) *sense-giving the seemingly urgent*, and (c) *sense-making from the past and future in order to understand the present*. We now apply the phenomenological approach for sense-giving and sense-making, to explore how these forms of contemporaneous reflection and learning can elaborate ADR as a reflective practice.

For example, when the authors reflected upon "What" questions, eidetic insights about sense-making of meaning through contemporaneous reflection and learning, were primarily related to first and second forms. Here, the phenomenological reflection concerned examples about the "distribution of situated meaning", and "enacting intersubjective meaning-making":

"Workshops with stakeholders that allow them to test a version of the prototype, reflect, and talk out loud about their reflections, have been useful for reflecting in the moment. Another technique we adopted was gamification-based roleplays in the physical room with stop-and-think points, which deliberately facilitated reflective moments during roleplay scenarios to understand the situated meaning of a virtual training scenario, played out in a non-virtual environment." (Author 1)

"I think that making sense of the here and now is more difficult to fabricate, than it is to reflect upon the past or the future. The 'here and now' is spontaneous and emerges from in situ actions and interactions with each other. Giving sense to the here and now is also something that happens through enacting with the others' reflection. There is a sense of co-reflection here that we [researchers and stakeholders] can engage with via something that triggers us to think about." (Author 1)

"Sense-making in the moment often revolved around navigating the ambiguity of sustainability and the diversity in perspectives. During stakeholder workshops, real-time adjustments to the BDN helped align these perspectives and connect meaning. These moments of reflection shaped immediate decisions and offered clarity in addressing emergent challenges providing guidance for the next cycles." (Author 2)

> *"During the workshops, we constantly experienced how rich yet challenging it was to engage in collective design with our diverse ADR team. For instance, some team members had little to no familiarity with the technology—the means—but were essential for representing the sustainability perspective—the ends—and vice versa. A critical skill we had to rely on a lot 'in the moment' was actively finding ways to connect meaning somewhere 'in the middle.' I remember that, rather early in the project, we used a drawing with 'the ends' on one side, 'the means' on the other, and a big question mark on the line connecting them, to signal the challenge."* (Author 3)

When reflecting upon "When" questions, the authors' reflection exemplified insights that were primarily related to the second form, with respect to reflections concerning examples about "framing meaning structures", and "re-defining meaning expressions":

> *"The here-and-now, stop-and-think kind of reflection, helped us in the project to frame what we think is meaningful for the activity we are encountering. This kind of reflection is different from a retrospective one which is more of an exploration of embodied information from the past. The here-and-now reflection is more confrontative, urging the team to give sense to what is going on in the room"* (Author 1)

> *During discussion with my supervisor, I was often challenged on my assumptions on how I tried to make sense of the observations from the workshops. I needed to rethink my I needed to rethink my interpretations and consider alternative perspectives. This process of re-evaluation was crucial in refining my understanding of the meaning behind 'sustainability' and 'blockchain'. By critically examining my initial assumptions and being open to different viewpoints, I was able to develop a more nuanced and comprehensive understanding of these complex concepts, guided by my supervisor.* (Author 2)

> *"I paid close attention to people's body language during the meetings—the way they shared their ideas, spoke about their experiences, responded to questions, and expressed their opinions. These interactions revealed subtle signs of underlying issues with meaning. We needed to address them in the moment, not later, because we aimed to co-create meaning directly, with everyone in the room. This way, the meaning would be co-owned"* (Author 3)

Finally, when reflecting upon "Why" questions, the authors' reflection exemplified insights that were related to the third form of contemporaneous reflection and learning, with respect to reflections about "re-viewing meaning of past problem spaces from present problem perspectives":

> *"After completing the project, we realized there was more to the story—particularly around the process itself and the role of constant reflection throughout. We realized there was an extra layer to our principles that focused on the iterative, reflective nature of our work. This addition aims to inform future projects by emphasizing how ongoing reflection shaped our approach and decision-making,*

providing a reflective framework for managing uncertainty and complex challenges in future challenges." (Author 2)

"I guess what really made us decide to pivot to an affordances conceptualization of meaning on this ADR project was not an anticipatory or retrospective theoretical consideration, but rather a very tangible feeling of discomfort and difficulty with a live exercise of making sense of a capabilities-based conceptualization by the practitioners during one of the workshops." (Author 3)

6 Concluding Discussion

This study explored the research question: *how can ADR be used as a reflective practice that engages scholars with sense-giving and sense-making of meaning?* The question was prompted due to the lack of extensive research nor insights on how the reflection and learning stage is facilitated in an ADR project [8], and thus the possibility of producing insights that can help ADR scholars facilitate the third ADR stage as reflective practice. As a result, the study employed a phenomenological approach inspired mainly by phenomenologists such as Van Manen and Zahavi, but also others (e.g., [57, 58, 61]) that inspired this study to explore a phenomenological approach for sense-giving and sense-making of meaning. Consequently, the study followed the phenomenological tradition of prompting questions that enable a self-reflective practice for generating eidetic insights that were presented as phenomenological themes for engaging with ADR as a reflective practice. In this section, we will discuss the themes' implications for practice and theory by connecting them to Schön's [13] notions of "reflective activity", "reflection-in-action", and "knowing-in-action". The discussion will also highlight the viability of phenomenology for centralizing a clear understanding of 'meaning', the variances of it, and why it is fruitful for IS researchers to engage with a self-reflexive practice about meaning in DSR (in this case, ADR). The section ends with outlining the limitations of this study and an outlook on future research.

6.1 Implications for Practice

Practicing ADR is typically guided by principles of ADR along with tasks for each ADR stage (see [5], pp. 40–44). At the same time, as indicated by ADR scholars (e.g., [8, 11]), not everyone who use ADR report how they have followed the principles or engaged with every task across the ADR stages. Nor is it completely obvious what kind of overarching principles that govern a successful ADR project, given the emerging nature of challenges and problems that an ADR scholar must learn how to navigate in a project [7]. It is against this background, that we discuss what implications of our study has for practicing ADR as a reflective practice.

First, our study mainly contributes to elaborating how the third ADR stage of reflection and learning can be elaborated in relation to the phenomenological concept of temporality. An ADR project exists over a period that stretches from 2–4 years depending on the complexity of the project [5]. During this time, reflection and learning occurs as an integrated process, cyclically, through an interplay with BIE-activities that, to use the phenomenological terminology, "open up" and "close down" for a reflective practice; e.g., opens up through the need of reflecting the design and redesign during the project, and closes down after analyzing intervention results according to stated design goals. In other words, the reflective practice occurs if there is a reason for reflection and learning to occur (e.g., need for refining design goals, prototype improvement), and that reason generally emerges and is identified via cycles of BIE. The BIE cycles are thus important for giving the ADR scholar an impulse to reflect and learn continuously. It is in the context of this on-going interplay that our work has implications for practicing reflection and learning over time as proposed by the phenomenological themes. For example, the themes provide ADR scholars a temporal structure to explain how they reflected upon their work, what reflections they did before a BIE cycle, after a milestone in a project, and in the moment of conducting a design process. Another example deals with the temporal nature of reflection, something that both Schön [66] and Van Manen [17] point out as inevitable for a reflective practice to happen. The phenomenological themes thus help ADR scholars to organize their reflection and learning stage accordingly to the three different aspects of temporality (anticipatory, retrospective, and contemporaneous).

Second, our study contributes to the practice of ADR by demonstrating how ADR scholars can ask phenomenological questions to pursue a self-reflexive practice, which is similar as doing a reflection about the reflection and learning stage. The prompted questions of this study can be used as guidelines for how to formulate similar questions that address the "What", "When", and "Why" aspects of a self-reflexive practice. As advocated by Van Manen [35], only what is given or what gives itself in lived experiences are proper phenomenological data for reflection and eidetic insights about the quality of the lived experience. The "lived" in turn is, here, referring to the experiences that carry the meaningfulness character of concrete, contextualized, and situated events in an ADR project, which triggered the necessity of thinking through reflection. The phenomenological gesture, which we proposed in this study, is thus to lift up and bring into focus with language any such raw moments of lived experiences, and help the ADR scholar to orient himself/herself to the lived meanings that arise in their experiences. It is this latter aspect that, as demonstrated in our study, phenomenological questions help an ADR scholar to conduct on a meta-level.

Finally, our study contributes to practicing reflection and learning in ADR by emphasizing the notions of sense-giving and sense-making, both of which are central to both phenomenology [18] as well as studies in organizations theory (e.g., [58]). By pursuing in a reflective practice through ADR, the scholar can use the phenomenological approach demonstrated in this study to give sense to, and make sense of, his/her eidetic insights on what makes their learning outcomes meaningful, and how their sense-making gives sense to the formalization of learning outcomes (e.g., influencing the development of design principles by describing what makes them meaningful).

6.2 Implications for Theory

Promoting ADR as a reflective practice has implications for how to understand the potentials of other DSR methods to emphasize the importance of reflection. Phenomenology can be used to guide DSR scholars in their reflective practice by centralizing the importance of "meaning" through a sense-giving and sense-making process. As such, the phenomenological approach of this study demonstrates clear concepts and aspects of both sense-giving, sense-making, and embodiment of meaning variances, which together help other scholars to conceptualize the significance of their reflective practice. This contribution has implications for theory in a number of ways.

First, our study contributes theoretically to the ADR method by extending the reflection and learning stage with three phenomenological themes, which unveil qualitative and temporal aspects of the stage to engage with. The contribution has, to some degree, similar implications as prior work that aimed to extend the ADR framework with both new and additional stages (e.g., [64]), or work that emphasized a particular component of the ADR framework (e.g., [9, 65]). Our proposed themes flesh out a nuanced way to theoretically understand the subtle aspects of reflection as an activity over time by providing specific concepts that enable the ADR scholar to practice reflection through sense-giving and sense-making of meaning. For instance, an anticipatory form of reflection can be done in relation to a typical DSR activity such as evaluation, where ex-ante evaluations emphasize the importance of identifying future evaluands (objects of evaluation) and techniques for evaluation [19]. Here, an anticipatory form of reflection can for example be used to conceptually entail the nature of ex-ante evaluations into sense-giving of what makes the evaluation meaningful, or sense-making of how reflection in itself constitutes an important part of evaluating emerging design knowledge (e.g., design principles) prior to the actual design of prototypes.

Second, the phenomenological approach in this study introduced the notion of "meaning" to the DSR community by unveiling the different phenomenological variances that can be useful for scholars that want to supplement the DSR notions "efficiency" and "sufficiency" with meaning. Doing so, one can for instance go beyond instrumental values of reflection and learning (e.g., causality of a reflected learning outcome and a refined design goal) to *"[...] express the exemplary aspects of meaning of a phenomenon."* ([35], p. 814). An aspect of meaning could in this case deal with concrete accounts of an experienced conflicting perspective between researchers and stakeholders, or researchers themselves. As pointed out by [5], the ways of which an artifact is shaped cannot be done without friction and conflicts in the organizational use, perspectives, and participants, especially if the project includes interventions. The meaning of the conflicts, how they hold a certain tension for making the singular intelligible, are aspects that the ADR scholar open up through a sense-giving and sense-making process. Implications of such process is for instance relevant for the guided emergence principle of ADR ([5], p. 44) as variances of meaning capture vital traits of describing culminating change that causes anticipated and unanticipated consequences—e.g., consequences that indicate how an ongoing refinement of design principles might be meaningful over time due to their significance for facilitating the design process as a reflective practice.

Finally, our work has theoretical implications for understanding ADR as a reflective practice by incorporating phenomenological reasonings around Schön's [13] notions of "reflective activity", "reflection-in-action", and "knowing-in-action", all of which are relevant for the reflection and learning stage of ADR. For example, a reflective activity stretches across a temporality of reflection and can thus not be considered as an isolated activity alone, especially because reflections might overlap as being anticipatory and retrospective (e.g., basing an anticipatory reflection on the reflection from the past). In phenomenological terms, the "intentionality" (direction) of a reflective activity is thus always in relation to time and space as influencing factors, whereas the content of the reflection might happen in action. As described by Van Manen ([45], p. 814), *"[...] methodologically speaking, phenomenology does not rely on (numerical, coded or objectifying) data but rather on data as 'phenomenological examples'"*. A reflection-in-action is thus a reflection on the examples that unveil meaning in-action through for instance sense-making, as was exemplified by the authors of this study when describing the third phenomenological theme of contemporaneous reflection and learning. A "stop-and-think" type of reflection also includes a mode of "knowing-in-action" as the reflective ADR practitioner have to be confronted with meanings of a lived experience that are not always rooted in a theoretical concept—e.g., evaluating adherence to design principles a-theoretically [8].

6.3 Limitations and Future Research

The limitation of our study is that we have followed the phenomenological approach along with a set of formulated phenomenological questions to only three scholars from two ADR projects. For future research, we thus propose that both ADR and DSR scholars test to apply the phenomenological approach, together with the proposed themes for reflection and learning, to come up with a set of own original questions that help them to engage with a reflective practice that is based on sense-giving and sense-making of meaning.

References

1. Gregor, S., Hevner, A.R.: Positioning and presenting design science research for maximum impact. MIS Q. **37**, 337–355 (2013)
2. Hevner, A.R., March, S.T., Park, J., Ram, S.: Design science in information systems research. MIS Q. **28**, 75–105 (2004)
3. Baskerville, R., Myers, M.D.: Special issue on action research in information systems: making IS research relevant to practice: foreword. MIS Q. **28**, 329–335 (2004)
4. Davison, R., Martinsons, M.G., Kock, N.: Principles of canonical action research. Inf. Syst. J. **14**(1), 65–86 (2004)
5. Sein, M.K., Henfridsson, O., Purao, S., Rossi, M., Lindgren, R.: Action design research. MIS Q. **35**, 37–56 (2011)
6. Pan, S.L., Carter, L., Tim, Y., Sandeep, M.S.: Digital sustainability, climate change, and information systems solutions: opportunities for future research. Int. J. Inf. Manag. **63**, 102444 (2022)
7. Haj-Bolouri, A., Purao, S., Rossi, M., & Bernhardsson, L.. Action Design Research in Practice: Lessons and Concerns. In ECIS (p. 131) (2018, June).
8. Twomey, M.B., Sammon, D., Nagle, T.: The tango of problem formulation: a patient's/researcher's reflection on an action design research journey. J. Med. Internet Res. **22**(7), e16916 (2020)

9. Haj-Bolouri, A., Bernhardsson, L., Rossi, M.: PADRE: a method for participatory action design research. In: Tackling Society's Grand Challenges with Design Science: 11th International Conference, DESRIST 2016, St. John's, NL, Canada, May 23-25, 2016, Proceedings 11, pp. 19–36. Springer International Publishing (2016)
10. Mullarkey, M.T., Hevner, A.R.: An elaborated action design research process model. Eur. J. Inf. Syst. **28**(1), 6–20 (2019)
11. Cronholm, S., Göbel, H.: Evaluation of action design research. Scand. J. Inf. Syst. **31**(2), 2 (2019)
12. Bødker, K., Kensing, F., Simonsen, J.: Participatory design in information systems development. In: Reframing Humans in Information Systems development, pp. 115–134. Springer, London (2011)
13. Schön, D.A.: The Reflective Practitioner, New York (1979)
14. Van Rensburg, J.J., Goede, R.: A model for improving knowledge generation in design science research through reflective practice. Electron. J. Bus. Res. Methods **17**(4), 192–211 (2019)
15. Visser, W.: Schön: design as a reflective practice. Collections. **2**, 21–25 (2010)
16. Vagle, M.D.: Re-framing Schön's call for a phenomenology of practice: a post-intentional approach. Reflective Pract. **11**(3), 393–407 (2010)
17. Van Manen, M.: On the epistemology of reflective practice. Teacher. Teach. **1**(1), 33–50 (1995)
18. Zahavi, D.: Phenomenology: the Basics. Routledge (2018)
19. Venable, J., Pries-Heje, J., Baskerville, R.: FEDS: a framework for evaluation in design science research. Eur. J. Inf. Syst. **25**(1), 77–89 (2016)
20. Peffers, K., Tuunanen, T., Rothenberger, M.A., Chatterjee, S.: A design science research methodology for information systems research. J. Manag. Inf. Syst. **24**(3), 45–77 (2007)
21. Gregor, S., & Jones, D. (2007). The Anatomy of a Design Theory
22. Gibbs, G.: Learning by Doing: a Guide to Teaching and Learning Methods. Further Education Unit (1988)
23. Dewey, J. (1934). Having an Experience
24. Wade, R.C., Yarbrough, D.B.: Portfolios: a tool for reflective thinking in teacher education? Teach. Teach. Educ. **12**(1), 63–79 (1996)
25. Schön, D. A. (1987). Educating the Reflective Practitioner
26. Gill, G.S.: The nature of reflective practice and emotional intelligence in tutorial settings. J. Educ. Learn. **3**(1), 86–100 (2014)
27. Dias, M., Pan, S.L., Tim, Y., Land, L.: Managing historical conditions in information systems strategizing: an imprinting perspective. J. Strateg. Inf. Syst. **32**(4), 101794 (2023)
28. Buyssens, H., Viaene, S.: Design principles for a blockchain-based multi-sided platform for the sustainable trade of water: an affordance approach. J. Clean. Prod. **471**, 143212 (2024)
29. Pathirannehelage, S.H., Shrestha, Y.R., von Krogh, G.: Design principles for artificial intelligence-augmented decision making: an action design research study. Eur. J. Inf. Syst., 1–23 (2024)
30. Driscoll, J., Teh, B.: The potential of reflective practice to develop individual orthopaedic nurse practitioners and their practice. J. Orthop. Nurs. **5**(2), 95–103 (2001)
31. Simon, H.A.: The Sciences of the Artificial, Reissue of the Third Edition with a New Introduction by John Laird. MIT Press (2019)
32. Greeno, J.G.: The situativity of knowing, learning, and research. Am. Psychol. **53**(1), 5–26 (1998)
33. Binks, C., Jones, F.W., Knight, K.: Facilitating reflective practice groups in clinical psychology training: a phenomenological study. Reflective Pract. **14**(3), 305–318 (2013)
34. Westoby, P.: Understanding Phenomenological Reflective Practice in the Social and Ecological Fields: Three Rivers Flowing. Routledge (2022)

35. Van Manen, M.: Phenomenology in its original sense. Qual. Health Res. **27**(6), 810–825 (2017)
36. Van Manen, M.: The Tact of Teaching: the Meaning of Pedagogical Thoughtfulness. Routledge (2016)
37. Schutz, A.: The Phenomenology of the Social World. Northwestern University Press (1967)
38. Riemer, K., Johnston, R.B.: Clarifying ontological inseparability with Heidegger's analysis of equipment. MIS Q. **41**(4), 1059–1082 (2017)
39. Monod, E., Boland, R., Santoro, F., Joyce, E.: The philosopher's corner: the duality of Heidegger in information systems research. ACM SIGMIS Datab.Adv. Inform. Syst. **53**(2), 26–40 (2022)
40. Haj-Bolouri, A.: The experience of immersive virtual reality: a phenomenology inspired inquiry. Commun. Assoc. Inf. Syst. **52**(1), 782–814 (2023)
41. Haj-Bolouri, A.: The philosopher's corner: The "immersed flesh": A phenomenological conceptualization of immersive virtual reality embodiment. The DATA BASE for Advances in Information Systems (Forthcoming)
42. Haj-Bolouri, A.: Wickedness in designing IT for integration work. A phenomenological account. Scand. J. Inf. Syst. **33**(1), 9 (2021)
43. Introna, L.D.: Hermeneutics and meaning-making in information systems. In: The Oxford Handbook of Management Information Systems: Critical Perspectives and New Directions, pp. 229–252 (2011)
44. Manen, M.V.: From meaning to method. Qual. Health Res. **7**(3), 345–369 (1997)
45. Van Manen, M.: Phenomenology of Practice: Meaning-Giving Methods in Phenomenological Research and Writing. Routledge (2023)
46. Husserl, E.: Ideas for a Pure Phenomenology and Phenomenological Philosophy: First Book: General Introduction to Pure Phenomenology. Hackett Publishing (2014)
47. Irwin, W.: Avatar and Philosophy: Learning to See. John Wiley & Sons (2014)
48. Spangenberger, P., Geiger, S.M., Freytag, S.C.: Becoming nature: effects of embodying a tree in immersive virtual reality on nature relatedness. Sci. Rep. **12**(1), 1311 (2022)
49. Heidegger, M.: The Question Concerning Technology. Garland Publishing, INC, New York/London (1977)
50. Ferro, F.: Beyond the Digital: The Virtuality of the Flesh in Merleau-Ponty's The Visibile and the Invisible (2024)
51. Tham, J., Howard, T., Verhulsdonck, G.: Extending design thinking, content strategy, and artificial intelligence into technical communication and user experience design programs: further pedagogical implications. J. Tech. Writ. Commun. **52**(4), 428–459 (2022)
52. Merleau-Ponty, M.: Phenomenology of Perception. Translated by Colin Smith (1965).
53. Saker, M., Frith, J.: Coextensive space: virtual reality and the developing relationship between the body, the digital and physical space. Media Cult. Soc. **42**(7–8), 1427–1442 (2020)
54. Verbeek, P.P.: What Things Do: Philosophical Reflections on Technology, Agency, and Design. Penn State Press (2005)
55. Hermberg, K.: Husserl's Phenomenology: Knowledge, Objectivity and Others. Bloomsbury Publishing (2006)
56. Gioia, D.A., Chittipeddi, K.: Sensemaking and sensegiving in strategic change initiation. Strateg. Manag. J. **12**(6), 433–448 (1991)
57. Dreyfus, H.L.: Essays in Honor of Hubert L. Dreyfus: Heidegger, Authenticity, and Modernity, vol. 1. MIT Press (2000)
58. Sandberg, J., Tsoukas, H.: Sensemaking reconsidered: towards a broader understanding through phenomenology. Organiz. Theory. **1**(1), 2631787719879937 (2020)
59. Carman, J.G.: Understanding evaluation in nonprofit organizations. Public Perform. Manag. Rev. **34**(3), 350–377 (2011)

60. Weick, K.E.: Reflections on enacted sensemaking in the Bhopal disaster. J. Manag. Stud. **47**(3), 537–550 (2010)
61. Woroniecki, S., Wibeck, V., Zeiler, K., Linnér, B.O.: The lived experiences of transformations: the role of sense-making and phenomenology analyses. Environ. Sci. Pol. **159**, 103797 (2024)
62. Casey, E.S.: Comparative phenomenology of mental activity: memory, hallucination, and fantasy contrasted with imagination. Res. Phenomenol. **6**, 1–25 (1976)
63. Van Manen, M.: But is it phenomenology? Qual. Health Res. **27**(6), 775–779 (2017)
64. Keijzer-Broers, W.J., de Reuver, M.: Applying agile design sprint methods in action design research: prototyping a health and wellbeing platform. In: Tackling Society's Grand Challenges with Design Science: 11th International Conference, DESRIST 2016, St. John's, NL, Canada, May 23–25, 2016, Proceedings 11, pp. 68–80. Springer International Publishing (2016)
65. Bilandzic, M., Venable, J.: Towards participatory action design research: adapting action research and design science research methods for urban informatics. J. Commun. Inform. **7**(3) (2011)
66. Schön, D.: Donald schon (schön): learning, reflection and change (1983). Accessed 11 Apr 2004

On the Role of Vision in Design Science Research

Bijan Khosrawi-Rad[1](✉) [iD], Susanne Robra-Bissantz[1] [iD], Timo Strohmann[1,2] [iD], and Jan vom Brocke[2] [iD]

[1] TU Braunschweig, Braunschweig, Germany
{b.khosrawi-rad,s.robra-bissantz,t.strohmann}@tu-bs.de,
timo.strohmann@uni-muenster.de
[2] University of Münster, Münster, Germany
jan.vom.brocke@uni-muenster.de

Abstract. Design science research (DSR) creates novel artifacts to address real-world challenges. Yet, DSR often overlooks explicit articulation of research projects' underlying values and future visions. This gap hinders effective communication, reduces design knowledge reusability, and may lead to questionable results. To address this issue, we shed light on the role of vision in DSR. We propose a *vision cycle* and exemplarily show its integration into Hevner's (2007) three-cycle view by emphasizing the importance of clearly formulating, reflecting on, and communicating a DSR project's vision, especially the direction in which solutions are explored. Drawing on vision communication literature, the vision cycle guides researchers to define overarching values, envision a preferred future, and outline a mission for realizing that vision. We contribute to the discussion on design knowledge communication by highlighting the importance of vision articulation and reflection to address grand societal challenges, offering methodological guidance, and promoting transparency in DSR.

Keywords: Design Science Research · Communication · Vision · Cycle

1 Introduction

Design science research (DSR) enables the creation of artifacts that solve practical problems while ensuring scientific rigor [1, 2]. An important phase in DSR is the communication of contributions to the outside world to enable further researchers to build on the acquired knowledge and to solve real-world problems [1, 2]. Although scholars stress the importance of DSR communication (ibid.), we have identified severe challenges relating to this and the contribution that DSR can provide for science and practice. We discovered these challenges during a DSR meta-study project that aimed at bringing together design knowledge of different research groups engaged in solving similar real-world problems [3]. While we systematically analyzed and synthesized contributions of prior DSR projects, we observed contradictions in the communicated design knowledge. Although the creative approach of DSR may lead to diverse solutions [4], design principles (DPs) that contradict are neither applicable in practical contexts nor can they be built upon in further research. We found that the occurrence of contradictory design knowledge shows that researchers often disagree on their picture of a future world. For example, in reviewing learning technology literature, we found DPs for promoting learners' autonomy (e.g., [5, 6]), while others advocate controlling students via learning analytics (e.g., [7, 8]). Although practitioners or researchers may agree on the one or the other worldview, we argue that the latter should be communicated because clear communication is vital for making DSR artifacts reusable [2]. Without an explicit objective, practitioners and researchers struggle to understand the intended benefits and underlying values, which reduces adoption. We consider this lack of communication a limitation of current research, as scholars should not only discuss *how* to achieve a goal but also *which* goal they pursue [9, 10]. Given that theorizing through design often leads to artifacts that are tied to specific conditions and serve dedicated low-range outcome variables, we consider it a drawback that it is rarely explained how gradual advances align with broader, for example, societal developments [9, 11]. Although this seems to be an inherent problem of (design) research that reduces the potential of design contributions [12], we advocate for adopting a holistic perspective on DSR as a method for creating a better future [9]. We argue that DSR projects always need something like a vision of the future and better world that is supposed to be achieved via artifacts and corresponding design knowledge. A vision is an idealistic depiction of a future scenario that directs long-term impact and meaningful change [13].

In DSR, a focus on a vision is hardly pronounced [9]. Organizations in practice instead typically articulate their vision explicitly, plan 3–5 years ahead, and continuously review their vision [14, 15]. In this research-in-progress paper, we adapt this practice-oriented perspective on visions to DSR. A vision should help researchers to articulate, continuously refine and communicate their view of a better world. Hence, we address a **first research question (RQ1):** *How can we introduce a vision of a future world into DSR?* As we strive for a first applicable showcase, we formulate a **second research question (RQ2)**: *How can we conceptualize a vision cycle that supplements Hevner's* [1] *overall accepted three-cycle-concept of DSR to adopt, apply, and communicate research visions in DSR projects?* In the following, we justify the need for a vision in DSR and share our insights concerning the relevance of a vision in different methodological DSR approaches. We then exemplary show for the three-cycle view of Hevner [1], how a vision can be anchored in a DSR project. We finish our paper with an example of a research project that brings the vision cycle into a researcher's life.

2 Research Background

2.1 Visions in DSR

DSR, as a key approach in information systems (IS) research, cannot be value-free [16]. While explanatory research in the natural sciences focuses on understanding how things are, design science is concerned with how things ought to be, meaning the development of artifacts to achieve specific goals [17]. DSR seeks prescriptive knowledge on how to design and implement artifacts to solve specific problems [18]. It is necessary in DSR to explicitly specify the goals of artifact development in scientific contributions [18]. Concerning its goals, aims or problem solving, however, it is recently discussed that DRS should emphasize broader objectives and even visions for developing different types of design knowledge [16]. Given DSR's openness to diverse theoretical and philosophical streams, personal values and worldviews inherently influence the design process [4] without being explicitly stated [19]. Apart from personal worldviews, researchers argue that great challenges of the IS field should be leading its research [20]. Also critically reflected IS visions, such as full virtualization, increasingly integrate IS discipline goals into broader economic and societal contexts [21]. Consequently, DSR is expected not only to focus on individual projects but also to serve as a "supermethodology" addressing global challenges [9]. This perspective is reinforced by conferences like *WI2022*, which addressed both *"Grand Challenges for IS"* and *"IS for Grand Challenges"*. Regarding visions, the perspective of "organizing visions" highlights the role of shared visions in legitimizing, diffusing, and applying IT innovations and supports the need for collective, cross-disciplinary future visions in IS research [22]. Here, visions that relate to a fundamental value system are already incorporated in value-sensitive design [23], that argues for embedding ethical considerations early in a value-based engineering process. Closer to the DSR paradigm, incorporating digital responsibility in IS research entails aligning the DSR process itself as well as the evaluation of artifacts with underlying values and asks for transparency in key decision-making during artifact creation process [10, 24].

While IS research step by step recognizes the need to consider vision, a systematic method for communicating vision in DSR remains absent. Guiding visions that most likely drive researchers and research groups, are neither systematically assessed for alignment with economic or societal future scenarios nor integrated into widely accepted guidelines for presenting research contributions. This omission not only raises challenges regarding their practical impact on organizations but also threatens the anchoring of design knowledge in a sustainable knowledge base, hindering its further development. To integrate the vision perspective in DSR, we acknowledge that multiple DSR frameworks exist (e.g., [19, 25, 26]). We focused on Hevner's [1] three-cycle view, as its emphasis on balancing relevance with rigor makes it an ideal foundation for demonstrating how broader aspirations and values can inform each DSR project phase.

2.2 Vision Communication in Practice

Our conceptualization of vision's role in DSR draws on literature about vision communication in practice. The vision is based on the interplay of the vision statement, mission, and value system. Practitioners use the articulation of an overarching *vision* to set strategic directions and inspire change [14, 15]. These visions not only impact individual organizations but also provide a foundation for addressing grand societal challenges [10]. A vision is a forward-looking depiction of the desired long-term impact that aims for meaningful transformation [13]. Forming and implementing a shared vision is often challenging due to contrasting stakeholder interests, different worldviews and established processes [13, 14]. Hence, the vision's enactment should be preceded by a systematic forming process (ibid.). Practitioners use *vision statements* to communicate this vision effectively, which they derive from core values [15, 27]. They clearly articulate the long-term goals of an endeavor. Underlying these statements are *values*, which are fundamental (ethical) guidelines that direct actions toward realizing the vision [13, 28]. Values represent normative anchors for guiding action, while a vision translates them into a desired future scenario [13]. Closely linked to the vision is the *mission*. The mission describes specific strategies for transforming certain overarching (e.g., societal) phenomena and outlines how the vision will be achieved [13, 29].

3 Integration of a Vision in DSR Projects

In the following, we first illustrate how the vision cycle can be integrated into different DSR frameworks and then demonstrate the integration for Hevner's [1] model.

3.1 Positioning the Vision Cycle in DSR Frameworks

Yet, current DSR frameworks would benefit from a systematic way to articulate an overarching vision to guide project evolution (see Sect. 2.1). Hevner's [1] widely cited three-cycle view organizes research into the relevance, rigor, and design cycles. Nonetheless, while each cycle may be influenced by underlying values, the framework does not explicitly incorporate a mechanism for continuously articulating and refining a project's vision. An added "vision" cycle would systematically unify these existing cycles around a shared mission, ensuring that broader ambitions, ethical stance, and forward perspectives inform design decisions. In such a configuration, the relevance cycle would not only address immediate, practice-based problems but also ensure that the externally derived vision aligns with the design intentions of the researcher. In the rigor cycle, only those established theories and strands of design knowledge that are coherent with the overall vision would be employed, ensuring that long-term aspirations guide theoretical contributions. Moreover, because the design cycle inherently connects with both the relevance and rigor cycles, positioning the vision as an overarching layer over the design cycle reinforces the idea that ethical and societal considerations, as well as the researcher's creative stance, should permeate the artifact development.

Process models such as those proposed by Peffers et al. [25] and Kuechler & Vaishnavi [30] outline iterative steps, from problem identification and motivation, to conclusion or communication, but these models rarely translate their initial problem orientation into an explicit, value-based vision. They often treat grand challenges, such as sustainability or digital responsibility, as implicit aspects of the problem statement, rather than as clearly articulated long-term visions that guide development. By integrating a unifying vision, these models would anchor the entire design process in ethical and societal objectives, ensuring each step tangibly contributes to a future-oriented mission. Notably, although the Peffers et al. [25] model includes a dedicated communication phase, it does not explicitly integrate the underlying vision into this process.

Similarly, the eDSR methodology [26] breaks complex projects into hierarchical echelons to manage intricacy, a strength that supports design knowledge accumulation. Nonetheless, a clear vision that transcends these echelons could unify short-term objectives with ethical or societal goals, making the project's evolution more transparent. The BAUSTEIN approach [19] includes a vision component ('vision BAUSTEIN') that mainly reflects the researcher's personal creativity without a systematic method to continuously capture, refine, and integrate an overarching vision. By extending this component into a sustained, guiding vision, BAUSTEIN could better align personal creativity with long-term impact and foster consistent decision-making across the project.

According to vom Brocke et al. [2], design knowledge hinges on the relationship between problem and solution spaces, a dynamic interplay where each DSR project contributes to a broader, evolving body of knowledge. A vision cycle could make these relationships explicit by aligning each design decision with a unifying vision, addressing both immediate problems and long-term values. By incorporating a dedicated vision, researchers could continuously articulate long-term aspirations that explicitly bind the problem and solution spaces. This approach would ensure that each contribution is not only evaluated on its immediate projectability but also on how it advances a future vision. In doing so, the vision would contribute to transparency, guide iterative refinement, and foster ethically and socially aligned knowledge accumulation.

In line with prior insights on vision articulation [9, 22], we argue that the absence of a clearly defined vision may hamper the ability to articulate overarching aspirations, track the evolution of goals, and communicate the foundational worldviews that underpin diverse design artifacts. By explicitly formulating such a vision and continuously refining it throughout the project lifecycle, existing frameworks could better unify disparate sub-problems, align artifact designs with long-term ethical and societal objectives, and guide ongoing communication among stakeholders. This integration is not only applicable to Hevner's [1] three-cycle view but also extendable to methodologies like eDSR [26] and BAUSTEIN [19], thereby enhancing transparency, future orientation, and consistency across diverse stakeholders in complex, multi-year projects.

3.2 Exemplary Conceptualization of the Vision Cycle

In the following, we first show exemplarily how the vision cycle can be integrated into Hevner's [1] three-cycle view as an overarching DSR framework (see Fig. 1).

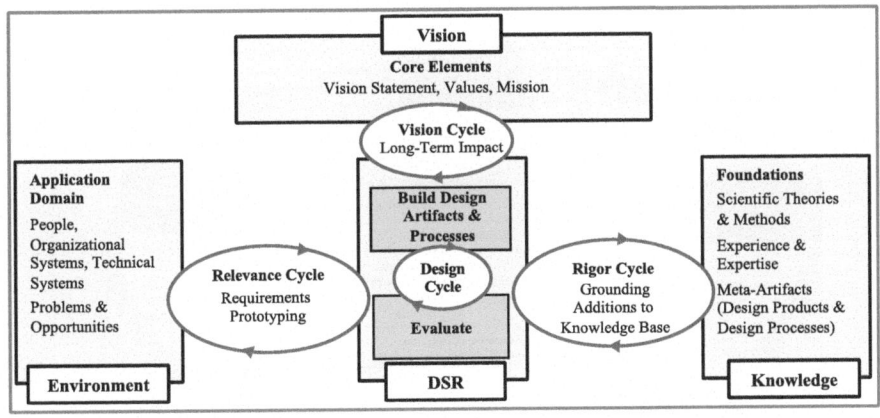

Fig. 1. An extension of Hevner's [1] three-cycle view through the vision cycle

Since designers typically implement the design cycle with a process framework, we then draw on Kuechler and Vaishnavi's [30] framework to illustrate how the vision cycle accompanies each of the steps of the design cycle. We position the vision cycle on top of the research framework. With this decision, we emphasize that researchers can guide their activities in the design cycle by the overall vision and can adapt the vision during or after artifact evaluations. By cutting across the design cycle, the vision cycle also integrates with both the relevance and rigor cycles (as detailed in Sect. 3.1). The vision cycle serves to clearly communicate and achieve the long-term impact on a societal phenomenon [27, 29]. We base the research activities in the vision cycle on literature on how practitioners communicate visions [13, 29] and have adapted them to the DSR context. These activities are routed into the core elements *vision statement, values, and mission*, which we will explain in more detail in the following. The vision cycle centers on the *vision* for a future world [27, 29]. A vision can be generalized or specific [13]. The researchers' creativity shapes the vision, which is influenced by existing worldviews and broader research philosophies [4]. A *vision statement* expresses the vision. This statement is a concise formulation that emphasizes the vision's long-term impact [13, 29]. The vision statement aligns with fundamental values held by the researchers [31]. These values are both individually and ethically grounded [32]. It is crucial to ensure these values align with fundamental human values since new technologies can cause unexpected negative effects [10]. For learning technologies, the OECD highlights, for instance, that these values relate to positivity in learning, collaboration, or resilient and sustainable education [33]. The mission explains how the vision can be achieved. It describes the concrete activities to achieve the overarching goal [13]. The mission defines key steps, actions, and mechanisms to drive overarching societal change (ibid.). While the vision specifies *"what"* to achieve, the mission describes *"how"* to achieve something [29]. For learning technology, the mission could involve adopting specific innovations, such as transforming the education system through motivating pedagogical conversational agents (PCAs) like chatbots for student support. Figure 2 visualizes the relationship between *vision, vision statement, values and mission*.

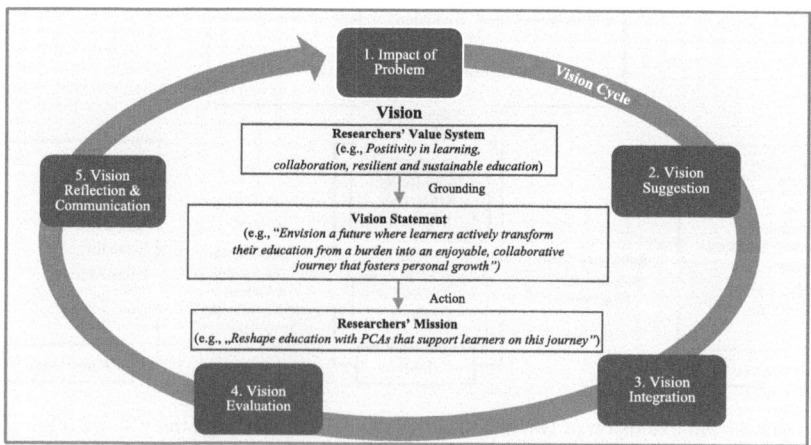

Fig. 2. Research activities in the vision cycle

The figure also shows five phases of research activities in the vision cycle, which we explain in the following. The examples for the researchers' value system, vision statement, and mission relate to our demonstration case which will be explained in more detail later. To apply the vision cycle, we suggest that researchers integrate a vision lens into each phase of the design cycle—using, for example, the process model proposed by Kuechler and Vaishnavi [30]—to steer the project's direction. Figure 2 above exemplarily shows how the vision accompanies each of Kuechler & Vaishnavi's [30] original DSR phases *(awareness of problem, suggestion, development, evaluation, and conclusion)* with phases of a vision cycle *(impact of problem, vision suggestion, vision integration, vision evaluation, and vision reflection and communication)*. Following the iterative perspective on DSR [30], the vision cycle can involve circumscriptions, meaning that a formulated vision statement can be reviewed, refined, or modified throughout the process. Involving practitioners is advisable to ensure the vision addresses real-world needs. In the **first phase (impact of problem)**, researchers prove if their suggested problem has a visionary impact. This step includes checking whether the problem described is based on fundamental values and if the problem pursues a vision that aligns with the one of the practice [9]. In the **second phase (vision suggestion)**, scholars formulate a desired future scenario that directs the DSR project. This vision statement should align with their value system and mission [13, 29]. To ensure the vision adheres to ethical and societal principles, researchers can assess how their findings align with established frameworks like the "Universal Declaration of Human Rights", ethical guidelines, or sustainability standards. This step also involves actively questioning which values one consciously rejects. These decisions influence which suggestion researchers choose in the design cycle (e.g., in the case of digital learning, whether they ground the artifact with theories of autonomy or control). The **third phase (vision integration)** aligns the development in the design cycle with the defined vision. For learning technologies, researchers could, for example, consider whether the instantiated mechanisms fulfill autonomy or control. This step ensures that the development activities align with the vision. The **fourth phase (vision evaluation)** aims to assess whether the results of the artifact evaluation in the design cycle contribute to the validation of the vision [31]. This decision involves justifying the evaluation strategy by referring to the vision (e.g., to consciously choose constructs that serve to test the vision). The **fifth phase (vision reflection and communication)** involves a final review and communication of the vision. This review captures lessons learned and provides an outlook for future iterations [34]. Researchers generate insights on how their overarching vision can be fulfilled or how it might need to be expanded or adjusted. For the reflection, possible methods include proving whether the outcome aligns with ethical guidelines, discussing the outcomes with stakeholders regarding the vision, and considering potential global changes of the examined designs. The reflection could also lead to the conclusion that, based on (potentially negative or undesirable) outcomes, researchers discover that their suggested solution does not fulfill the vision or is not in line with their value system. Overall, this approach helps link the long-term impact of a research idea with practical studies and adjust it in new research iterations.

4 Demonstration of the Vision Cycle

The use case centers on a dissertation project on "game-inspired PCAs", which encompass educational chatbots that apply gamification or serious games [35]. The research on game-inspired PCAs in different roles emerged in several design cycles, accompanied by vision cycles. The research comprises seven projects, from the identification of target group's challenges and research gaps to DP derivation, evaluation and synthesis. Parallel to each design cycle, the author used the vision cycle to reflect on how the results contributed to the further development of the vision. Figure 3 shows an excerpt of the vision cycle application; the **digital appendix** details all seven projects: https://doi.org/10.6084/m9.figshare.28334984. In the following, we explain how the vision cycles informed the communication of the findings in this endeavor.

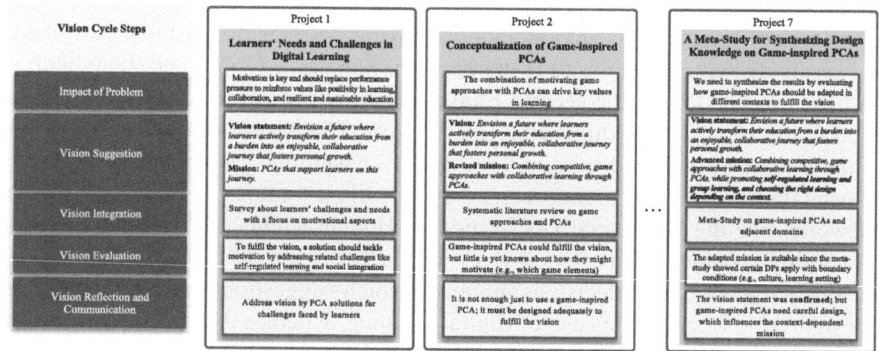

Fig. 3. Excerpt: Vision cycle applied to a research endeavor on designing game-inspired PCAs

The author started the research endeavor by addressing the problem of students' low motivation in digital learning [6]. Based on this problem, the first project started with an initial statement, namely, *"Envision a future where learners actively transform their education from a burden into an enjoyable, collaborative journey that fosters personal growth"*. This decision was informed by an initial stakeholder workshop. Since the research is part of a broader project on PCAs, the mission was defined as deploying PCAs to support learners during this journey. The research focused on PCAs since technological advances enable them to guide students individually, offering potentials for better equity and broadly accessible learning support [6]. Given that existing PCAs in practice do not sufficiently fulfill the overarching vision despite the potentials mentioned in literature (ibid.), the research investigated the connection of PCAs with game approaches. The author grounded the vision and mission in values deemed vital, specifically *"positivity in learning, collaboration, as well as resilient and sustainable education"*. These values align with current guidelines like the OECD guidelines on twenty-first-century skills [33]. The author chose „*positivity in learning*" to highlight that learning is seen as an engaging experience rather than a stressful and unmotivating activity. "*Collaboration*" was chosen to express the important role of social relatedness in learning [6]. "*Resilient and sustainable education*" highlights that the solution should not only contribute to motivating the individual, but also to creating a sustainable education system at all that is resilient to dynamic societal changes. To ensure an effective vision communication, the author limited the selection to values most relevant to the context. This reflection involved deliberately rejecting certain values, such as strict performance optimization and student control, which might reduce motivation. The first project deepened the understanding of target groups' challenges. It provided insights into their issues such as motivation in self-regulated and social learning. Subsequent projects built on this foundation and adjusted the mission based on the research findings. For example, reflecting on the findings from the first project, the author decided to focus on game approaches, as they are established for fostering motivation, which aligns with the value of positivity in learning [6, 35]. The literature review highlighted challenges, such as the lack of clarity on how game-inspired PCAs motivate self-regulated and collaborative learning in different contexts. The author evaluated game-inspired PCA artifacts in projects 3 to 6, including the contexts of self-regulated English education, collaborative business IS education, and creativity in entrepreneurship education. These projects validated whether the solutions contributed to the vision and helped sharpen it. The artifact evaluations confirmed game-inspired PCAs' effectiveness in fostering motivation as well as an enjoyable and collaborative learning journey. The studies also revealed boundary conditions, such as the dependence of vision fulfillment on cultural, individual, and learning-context-specific factors. For instance, Chinese learners had different expectations regarding the social role of a game-inspired PCA. Moreover, the results indicated that collaborative and competitive game mechanics should be balanced, and learners exhibited varying preferences regarding autonomy. While these findings did not alter the vision, they provided new insights for the mission. Finally, a meta-study in project 7 synthesized insights from all projects and related literature and identified boundary conditions influencing the effectiveness of game-inspired PCAs. This final project confirmed the vision's adaptability to diverse educational contexts. Since game-inspired PCAs require contextual adaptation, the mission evolved across projects as follows: *"Combining competitive, game approaches with collaborative learning through PCAs, while promoting self-regulated learning and group learning, and choosing the right design depending on the context"*.

5 Conclusion and Outlook

Regarding our contribution, we address RQ1 by emphasizing the need to explicitly formulate and reflect on visions in DSR projects and address RQ2 by demonstrating how integrating the vision cycle with Hevner's [1] three-cycle view links individual artifacts to their broader impact. Articulating vision is crucial to highlight the impact of IS for a responsible future world grounded in core human values (which is often not clear in times of dynamic change). Incorporating a vision enhances transferability and the further development of DSR contributions. By explicitly documenting visions, subsequent researchers can quickly assess synergies or divergences in values and goals. We also provide methodological guidance for the vision cycle, which suits both individual paper projects and entire research pipelines, such as dissertations, where perspectives may evolve over time. Moreover, we respond to the DSR community's call for greater transparency [24] by presenting the vision cycle as a means to clearly document changes in research visions. We acknowledge the limitations of our ongoing research. In our exemplary case, the overarching vision was considered from the outset but documented only near the end, indicating that additional guidance is needed for developing visions from scratch. While this paper primarily focuses on articulating the role of vision in DSR and offers only initial suggestions for its integration, future work will refine the vision cycle in collaboration with other DSR scholars (e.g., through workshops that systematically capture and reflect on potential visions in IS research). We will also explore methods to rigorously test visions and substantiate the relationship between the vision cycle and the rigor and relevance cycles (e.g., checklists to assess the fit between research visions and overarching philosophies). Finally, we intend to investigate how stakeholders can be integrated into the vision cycle.

References

1. Hevner, A.: A three cycle view of design science research. Scand. J. Inf. Syst. **19**, 87–92 (2007)
2. vom Brocke, J., Winter, R., Hevner, A., Maedche, A.: Special issue editorial–accumulation and evolution of design knowledge in design science research: a journey through time and space. JAIS. **21**, 520–544 (2020)
3. Khosrawi-Rad, B., Grogorick, L., Strohmann, T., Robra-Bissantz, S.: Toward a method for design science research meta-studies to improve the reusability of design principles. In: DESRIST 2024 Proceedings. Springer Nature Switzerland, Trollhättan (2024)
4. Baskerville, R., Kaul, M., Pries-Heje, J., Storey, V., Kristiansen, E.: Bounded creativity in design science research: thirty seventh international conference on information systems. In: ICIS 2016 Proceedings, Dublin (2016)
5. Jokisch, C., Hobert, S., Schumann, M.: Increasing students' engagement: designing a gamified peer feedback systems. In: ECIS 2023 Proceedings, Kristiansand (2023)
6. Schlimbach, R., Khosrawi-Rad, B., Lange, T., Strohmann, T., Robra-Bissantz, S.: Design knowledge for virtual learning companions from a value-centered perspective. Commun. Assoc. Inf. Syst. **54**, 293–330 (2024)
7. Haag, F., Günther, S.A., Hopf, K., Handschuh, P., Klose, M., Staake, T.: Addressing learners' heterogeneity in higher education: an explainable AI-based feedback artifact for digital learning environments. In: Wirtschaftsinformatik 2023 Proceedings, Paderborn (2023)
8. Nguyen, A., Tuunanen, T., Gardner, L., Sheridan, D.: Design principles for learning analytics information systems in higher education. Eur. J. Inf. Syst. **30**, 541–568 (2021)
9. Herwix, A.: Toward a Responsible Design Science Research Ecosystem for the Digital Age: A Critical Pragmatist Perspective. (2024)
10. Trier, M., et al.: Digital responsibility. Bus. Inf. Syst. Eng. **65**, 463–474 (2023)
11. Gregor, S., Chandra Kruse, L., Seidel, S.: The anatomy of a design principle. J. Assoc. Inf. Syst. **21**, 1622–1652 (2020)
12. Wieringa, R., Daneva, M.: Six strategies for generalizing software engineering theories. Sci. Comput. Program. **101**, 136–152 (2015)
13. Kirkpatrick, S.A.: Understanding the role of vision, mission, and values in the HPT model. Perform. Improv. **56**, 6–14 (2017)
14. Kantabutra, S., Avery, G.C.: The power of vision: statements that resonate. J. Bus. Strateg. **31**, 37–45 (2010)
15. Lucas, J.R.: Anatomy of a vision statement. Manag. Rev. **87**, 22 (1998)
16. Iivari, J.: A paradigmatic analysis of information systems as a design science. Scand. J. Inf. Syst. **19**, 39–64 (2007)

17. Simon, H.A.: The Sciences of the Artificial. MIT Press, Cambridge, MA (1996)
18. Gregor, S., Hevner, A.R.: Positioning and presenting design science research for maximum impact. MISQ. **37**, 337–355 (2013)
19. Schoormann, T., Möller, F., Chandra Kruse, L., Otto, B.: BAUSTEIN—A design tool for configuring and representing design research. Inform. Syst. J., 1–31 (2024)
20. Mertens, P., Barbian, D.: Researching "Grand Challenges"—A "Grand Challenge". Bus. Inf. Syst. Eng. **57**, 391–403 (2015)
21. Buhl, H.U., Winter, R.: Vollvirtualisierung—Beitrag der Wirtschaftsinformatik zu einer Vision. Wirtsch. Inform. **51**, 157–160 (2009)
22. Swanson, E.B., Ramiller, N., Wang, P.: Organizing vision revisited and reimagined for a changing world. J. Inf. Technol., 1–21 (2025)
23. Spiekermann, S., Winkler, T.: Value-based engineering for ethics by design. http://arxiv.org/abs/2004.13676 (2020)
24. Hevner, A.R., et al.: Transparency in design science research. Decis. Support. Syst. **182**, 114236 (2024)
25. Peffers, K., Tuunanen, T., Rothenberger, M.A., Chatterjee, S.: A design science research methodology for information systems research. J. Manag. Inf. Syst. **24**, 45–77 (2007)
26. Tuunanen, T., Winter, R., vom Brocke, J.: Dealing with complexity in design science research: using design echelons to support planning, conducting, and communicating design knowledge contributions. MIS Q. **48**, 427–458 (2024)
27. House, R.J.: A theory of charismatic leadership. Leadership: The cutting egde (1977)
28. Baum, J.R., Locke, E.A.: The relationship of entrepreneurial traits, skill, and motivation to subsequent venture growth. J. Appl. Psychol. **89**, 587–598 (2004)
29. Kirkpatrick, S.A.: Build a Better Vision Statement: Extending Research with Practical Advice. Rowman & Littlefield (2016)
30. Kuechler, B., Vaishnavi, V.: On theory development in design science research: anatomy of a research project. Eur. J. Inf. Syst. **17**, 489–504 (2008)
31. Baum, J.R., Locke, E.A., Kirkpatrick, S.A.: A longitudinal study of the relation of vision and vision communication to venture growth in entrepreneurial firms. J. Appl. Psychol. **83**, 43–54 (1998)
32. Podsakoff, P.M., MacKenzie, S.B., Moorman, R.H., Fetter, R.: Transformational leader behaviors and their effects on followers' trust in leader, satisfaction, and organizational citizenship behaviors. Leadersh. Q. **1**, 107–142 (1990)
33. OECD: The future of education and skills: education 2030. Organisation for Economic Co-operation and Development. https://www.oecd.org/education/2030-project/ (2018)
34. Crossan, M.M., Lane, H.W., White, R.E.: An organizational learning framework: from intuition to institution. Acad. Manag. Rev. **24**, 522 (1999)
35. Khosrawi-Rad, B., Grogorick, L., Robra-Bissantz, S.: Game-inspired pedagogical conversational agents: a systematic literature review. AIS Trans. Human-Comput. Interact. **15**, 146–192 (2023)

Enacting Creativity Rigorously in Design Science Research: Towards a Typology of Creativity Strategies

Marc E. Kratz[1(✉)], Christoph Seckler[1], and Jan vom Brocke[2,3]

[1] ESCP Business School, Berlin, Germany
{mkratz,cseckler}@escp.eu
[2] University of Münster, Münster, Germany
jan.vom.brocke@uni-muenster.de, jan.vom.brocke@ercis.org
[3] ERCIS - European Research Center for Information Systems, Münster, Germany

Abstract. Design Science Research (DSR) holds substantial promise for entrepreneurship by aiming to advance knowledge through innovative problem-solving approaches grounded in methodologically rigorous frameworks. While substantial progress has been made in advancing analytical and evaluative methods in DSR, there remains a lack of structured guidance on how to systematically integrate creativity into the design science process. This gap is particularly critical for entrepreneurship, where innovation and adaptability are essential for solving challenges unique to specific contexts. This study proposes a typology of creativity strategies, outlining six distinct approaches to creativity. We draw on the componential theory of creativity to ground these strategies in a theoretical framework. We demonstrate the applicability of the strategies across the main activities of DSR providing guidance for deploying creativity methods in DSR. This study contributes by advancing the methodical repertoire of creativity methods in entrepreneurship.

Keywords: Design science research · Creativity · Entrepreneurship

1 Introduction

Design Science [DS] scholars can leverage a matured methodological repertoire for facilitating rigorous DS [1–6]. By methodological repertoire, we refer to any procedures related to analyzing [problems], creating artifacts, and subsequently evaluating their usefulness. Advances have been made in the area of analytical methods [1–3] and evaluative methods [4–6]. Overall, the DSR community significantly advanced in offering both analytical and evaluative guidance.

However, despite these important contributions, what remains underdeveloped is a methodological creativity repertoire [7]. By methodological creativity repertoire, we refer to explicit guidance, methods, or knowledge to utilize and enhance creativity in DSR. Creativity, defined as producing novel and fitting solutions [8], translatable to a process of producing new, original, human-caused novelties through deliberate actions

[9], is central to innovative problem solving. The latter is central to the design phase and relies on creativity, which in turn complements rigor [10, 11]. Furthermore, creativity addresses ambiguity and uncertainty in DSR, which can be helpful during the phase of framing the problem or solution space to be solved [10]. Overall, creativity has an essential role within DSR in enhancing the theoretical soundness [12] and practical applicability of research outcomes [13]. Yet, despite its critical relevance - especially to DSR in entrepreneurship, specific creativity guidance remains scarce, unlike in other disciplines such as Management [14].

As Dimov et al. [15] argue, entrepreneurship inherently embraces creativity and disruption, posing unique challenges for design science [15]. This highlights the critical need for a methodological repertoire that provides sound, theoretically grounded tools to effectively leverage creativity—an essential element in entrepreneurship [16, 17]—within the context of design science research. As main contribution, the outlined strategies intend to provide tools to address practical challenges, foster innovation and design impactful solutions. These goals align with entrepreneurship and DSR: emphasizing actionable frameworks and artifacts that bridge theory and practice to solve complex, real-world problems [17, 18].

The purpose of this article is to provide concrete methodical guidance in the form of a typology for using creativity methods in DSR. We introduce Teresa Amabile's seminal creativity theory to the DS discourse. Amabile's componential theory [8] details the creativity process and its internal and external components. Building on these insights, we define distinct creativity strategies, characterized by a common core mechanism [19], the degree of structuredness, established creativity methods, connected to creativity theory [8, 20] as well as an evaluation of strengths and weaknesses [21, 22]. We demonstrate the applicability of these strategies across the DSR phases [18] using an entrepreneurship-focused example.

This article has three contributions. First, it shifts the focus from evaluative (e.g., [15, 23]) and analytical (e.g., [4, 6, 24]) methods to developing a creativity repertoire. Second, we provide specific guidance for scholars in choosing, utilizing, and evaluating relevant creativity methods. This manifests by our suggestion of a novel and comprehensive typology of creativity strategies, supported by the demonstration of applicability. Third, this study contributes to reconciling the often-discussed rigor and creativity dichotomy [10]. While rigor is often associated with evaluative methods, rigor refers to the "adherence to state-of-the- art-rules" ([18], p. 9). Thus, creativity methods need to be performed rigorously, leading us to the title of our paper.

2 Componential Theory of Creativity

To enable the theorization necessary for the development of creativity strategies, we draw on Amabile's Componentional Theory of Creativity (CToC) [8]. Understanding CToC's components is crucial for unlocking creativity and advancing diverse domains. CToC explicates the creative process and its influencing components [8]. CToC's components act within or outside the individual: domain-relevant skills, intrinsic motivation, creativity-relevant processes are the internal components, whereas the social environment acts externally. We find CToC especially well-suited for practical guidance in DSR contexts: it clarifies creativity's essential building blocks [8], whereas other theories emphasize cognition or broader theoretical or cognitive approaches [25–27].

Amabile's model identifies the social environment—including factors like motivation, resources, and management—as an external creativity influence [28]. The social environment influences creativity by stimulating or obstructing intrinsic motivation through extrinsic factors, such as collaborative teams, supportive leadership, and freedom in task execution. Social networks, especially weak ties, provide diverse perspectives that foster problem-solving and enhance creativity [29]. Team creativity surpasses the sum of individual creativity, emerging through group interactions [30, 31]. Both composition [32, 33] and leadership [34, 35] shape external conditions, enabling autonomy, resource management, and effective collaboration to foster synergy. Over time, aggregated efforts amplify creativity [30, 36].

Amabile's componential theory of creativity identifies three key internal components influencing the creativity process: domain-relevant skills, intrinsic task motivation, and creativity-relevant processes [8]. Domain-relevant skills are defined as skills that *"include knowledge, expertise, technical skills, intelligence, and talent in the particular domain where the problem solver is working - such as product design or electrical engineering."* ([37], p. 135). These skills are critical for enabling creativity, as they provide the raw ingredients for problem-solving and have been empirically linked to creative outcomes [38, 39].

Intrinsic task motivation is defined as *"passion: the motivation to undertake a task or solve a problem because it is interesting, involving…or satisfying - rather than undertaking it out of the extrinsic motivation arising from contracted-for rewards, …, or requirements to do something in a certain way."* ([37], p. 135). According to Amabile, this intrinsic drive lies at the core of creativity, as individuals are most creative when personally engaged [37]. However, it can be complemented by synergistic extrinsic motivators, such as inspirational leadership, which has been shown to enhance creativity through team identification [31, 40].

Creativity-relevant processes involve *"include a cognitive style and personality characteristics that are conducive to independence, risk-taking, and taking new perspectives on problems, as well as a disciplined work style and skills in generating ideas."* ([37], p. 135). These processes empower problem solvers to explore unconventional solutions iteratively while resisting conformity [31].

3 Towards a Typology of Creativity Strategies

To provide structured guidance to DSR scholars on leveraging creativity [37], we introduce a coherent typology of creativity strategies (see Table 1). By *creativity strategies*, we refer to strategic groupings of creativity techniques, organized by shared mechanisms, commonalities from theoretical underpinnings, and application characteristics. This coherent typology offers DS researchers orientation on how to purposefully select and apply creativity-enhancing approaches across the different phases of a DSR project—such as problem framing, cause analysis, and artifact design.

The underlying structure of the typology is threefold. First, each strategy is defined by a core creativity mechanism, representing the process that drives change, aligned

Table 1. Creativity strategies

Strategy	Guided strategy	Exploratory strategy	Facilitated ideation strategy	Visualization strategy	Stimulus strategy	Access strategy
Core mechanism	Systematizing	Envisioning	Enabling	Mapping	Associating	Priming
Structuredness	High	High	Medium	Medium	Low	Low
Creativity methods (examples)	Six thinking hats; Morphological box; TRIZ	Thought experiments; Scenario planning; Pre-mortem analysis	Brain-, Game-, Groupstorming; Brainwriting; Nominal Group Technique (NGT)	Conceptual diagrams; Mind mapping; Storyboards	Analogy; Metaphors; Random stimulus	Mindfulness; Gratitude; Meditation
Example papers	[41–43]	[44–46]	[47–49]	[50–52]	[53–55]	[57–59]
Primary CToC component	Creativity-relevant processes	Creativity-relevant processes	Domain-relevant skills	Domain-relevant skills	Creativity-relevant processes	Intrinsic task motivation
Type of creativity	Transformational	Exploratory	Combinational Exploratory	Exploratory	Combinational	Combinational
Strengths and weaknesses	High on accuracy, lower on generality—Simplicity depends on specifics	High on generality, lower on accuracy and simplicity depending on specifics	High on generality, lower on accuracy and simplicity due to group dynamics	High on simplicity and accuracy, lower on generality	High on generality, lower on accuracy & simplicity due to subjective participants	High on generality, low on simplicity and accuracy

with Bunge's understanding of mechanisms as "how something ticks" [19]. This links each strategy to a distinct logic of how creativity is enacted.

Second, we to offer practitioners guidance on when to use which strategy, we evaluate the strategies based on their degree of structuredness. We define structuredness as the extent to which a creativity strategy utilizes predefined processes and guidelines to address a problem, balancing flexibility with established methods. The utility of this measure lies in understanding when to use which strategy. Strategies with a higher degree of structuredness are helpful in situations that are well-defined and benefit from systematic approaches. In contrast, a lower degree of structuredness is helpful in open-ended situations that demand flexibility and exploration. Each strategy is exemplified by three illustrative methods, whose effectiveness in enhancing creativity is demonstrated through the provided example papers.

Third, as seen in rows 4 and 5, we elaborate how these strategies are informed by creativity theory. We evaluate which component of CToC has the largest role in enabling success for the strategy [37]. Furthermore, we categorize each strategy along the type of creativity enabled: combinational, explorational, or transformational [20]. Last, in row five of Table 1, we offer an assessment of the strengths and weaknesses of each creativity strategy. With broad reference to the works of Thorngate [21] and Weick [22], we evaluate the strategies based on their accuracy of use, the simplicity of deployment, and the generality of applicability.

3.1 Guided Strategy

The core mechanism of the guided strategy is systematizing. Systematizing is representative as the respective creativity methods provide a structured set of instructions and guidelines for a process that systematically approaches and aims to resolve well-structured problems. Systematizing acts here as a mechanism by affecting change through leading the creative process through an orderly progression to enable organized ideation. Methods like Six Thinking Hats, morphological box, and TRIZ - all with a structured set of instructions - exemplify this strategy and have been shown to boost creativity [41–43]. Consequently, the guided strategy has a high degree of structuredness.

The guided strategy is primarily informed by creativity-relevant processes [37]. The guided strategy primarily relies on creativity-relevant processes [37], including disciplined work styles and systematic exploration. It deploys transformational creativity, which encompasses the alteration of fundamental dimensions or parameters of a problem space. It aims to generate entirely new structures and previously inconceivable ideas [20]. The transformational aspect can be exemplified by viewing the creativity method six thinking hats. It shifts perspectives to transform how researchers view problems, leading to novel insights. We evaluate the guided strategy as high on accuracy and simplicity but moderately lower on generality.

Grounded in the works of Thorngate [21] and Weick [22], we define accuracy, generality, and simplicity as follows. Accuracy is dependent on how precisely a strategy manages to address the specifics of a creative problem or design at hand. Simplicity refers to the ease of understanding and implementation of the strategy. It considers the number of involved elements, relationships, or special knowledge required. Generality refers to the breadth of applicability of the strategy across distinct types of problems or situations [21, 22]. The creativity methods of this strategy are high in accuracy, as they are designed to examine a specific problem or situation closely. These methods are versatile regarding their application area. However, their generality is relatively lower, as they need to be tailored to the specific type of problem or designed artifact. We argue for a high score on simplicity due to the inherent nature of having clear and structured instructions. However, the simplicity depends on the specific context and the familiarity with the method.

3.2 Exploratory Strategy

Central to the exploratory strategy is the mechanism of envisioning. It facilitates imagining diverse possibilities through creativity methods like thought experiments, scenario planning, and pre-mortem analysis. Previous research either listed these methods as tools for creativity or demonstrated a positive impact on creativity [44–46]. This mechanism leads to change by encouraging practitioners to explore and evaluate potential outcomes before they occur, shaping the analysis, problem space, solution space and design choices. As the strategy requires a specific topic to explore, and the methods are based on clear instructions, the level of structuredness is high.

The strategy is strongly informed by creativity-relevant processes [37], requiring new perspectives, and enabling researchers to systematically envision innovative scenarios. When deploying the exploratory strategy, the type of creativity leveraged is explorational. Explorational creativity is defined as the process of generating novel and unexpected ideas by thoroughly exploring and experimenting within a conceptual space [20]. This is innately given through the nature of how the creativity methods of the exploratory strategy intend to work.

Exploratory strategy scores high on generality [21, 22]. The creativity methods are designed to enable the exploration of a broad range of scenarios. They are not limited to specific artifact types or problem areas. Thus, they are applicable across a wide section of research-related evaluative instances. Simplicity and accuracy scores are relatively lower [21, 22]. Envisioning future possibilities inherently negates the ability to have an accurate view. As for simplicity, the scoring is shaped by the specifics of the designed artifact to be evaluated. Depending on the artifact, the researcher may be confronted with the requirement of a deep and nuanced understanding of multiple variables interacting with the artifact in hypothetical scenarios.

3.3 Facilitated Ideation Strategy

The core mechanism - enabling - of facilitated ideation strategy (FIS) is representative of how creativity methods such as Brain-, Group-, or Gamestorming, Brainwriting and nominal group technique (NGT) function. Various researchers across disciplines have shown the positive impact of these methods on creativity both conceptually and empirically [47–49]. Enabling as a mechanism, fosters change by creating an environment conducive to the free flow of ideation, removing psychological or procedural barriers that hinder creativity. It offers structured guidance for a targeted ideation process, balancing creative freedom with structure for individuals or groups. Though these methods suggest high structuredness, the strategy allows flexibility, resulting in a medium degree of structuredness.

FIS is primarily informed by domain-relevant skills [37], as participants' knowledge, expertise and skills are necessary to ensure ideation. The FIS utilizes both explorational and combinational creativity. The creativity demonstrated via a groupstorming session is explorational as it allows the team members to explore structured conceptual areas within their domains of expertise. However, it involved combining elements that were familiar, at least to the respective expert of the field. Thus, it can be argued that it is also combinational, which is defined as the novel combination of familiar concepts, often through structural mapping, to generate unique and insightful ideas [20].

As the associated creativity methods are versatile and can be applied across broad problems and groups, FIS scores high on generality [21, 22]. It scores lower yet moderately high on accuracy [21, 22]. The inherent focus on ideation within a structured process can lead to relevant and specific ideas. The accuracy can be impacted by the specifics of the group dynamic as it may introduce variability or bias. The basic concepts of these creativity methods are easy to execute, yet the facilitation of the process may require experience, skill, or specific knowledge. Thus, the simplicity score is lower [21, 22].

3.4 Visualization Strategy

Regarding the visualization strategy, the core mechanism is mapping. Mapping effectively represents the visualization strategy as it deploys creativity methods such as conceptual diagrams, mind mapping, and storyboards. A range of publications support the notion that these creativity methods are intricately linked to an increase in creativity or used in creative-related activities [50–52]. The mechanism fosters clarity by organizing and visualizing ideas or complex relationships, enhancing understanding. Enhanced understanding is pivotal to creativity, simplifying complex ideas for further development. Leaning more toward flexibility, even when following a specific method, the visualization strategy has a moderate level of structuredness.

Theorizing on the impact this strategy can have; we conclude that understanding is paramount. Hence, this strategy is also informed primarily by domain-relevant skills, as successful visualization hinges on the ability to structure, organize and interpret the relevant information of the problem or solution space. In a mind map, the identified main topic or problem is used as the central node, from which branches are added to sub-nodes that represent subtopics, data, theories, and ideas. In visually organizing a plethora of information, creative connections and insights are enabled. However, domain-specific expertise is necessary to ensure truthful representation. Visualization strategy mainly uses explorational creativity [20]. The creativity methods of this strategy involve systematically mapping out and exploring a multitude of aspects of a complex issue along a structured visual framework, facilitating the discovery of novel insights, which is a characteristic of explorational creativity [20].

The highest-scoring characteristic of the visualization strategy is simplicity [21, 22]. The creativity methods are user-friendly and easily understood. As they enable clarifying and structuring thoughts, their inherent focus is simplification or, in other words, simplicity. Accuracy also earns a high score, as these methods aim to represent complex ideas, processes, or systems accurately, leading to a precise understanding of the subject matter [21, 22]. Moderately lower is the score on generality [21, 22]. While these methods can be applied across a breadth of fields, they are the most effective if the need for clarity and visualization emerges.

3.5 Stimulus Strategy

The stimulus strategy's core mechanism, associating, expands cognitive boundaries by linking disparate ideas (e.g., analogy, metaphors, random stimulus) [53–55]. These methods connect unrelated concepts to spark innovation. Because it depends on spontaneous, unpredictable connections rather than a prescribed process, the strategy has lower structuredness.

Requiring risk-taking and diverse perspectives, the stimulus strategy aligns with creativity-relevant processes [37]. The stimulus strategy can be assigned to combinational creativity [20]. It maps parallels between core concepts and random elements, aiming to yield novel insights by linking familiar and unfamiliar ideas, in line with the core definition of combinational creativity [20].

Regarding generality [21, 22], the stimulus strategy scores high, as it demonstrates a high adaptability across various domains. Both, accuracy, and simplicity [21, 22], score relatively lower. These methods can enable the ideation of novel concepts. However, the reliance on subjective interpretations of the associations made, could lead to less precise or relevant outcomes. Furthermore, an adept mind and an aptitude for creative thinking are required. Hence, the utilization of these methods is not simple.

3.6 Access Strategy

The access strategy's core mechanism, priming, fosters mental clarity and flexibility for creative thinking [56]. Creativity methods that are exemplary of the potential of the access strategy are mindfulness, gratitude, and meditation. Mindfulness practices have been shown to increase aptitude or behavioral inclination for creativity [57, 58]. Meditation has been shown to enhance creativity performance [59, 60]. The level of structuredness is low, as even though all three methods require a specific method, these depend on individual experiences and subjective mental states. The execution or the outcome is undefined, self-directed, and fluid, thus unstructured.

The sole requirement is that the researcher or group of researchers want to enhance their mindset regarding creativity. Hence an intrinsic task motivation is the main relevant creativity component [37]. Being motivated by a task offers the opportunity for individuals to also venture into different paths such as practicing mindfulness. It can be argued that the access strategy deploys combinational creativity [20] as, for example, mindfulness involves the synthesis of thoughts and sensations, which can be hypothesized to lead to new combinations. To deploy this strategy, there should be a prevalent need to attune the researcher's mindset towards creativity, which, in turn, can be said to hinge on open-mindedness.

As this strategy can be applied to various contexts, it is high on generality [21, 22]. However, as it involves internal mental processes involving potentially complex techniques, it is moderately lower on accuracy and simplicity [21, 22].

4 Demonstration

The utility and necessity of creativity during design-related activities within DSR is undisputed [10, 11, 61, 62]. However, we argue, these strategies can be applied across the entire DSR spectrum. Following Seckler et al. [18], DSR comprises three main phases: analysis, design, and evaluation The analytical phase addresses problem identification, while the design phase refines new artifacts or solutions using existing scientific knowledge and theoretical principles [18]. Finally, the evaluation phase assesses an artifact's usefulness [18].

4.1 Analytical Phase

In the analytical phase, a deep understanding of the problem space is essential for DSR success. Domain-relevant skills, as emphasized by Amabile [8], play a key role and must be paired with broader perspectives to uncover hidden challenges. We illustrate this with a DSR use case on renewable energy rural SMEs, where DSR team is analyzing the adoption barriers of renewable energy solutions. During the analytical phase, their objective is to identify the underlying challenges to later design an actionable framework for improving adoption. The guided strategy supports structured exploration. For instance, Six Thinking Hats offers sequential, role-based perspectives [63]: the white hat collects facts (e.g., energy costs), the black hat highlights risks (e.g., financial barriers), and the red hat captures emotional aspects (e.g., perception of sustainability). This method fosters creativity by prompting structured, role-based thinking—enabling the DS research team to analyze the energy adoption challenge through various lenses. Leveraging the systematizing mechanism of the guided strategy enables the research team to enhance analytical depth when exploring complex problem spaces.

To complement such a structured approach, applying combinational creativity via the stimulus strategy shows further potential during the analytical phase. Linking unrelated concepts via metaphor exemplifies the stimulus strategy [55]. To use this method, researchers must first identify the core concept of the research project and then envision random elements that share similarities with it. These elements could include everyday objects, newspaper articles, or video clips. By drawing parallels between the core concept and these elements, a metaphor is created, which can lead to new insights and connections [55]. For example, a "river" metaphor frames adoption as "boats" navigating regulatory "currents" and financial "rocks," revealing insights for improving the design framework. The strategy is chosen here as the associating mechanism supports creativity relevant processes, which in turn enables in-depth insight generation of the problem space.

4.2 Design Phase

To guide the initial search for suitable solution types, as the design phase creates and refines new artifacts or solutions using existing scientific knowledge and theoretical principles [18], the team applies the facilitated ideation strategy using the Nominal Group Technique (NGT). This structured group method ensures that diverse perspectives—such as those from policy experts, rural entrepreneurs, and technical specialists—are equally considered. Each participant first generates ideas individually before sharing them in a in the plenary [47]. This approach promotes a wide exploration of potential directions, such as financing platforms, shared ownership schemes, or bundled service offerings. By combining structure with inclusive participation, NGT supports creative yet focused generation of solution concepts in the early design phase. FIS is selected here due to its enabling mechanism, supporting creativity relevant processes (e.g., divergent thinking) to surface and refine solutions/artifacts in a complex, multi-perspective environment.

To deepen understanding of how these preliminary ideas might unfold in practice, the team uses the visualization strategy via storyboarding. This technique helps represent potential user interactions with each idea in a narrative, scenario-based format [52]. For instance, one storyboard might depict a small business owner navigating a local cooperative platform to access solar equipment, while another might show a government-backed grant service embedded into an SME financing portal. Mapping these imagined experiences visually highlights touchpoints, emotional reactions, and feasibility issues that may not surface through discussion alone. By visualizing usage scenarios early, the team refines their understanding of what types of solutions might resonate most with the target context. The strategy is chosen here as its mapping mechanism leverages domain-relevant skills necessary to support iterative refinements and deconstruction of complex potential artifacts.

4.3 Evaluative Phase

Although creativity is often linked with the design phase, it also offers value in evaluation. This phase assesses the artifact's usefulness, effectiveness, and practicality [18] using rigorous metrics and data collection [4]. Continuing the renewable energy example, the DS team evaluates a leasing model for solar panels in rural businesses. During the evaluative phase, the researchers must rigorously assess the viability and usefulness. The exploratory strategy offers significant potential during this phase. By leveraging thought experiments, researchers can anticipate challenges and assess the utility of the designed artifact. Thought experiments, defined as reasoning about the real impact of imagined scenarios [64], induce creativity by encouraging scenario-based thinking. These imagined scenarios (e.g., policy shifts or demand spikes) can foster creative foresight and support robust evaluation. This structured reflection enables researchers to explore potential weaknesses and adapt designs accordingly. The envisioning mechanism of this strategy leverages creativity-relevant processes to anticipate hypothetical scenarios, which in turn can help to uncover artifact weaknesses.

Although usable in any phase, the access strategy particularly aids evaluation by enhancing researcher's ability to engage in critical yet open-minded reflection. The strict and necessary requirement for rigor in evaluations [4] can introduce the risk of dismissing unexpected findings or alternative interpretations. The access strategy fosters mental clarity and openness, enabling researchers to approach evaluation with a balanced mindset. The exemplary DS research team can leverage mindfulness and meditation techniques to remain attentive and reduce bias during user feedback analysis. For example, rather than ignoring negative input about financial flaws due to confirmation bias, a creativity-primed mindset might uncover improvements like peer-to-peer lending or dynamic pricing. The underlying priming mechanism of the access strategy enables a focus on the intrinsic task motivation, counteracting potential cognitive biases which could impact the evaluation.

With these strategies, researchers gain practical guidance on deploying creativity across DSR phases [18], understanding when and how to apply each strategy—and what kind of value it can unlock.

5 Concluding Discussion

While many scholars have highlighted the importance of creativity in DSR [10, 65, 66], concrete guidance for DS scholars remains scarce. Whilst we recognize the significant advancement in both analytical (e.g., [1–3, 15, 23]) and evaluative (e.g., [4–6, 24]) methodological repertoire, we address creativity's underdevelopment and provide explicit guidance integrating creativity in DSR.

Our research extends DSR creativity research [10, 65, 66], particularly in entrepreneurship [15], providing a structured methodical contribution that complements existing analytical and evaluative approaches. Building on Amabile's theoretical foundation, we advance the discourse towards incorporating creativity methods in DS research. Our proposed typology of creativity strategies is designed to enhance creativity across all phases of DSR [18], shifting the focus from purely evaluative and analytical approaches to an explicit creativity repertoire through structured strategies.

We go beyond proposing a typology by demonstrating the feasibility of creativity strategies in DSR processes. In line with an initial design evaluation, we demonstrate the applicability of the different strategies across the three phases of DSR [18]. The typology represents a framework for future empirical evaluation. To successfully enrich the methodical diversity within DSR, balancing rigor and creativity is necessary. The creativity strategies and their associated methods should be applied rigorously. For example, following established procedures—such as conducting individual brainstorming before team brainstorming—can maximize effectiveness. By introducing a structured typology of creativity strategies, we provide explicit methodological repertoire for creativity in DSR contributing to the reconciliation of rigor and creativity.

Despite our contributions, we acknowledge several limitations in our study. These stem from the conceptual nature of this research effort, the complexity of measuring creativity impact as well as the dependency on different contextual variations across DSR application possibilities. While recognizing these limitations, we believe our typology of creativity strategies represents a first methodological guidance and a conceptual foundation to enable the DS community to leverage the potential of creativity.

Future research should focus on empirically validating and exploring the effectiveness of the proposed creativity strategies in real-world DSR projects. Understanding the effectiveness of these strategies can be achieved by applying the strategies in controlled settings and evaluating the impact. Furthermore, an assessment of their longitudinal impact would increase understanding of how creativity can enhance the DSR approach. Lastly, an exploration of possible influencing factors e.g., context or varying research team compositions could enhance the practical utility of the strategies. Refinement of the typology based on empirical evidence can further the strategy typology.

Disclosure of Interests. The authors have no competing interests to declare that are relevant to the content of this article.

References

1. Walls, J.G., Widmeyer, G.R., El Sawy, O.A.: Building an information system design theory for vigilant EIS. Inf. Syst. Res. **3**, 36–59 (1992). https://doi.org/10.1287/isre.3.1.36
2. Gregor, S.: The nature of theory in information systems. MIS Q. **30**, 611–642 (2006). https://doi.org/10.2307/25148742
3. Jones, D., Gregor, S.: The anatomy of a design theory. JAIS. **8**, 312–335 (2007). https://doi.org/10.17705/1jais.00129
4. Hevner, A.R.: A three cycle view of design science research. Scand. J. Inf. Syst. **19**(2), 4 (2007)
5. da Moutinho, J., Fernandes, G., Rabechini, R.: Evaluation in design science: A framework to support project studies in the context of university research Centres. Eval. Program Plann. **102**, 102366 (2024). https://doi.org/10.1016/j.evalprogplan.2023.102366
6. Venable, J., Pries-Heje, J., Baskerville, R.: FEDS: a framework for evaluation in design science research. Eur. J. Inf. Syst. **25**, 77–89 (2016). https://doi.org/10.1057/ejis.2014.36
7. Hevner, A.R.: A Three Cycle View of Design Science Research. Scand. J. Inform. Syst. **19** (2007)
8. Amabile, T.M.: The social psychology of creativity: A componential conceptualization. J. Pers. Soc. Psychol. **45**, 357–376 (1983). https://doi.org/10.1037/0022-3514.45.2.357
9. Bunge, M.: Scientific Realism: Selected Essays of Mario Bunge. Prometheus Books, Amherst, NY (2001)
10. Baskerville, R., Kaul, M., Pries-Heje, J., Storey, V.: Inducing creativity in design science research. In: Tulu, B., Djamasbi, S., Leroy, G. (eds.) Extending the Boundaries of Design Science Theory and Practice, pp. 3–17. Springer International Publishing, Cham (2019). https://doi.org/10.1007/978-3-030-19504-5_1
11. Thompson, G., Lordan, M.: A review of creativity principles applied to engineering design. Proc. Inst. Mech. Eng. E J. Process Mech. Eng. **213**, 17–31 (1999). https://doi.org/10.1243/0954408991529960
12. Voigt, M., Niehaves, B., Becker, J.: Towards a unified design theory for creativity support systems. In: Peffers, K., Rothenberger, M., Kuechler, B. (eds.) Design Science Research in Information Systems. Advances in Theory and Practice, pp. 152–173. Springer, Berlin Heidelberg (2012). https://doi.org/10.1007/978-3-642-29863-9_13
13. Sarkar, P., Chakrabarti, A.: Assessing design creativity. Des. Stud. **32**, 348–383 (2011). https://doi.org/10.1016/j.destud.2011.01.002
14. Xu, F.: Creative management. In: Carayannis, E.G. (ed.) Encyclopedia of Creativity, Invention, Innovation and Entrepreneurship, pp. 317–321. Springer, New York (2013). https://doi.org/10.1007/978-1-4614-3858-8_3
15. Dimov, D., Maula, M., Romme, A.G.L.: Crafting and assessing design science research for entrepreneurship. Entrep. Theory Pract. **47**, 1543–1567 (2023). https://doi.org/10.1177/10422587221128271
16. Amabile, T.M.: Entrepreneurial creativity through motivational synergy. J. Creat. Behav. **31**, 18–26 (1997). https://doi.org/10.1002/j.2162-6057.1997.tb00778.x
17. Dimov, D.: Beyond the single-person, single-insight attribution in understanding entrepreneurial opportunities. Entrep. Theory Pract. **31**, 713–731 (2007). https://doi.org/10.1111/j.1540-6520.2007.00196.x

18. Seckler, C., Mauer, R., vom Brocke, J.: Design science in entrepreneurship: conceptual foundations and guiding principles. J. Busi. Venturing Design. **1**, 100004 (2021). https://doi.org/10.1016/j.jbvd.2022.100004
19. Bunge, M.: How does it work?: the search for explanatory mechanisms. Philos. Soc. Sci. **34**, 182–210 (2004). https://doi.org/10.1177/0048393103262550
20. Boden, M.A.: Creativity and artificial intelligence. Artif. Intell. **103**, 347–356 (1998). https://doi.org/10.1016/S0004-3702(98)00055-1
21. Thorngate, W.: Possible limits on a science of social behavior. In: Strickland, L.H., Aboud, F.E., Gergen, K.J. (eds.) Social Psychology in Transition, pp. 121–139. Springer US, Boston, MA (1976). https://doi.org/10.1007/978-1-4615-8765-1_9
22. Weick, K.E.: Theory construction as disciplined imagination. Acad. Manag. Rev. **14**, 516–531 (1989). https://doi.org/10.2307/258556
23. Hevner, A., Gregor, S.: Envisioning entrepreneurship and digital innovation through a design science research lens: A matrix approach. Inf. Manag. **59**, 103350 (2022). https://doi.org/10.1016/j.im.2020.103350
24. Magistretti, S., Sanasi, S., Dell'Era, C., Ghezzi, A.: Entrepreneurship as design: A design process for the emergence and development of entrepreneurial opportunities. Creat. Innov. Manage. **32**, 5–21 (2023). https://doi.org/10.1111/caim.12529
25. Sternberg, R.J., Lubart, T.I.: An investment theory of creativity and its development. Hum. Dev. **34**, 1–31 (1991). https://doi.org/10.1159/000277029
26. Guilford, J.P.: The Nature of Human Intelligence. McGraw-Hill, New York (1967)
27. Csikszentmihalyi, M.: Flow: the Psychology of Optimal Experience. Harper & Row, New York (1990)
28. Amabile, T.M., Conti, R., Coon, H., Lazenby, J., Herron, M.: Assessing the work environment for creativity. Acad. Manag. J. **39**, 1154–1184 (1996). https://doi.org/10.2307/256995
29. Kim, S.K., Shin, S.J., Shin, J., Miller, D.R.: Social networks and individual creativity: the role of individual differences. J. Creat. Behav. **52**, 285–296 (2018). https://doi.org/10.1002/jocb.153
30. Hargadon, A.B., Bechky, B.A.: When collections of creatives become creative collectives: A field study of problem solving at work. Organ. Sci. **17**, 484–500 (2006). https://doi.org/10.1287/orsc.1060.0200
31. Amabile, T.M., Pratt, M.G.: The dynamic componential model of creativity and innovation in organizations: making progress, making meaning. Res. Organ. Behav. **36**, 157–183 (2016). https://doi.org/10.1016/j.riob.2016.10.001
32. Baer, M., Oldham, G.R., Jacobsohn, G.C., Hollingshead, A.B.: The personality composition of teams and creativity: the moderating role of team creative confidence. J. Creat. Behav. **42**, 255–282 (2008). https://doi.org/10.1002/j.2162-6057.2008.tb01299.x
33. Im, S., Montoya, M.M., Workman, J.P.: Antecedents and consequences of creativity in product innovation teams. J. Product. Innov. Manag. **30**, 170–185 (2013). https://doi.org/10.1111/j.1540-5885.2012.00887.x
34. Kolb, J.A.: Leadership of creative teams*. J. Creat. Behav. **26**, 1–9 (1992). https://doi.org/10.1002/j.2162-6057.1992.tb01151.x
35. Paulus, P.: Groups, teams, and creativity: the creative potential of idea-generating groups. Appl. Psychol. **49**, 237–262 (2000). https://doi.org/10.1111/1464-0597.00013
36. Pirola-Merlo, A., Mann, L.: The relationship between individual creativity and team creativity: aggregating across people and time. J. Organ. Behavior. **25**, 235–257 (2004). https://doi.org/10.1002/job.240
37. Amabile, T.M.: Componential theory of creativity. In: Kessler, E.H. (ed.) Encyclopedia of Management Theory, pp. 134–139. Sage Publications, London (2013). https://doi.org/10.4135/9781452276090.n42

38. Conti, R., Coon, H., Amabile, T.M.: Evidence to support the componential model of creativity: secondary analyses of three studies. Creat. Res. J. **9**, 385–389 (1996). https://doi.org/10.1207/s15326934crj0904_9
39. Baer, J.: Domain specificity and the limits of creativity theory. J. Creat. Behav. **46**, 16–29 (2012). https://doi.org/10.1002/jocb.002
40. Hirst, G., van Dick, R., van Knippenberg, D.: A social identity perspective on leadership and employee creativity. J. Organ. Behavior. **30**, 963–982 (2009). https://doi.org/10.1002/job.600
41. Birdi, K., Leach, D., Magadley, W.: Evaluating the impact of TRIZ creativity training: an organizational field study. R&D Manag. **42**, 315–326 (2012). https://doi.org/10.1111/j.1467-9310.2012.00686.x
42. Chang, Y.-S., Chien, Y.-H., Yu, K.-C., Chu, Y.-H., Chen, M.Y.: Effect of TRIZ on the creativity of engineering students. Think. Skills Creat. **19**, 112–122 (2016). https://doi.org/10.1016/j.tsc.2015.10.003
43. Álvarez, A., Ritchey, T.: Applications of general morphological. Analysis. **4** (2015)
44. Gardner, W.L.: Thought experiments: no argument here—we need more of them. J. Organ. Behavior. **44**, 563–568 (2023). https://doi.org/10.1002/job.2684
45. Latham, G.P.: The upsides and downsides of thought experiments in I-O/OB. J. Organ. Behavior. **44**, 569–571 (2023). https://doi.org/10.1002/job.2701
46. MacKay, B., McKiernan, P.: Creativity and dysfunction in strategic processes: the case of scenario planning. Futures. **42**, 271–281 (2010). https://doi.org/10.1016/j.futures.2009.11.013
47. Gallagher, M., Hares, T., Spencer, J., Bradshaw, C., Webb, I.: The nominal group technique: A research tool for general practice? Fam. Pract. **10**, 76–81 (1993). https://doi.org/10.1093/fampra/10.1.76
48. Parnes, S.J., Meadow, A.: Evaluation of persistence of effects produced by a creative problem-solving course. Psychol. Rep. **7**, 357–361 (1960). https://doi.org/10.2466/pr0.1960.7.2.357
49. VanGundy, A.B.: Brain writing for new product ideas: an alternative to brainstorming. J. Consum. Mark. **1**, 67–74 (1984). https://doi.org/10.1108/eb008097
50. Eppler, M.J.: A comparison between concept maps, mind maps, conceptual diagrams, and visual metaphors as complementary tools for knowledge construction and sharing. Inf. Vis. **5**, 202–210 (2006). https://doi.org/10.1057/palgrave.ivs.9500131
51. Sun, M., Wang, M., Wegerif, R., Peng, J.: How do students generate ideas together in scientific creativity tasks through computer-based mind mapping? Comput. Educ. **176**, 104359 (2022). https://doi.org/10.1016/j.compedu.2021.104359
52. Taylor, C.L., Kaufman, J.C., Barbot, B.: Measuring creative writing with the storyboard task: the role of effort and story length. J. Creat. Behav. **55**, 476–488 (2021). https://doi.org/10.1002/jocb.467
53. Johannessen, J.-A.: Creative Strategies as a Prerequisite for Process Pedagogy. Leadership and Organization in the Innovation Economy, pp. 103–126. Emerald Publishing Limited, Leeds (2019). https://doi.org/10.1108/978-1-78973-857-520191013
54. Lockton, D., Singh, D., Sabnis, S., Chou, M., Foley, S., Pantoja, A.: New metaphors: A workshop method for generating ideas and reframing problems in design and beyond. In: Proceedings of the 2019 on Creativity and Cognition, pp. 319–332. ACM, San Diego, CA (2019). https://doi.org/10.1145/3325480.3326570
55. Marin, A., Reimann, M., Castaño, R.: Metaphors and creativity: direct, moderating, and mediating effects. J. Consum. Psychol. **24**, 290–297 (2014). https://doi.org/10.1016/j.jcps.2013.11.001
56. Claxton, G., Edwards, L., Scale-Constantinou, V.: Cultivating creative mentalities: A framework for education. Think. Skills Creat. **1**, 57–61 (2006). https://doi.org/10.1016/j.tsc.2005.11.001

57. Henriksen, D., Richardson, C., Shack, K.: Mindfulness and creativity: implications for thinking and learning. Think. Skills Creat. **37**, 100689 (2020). https://doi.org/10.1016/j.tsc.2020.100689
58. Lebuda, I., Zabelina, D.L., Karwowski, M.: Mind full of ideas: A meta-analysis of the mindfulness–creativity link. Personal. Individ. Differ. **93**, 22–26 (2016). https://doi.org/10.1016/j.paid.2015.09.040
59. Ding, X., Tang, Y.-Y., Tang, R., Posner, M.I.: Improving creativity performance by short-term meditation. Behav. Brain Funct. **10**, 9 (2014). https://doi.org/10.1186/1744-9081-10-9
60. Chen, L., Guo, Y., Song, L.J., Lyu, B.: From errors to OCBs and creativity: A multilevel mediation mechanism of workplace gratitude. Curr. Psychol. **41**, 6170–6184 (2022). https://doi.org/10.1007/s12144-020-01120-5
61. Gregor, S., Hevner, A.R.: The front end of innovation: perspectives on creativity, knowledge and design. In: Donnellan, B., Helfert, M., Kenneally, J., VanderMeer, D., Rothenberger, M., Winter, R. (eds.) New Horizons in Design Science: Broadening the Research Agenda, pp. 249–263. Springer International Publishing, Cham (2015). https://doi.org/10.1007/978-3-319-18714-3_16
62. Hevner, A., Chatterjee, S.: Design and creativity. In: Design Research in Information Systems, pp. 145–156. Springer US, Boston, MA (2010). https://doi.org/10.1007/978-1-4419-5653-8_11
63. De Bono, E.: Six Thinking Hats. Penguin Books, London (1985)
64. Aguinis, H., Beltran, J.R., Archibold, E.E., Jean, E.L., Rice, D.B.: Thought experiments: review and recommendations. J. Organ. Behavior. **44**, 544–560 (2023). https://doi.org/10.1002/job.2658
65. vom Brocke, J., Maedche, A.: The DSR grid: six core dimensions for effectively planning and communicating design science research projects. Electron. Markets. **29**, 379–385 (2019). https://doi.org/10.1007/s12525-019-00358-7
66. Knapp, D., Seckler, C., & vom Brocke, J.. Creativity in design science research: how to use divergent and convergent methods effectively. Presented at the 18th International Conference on Design Science Research in Information Systems and Technology (DESRIST 2023), Pretoria, ZA (2023)

GALEA – Leveraging Generative Agents in Artifact Evaluation

Nicolas Prat[1](✉) , John P. Lalor[2] , and Ahmed Abbasi[2]

[1] ESSEC Business School, Cergy-Pontoise, France
prat@essec.edu
[2] Human-centered Analytics Lab (HAL), University of Notre Dame, Notre Dame, IN, USA
{jlalor1,aabbasi}@nd.edu

Abstract. Large language models and generative artificial intelligence are disrupting academic research. They have reached a stage of maturity that enables them to function as proxies for humans in certain tasks and domains. This ability to simulate humans has major implications for the production and evaluation of knowledge. When coupled with agents, large language models become even more powerful proxies for humans. However, several authors have warned against the risks and limitations of using large language models to simulate humans in academic research. In this research, we focus on artifact evaluation leveraging generative agents. We argue that current research lacks a nuanced approach required in the application of generative agents in artifact evaluation, and that the methodological apparatus developed in design science research can provide a basis for this nuanced approach. Building upon this methodological apparatus, we develop a framework for artifact evaluation with generative agents. The main components of the framework are three design principles (applicability depending on artifact and evaluation methods, objectives of evaluation methods with generative agents, implementation choices aligning generative agents with artifact evaluation process), a typology of artifacts, and a matrix of augmentation. We apply the framework to two recent paper exemplars.

Keywords: Artifact · Evaluation · Generative AI · Agents · Generative agents

1 Introduction

Large language models (LLMs), and generative artificial intelligence (AI) more generally, are revolutionizing several domains, including research in information systems [1]. A recent application of LLMs in research is the simulation of humans. Current models can, in certain domains or tasks, function as believable proxies for humans. This has major implications for evaluating research outputs, including artifacts.

When generative AI is coupled with agent-based modeling (ABM), it becomes even more powerful for evaluating research outcomes. LLM-based agents or, more generally, generative agents [2], have thus emerged as a research topic, including applications of these agents to the production or evaluation of research outcomes.

Despite the promises of generative agents as "simulacra of human behavior" [2], several papers have warned against the potential risks of using LLMs as substitutes for humans in research, some even pointing out that the very nature of LLMs makes them unable to reproduce all the subtleties of human cognition [3].

This research focuses on the application of generative agents to artifact evaluation. As argued by Abbasi et al. [4], evaluation *of* generative AI artifacts is a complex issue. Similarly, artifact evaluation *with* generative AI, including generative agents, is a complex issue. Current approaches do not capture all the nuances required in this context. We need to consider what artifacts and evaluation methods are amenable to generative agents, what may be augmented by generative agents depending on objectives, and what criteria to consider when implementing generative agents in artifact evaluation. Design science research (DSR) is well equipped to answer these questions. It has developed a methodological apparatus for evaluating artifacts and, more generally, knowledge processes and outcomes [5–7]. Building upon this apparatus, we propose a framework, named GALEA[1] (Generative Agents Leveraged in the Evaluation of Artifacts). The framework comprises three design principles (applicability depending on artifact and evaluation methods, objectives of evaluation methods with generative agents, implementation choices aligning generative agents with artifact evaluation process), a typology of artifacts, and a matrix of augmentation. The typology of artifacts is based on the DOLCE ontology [8]. The matrix of augmentation considers the categories and levels of augmentation. To illustrate how GALEA captures the nuances of artifact evaluation with generative agents, we apply it to two recent exemplar papers.

The paper is structured as follows. Section 2 reviews previous research. Section 3 presents the typology of artifacts used in the GALEA framework. Section 4 presents the framework and Sect. 5 demonstrates its application. Section 6 concludes.

2 Literature Review

LLMs can simulate personality types. For example, the "big five" personality traits (extroversion, agreeableness, conscientiousness, emotional stability, openness to experience) can be used to define different personas with LLMs. Once initiated, the personas can behave in a predictable way according to their personality [9].

Beyond simulating individual personas, LLMs may simulate potentially large samples of humans ("silico samples") in academic research. These samples may be used to produce or evaluate knowledge, for example in social science research [10], marketing [11], and computer information systems [12]. There can be many advantages in using LLMs as proxies for humans in research: speed, scale, cost reduction, and better handling of the complexity and dynamics of social phenomena. With LLMs as proxies for humans, multiple simulations may be produced, testing many different parameters without being constrained by the limited attention span of human subjects; replacing human subjects with LLMs is also relevant in high-risk projects [13].

---

[1] Galea is the Latin word for *helmet*. It is used in anatomy or botany to refer to a helmet-shaped structure or organ. Source: https://www.wordreference.com/definition/galea.

Despite the promises and benefits of LLMs, several authors have warned against the risks and limitations of using them as proxies for humans in academic research [3, 11, 13, 14]. More specifically:

- LLMs differ fundamentally from humans. They rely on probabilistic patterns to predict the next word and fail to reproduce all the subtleties of human cognition.
- The samples on which LLMs are trained may differ from the samples of humans that they are supposed to simulate. In particular, several LLMs are trained mostly with data from Western, Educated, Industrialized, Rich, and Democratic countries (WEIRD). Moreover, LLMs may be smarter (e.g., GPT 4o as opposed to GPT 3.5) or less toxic/more prosocial than the humans they are supposed to represent. They also struggle with tasks not encountered in their training data [3]. Therefore, rather than algorithmic bias, the fundamental issue is algorithmic fidelity [10], which should be estimated for a given model, sample, and topic or domain.
- The results obtained by simulating humans with LLMs may be sensitive not only to the model, but also the model version, training data, prompts, model parameters (e.g., Softmax temperature), and fine-tuning.
- Several issues are issues generally encountered with LLMs, e.g., hallucinations, privacy concerns and more generally ethical issues, copyright, transparency and replicability, data quality, and environmental cost.
- There is generally a trade-off between internal and external validity [13]: big models trained with a lot of data but with little transparency and control possibilities (priority to external validity), versus models trained with less data, but with more transparency and control (priority to internal validity).

When using LLMs as proxies for humans in research, one size does not fit all. For example, in psychological science, LLMs as proxies for participants may be most useful for specific topics, specific tasks, specific research stages, and specific samples [14].

To make LLMs even more powerful in simulating humans, generative agents have been proposed [2], combining generative AI with agent-based modeling (ABM). Park et al. [2] define generative agents as "computational software agents that simulate believable human behavior" and present an architecture for generative agents with three components: memory stream, reflection, and planning. Generative agents interact with their environment (including other agents), make decisions, plan, and act on their environment. Interactions with and between generative agents are in natural language. Agents may cooperate with each other to execute complex tasks (multi-agent systems [15, 16]). Chain-of-Thought (CoT) strategies may be used [17], prompting agents to decompose complex tasks. Thanks to their LLM component, generative agents may react dynamically depending on context [18], instead of being limited by pre-specified and often limited rules [19]. Generative agents may reflect personality types, demographic characteristics, attitudes, and values. Simulating humans with generative agents (a.k.a. LLM-agent hybrids) is particularly relevant in social science research [13], including for simulating social interactions, cooperation, and emotion [20, 21]. When generative agents are the counterparts of real individuals, this facilitates the assessment of their believability, by comparing their responses with those of the human they represent [22]. Several papers have already applied generative agents to evaluating research outcomes (including artifacts) or mentioned potential applications [2, 15–25]. The risks associated with using generative agents as proxies for humans in research are essentially the same as those regarding the use of LLMs not combined with agents.

This research focuses on artifact evaluation with generative agents. Artifact evaluation with generative agents is a complex issue, and current research does not capture the nuances required to address this complexity. DSR has developed a rich methodological apparatus regarding the evaluation of artifacts, and the validity of DSR knowledge more generally [5–7]. Building upon this apparatus, we propose a framework to capture the nuances of artifact evaluation with generative agents. Next, we present the typology of artifacts that we use in this framework.

3 Typology of Artifacts

Traditionally, DSR in information systems (IS) has focused on information technology (IT) or IS artifacts. However, as illustrated below, generative agents have been used or proposed for evaluating a variety of artifacts beyond IT and IS. Examples include government policies and architectural design. We contend that the methodological apparatus developed in DSR in IS is applicable to a variety of artifacts, in the social sciences in particular. Consequently, GALEA may be applied to artifacts in a broad sense. We are interested in leveraging an IT artifact (generative agents) to evaluate other artifacts, which may be non-IT or IS artifacts themselves. DSR, with the methodological apparatus it has developed regarding artifact evaluation, is perfectly suited to address this issue, even if this requires adaptations to consider the wider range of artifacts addressed.

Consistent with the intended scope of GALEA, we need a typology of artifacts not limited to IS, IT, or technical artifacts. This typology needs to be detailed enough to account for the variety of artifacts. It will be used in the first design principle of GALEA. The typology of March and Smith [26] is widely used. However, it is defined at a high level (distinguishing between constructs, models, methods, and instantiations) and specific to DSR in IS. Other typologies are either specific to DSR in IS or focused on technical artifacts [27–30]. Therefore, we need to define our typology of artifacts. Instead of defining it from scratch, we reuse a foundational ontology.

The ontology that we use is DOLCE, a Descriptive Ontology for Linguistic and Cognitive Engineering [8, 31]. We define an artifact as an entity intentionally produced by a human or a collective of humans to fulfill a function [29, 32]. Our typology of artifacts is a subset of DOLCE (Fig. 1). The concepts of DOLCE are explained in [8, 31, 33, 34]. At a high level, endurants are distinguished from perdurants. Endurants represent physical or non-physical objects. Perdurants typically represent events or processes. The fundamental difference between endurants and perdurants is temporal: endurants (e.g., a table) are wholly present any time they are present, while perdurants (e.g., a manufacturing process) unfold progressively through time. We content that for an artifact to be qualified as such, it should be present completely at any time it is present; therefore, all artifacts are endurants. Within the category of endurants, non-physical objects are decomposed into mental objects and social objects. Since mental objects are specific to the minds of individuals, they are not artifacts. A social object is the product of a community. It may have agency or not. Institutions are examples of agentive social objects. Non-agentive social objects that qualify as artifacts are concepts, descriptions, and information objects. Descriptions define or use concepts. They include information encoding systems (e.g., classification systems or grammars), methods (descriptions "that contain a specification to do, realize, behave, etc."), social descriptions (e.g., laws, norms, or peace treaties), systems as descriptions ("the descriptive, unifying aspect of a system (usually it includes at least a design, or project, plan, etc.)."), and theories. Examples of information objects are diagrams, words, or text. Physical objects may be agentive or non-agentive. Robots with agency are examples of agentive physical objects that qualify as artifacts. According to the DOLCE terminology, non-agentive physical objects are the only ones that qualify as material artifacts.

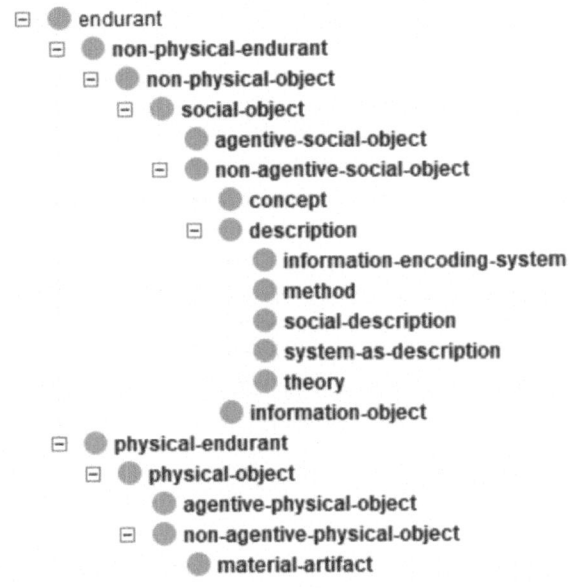

Fig. 1. Typology of artifacts based on the DOLCE ontology [33].

Table 1 shows the lowest levels of the typology of artifacts (leaf nodes in Fig. 1), with examples for each artifact type, and examples of applications of generative agents to evaluate artifacts of this type. For some artifact types, we did not find examples of applications of generative agents to evaluate artifacts of these types. We will provide explanations for this when detailing the first design principle of GALEA.

Table 2 maps the typology of artifacts of GALEA with the typology of March and Smith [26]. "?" denotes ambiguity in mapping a concept of a typology into concepts of the other typology, and ∅ indicates that a concept of a typology cannot be mapped or can only be partially mapped into concepts of the other typology.

Mapping the typology of GALEA into the one of March and Smith [26] (left column of Table 2), we note that some agentive social objects may not be mapped easily. For example, it is unclear if organizations should be defined as instantiations, models, or methods. Similarly, it is unclear if social descriptions such as laws should be characterized as models or methods, and the distinction between models and methods does

Table 1. Typology of artifacts: examples of artifacts and evaluation with generative agents.

Artifact type	Examples	Evaluation with generative agents
Agentive social object	Organization, institution, generative agent	Holacracy (a decentralized form of organization) [23] Generative agents [16]
Concept	Concept in a language, construct in a theory	
Information-encoding system	Taxonomy, grammar of a programming language, query language	
Method	Project management methodology, conceptual modeling methodology, specification of an algorithm	Hiring methods [15] Recommendation algorithms [20]
Social description	Regulation, law, norm, policy	Scare resource allocation policies [21] Government policies [22]
System as description	Conceptual model, business process model, system architecture	Spatial designs in urban planning [19]
Theory	Explanatory theory, predictive theory, prescriptive (DSR) theory [35]	Social science theories [2, 18]* Filter bubble effect [20]
Information object	Text, diagram, software, implemented algorithm	Artificially generated text (e.g., chatbot, LLM) [24] LLM-generated text [17] Digital services [25]
Agentive physical object	Robot with agency	
Material artifact	Robot without agency, building, shirt, computer, smartphone	

*Theory development, which implicitly includes theory evaluation.

not appear relevant here. Theories have no equivalent in March and Smith [26]. When mapping the typology of March and Smith [26] into the one of GALEA (right column of Table 2), some instantiations may not be mapped into any concept in the typology of GALEA. For example, an information systems development method is a method according to March and Smith [26] (and according to GALEA); its execution is an instantiation according to March and Smith [26]. However, according to the typology of GALEA, this execution is not an artifact, because it would be characterized as a perdurant in DOLCE. Summing up, there is only partial mapping between the two typologies, which have different scopes and levels of detail.

Table 2. Mapping the typology of artifacts to and from the typology of March and Smith [26].

To March and Smith [26]	From March and Smith [26]
Agentive social object → instantiation,? Concept → construct Information-encoding system → construct Method → method Social description →? System as description → model Theory → ∅ Information object → instantiation, model, method Agentive physical object → instantiation Material artifact → instantiation	Construct → concept, information-encoding system Model → system as description, information object Method → method, information object Instantiation → agentive social object, information object, agentive physical object, material artifact, ∅

We now turn to the description of the GALEA framework.

4 A Framework for Leveraging Generative Agents in Artifact Evaluation

We propose the GALEA framework for leveraging generative agents in artifact evaluation (Fig. 2). "Leveraging" implies that generative agents should "complement rather than replace human stakeholders in design processes." [2]: they should augment the artifact evaluation process, rather than automate it completely. There should be at least one researcher controlling the evaluation process. Generative agents play the role of secondary participants [5] in evaluation, as proxies for human subjects and/or human evaluators. For example, they may evaluate artificially generated text [17, 24].

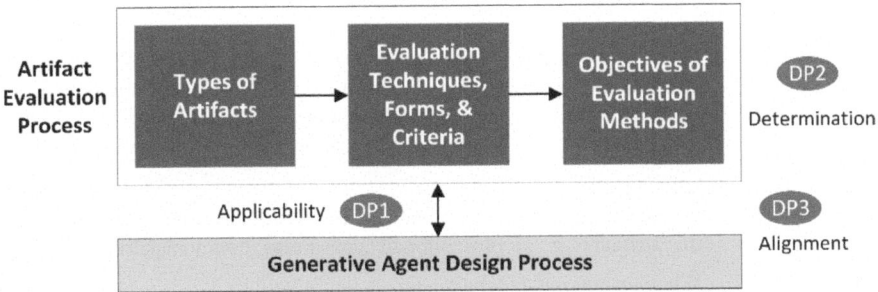

Fig. 2. The Generative Agents Leveraged in the Evaluation of Artifacts (GALEA) framework.

GALEA builds upon prior work on knowledge evaluation and validity in DSR [5–7]. At a higher level, program theory proved useful to structure the framework. A program theory is "an explicit theory or model of how an intervention, such as a project, a program, a strategy, an initiative, or a policy, contributes to a chain of intermediate results and finally to the intended or observed outcomes" [36, p.xix]. Program theory facilitates evaluation (a.k.a. theory-based evaluation) by making causal links explicit, e.g., from inputs to activities to outputs to outcomes (for participants) to impacts (for the broader community). In GALEA, essential inputs are types of artifacts and evaluation methods (evaluation techniques, forms, and criteria). The intended outcome (objective) is to improve the resource efficiency or validity of evaluation. The three design principles (described below) may be considered as activities to be applied sequentially.

FEDS [6] distinguishes between formative and summative evaluation, and between artificial and naturalistic evaluation. We agree with Sarstedt et al. [11, p.1254] that "silicon samples hold particular promise in upstream parts of the research process [..], where researchers collect external information to safeguard follow-up design choices." In other words, generative agents are primarily for formative evaluation. Regarding the distinction between artificial and naturalistic evaluation, generative agents are artificial but are in some cases hardly distinguishable from human subjects or evaluators.

4.1 Design Principles

Table 3 presents the design principles, using the schema of Gregor et al. [37].

As mentioned above, applying LLMs (and generative agents) in research requires considering the specificities of topics/domains, tasks, research stages, and samples. The specificity of the topic or domain is taken into consideration in DP1, which determines the applicability of generative agents for evaluating the artifact at hand. The specificity of tasks (evaluation methods, in our case) is considered in DP2. The specificity of research stages is taken into consideration by applying generative agents to formative evaluation primarily. The specificity of samples is considered in DP3, as a criterion to choose between several alternative solutions for implementing generative agents.

We now detail each design principle.

Table 3. Design principles in GALEA.

Design principle title	DP1: Applicability depending on artifact and evaluation methods	DP2: Determine objectives of using generative agents in evaluation methods	DP3: Implementation choices aligning generative agents with artifact evaluation process
Aim, implementer and user	For artifact designers to evaluate an artifact for the target population of this artifact (e.g., IT professionals, consumers, policy makers)		
Context	When leveraging generative agents in evaluation		

(continued)

Table 3. (*continued*)

Design principle title	DP1: Applicability depending on artifact and evaluation methods	DP2: Determine objectives of using generative agents in evaluation methods	DP3: Implementation choices aligning generative agents with artifact evaluation process
Mechanism	Determine applicability of generative agents to artifact evaluation depending on the artifact and the evaluation methods	Based on the applicability of generative agents and on the objectives, choose the evaluation methods to which generative agents will be applied, and what will be augmented by generative agents	Based on the objectives and specific context (e.g., research transparency and replicability constraints, available resources, target population of the artifact), choose the LLM, library, or off-the-shelf software for generative agents, aligning the generative agents with the artifact evaluation process
Rationale	Because applicability of generative agents to artifact evaluation depends on the artifact (and more generally on its type), on the evaluation criteria, evaluation techniques, and form of evaluation	Because the objectives of using generative agents in artifact evaluation should be to improve the resource efficiency and/or validity of evaluation, which helps determine what evaluation methods will be augmented with generative agents and how they will be augmented (matrix of augmentation)	Because several solutions are available to implement generative agents for artifact evaluation, and the choice of the solution and its alignment with the evaluation process depend on several criteria (e.g., sample of population on which the LLM has been trained, necessity for fine-tuning, transparency requirements, cost of adapting reusable libraries, specific topics or domains to which the libraries apply)

4.2 Applicability Depending on Artifact and Evaluation Methods

The applicability of generative agents depends on the artifact. It also depends on the evaluation methods and, more specifically, on criteria, techniques, and form of evaluation, as defined in Prat et al. [5]. "Applicability" means that generative agents may be applied, but also that they add value (e.g., compared to using LLMs without ABM).

The applicability of generative agents depends on the type of evaluated artifact. For most artifact types, there are papers that mention applications or potential applications of generative agents to evaluate artifacts of this type (Table 1). However, we did not find examples for the following artifact types: concept, information encoding system, agentive physical object, and material artifact. Regarding concepts, it is not surprising: evaluating a single concept is not common. For evaluating information encoding systems, e.g., query languages, we could consider applying generative agents. For physical artifacts (agentive physical object and material artifact), we could in theory consider applying generative agents (e.g., to evaluate product prototypes). However, the fact that we found no examples is consistent with the observation that using generative agents for evaluation makes most sense in the upstream research stages, before decisive design choices are made and products are put into production. Beyond the artifact type, the applicability of generative agents for evaluation may depend on the artifact itself: as mentioned above, the topic or domain of the artifact should be considered.

Regarding the applicability of generative agents to evaluation criteria, for the sake of space, we focus on the criteria in the hierarchy of Prat et al. [5, p. 258] that are not amenable to evaluation with generative agents. Within the goal dimension, technical and economic feasibility are difficult to evaluate with generative agents, which likely do not have the required specialized knowledge to evaluate technical feasibility or to make cost-benefit computations. In the environment dimension, generative agents, as proxies for people, appear most relevant to evaluate this category of criteria, although using generative agents to evaluate ethicality is not recommended. Most criteria in structure and activity are amenable to evaluation with generative agents. Completeness is hard to evaluate without a notion of what "complete" means. Fidelity to modeled phenomena requires comparing a model with reality, a challenge for LLMs. Similarly to ethicality, we would not recommend using generative agents to evaluate trustworthiness. In evolution, learning capability appears difficult to assess by generative agents, and generative agents have little potential added value for evaluating robustness and scalability (of algorithms, typically).

Figure 3 shows what evaluation techniques may use generative agents (greyed rectangles). As mentioned above, generative agents may be used as substitutes for human subjects or evaluators. Therefore, they can be used even in organizational contexts (such as case studies, for example). Regarding field experiments, A/B testing with generative agents is a relevant substitute or complement to traditional A/B testing [20, 25]. Even though generative agents could be used in analytical evaluation techniques and informed argument, their added value, compared with plain LLMs, is not apparent.

Figure 4 shows the forms of evaluation compatible with generative agents. They have been used or may be used for most forms of evaluation. However, LLMs are often flawed reasoners [3], and generative agents are not recommended for formal proof.

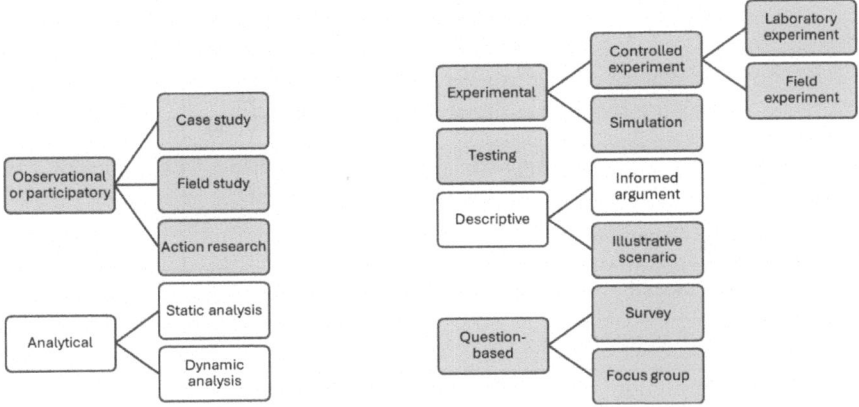

Fig. 3. Applicability depending on evaluation techniques (split into two parts for brevity).

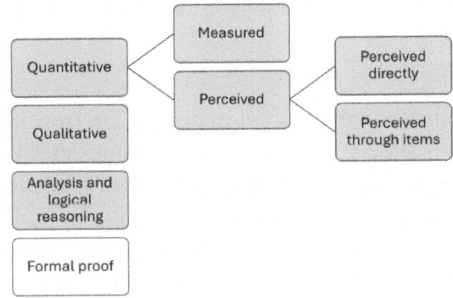

Fig. 4. Applicability depending on form of evaluation.

4.3 Determine Objectives of Evaluation Methods Using Generative Agents

Once the applicability of generative agents has been examined with DP1, the artifact designer should determine the objectives of using them in artifact evaluation. Depending on the objectives, he may choose the evaluation methods that will use generative agents, and what will be augmented by these agents. Applying generative agents to an evaluation method may pursue such objectives as: reduce evaluation costs and time, increase evaluation scale, release constraints of time and space met in physical environments, or improve external or internal validity of evaluation. Artifact evaluation should balance rigor and resource efficiency [6]. Therefore, using generative agents in an evaluation should improve resource efficiency and/or evaluation validity. As design knowledge, the validity of evaluation knowledge may be assessed with design science validity criteria [7], e.g., internal or external validity. When considering the benefits of generative agents, the comparison is not always between evaluation with humans and with generative agents. For example, one may consider the benefits of generative agents compared to rule-based ABM. To decide what should be augmented when applying generative agents to an evaluation method, Fig. 5 proposes a matrix of augmentation.

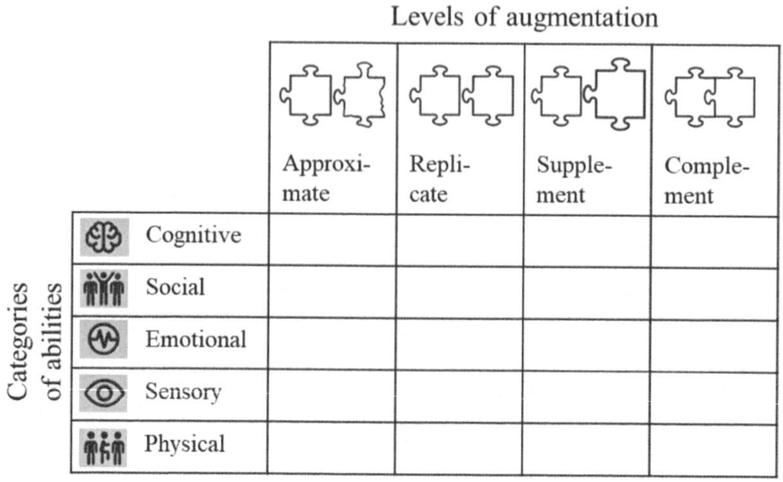

		Levels of augmentation			
		Approximate	Replicate	Supplement	Complement
Categories of abilities	Cognitive				
	Social				
	Emotional				
	Sensory				
	Physical				

Fig. 5. Matrix of augmentation (The icons for the categories of abilities were generated with DALL·E 3).

This matrix draws on the augmentation matrix of De Boeck and Vaes [38, p. 71]. Its first dimension is the category of abilities. We consider five categories [38–40]: cognitive, social, emotional, sensory and physical. The second dimension is the level of augmentation. De Boeck and Vaes [38] distinguish between replicate, supplement and exceed. We consider four levels. Replicate is the replication of a human ability (without changes). Supplement is the extension/improvement of a human ability. Complement (exceed) is augmentation through an ability not possessed by humans. We add the level "approximate," since approximating capabilities may sometimes be sufficient. With the matrix of Fig. 5, for each evaluation method using generative agents, the artifact designer specifies the level of augmentation for each required capability.

4.4 Implementation Choices Aligning Generative Agents with Artifact Evaluation Process

Depending on objectives and context (e.g., research transparency and replicability constraints, available resources, target population), the artifact designer chooses the technical solution for generative agents, aligning the generative agents with the artifact evaluation process. Several solutions are available: using existing LLMs, writing code to complement an existing library, accessing a library through an API, or buying off-the-shelf software. The choice of the solution and its alignment with the artifact evaluation process depend on several criteria (e.g., transparency requirements and tradeoffs between internal and external validity). Multimodal models, 3D virtual environments or metaverses enable interactions beyond natural language (e.g., visual abilities).

5 Application of the Framework

To illustrate how GALEA captures the nuances of artifact evaluation with generative agents, we apply it to two papers (Table 4). The first paper [24] presents a generative agent for scoring LLM-generated text, ChatEval. The generative agents serve as proxies for human raters and are tasked with assessing the quality of generated text for one task and rating the generated text on four dimensions (naturalness, coherence, engagingness, and

Table 4. Examples applying GALEA.

	ChatEval [24]	Agent4Rec [20]
Summary	LLM agents as proxies for human evaluators. Agents simulate a debate to evaluate generated text	LLM agents as proxies for human subjects (users) with the goal of eliciting preferences and interpretable feedback for the evaluation of recommender systems
DP1	Evaluation of information objects (generated text) Replace human evaluators to efficiently score generated data for system testing Quantitative-measured and quantitative-perceived	Evaluation of a method (recommendation algorithm) and theory (filter bubble effect) Replace human subjects to generate data for system testing Quantitative-measured and qualitative
DP2	Cognitive approximation. The agents are evaluating text, and their evaluations are themselves scored against a human gold standard	Cognitive replication: Ratings Social approximation: Free-text feedback Emotional/social supplement: Post-exit interviews
DP3	Proxies for human raters are generative agents based on OpenAI GPT-3.5-turbo and GPT-4. Evaluation scenarios include single-agent and multi-agent simulations	Implemented with existing framework for deploying generative agents (LangChain) LLM is closed-source GPT-3.5-turbo model from ChatGPT
Remarks	Operates at lower levels of augmentation (approximation) with a goal of achieving replication The datasets used include texts generated by multiple LLM agents, however the analysis is done at the aggregate level. There is an opportunity here to evaluate not only the generated text, but also the text generation models themselves Reliance on GPT-3.5-turbo means lack of transparency and less understanding of generalization across LLM models and architectures	Reliance on GPT-3.5-turbo means lack of transparency and less understanding of generalization across LLM models and architectures Only using one LLM model for the generative agents may introduce external threats to validity regarding generalization

groundedness) for the other task. The objective is cognitive replication of human raters. The second paper [20] proposes Agent4Rec, a generative agent that simulates human raters of items (e.g., movies or books). In this work, a method is evaluated (i.e., recommender systems), and the filter bubble effect is replicated using agent-generated data. While this work is more robust in its adherence to GALEA, implementation choices—specifically the use of closed-source LLM models from OpenAI—may introduce threats to the validity of the study as the models are not transparent and there was not a triangulation of results with other LLM models (closed- or open-source). These examples implicitly address DP1 and DP2 through their motivation and experimental setup. Future work can build on these exemplars by using GALEA to define and describe decisions based on the design principles to achieve stated aims regarding using generative agents in evaluation. For example, stating the goals of using generative agents (DP2) and what is to be achieved by their inclusion can help place the use of generative agents in context of the research question being addressed. The implementation decisions should also be carefully considered and explicitly described (DP3).

6 Conclusion

Recognizing the potential of generative agents as proxies for humans and the complexity of using them in artifact evaluation, we have proposed and illustrated the GALEA framework to leverage generative agents when evaluating artifacts. We acknowledge that the hierarchy of criteria used in DP1 was originally defined in the context of DSR in IS and may need to be extended for application to other types of artifacts. Moreover, the design principles will need to be completed, as they do not consider all evaluation steps (they stop at implementation choices). Finally, beyond illustration of the framework with published research, we will apply it in actual projects building artifacts.

References

1. Susarla, A., Gopal, R., Thatcher, J.B., Sarker, S.: The Janus effect of generative AI: charting the path for responsible conduct of scholarly activities in information systems. Inf. Syst. Res. **34**, 399–408 (2023)
2. Park, J.S., O'Brien, J., Cai, C.J., Morris, M.R., Liang, P., Bernstein, M.S.: Generative agents: interactive simulacra of human behavior. In: Proc. UIST, pp. 1–22. ACM (2023)
3. Gao, Y., Lee, D., Burtch, G., Fazelpour, S.: Take caution in using LLMs as human surrogates: Scylla ex machina. arXiv preprint arXiv:2410.19599 (2024)
4. Abbasi, A., Parsons, J., Pant, G., Sheng, O.R.L., Sarker, S.: Pathways for design research on artificial intelligence. Inf. Syst. Res. **35**, 441–459 (2024)
5. Prat, N., Comyn-Wattiau, I., Akoka, J.: A taxonomy of evaluation methods for information systems artifacts. J. Manag. Inf. Syst. **32**, 229–267 (2015)
6. Venable, J., Pries-Heje, J., Baskerville, R.: FEDS: a framework for evaluation in design science research. Eur. J. Inf. Syst. **25**, 77–89 (2016)
7. Larsen, K.R., et al.: Validity in design science. MIS Quart.. Forthcoming. (2025)
8. Borgo, S., et al.: DOLCE: a descriptive ontology for linguistic and cognitive engineering. Appl. Ontol. **17**, 45–69 (2022)

9. Caron, G., Srivastava, S.: Manipulating the perceived personality traits of language models. In: Proc. EMNLP, pp. 2370–2386. ACL (2023)
10. Argyle, L.P., Busby, E.C., Fulda, N., Gubler, J.R., Rytting, C., Wingate, D.: Out of one, many: using language models to simulate human samples. Polit. Anal. **31**, 337–351 (2023)
11. Sarstedt, M., Adler, S.J., Rau, L., Schmitt, B.: Using large language models to generate silicon samples in consumer and marketing research: challenges, opportunities, and guidelines. Psychol. Mark. **41**, 1254–1270 (2024)
12. Park, J.S., Popowski, L., Cai, C., Morris, M.R., Liang, P., Bernstein, M.S.: Cocial simulacra: creating populated prototypes for social computing systems. In: Proc. UIST, pp. 1–18. ACM (2022)
13. Grossmann, I., Feinberg, M., Parker, D.C., Christakis, N.A., Tetlock, P.E., Cunningham, W.A.: AI and the transformation of social science research. Science. **380**, 1108–1109 (2023)
14. Dillion, D., Tandon, N., Gu, Y., Gray, K.: Can AI language models replace human participants? Trends Cogn. Sci. **27**, 597–600 (2023)
15. Li, Y., Zhang, Y., Sun, L.: Metaagents: Simulating interactions of human behaviors for llm-based task-oriented coordination via collaborative generative agents. arXiv preprint arXiv:2310.06500 (2023)
16. Talebirad, Y., Nadiri, A.: Multi-agent collaboration: Harnessing the power of intelligent LLM agents. arXiv preprint arXiv:2306.03314 (2023)
17. Li, Y., et al.: MATEval: a multi-agent discussion framework for advancing open-ended text evaluation. In: Proc. DASFAA, pp. 415–426. Springer Nature, Singapore (2024)
18. Mitsopoulos, K., et al.: Psychologically-valid generative agents: a novel approach to agent-based modeling in social sciences. In: Proc. AAAI FSS, pp. 340–348. AAAI Press (2023)
19. Noyman, A., Hu, K., Larson, K.: TravelAgent: Generative Agents in the Built Environment. arXiv preprint arXiv:2412.18985 (2024)
20. Zhang, A., Chen, Y., Sheng, L., Wang, X., Chua, T.-S.: On generative agents in recommendation. In: Proc. SIGIR, pp. 1807–1817. ACM (2024)
21. Ji, J., et al.: SRAP-agent: Simulating and optimizing scarce resource allocation policy with LLM-based agent. arXiv preprint arXiv:2410.14152 (2024)
22. Park, J.S., et al.: Generative agent simulations of 1,000 people. arXiv preprint arXiv:2411.10109 (2024)
23. Zhu, C., Cheng, Y., Zhang, J., Qiu, Y., Xia, S., Zhu, H.: Generative organizational behavior simulation using large language model based autonomous agents: a holacracy perspective. arXiv preprint arXiv:2408.11826 (2024)
24. Chan, C.-M., et al: Chateval: Towards better LLM-based evaluators through multi-agent debate. arXiv preprint arXiv:2308.07201 (2023)
25. Vezhnevets, A.S., et al.: Generative agent-based modeling with actions grounded in physical, social, or digital space using Concordia. arXiv preprint arXiv:2312.03664 (2023)
26. March, S.T., Smith, G.F.: Design and natural science research on information technology. Decis. Support. Syst. **15**, 251–266 (1995)
27. Offermann, P., Blom, S., Schönherr, M., Bub, U.: Artifact types in information systems design science—a literature review. In: Proc. DESRIST, pp. 77–92. Springer, Berlin Heidelberg (2010)
28. Sangupamba Mwilu, O., Comyn-Wattiau, I., Prat, N.: Design science research contribution to business intelligence in the cloud—a systematic literature review. Futur. Gener. Comput. Syst. **63**, 108–122 (2016)
29. Kassel, G.: A formal ontology of artefacts. Appl. Ontol. **5**, 223–246 (2010)
30. Weigand, H., Johannesson, P., Andersson, B.: An artifact ontology for design science research. Data Knowl. Eng. **133**, 101878 (2021)
31. Masolo, C., Borgo, S., Gangemi, A., Guarino, N., Oltramari, A.: WonderWeb deliverable D18. Technical report, Laboratory For Applied Ontology—ISTC-CNR, (2003)

32. Hilpinen, R.: On artifacts and works of art. Theoria. **58**, 58–82 (1992)
33. ISTC-CNR Laboratory for Applied Ontology: DOLCE-Lite-Plus, Version 3.9.7. https://www.loa.istc.cnr.it/old/ontologies/DLP3971.zip (2006)
34. Masolo, C., Vieu, L., Bottazzi, E., Catenacci, C., Ferrario, R., Gangemi, A., Guarino, N.: Social roles and their descriptions. In: Proc. KR, pp. 267–277. AAAI (2004)
35. Gregor, S.: The nature of theory in information systems. MIS Q. **30**, 611–642 (2006)
36. Funnell, S.C., Rogers, P.J.: Purposeful Program Theory: Effective Use of Theories of Change and Logic Models. John Wiley & Sons, San Francisco, CA (2011)
37. Gregor, S., Kruse, L.C., Seidel, S.: Research perspectives: the anatomy of a design principle. J. Assoc. Inf. Syst. **21**, 1622–1652 (2020)
38. De Boeck, M., Vaes, K.: Human augmentation and its new design perspectives. Int. J. Des. Creat. Innov. **12**, 61–80 (2024)
39. Jain, H., Padmanabhan, B., Pavlou, P.A., Raghu, T.S.: Editorial for the special section on humans, algorithms, and augmented intelligence: the future of work, organizations, and society. Inf. Syst. Res. **32**, 675–687 (2021)
40. Pedersen, I., Duin, A.H.: Defining a classification system for augmentation technology in socio-technical terms. In: Proc. ISTAS, pp. 1–4. IEEE (2021)

Past Lessons, Future Directions: An Author-Informed Review of Design Science Research in Information Systems

Sebastian Reiners[1], Gregor Kipping[1,3], Fabian Tingelhoff[2], and Michael Gau[3,4](✉)

[1] European Research Center for Information Systems (ERCIS), University of Münster, Leonardo-Campus 3, 48149 Münster, Germany
{sebastian.reiners,gregor.kipping}@ercis.uni-muenster.de
[2] Institute for Information Systems and Digital Business, University of St. Gallen, Müller-Friedberg-Strasse 8, 9000 St. Gallen, Switzerland
fabian.tingelhoff@unisg.ch
[3] Liechtenstein Business School, University of Liechtenstein, Fürst-Franz-Josef-Strasse, 9490 Vaduz, Liechtenstein
michael.gau@uni.li
[4] Human-Centered Systems Lab, Karlsruhe Institute of Technology (KIT), Kaiserstrasse 93, 76131 Karlsruhe, Germany

Abstract. This paper explores the foundational insights and evolving perspectives within Design Science Research (DSR) by analyzing the reflections of authors who contributed some of the most pivotal and cited works in the field. Through in-depth interviews with 14 DSR experts, each representing a seminal and impactful publication, we investigate the motivations, challenges, and retrospective viewpoints that shaped their research contributions. Key themes include the authors' reflections on the original aims and main contributions of their work, considerations on what they might alter if revisiting their studies today, and advice for aspiring DSR researchers. These perspectives provide a unique lens into the evolution of DSR, highlighting both enduring principles and areas ripe for innovation. This study chronicles significant milestones in DSR as well as offers guidance for future research and practice, charting a path forward for scholars navigating this dynamic and impactful paradigm.

Keywords: Design Science Research · Expert Interviews · Philosophy of DSR · Research Challenges · Trends in DSR

1 Introduction

Design Science Research (DSR) has received significant attention as a vital research paradigm in the field of Information Systems (IS) ever since its widespread establishment [16, 22, 29]. It provides a structured approach to designing and evaluating artifacts that can be applied to the solution of real-world problems. As the field matured, seminal works shaped and defined its trajectory, influencing both how research is conducted and how findings are applied [13,16,23]. However, less is known about how the field and philosophy of DSR have changed over time. A recent study sheds light on the characteristics of DSR research based on a bibliometric analysis [3]. Our study aims to illuminate the development and enduring impact of influential DSR contributions by examining the insights and reflections of its prominent authors. Through their reflections, we gain a nuanced and more personalized perspective than standard literature reviews of the field's foundational principles, current challenges, and fresh perspectives in DSR.

In this work, we investigate the long-term relevance of original methods or frameworks regarding whether they still effectively address the initial challenges in light of technological and methodological advancements. Another consideration involves unintended applications, wherein contributions are used beyond their intended scope, prompting exploration of how authors perceive these adaptations.

We conducted 14 in-depth interviews with authors[1] of some of the most cited and widely referenced papers[2] in DSR. The findings of this study reveal recurring themes across the interviews, including the authors' emphasis on complexity, transdisciplinary research, and the role of DSR in bridging theoretical growth with practical impact. By charting the collective experiences of these authors, this paper contributes to the ongoing discourse on the future directions of DSR. Following a qualitative research approach, we propose directions for the future of DSR and seek to provide emerging researchers and practitioners with guidance grounded in the field's legacy. Moreover, this study underscores the adaptability and transdisciplinary nature of DSR as it continues to respond to contemporary challenges in IS and beyond.

2 A History of Design Science Research

DSR is an important research paradigm in the field of IS [13]. It is rooted in engineering and the science of the artificial [26]. Over the past decades, the recognition of DSR has grown due to the practical nature of IS problems and its relevance to research outcomes while maintaining scientific rigor. DSR aims to solve real-world problems by designing innovative artifacts [15]. One of the main purposes of DSR is to generate design knowledge and contribute to the scientific knowledge base by providing descriptive explanations of "how to do something to achieve a goal" [12, p. 1622]. DSR projects typically produce design knowledge describing the means-end relationship between the problem and the solution space while novel artifacts are represented in the form of constructs, models, methods, and instantiations [13,16]. Because of its problem-solving nature, DSR has a central role in disciplines such as engineering, architecture, and IS as well as information technology-related disciplines, promoting the development of

---

[1] Cumulative citation count of 227,947 on Google Scholar [25.03.2025].
[2] Cumulative citation count of 42,902 on Google Scholar [25.03.2025].

innovative solutions. However, the application of DSR methodology is not limited to these fields. It can be applied in many disciplines to solve real-world problems, for instance, in operations management [2] or in the field of entrepreneurship [24].

The methodological discourse of DSR has advanced over the past few years. There exist many frameworks, guidelines, and process models supporting design science researchers in conducting DSR projects and structuring the design process (e.g., Sein et al. [25], Kuechler and Vaishnavi [17], Gregor and Jones [14], Peffers et al. [23], Tuuanen et al. [28] and more). However, these guidelines support researchers on the meta level. On the instantiation level, DSR is highly context dependent and does not follow a cookbook [7]. With the growth of the DSR knowledge base and constant change, the complexity of DSR projects is increasing [28]. Due to emerging technologies and the advancing prevalence of DSR, new challenges are arising that need to be addressed. In order to better understand the past and what is missing to address future challenges we present future DSR themes based on the authors' perspectives of the most pivotal and cited works.

3 Method

We pursued a qualitative research approach to derive our insights from 14 in-depth, semi-structured interviews [10,20].

3.1 Ensuring Validity and Reliability of Interview Data

To ensure the validity and reliability of the qualitative data, we followed the four widely established quality criteria [18]: credibility, transferability, dependability, and confirmability.

Credibility, measures how well the qualitative data aligns with reality [20]. To ensure the interview partners are "knowledgeable agents" [10], we selected and interviewed authors (A1–A14) who actively shaped DSR through purposive sampling [8]. We ensured the credibility of our informants by verifying that their papers were either published in highly ranked journals (e.g., MIS Quarterly for A2, 10, and 12), cited extensively (e.g., A3 and 7), or both. *Transferability* refers to the degree to which the generated knowledge can be abstracted to another context with different interview partners. We provide contextual information about our interview partners' papers in Table 1. *Dependability* concerns the replicability of research findings. By making all our data publicly available and presenting in-depth information on our methods, we promote replicability through systematism and transparency [20]. Lastly, *confirmability* regards the results' objectivity [18]. We proactively addressed potential biases throughout the research process, especially during the data analysis and coding. Foremost, through iterative discussions, we ensured that all researchers were aware of their potential biases (e.g., opinions on what constitutes DSR) and knew methods to counter them actively. Moreover, all of the current study's authors conducted the interviews to further prohibit systematic biases and ensure data diversity. In the following, we provide detailed information on how we ensured confirmability in our data collection and analysis.

Table 1. Papers of Interviewed Authors

Acro.	Author	Title	Year
A1	Abbasi, A., Parsons, J., Pant, G., Sheng, O. R. L., & Sarker, S.	Pathways for Design Research on Artificial Intelligence	2024
A2	Gregor, S., & Hevner, A. R.	Positioning and presenting design science research for maximum impact	2013
A3	Maedche, A., Gregor, S., Morana, S., & Feine, J.	Conceptualization of the problem space in design science research	2019
A4	Mandviwalla, M.	Generating and justifying design theory	2015
A5	Mullarkey, M. T., & Hevner, A. R.	An elaborated action design research process model	2019
A6	Seckler, C., Mauer, R., & vom Brocke, J.	Design science in entrepreneurship: conceptual foundations and guiding principles	2021
A7	Tremblay, M. C., Hevner, A. R., & Berndt, D. J.	Focus groups for artifact refinement and evaluation in design research	2010
A8	Peffers, K., Tuunanen, T., Rothenberger, M. A., & Chatterjee, S.	A design science research methodology for information systems research	2007
A9	Venable, J., Pries-Heje, J., & Baskerville, R.	FEDS: A framework for evaluation in design science research	2016
A10	Tuunanen, T., Winter, R., & vom Brocke, J.	Dealing with Complexity in Design Science Research: A Methodology Using Design Echelons	2024
A11	vom Brocke, J., Winter, R., Hevner, A., & Maedche, A.	Accumulation and evolution of design knowledge in design science research: a journey through time and space	2020
A12	Baskerville, R. L., Kaul, M., & Storey, V. C.	Genres of inquiry in design-science research	2015
A13	Hevner, A. R., March, S. T., Park, J., & Ram, S.	Design science in information systems research	2004
A14	Zolbanin, H., & Aubert, B.	A process model for design-oriented machine learning research in information systems	2025

3.2 Data Collection and Analysis

Our qualitative data collection comprised 14 interviews with authors of some of the most influential DSR papers. Interviews had an average duration of around 30 min. We conducted the interviews online via digital video communication tools. Moreover, we interviewed only one author of each paper as to not skew the results to reflect one paper's views over others disproportionally. We used a semi-structured interview guideline, maintaining researcher-participant reciprocity and reflexivity [9]. First, we asked interview partners about their expertise in the domain. Then, in the central part, we asked questions about the motivation, challenges, and contributions behind their publications. Notably, we also asked reflexive questions, such as, "Would you change something in the paper if you wrote it today?" We closed the interview by asking our interview partners about their future hopes and aspirations for the DSR discipline. Throughout the interview, interviewers were free to follow up on any comments. Once we completed the interviews, we transcribed each one[3]. Following the approach outlined by Gioia et al. [10], we initially conducted our inductive coding comparable to Strauss and Corbin's [27] open coding, which resulted in a dataset of 508 1st-order concepts while remaining faithful to our informants' wording. As we realized that many informants referred to similar concepts using different words, we aggregated our 1st-order concepts into 10 2nd-order themes corresponding to Strauss and Corbin's [27] axial coding within iterative discussions among this study's authors. In line with Strauss and Corbin's [27] notion of selective coding, we aggregated the discovered 2nd-order themes into three overarching dimensions. These groupings have enabled us and empower readers to identify, link, and interpret relevant themes in our data between interviewees and abstract these into novel knowledge. By adopting this approach, we were able to investigate multiple perspectives and gain a comprehensive understanding of the dataset's scope and depth [10, 27]. Our data collection and analysis approach is illustrated in Fig. 1.

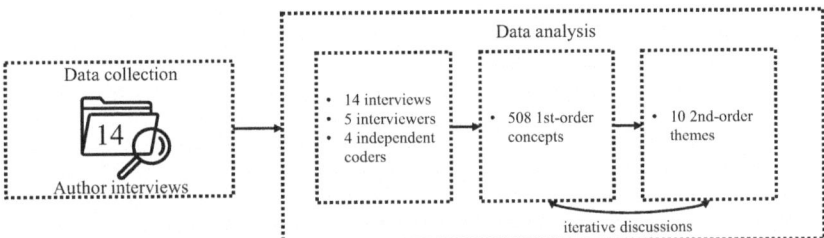

Fig. 1. Data Collection and Analysis

4 Author-Informed Review of Design Science Research

The author-informed review we conducted reveals a variety of relevant themes discussing DSR. By an author-informed review, we refer to engaging in interviews with the authors (A1–A14) to reflect on their research. The findings can be categorized into three overarching dimensions: the learnings from the past,

---

[3] Repository of all transcripts and videos: https://github.com/Ebas0/DESRIST25-P-L-F-D.

current challenges, and future directions. The adjacent 2nd-order themes are displayed in Table 2. The additional columns aggregate the sum of the 1st-order concepts for the respective theme as well as an exemplary 1st-order concept for this theme.

Table 2. 2nd-Order Themes and 1st-Order Concepts

2nd-Order	Exemplary 1st-Order	Sum 1st-Order
Complexity	Cannot plan the whole DSR process in the beginning of the project	110
Transdisciplinarity	DSR is a combination of different research streams	69
Maturity	Historically, DSR was not established as a scientific approach	55
Positioning	Different IS communities have different perspectives of what abstraction means	49
Rigor	Design process must be transparent	48
Guidance	Missing guidance for conducting DSR	48
Eligibility	DSR did not exist as a term but people were doing it	25
Clinical Inquiry	Build artifacts that are meaningful for practice	20
Value Creation	Change the world but change it for the better	19
Evolution	Use modern solutions for DSR and do not always rely on the "old" stuff	9
Total		508

4.1 Learning from the Past

Eligibility. The methodologies and approaches foundational to DSR were applied long before the term gained traction: "The term didn't exist at the time. Yet that was what I was doing" (A9). Reflecting on the roots, an author noted they performed "design-oriented research, even before it was called that name, back in the 80s and 90s" (A10). Despite the lack of explicit nomenclature, these efforts laid the groundwork for what would become a recognized IS research paradigm. A sense of perpetuity is captured in the assertion, "I sort of disagree that we're doing something new here. We're doing something that has been done [...] since the beginning of time" (A13).

The publication by Hevner and colleagues in 2004 marked a pivotal moment in the formalization of DSR for IS [16]. This was explicitly recognized by numerous scholars who credit it with crystallizing the domain. One interviewee noted, "I was a first-year PhD student when the Hevner et al. paper came out [...] and so that really just changed my life" (A1), signifying the profound impact it had on shaping academic trajectories. Overall, the contributions of the seminal paper provided much-needed clarity and eligibility [16]. It clarified the terminology of DSR, whose the principles and practices have deep and enduring origins. In doing so, they established "the tension that exists between scientific theory and [...] pragmatic design" (A13) which shapes the field to this day.

Maturity. There was considerable debate surrounding DSR's fundamental nature. As one interviewee noted, "there were multiple views of what this design science research was" (A12). This uncertainty was compounded by fundamental ambiguity among scholars who questioned whether theory should precede or follow practice and whether the discipline retained its pragmatic essence: "Does theory come first or second? [...] Are we still a pragmatic discipline?" (A5). Furthermore, the very core of the emerging paradigm was scrutinized, with critical inquiries such as, "is this science or is this just consulting?" (A6).

Multiple researchers reflected that the idea for their own influential paper was born from a personal and collective academic journey. As one author noted, the paper began "in my head, at least when I was working on my PhD" (A4). The goals were to "clarify why design science is a scientific approach" (A6) while still signifying "how it is related but different from practice or consulting" (A6). Further, there was a need to clarify why "design science is a distinct scientific approach on par and complementary to explanatory research" (A6). In that regard, DSR evolved as a "paradigm with multiple methodologies within it and multiple approaches" (A12).

The pivotal aim, as articulated by the researchers, was to "legitimize doing design-oriented research" (A10) within IS, recognizing DSR as a "scientific approach" (A10) that leverages the "scientific method" (A6). The validation was especially crucial given that in the early 2000s many young scholars faced difficulties when their work was evaluated by reviewers unfamiliar with or biased against this emerging paradigm. Prior to the aforementioned milestone, "thousands of researchers did design-oriented research in the 1980s and 1990s, especially in Europe" (A10), but they faced challenges in gaining recognition in top IS journals. Authors hoped to provide a theoretical foundation that could be easily recognized by reviewers and editors alike, who previously struggled with a lack of expertise in the area. One interviewee noted the initial resistance and the need for a concerted effort to educate and convince the academic community of DSR's validity. The challenge was further compounded by the novelty of DSR, as it "required a lot of expertise from the editors, and in many cases, it was new. The expertise in the editors just wasn't there" (A12). Therefore, the quest to establish DSR as a recognized scientific discipline was as much about advancing research practices as it was about fostering understanding and acceptance within the academic publishing landscape.

Guidance. DSR evolved through the efforts of scholars grappling with its methodological foundations. One researcher reflected, "I was struggling a bit because there was no guidance for doing design science research" (A9). Others noted challenges of existing approaches: "I don't really like this model. It was too, too abstract, too high level, and it was difficult to sort of think about how would I plan my PhD study if I would start with this figure" (A10). This situation inspired the development of new articles, particularly for novices, where a "part was needed, that is a set of steps. First do this, then do this, then do this, then do that" (A9). The aim has been to foster a shared language in the DSR community without imposing unnecessary gatekeeping. These reflections highlight the ongoing dialogue in DSR about balancing structure, flexibility, and inclusivity.

Reflecting on whether the authors would change their works in hindsight, most concluded their work represents "a product of its time" (A8) encapsulating contemporary thinking. One author articulated, "I don't think we'd change anything. [...] I think it provided the right, if you will, foundation for additional thinking" (A13). Another noted, "I'm not sure there's anything I would change at this point in time in the paper. It seems to be enduring" (A12). Furthermore, the timeless nature of conceptual papers is underscored by the thought that they are "independent of technology and time, more or less" (A3). As another interviewee reflected, "I wouldn't change the paper that much [...] it sort of captures our thinking in years 2005, 2007 [...] and it has lasted quite well" (A8).

4.2 Current Challenges

Complexity. The complexity of the design process is a diverse theme. It can be further split into the topics planning & organizing, intermediate artifacts, iterative, agility, and stopping. These individual topics are illustrated in the following.

Planning and Organizing. While planning is critical, it must be flexible enough to accommodate the unpredictability of real-world dynamics. One scholar highlighted this balance, noting, "I mean, you have to have a discipline of planning. But as Mike Tyson would say, once you get punched in the face, the plan goes out the window. Well, it doesn't really go out the window because the discipline of planning is still there. However, you need to be cognizant of the emergent capabilities of the real world" (A13). The complexity increases when planning over extended timelines. As one researcher reflected, "if I need to set out the layout for design research, which goes through all those phases, and today I plan how I am going to evaluate it in two years or three years' time [...] I have hardly understood [the problem] in the very beginning. And of course, I have no clue of the solution, really" (A11). This underscores the need to blend structured methods with openness to change, allowing researchers to align their work with objectives, constraints, and emerging opportunities: "I've always been a great fan of doing design science research the way you would like to do it [...] Regarding your objective, your constraints, and the opportunities you also face in a certain project" (A11).

Intermediate Artifacts. Researchers struggle to package their work. As one scholar noted, if "you have a complex artifact, a complex process, lots of stakeholders, and a complex problem, it's really hard to document the complete process from problem analysis" (A10). Under this light, another author warned to not "lose the whole complexity and the whole interesting problem only because you cannot publish it in a simple conference paper" (A11). It is crucial to "not oversimplify and go the simple way and the easy way, because at the end, the simplistic and easy artifacts won't really help society and won't really help the discipline" (A11). The concept of intermediate artifacts emerged in our author-informed review to address these challenges. One scholar emphasized, "in our paper, we call this intermediate artifacts" (A10), advocating for their legitimacy in scholarly publications: "I [...] hope that this paper [...] legitimizes that people submit intermediate artifacts and portions of the design process" (A10). This approach not only accommodates the complexity of DSR but also encourages researchers to "cut out a piece of the design project and publish it as a separate contribution" (A10), thereby creating opportunities for cumulative knowledge building and reusing of knowledge. These pieces (also called "chunks" (A11) or "echelons" (A10)) allow researchers to focus on specific parts of the design process (e.g., problem understanding).

Iterative. As one scholar observed, "design science research really is not a linear process" (A11), emphasizing that "the real design science research in the real world is never that linear" (A11). This iterative nature allows researchers to adapt to emergent insights, revisiting earlier phases upon finding "that you're designing for the wrong thing" (A5). A central characteristic of this approach is the build-evaluate-intervene cycle, where each iteration transforms both the solution and its environment: "Once you build something, you evaluate it. You feel that it has potential to improve an environment. Once you intervene in that environment, you've changed the environment. You've changed the problem for the next cycle" (A13).

Agility. Iterative methods also enable researchers to integrate lessons learned from one phase into subsequent activities, fostering agility: "If you run through those phases in a linear way, you kind of do not learn much from the result of the one phase" (A11). Instead, the iterative approach encourages agility and responsiveness, embodying the philosophy that "design science is a journey through space and time" (A11). This perspective aligns with the principles of agile methods, which, as another scholar noted, contrasts sharply with the "waterfall-y" (A11) tendencies sometimes seen in DSR: "We teach agile methods in software engineering. I always thought, Why are we so non-agile?" (A11). One author remarked "you have to be also always agile with your feet when you're doing these DSR, because things will not go in the way that you have planned always. Sometimes they do, but most often not. Especially if you're working with industry, you know, surprising things happen, always" (A8).

Stopping. The complexity inherent in DSR extends not only to planning, iterative cycles, and intermediate artifacts but also to determining when to stop. As one scholar noted, "I think it's still an opportunity for folks to work on the stopping rule. [...] When is [the artifact] ready to be unveiled? When is it ready to be tested? We don't know that. We all just guess right now" (A4). This uncertainty reflects the ongoing tension between achieving sufficient refinement and avoiding overinvestment in endless iterations.

Rigor. The challenge of rigorous evaluation reflects the dual nature of DSR, where design and evaluation must coexist in a productive tension. This tension was reflected by one author: "You've got to sometimes make a decision. Do you focus on the actual artifact, and then the people will say, Well, you haven't tested it properly. And if you go too much into the testing, then they'll start to look for a full-blown behavioral science experimental setup. And sometimes, for our people, it's hard for them to do that properly" (A2). As one scholar succinctly put it, "we try to design and evaluate concurrently innovative solutions to real-world problems" (A11), underscoring the importance of navigating this complexity to produce impactful, credible research outcomes. Evaluation is not merely a concluding step but an integral part of the entire research process. As one expert noted, "I found it very important to evaluate not only at the end of the process but also during the process" (A10). However, achieving this level of rigor often feels overwhelming: "In effect, [you] conduct two research projects: A design project and an evaluation project" (A9). Despite its importance, evaluation is resource-intensive and can strain researchers' capacity: "You can't just spend massive amounts of resources on conducting evaluations" (A9). It often becomes a balancing act, where compromises must be made between depth of evaluation and the practicality of conducting a comprehensive study. At the same time, building and testing are inherently interconnected, as "how much evaluation is built into [the building process]" (A4) can itself be a marker of rigor, showing that evaluation is not merely a separate phase but an embedded contribution.

Positioning. Effective positioning begins with identifying where to start and how the research builds on existing work: "We argue towards starting somewhere where it makes sense, also where others have stopped, and kind of you stand on the shoulders of giants" (A11). This requires researchers to ground their work in prior knowledge, carefully defining the boundaries of their contributions and clearly articulating the advancements made. Positioning also involves moving from a specific problem toward generalizable insights. As one expert noted, "why we also did talk about abstraction a lot, which is a key theme here, where abstraction is important to help build a cumulative tradition" (A1). The process of defining and articulating the problem is foundational for effective positioning: "The first real artifact that you build is a representation of your problem with appropriate boundaries, with appropriate goals for your project" (A13). Understanding the problem deeply and aligning the research objectives with the intended contribution ensures that the resulting work is both relevant and impactful: "In the end, the contribution needs to be very clear and say, Okay, that's really the advancement this design research has made" (A11).

4.3 Future Directions

The future of DSR holds immense potential, with opportunities limited only by the ambition and creativity of its adjacent researchers. As one expert noted, "the sky is the limit in terms of what somebody starting out today can do" (A4). In the following section, we describe, through the lens of the interviewed authors, how the challenges of the previous chapter relate to potential advancements in the field of DSR. The future directions sourcing from these challenges are supplemented with comments from authors on the future of the field. They are presented in Table 3 with a short description.

Table 3. Themes for the Future of DSR

Direction	Description
Advance the Concept of Intermediate Artifacts	Promote the legitimacy of intermediate artifacts as scholarly contributions. It encourages publishing reusable components of the design process to foster cumulative knowledge building and broader applicability of findings.
Encourage Diversity in Research Approaches	Foundational works like [16,23] are pivotal but may limit innovation. Researchers should embrace diverse and modern approaches to advance DSR.
Foster Iterative and Adaptive Approaches	Iterative processes should be recognized and further explored as a core characteristic of DSR. By moving away from linear approaches, researchers can navigate the unpredictability of real-world projects and incorporate lessons learned at every stage of the research process.
Foster Transdisciplinarity Integration	Extend DSR beyond its traditional domains. By balancing explanatory and design-focused approaches, DSR can cross-fertilize with other disciplines.
Strengthen Clinical Inquiry	Prioritize clinical inquiry by fostering deeper collaborations with practitioners. Shift from theoretical discussions to impactful, hands-on projects, bridging the rich problem and solution spaces of today's socio-technical landscape.
Leveraging Technology for Societal Impact	Leverage emerging technologies to design artifacts addressing societal and business challenges, balancing specificity with generalizability.

Value Creation. DSR has transformative potential for driving meaningful change in society. As one expert passionately advocated, "let's do world domination with design" (A1), reflecting the ambition to extend DSR's influence. Central to this ambition is the goal of making a tangible difference, as another expert noted, "we want to make a difference in the world" (A13). This involves not just solving problems but addressing broader societal challenges—ethical considerations included. As one participant reflected, "we change the world, but do we always change it for the better?" (A13), emphasizing the responsibility inherent in DSR to contribute positively. "It's great to take tiny steps that eventually lead to something bigger," one expert noted (A11), illustrating the cumulative impact of DSR initiatives. Beyond societal contributions, DSR holds promise for the IS field itself, as it has strong relevance and impact: "Can be more recognized for the great things we are doing" (A11). Ultimately, DSR is positioned as "a recipe for a future world" (A12), crafting pathways to a better, more equitable future while cementing its place as a pivotal research approach. Furthermore, DSR aligns naturally with global initiatives, such as the UN Sustainable Development Goals, providing a framework for improving health, education, poverty reduction, and environmental sustainability. A participant highlights its role in this context, stating, "Improving the quality of life [...] building and developing new artifacts for doing it is, of course, an important thing to do" (A9).

One of the defining strengths of DSR lies in its holistic approach, combining technological innovation with a deep understanding of environmental, behavioral, and organizational factors. "With the training that people in DSR get [...] we have the ability to create new things" (A4). The accelerating pace of technological change further amplifies the relevance and urgency of DSR. While technology can sometimes constrain creativity, it also offers unprecedented opportunities for innovation: "Technology is running at warp speed. Our work is never done" (A7); "There is so much you can do" (A4). This duality requires researchers to embrace both the challenges and possibilities of the technological landscape. As one participant emphasized, "I want to see more and more excitement about the creative nature of DSR [...] If we do that, we can start or continue or even more effectively influence the major trends that are happening in the world today" (A5).

Transdisciplinarity. DSR evolved as a combination of different research streams and has immense potential to transcend its traditional boundaries and contribute to a wide range of disciplines: "DSR has the opportunity to make contributions across multiple disciplines" (A5). One expert emphasizes the need for an ambidextrous approach, blending explanation with design: "With explanation, you can analyze a problem or a solution. But it is the design bit that actually gives you another means and relationship" (A6). This balance is critical to addressing the current imbalance in fields such as entrepreneurship, which are "dominated by descriptive and explanatory research" (A6). As one participant noted, "The concepts and ideas of design science research are relevant to all applied disciplines" (A9). The future of DSR lies in embracing transdisciplinarity by extending its methodologies and insights to diverse applied disciplines and fostering collaboration for sharing design and process knowledge across social sciences and beyond: "I think we're here to work and collaborate effectively to make an impact. So, you know, I don't think we dominate other methodologies. I think we collaborate with other methodologies very well. It's [...] not an either or decision" (A13). This approach not only enhances the relevance of DSR but also positions it as a critical enabler of impactful research across fields. As one expert noted, "there's a lot to learn from other applied disciplines, and there's a lot that we can cross-fertilize with other applied disciplines" (A9).

Clinical Inquiry. The future of DSR increasingly emphasizes clinical inquiry—engaging directly with real-world problems through collaborative, hands-on approaches [6]. One expert highlighted the value of co-creation: "Experimental processes and really co-create and co-deliver, co-evaluate with customers, both an understanding of the discovery of the problem customers are facing and the co-creation, co-development, and co-evaluation with customers of a novel product or service" (A5). This partnership-driven approach not only aligns with industry needs but also empowers researchers and students alike, demonstrating their ability to effect tangible change. Scholars are encouraged to focus on complex, practical challenges and actively work alongside practitioners. Moreover, DSR offers a unique opportunity to infuse rigor into industry innovation, with one practitioner remarking, "the industry is more than willing to engage with us. But we have to show up" (A4). By creating socio-technical solutions, scholars can bridge a "super-rich solution space" (A11) with a "super-rich [...] problem space" (A11) to address pressing societal and organizational challenges. Clinical inquiry also calls for a shift in academic practice. As one scholar suggested, "we should do more projects, not only papers [...] talking about how to do it, but actually do[ing] it" (A11). This vision for DSR is not merely aspirational—it represents a call to action for the community to deepen its impact, expand its engagement with industry, and deliver transformative innovations that resonate across society: "I would like to recommend everybody: stand up, leave your desk, go out there in the wild, engage with real people, and try to contribute what you can to joint solutions. And that, of course, also includes very many other disciplines and other regions around the world. The more, the merrier" (A11).

Evolution. While foundational works like [16,23] have provided crucial frameworks, there is a concern that they constrain innovation in DSR methodologies. As one expert highlighted, "most of the work that's done in design science research really anchors itself to about, I don't know, maybe four different methods" (A12), suggesting the need to explore beyond these commonly utilized approaches. Another added, "we don't have to have one method or even four methods. I think there's room for more than that" (A12). This recognition opens the door for experimentation and acceptance of new ways to conduct DSR. As one author put it, "I think it's about time for us to grow out of that and begin to accept that there are many different ways to do design science research" (A12). Circling back, one author commented "don't always look at Hevner et al. (2004) and Peffers et al. (2007). There is more modern stuff that we need and that we should use" (A10). Thus, the evolution of DSR requires researchers to move beyond relying on a limited set of methodologies, which will encourage diversity and adaptability in research approaches.

5 Discussion

The increase of emergent technologies and the growing adoption of DSR methodologies present novel methodological and theoretical challenges that require systematic investigation [7]. To establish a comprehensive understanding of how to address these future challenges, we conducted interviews with the authors of highly cited seminal DSR literature. We synthesized key themes and research directions based on the authors' perspectives. The comments and issues raised during the interviews often overlap, meaning they cannot be neatly categorized as specific to the past, present, or future. One of the pressing issues raised in our author-informed review relates to the dynamics of the author-editor-reviewer triangle [1]. This construct represents the vigorous and interdependent relationship among these roles in the academic publishing process.

DSR papers face diverse and, at times, inappropriate feedback during the review process [13]. This often stems from the varying levels of familiarity reviewers have with the methodological foundations and goals of DSR [11]. Even two decades after Hevner et al.'s [16] seminal paper on design science, authors still risk having their work evaluated by individuals who lack an understanding of its unique methodological underpinnings [1]. This pattern seems to reoccur as the field evolves. Authors proposing novel DSR approaches face similar issues to those encountered during the early days of the field [30]. Just as in the past, editors and reviewers unfamiliar with the innovation, e.g., design-oriented machine learning, struggle to evaluate it fairly, highlighting a persistent gap in understanding new methodologies [21]. This disconnect creates a cycle where innovative contributions are undervalued or misunderstood, hindering the field's growth [1]. Furthermore, there is a need for dedicated editorials or special issues in journals to establish and legitimize emerging research approaches, enabling others to build on them [5]. In turn, authors must familiarize themselves with these editorials and seminal papers of the field to avoid repeating the mistakes outlined within them [1,7,13].

In our review, the interviewed authors frequently emphasized that our world is not becoming simpler; rather, it is constantly changing and becoming increasingly complex, causing applicability issues of design knowledge in real-world settings [19,28]. Despite this, there is a noticeable trend within the field toward producing simpler, more easily publishable research. This trend is compounded by efforts to make DSR more accessible to young scholars, aiming to lower barriers and reduce complexity, which creates an intriguing ambivalence and duality: while simplification can open up the field, it risks oversimplifying complex realities. Historically, the mantra "complexity is death" (Chuck Thacker) notably echoed by Microsoft, has suggested that we avoid complexity at all costs. However, the current paradigm has shifted to embracing the intricacies of contemporary issues, suggesting that we must now design for complexity [7,28]. To address the potential drawbacks of oversimplification, it will become essential to foster a cumulative tradition within DSR. Embracing intermediate contributions can mitigate the risk of reducing complex societal and disciplinary challenges to oversimplified solutions [1]. These intermediate artifacts enable researchers to build a robust body of work that captures the complexity of issues and solutions over time, rather than compressing them into a single, simplified narrative [1].

This work is not free of limitations. Our study focuses primarily on authors of seminal and impactful DSR publications. While the selected experts represent influential contributions, the findings might not fully generalize to all DSR communities. Thus, we emphasize a potential selection bias, particularly relevant for less cited but innovative domains or emerging areas of research. While the advice shared by experts is valuable, it may reflect the career trajectories and contexts of seasoned scholars, which might not fully align with the challenges faced by early career researchers today. Further, authors might have rationalized or reinterpreted their past decisions based on current knowledge, rather than accurately recalling their original motivations and challenges. Hence, the retrospective nature of the interviews might be influenced by hindsight bias. We tried to counter this constraint by integrating recent works as well, but this limitation might still be present.

Based on the identified limitations, future research could broaden the scope of participant selection to include a wider array of DSR authors, especially those from less cited or emerging domains. Incorporating methodological triangulation by utilizing additional data sources, like bibliometric analyses or surveys, could enhance the robustness of findings by providing diverse perspectives and quantitative data [3,4,21]. Lastly, reflecting on the practical application of design science in IS could reveal the practical challenges and strategies involved in implementing DSR theories [11].

6 Conclusion

This study contributes to the ongoing evolution of DSR by engaging directly with the authors of these seminal works. By treating seminal works as evolving "artifacts," this review extends the iterative philosophy of DSR, ensuring these foundational contributions adapt over time. Through in-depth interviews, this research highlights the enduring relevance of past contributions as well as anticipates future developments, serving as a resource for understanding DSR's trajectory. We contribute to the field by identifying and synthesizing 10 key themes representing lessons from the past, current challenges, and future directions of DSR. We highlight that contemporary advancements of DSR are deeply rooted in the seminal contributions of pioneering thinkers. Many foundational papers in DSR emerged from scholars who, during their early academic careers, encountered significant hurdles in publishing their innovative ideas. The resulting seminal papers were motivated by a desire to help others navigate the intricacies of conducting and publishing in the field. Further, we offer a structured lens through which others can address the inherent challenges of DSR, from managing transdisciplinary collaboration to ensuring rigor and transparency in the design process. Moreover, the identified themes emphasize the importance of creating practical value and adapting to evolving methods. Looking to the future, explicit pathways for DSR include advancing the concept of intermediate artifacts to foster cumulative knowledge, encouraging diversity in research approaches to promote innovation, and fostering iterative and adaptive approaches for navigating real-world unpredictabilities.

Acknowledgments. This work was funded by the European Union [EU Funding Erasmus+ 2022-2-LI01-KA220-HED-000098911: "Design Science Research Academy"].

References

1. Abbasi, A., Parsons, J., Pant, G., Sheng, O., Sarker, S.: Pathways for design research on artificial intelligence. Inf. Syst. Res. **32**(2), 441–459 (2024). https://doi.org/10.1287/isre.2024.editorial.v35.n2
2. van Aken, J., Chandrasekaran, A., Halman, J.: Conducting and publishing design science research: inaugural essay of the design science department of the Journal of Operations Management. J. Oper. Manag. **47–48**, 1–8 (2016). https://doi.org/10.1016/j.jom.2016.06.004
3. Akoka, J., Comyn-Wattiau, I., Storey, V.C.: Design science research: progression, schools of thought and research themes. In: Gerber, A., Baskerville, R. (eds.) Design Science Research for a New Society: Society 5.0, pp. 235–249. Springer, Cham (2023). https://doi.org/10.1007/978-3-031-32808-4_15
4. Alvesson, M., Sandberg, J.: Generating research questions through problematization. Acad. Manag. Rev. **36**(2), 247–271 (2011). https://doi.org/10.5465/amr.2009.0188
5. Baskerville, R., Baiyere, A., Gregor, S., Hevner, A.R., Rossi, M.: Design science research contributions: finding a balance between artifact and theory. J. Assoc. Inf. Syst. **19**(5), 358–376 (2018). https://doi.org/10.17705/1jais.00495
6. Baskerville, R., vom Brocke, J., Mathiassen, L., Scheepers, H.: Clinical research from information systems practice. Eur. J. Inf. Syst. **32**(1), 1–9 (2023). https://doi.org/10.1080/0960085X.2022.2126030
7. vom Brocke, J., Winter, R., Hevner, A.R., Maedche, A.: Special issue editorial - accumulation and evolution of design knowledge in design science research: a journey through time and space. J. Assoc. Inf. Syst. **21**(3), 520–544 (2020). https://doi.org/10.17705/1jais.00611
8. Etikan, I., Musa, S.A., Alkassim, R.S.: Comparison of convenience sampling and purposive sampling. Am. J. Theor. Appl. Stat. **5**(1), 1–4 (2016). https://doi.org/10.11648/j.ajtas.20160501.11
9. Galletta, A., Cross, W.E.: Mastering the Semi-Structured Interview and Beyond: From Research Design to Analysis and Publication. NYU Press, New York (2013)
10. Gioia, D.A., Corley, K.G., Hamilton, A.L.: Seeking qualitative rigor in inductive research. Organ. Res. Methods **16**(1), 15–31 (2013). https://doi.org/10.1177/1094428112452151
11. Gregor, S.: Reflections on the practice of design science in information systems. In: Aier, S., Rohner, P., Schelp, J. (eds.) Engineering the Transformation of the Enterprise: A Design Science Research Perspective, pp. 101–113. Springer, Cham (2021). https://doi.org/10.1007/978-3-030-84655-8_7
12. Gregor, S., Chandra Kruse, L., Seidel, S.: Research perspectives: the anatomy of a design principle. J. Assoc. Inf. Syst. **21**(6), 1622–1652 (2020). https://doi.org/10.17705/1jais.00649
13. Gregor, S., Hevner, A.R.: Positioning and presenting design science research for maximum impact. MIS Q. **37**(2), 337–356 (2013). https://doi.org/10.25300/MISQ/2013/37.2.01
14. Gregor, S., Jones, D.: The anatomy of a design theory. J. Assoc. Inf. Syst. **8**(5) (2007). https://doi.org/10.17705/1jais.00129

15. Hevner, A.R.: A three cycle view of design science research. Scand. J. Inf. Syst. **19**(2), 87–92 (2007)
16. Hevner, A.R., March, S.T., Park, J., Ram, S.: Design science in information systems research. MIS Q. **28**(1), 75–105 (2004). https://doi.org/10.2307/25148625
17. Kuechler, W., Vaishnavi, V.: On theory development in design science research: anatomy of a research project. Eur. J. Inf. Syst. **17**(5), 489–504 (2008). https://doi.org/10.1057/ejis.2008.40
18. Lincoln, Y.S., Guba, E.G.: Naturalistic Inquiry. SAGE Publications, Thousand Oaks (1985)
19. Lukyanenko, R., Parsons, J.: Design theory indeterminacy: what is it, how can it be reduced, and why did the polar bear drown? J. Assoc. Inf. Syst. **21**(5), 1–59 (2020). https://doi.org/10.17705/1jais.00639
20. Merriam, S.B., Grenier, R.S.: Qualitative Research in Practice: Examples for Discussion and Analysis. Wiley, San Francisco (2019)
21. Nagle, T., Doyle, C., Alhassan, I.M., Sammon, D.: The research method we need or deserve? A literature review of the design science research landscape. Commun. Assoc. Inf. Syst. **50**, 358–395 (2022). https://doi.org/10.17705/1CAIS.05015
22. Nunamaker, J.F., Jr., Chen, M., Purdin, T.D.: Systems development in information systems research. J. Manag. Inf. Syst. **7**(3), 89–106 (1991). https://doi.org/10.1080/07421222.1990.11517898
23. Peffers, K., Tuunanen, T., Rothenberger, M.A., Chatterjee, S.: A design science research methodology for information systems research. J. Manag. Inf. Syst. **24**(3), 45–77 (2007). https://doi.org/10.2753/MIS0742-1222240302
24. Seckler, C., Mauer, R., vom Brocke, J.: Design science in entrepreneurship: conceptual foundations and guiding principles. J. Bus. Ventur. Des. **1**(1), 100004 (2021). https://doi.org/10.1016/j.jbvd.2022.100004
25. Sein, M.K., Henfridsson, O., Purao, S., Rossi, M., Lindgren, R.: Action design research. MIS Q. **35**(1), 37–56 (2011). https://doi.org/10.2307/23043488
26. Simon, H.A.: The Sciences of the Artificial, 3rd edn. MIT Press, Cambridge (1996)
27. Strauss, A., Corbin, J.: Basics of Qualitative Research: Techniques and Procedures for Developing Grounded Theory. SAGE Publications, Thousand Oaks (1998)
28. Tuunanen, T., Winter, R., vom Brocke, J.: Dealing with complexity in design science research: a methodology using design echelons. MIS Q. **48**(2), 427–458 (2024). https://doi.org/10.25300/MISQ/2023/16700
29. Walls, J.G., Widmeyer, G.R., El Sawy, O.A.: Building an information system design theory for vigilant EIS. Inf. Syst. Res. **3**(1), 36–59 (1992). https://doi.org/10.1287/isre.3.1.36
30. Zolbanin, H., Aubert, B.: A process model for design-oriented machine learning research in information systems. J. Strateg. Inf. Syst. **34**(1), 101868 (2025). https://doi.org/10.1016/j.jsis.2024.101868

The Relevance of Design Features: From Abstract Knowledge to Practical Implementation

Timo Strohmann[1](✉) and Bijan Khosrawi-Rad[2]

[1] University of Münster, Münster, Germany
timo.strohmann@uni-muenster.de
[2] TU Braunschweig, Braunschweig, Germany
b.khosrawi-rad@tu-braunschweig.de

Abstract. Design Science Research (DSR) aims to create rigorous, innovative artifacts and produce actionable design knowledge, but translating high-level prescriptions like design principles into tangible implementations remains challenging. We position design features as mid-level constructs that operationalize abstract guidance into concrete functionalities. Drawing on a systematic review of 34 DSR studies contributing 233 design features, we show how inconsistent characterizations complicate their reuse. To address this gap, we propose a two-dimensional framework across six artifact layers and three levels of abstraction, clarifying how design features link theoretical prescriptions to real-world instantiations while retaining flexibility. Building on these insights, we offer guidelines for formulating design features to enhance traceability, foster reusability, and support iterative refinement. We then illustrate their application in one case. By systematically documenting design features with clarity and precision, DSR scholars can more effectively bridge abstract knowledge and practical development, ultimately strengthening the rigor and impact of DSR.

Keywords: Design Science Research · Design Feature · Design Principle · Design Theory · Design Knowledge · Artifact · Abstraction

1 Introduction

Design Science Research (DSR) focuses on the creation of innovative artifacts, such as software systems, methods, and models, to address real-world problems while simultaneously producing actionable knowledge for both researchers and practitioners [1, 2]. A core challenge in DSR lies in translating the abstract design knowledge into practical implementations (e.g., software prototypes, organizational interventions). Although concepts like design principles (DPs) [3] provide high-level prescriptions, researchers have increasingly noted the difficulty of moving from these general guidelines to concrete artifact instantiations [4, 5]. This gap often limits the transferability and replicability of DSR findings, as practitioners may struggle to operationalize abstract prescriptions within specific contexts [6]. Against this backdrop, "design features" have emerged in

© The Author(s), under exclusive license to Springer Nature Switzerland AG 2025
S. Chatterjee et al. (Eds.): DESRIST 2025, LNCS 15703, pp. 116–134, 2025.
https://doi.org/10.1007/978-3-031-93976-1_8

multiple studies [7–9] as bridging elements: they reside between conceptual DPs and tangible artifacts, helping translate "what" should be done into the "how" of implementation [10]. By breaking down abstract guidance into systematic, feature-level elements, researchers and practitioners can more effectively specify, evaluate, and refine the concrete functionality or characteristics of an artifact [3, 7]. In turn, this mid-level abstraction facilitates traceability, linking DPs back to user needs and forward to working systems, and fosters cumulative knowledge building, as these documented features can be adapted and extended across subsequent projects [2].

Despite the growing interest in design features, there remains a lack of conceptual clarity regarding their exact nature, role, and relationship to other forms of design knowledge [11]. Existing literature uses a variety of terms (e.g., "technological rules," [10] "mechanisms," [3] "features," [7, 11] "design knowledge chunks" [2]), often leaving ambiguity about how these constructs compare and how best to conceptualize or implement them in DSR. Moreover, the inconsistent formulation of design features can hamper their reusability in practical settings, complicate collaboration between stakeholders, and limit the broader accumulation of design knowledge. To address this gap, this paper investigates the relevance of design features in DSR and their role in operationalizing abstract knowledge into tangible artifacts. We also propose recommendations for systematically formulating design features to mitigate inconsistencies and enhance their practical applicability. Specifically, we seek to answer the following **research question (RQ)**:

How can we conceptualize and define "design features" so that they effectively bridge abstract design knowledge (e.g., DPs) and tangible instantiations in DSR while ensuring greater clarity, consistency, and reusability?

In what follows, we first review the foundational concepts of design knowledge and the existing references to design features, establishing a common vocabulary and situating our work within prior research. We then present our methodology, which involved a systematic literature review of DSR publications that explicitly referred to or employed "design features." Through this process, we identified 34 relevant studies and extracted 233 unique design features. Next, we classified these features across two complementary dimensions: a six-layer classification to capture the primary functional or organizational domain of each feature and three levels of abstraction (high, medium, low) to assess how specific or generic each feature's formulation was. We then analyzed the resulting classification to understand where in the design stack each feature primarily operates and how broadly or narrowly it is prescribed. This analysis forms the basis for our subsequent discussion of design feature conceptualization, formulation recommendations, and their implications for bridging abstract design knowledge with tangible artifact implementations.

2 Background and Related Work

2.1 Types of Design Knowledge

DSR aims to create and evaluate IT artifacts while simultaneously generating design knowledge to guide future research and practice [1, 2]. In this paper, we draw on several interrelated concepts that capture different levels of abstraction and prescription in DSR. Although DSR includes various constructs (e.g., models, methods, frameworks), we focus here specifically on constructs that operationalize abstract design knowledge. Table 1 summarizes these selected constructs.

Table 1. Overview of Key Constructs Operationalizing Design Knowledge

Type	Classification	Definition and connection
User story [12]	**Not itself design knowledge** but *input* to forming design knowledge	**Definition:** A short, narrative statement capturing a user's need or requirement, often in an agile development context **Connection:** Provides contextual insights that influence MRs and DPs; contributes to refining design features to better serve end-user needs
Kernel theory [13]	**External theoretical knowledge** that *informs* design knowledge	**Definition:** Foundational theories from other disciplines (e.g., natural, social, or design sciences) that provide abstract constructs and empirical insights to inform design knowledge construction **Connection:** Informs the derivation of MRs and DPs—Linking validated external knowledge to the concrete design prescriptions and implementations
MR [5, 14]	**Design knowledge** (requirements-oriented)	**Definition:** High-level or abstract requirements describing the goals and needs that a class of artifacts should fulfill **Connection:** Captures underlying needs or problem statements guiding the solution space. Derived from user stories, kernel theories, or empirical studies; informs DPs and thereby influences the specification of design features

(continued)

Table 1. (*continued*)

Type	Classification	Definition and connection
DP [3]	**Design knowledge** (principles-level)	**Definition:** Prescriptive, abstract guidance linking design actions (means) to desired outcomes (ends) **Connection:** Provides actionable guidelines to implement artifacts that satisfy MRs; reflects theoretical underpinnings to ensure rigor in solution development. Directly influences which design features are selected and how they are instantiated
Design feature (see Table 2)	**Design knowledge** (feature-level)	**Definition:** Concrete, tangible characteristics of an artifact that operationalize one or more DPs **Connection:** Bridges the gap between abstract DPs and real-world artifact instantiations; enables practical realization of design knowledge. Shapes the final artifact's functionality, user experience, and overall design
Instantiation [15]	**Design entity** (embodiment of design knowledge)	**Definition:** A realized artifact (e.g., software system, prototype, process) embodying the MRs, DPs, and design features **Connection:** Demonstrates how DPs and design features function in practice, serving as an evaluable outcome of the design process. Represents the culmination of MRs, DPs, and design features in a tangible form; provides feedback for refinement of theories
Design theory [10, 14]	**Higher-level synthesis of design knowledge** and outcomes (the "product-framework")	**Definition:** A comprehensive, abstract representation of the relationships between constructs, principles, and outcomes in a design context **Connection:** Explains, predicts, and prescribes how design knowledge leads to effective solutions. Integrates MRs, DPs, justificatory knowledge, and instantiations; design features are a link from theory to artifact

At the most context-specific level, user stories [12] provide short, narrative statements capturing individual user needs or requirements. These stories often inform the derivation of meta-requirements (MRs) [5, 14], which shift from user-centric anecdotes to more abstract goals that a class of artifacts should fulfill. In practice, many DSR papers derive MRs from user stories, kernel theories, or a combination of both, thereby bridging practical stakeholder requirements with established theoretical knowledge. Likewise, kernel theories [14] can serve as foundational disciplinary knowledge that informs and justifies the derivation of meta-requirements and design principles. MRs, in turn, help researchers formulate DPs [3, 10], which prescribe how a solution's actions or mechanisms (means) can produce intended outcomes (ends) in a given context. To bridge these higher-level principles and the final system, design features translate abstract guidance into concrete, tangible characteristics of an artifact [7, 8]. Such features might specify system functionalities, user-interface patterns, or data-handling mechanisms, thus rendering the "how to implement" aspect of DPs more explicit. These design features then form the basis for creating instantiations—the realized artifacts, prototypes, or processes that embody all preceding forms of design knowledge [2, 15]. Finally, when researchers integrate the insights gained from evaluating these instantiations into broader explanatory and predictive frameworks, they create or refine design theory [10, 14]. By understanding how user stories, MRs, DPs, design features, and instantiations interrelate, scholars and practitioners can develop a cumulative body of DSR knowledge that remains both theoretically rigorous and practically transferable.

2.2 Design Feature Concepts

Numerous DSR studies use the term "design feature" (or a closely related notion) to denote a tangible, operational aspect of an artifact that arises from more abstract design knowledge such as DPs [7, 16–22]. Although the terminology and emphasis vary, scholars consistently position design features as bridging elements—converting high-level prescriptions (e.g., DPs) into concrete instantiations [7, 8]. Table 2 illustrates how various authors define or refer to these mid-level constructs and underscores their role in linking theoretical prescriptions to actual system functionalities, user-interface components, or process workflows. Taken together, these contributions suggest that design features represent a critical mid-level abstraction: more concrete than DPs, yet flexible enough to be adapted across different contexts. This duality not only facilitates traceability from principle to artifact, allowing researchers to pinpoint how abstract guidelines materialize in specific system elements, but also supports the accumulation and reuse of design knowledge [2, 4]. Because design features are documented and codified in a way that is readily understandable to practitioners [7, 8], they can be carried forward into subsequent projects or adapted to new domains, thereby promoting both theoretical rigor and practical applicability.

The table further reveals consistent themes regarding design features, despite the use of different terms such as "technological rules," "mechanisms," or "design entities." In each case, authors emphasize that features make abstract prescriptions actionable by offering more detailed guidance for artifact creation. Some studies elaborate on how specific design features can be derived directly from DPs [7], while others discuss these elements as a lower-level construct beneath broader design theories [9, 11]. In all instances, however, the shared implication is that design features expedite practical implementation, enabling researchers and practitioners to achieve consistent outcomes while refining their design knowledge in an iterative, reusable manner.

Table 2. Design feature related concepts

Design feature related concept	Definition	Implications for DSR
Gregor and Jones [10]: "**technological rules for implementation**"	Prescriptive statements specifying how to implement design theory in practice ("if you want Y in Z, do X")	Bridges abstract designs (principles) and real-world artifacts; clarifies actionable steps; promotes replicability and refinement
Möller et al. [8]: "**design features**"	Concrete system functionalities or attributes that operationalize higher-level prescriptions in a specific solution context	Offers greater granularity than abstract DPs; supports traceability and iterative refinement of tangible system elements
Möller et al. [11]: "**feature**"	Subsequent, more concrete element that follows DPs; part of a four-dimensional solution space taxonomy	Positions features after principles in design processes; underscores "bridge to implementation" while not treating them as a stand-alone mechanism
Meth et al. [7]: "**design features**" (operationalizing each DP)	Artifact capabilities that realize higher-level DPs (e.g., "manual mining," "automatic mining")	Demonstrates explicit mapping from principle to feature; highlights traceability and reusability in top-tier DSR publications
Gregor et al. [3]: "**mechanisms**"	In the "anatomy of a DP," mechanisms specify how an abstract principle can be operationalized, either via technological functions, human actions, or a combination of both, to achieve an intended outcome for a user in a given context. Mechanisms may thus be partly deterministic (e.g., automated system processes) or affordance-based (e.g., user actions enabled by the artifact)	Although mechanisms can serve a bridging function—Translating high-level prescriptions into implementable steps—They are not necessarily identical to "design features". In their usage, a mechanism might include both the technical artifact and user behaviors that enact it, highlighting sociotechnical interactions grounded in justificatory knowledge rather than purely technical functionalities

(*continued*)

Table 2. (*continued*)

Design feature related concept	Definition	Implications for DSR
Gregor and Hevner [15]: **"level 1 artifact"**, not explicitly named "feature"	Focus on five artifact forms (constructs, models, methods, instantiations, and design theories) and three level view; no separate feature-level concept	Encourages clarity about artifact maturity (from partial to full theory); sees "features" as embedded in concrete or abstract artifacts
Wache et al. [9]: **"design features"**	A more concrete level below DPs, used to implement broad prescriptions in actual chatbot systems	Emphasizes abstraction continuum; highlights reusability of general principles but underscores the need for concrete, contextual features
Iivari [5]: **"design decisions"**	Argues that not all design knowledge must be a full design theory; partial or lower-level design artifacts can be valuable	Encourages acknowledging smaller, practice-focused contributions without forcing them into "theory"; sees "features" as useful design knowledge
vom Brocke et al. [2]: **"design knowledge chunk"** and **"design entity"**	Modular prescriptive knowledge about how an artifact addresses a problem; not specifically labeled "feature"	Stresses iterative accumulation and evolution of modular design knowledge; features fit as part of an evolving solution space
Apel and Kästner [23]: **"feature"**	A cohesive unit of functionality that represents a design decision or stakeholder requirement. In feature-oriented software development, features serve as building blocks that can be combined, customized, or omitted to form different software variants in a product line	Although originating outside the traditional IS research domain, this work underscores how feature-based decomposition supports reusability and variability, aligning well with DSR'S goals of systematically creating and evaluating artifacts. By structuring code and design decisions into feature modules, the approach highlights traceability from stakeholder requirements to artifact functionality

Moreover, by making cross-project transfer more straightforward, e.g., "feature libraries" or "design feature catalogs" that can be selectively applied to new problems, design features directly address a longstanding challenge in DSR: how to move beyond ad-hoc solutions and develop systematic, replicable approaches [4, 7, 8]. Documenting design features along with their underlying rationale (i.e., the DPs they operationalize) empowers organizations to accelerate innovation, reduce design complexity, and ensure that lessons learned in one setting can positively inform others. Consequently, a well-defined set of design features not only strengthens the theoretical foundation of a DSR project but also heightens its practical impact by simplifying the adaptation of proven solutions across varied real-world scenarios.

Hence, building on these insights, we propose the **following working definition of a design feature:** *A design feature is a mid-level DSR construct that operationalizes one or more DPs by specifying tangible, context-relevant functionalities or characteristics of an artifact. By offering traceable, reusable guidance linking abstract prescriptions to actual implementation details, design features bridge higher-level theory and the creation of real-world systems. They can be adapted and refined iteratively, thereby facilitating cross-project knowledge transfer and promoting systematic design.*

3 Research Methodology

We used a dataset created in a prior literature review [24], which analyzed design knowledge in the information systems research domain between 2011 and 2022 and was conducted in early December 2022. That review applied a systematic literature review approach aligned with Webster and Watson's recommendations [6] and guided by PRISMA [7]. It yielded 3097 initial hits from the AIS eLibrary and selected basket-of-eight journals using queries such as "design principle" and conceptually related terms.

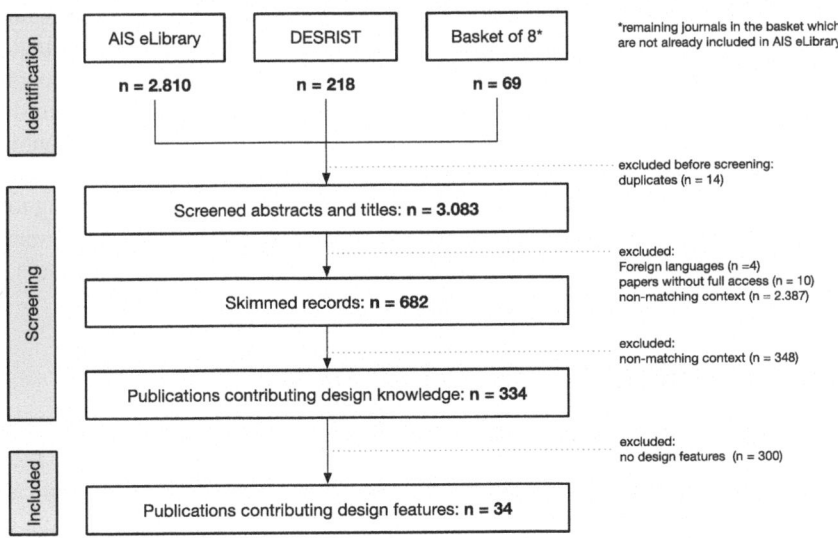

Fig. 1. PRISMA flow diagram based on Page et al. (2021) Fig. 1

After removing 14 duplicates, we screened 3083 abstracts and titles, retaining 682 publications that addressed design artifacts or mid-level constructs. Next, we skimmed these 682 papers in full text to exclude 348 that did not operationalize bridging elements between higher-level prescriptions and concrete artifact instantiations (i.e., "non-matching contexts"), leaving 334 that clearly contributed design knowledge. From those 334 studies, we selected those that explicitly used or reported "design features" as operational instantiations of abstract design knowledge, arriving at a final set of 34 publications. Two researchers then extracted every explicit design feature from these publications, assigning each a short descriptive name (e.g., "BERT-based final sequence extraction," "Adaptive communication orientation"). In total, 233 unique design features were identified, extracted and analyzed.

We then classified these 233 features according to two complementary dimensions. First, we mapped each feature onto a six-layer structure (see Table 3 in Sect. 4.1) that distinguishes which aspect of artifact design it addresses (e.g., user interface, data handling, workflow coordination). This layered perspective emerged partly inductively from our coding (e.g., identifying recurring patterns such as "interaction features" vs. "data features") and partly from multi-tier architecture thinking in software engineering, information systems research perspectives and a process-science view. Specifically, layers 1–3 (Interaction and engagement, functional/procedural, data and information Handling) mirror common user-interface, application logic, and data-management tiers [25]. Layer 4 (Process and workflow orchestration) integrates recent process-science considerations [26], and layers 5 and 6 (Organizational/ecosystem structuring, human and social Interventions) reflect an information systems perspective on the relevance of organizations and their impact on humans [1]. When a design feature spanned multiple layers, we coded it based on its most dominant or distinctive intent.

Second, building on the abstraction levels of vom Brocke et al. [2], we classified each feature by high, medium, or low, reflecting how broad or specific each feature's prescription is. High-level features remain conceptual (e.g., "Provide multi-language support"), while low-level features pin down explicit technologies or domain constraints (e.g., "Implement BERT-based extraction using version X of library Y"). Medium-level features lie in between, referencing certain domain or technology specifics without fully committing to one narrowly defined solution.

The full dataset of the extracted design features, their classification according to the two dimensions with a rationale for each classification, as well as a list of the 34 studies, can be downloaded from our digital appendix: https://doi.org/10.6084/m9.figshare.283 23194.

4 Analysis of Design Features in DSR Studies

4.1 Layered Classification of Design Features

We sorted each design feature into one of the six layers (Table 3). This classification helps clarify what aspect of artifact design a feature addresses—user interaction, core functionality, data handling, workflow orchestration, organizational structures, or sociobehavioral interventions. Where appropriate, some design features could arguably fit multiple layers (e.g., a chatbot feature that includes both a user interface component and an underlying workflow). In such cases, we coded each feature by its most dominant or distinctive layer. We identified 52 design features under (1) Interaction and Engagement,

86 under (2) Functional/Procedural, 36 under (3) Data and Information Handling, 14 under (4) Process and Workflow Orchestration, 12 under (5) Organizational/Ecosystem Structuring, and 33 under (6) Human and Social Interventions.

Most studies propose features in multiple layers, reflecting the interdisciplinary nature of DSR artifacts (e.g., a chatbot requiring both user-interface design and back-end

Table 3. Layer definition and illustrative design features

Layer	Definition/purpose	Example
1. Interaction and engagement	Covers how end-users or stakeholders perceive, navigate, and interact with the artifact (digital or otherwise). Encompasses interfaces (physical, graphical, conversational, etc.) and mechanisms that foster engagement or user involvement	"The enterprise chatbot should be able to display the current conversation context and its capabilities" [17]
2. Functional/procedural	Encompasses the "logic" or "mechanisms" that perform specific tasks, calculations, or procedures—Whether automated in software or carried out by humans. Represents the "how it works" aspect of the artifact	"To increase the precision of the sequence extraction, a final selection of sequences is conducted by applying a bidirectional encoder representations from transformers (BERT) language representation model (DP1/2)" [18]
3. Data and information handling	Focuses on how data is collected, managed, stored, transformed, and shared. Also addresses data governance, privacy, security, and integration with external systems or data sources	"Use APIs to create interfaces to existing data sources" [19]
4. Process and workflow orchestration	Encompasses coordination of tasks or activities across time and among different stakeholders or system components. May include business processes, organizational workflows, or collaborative routines	"…enable actors to (re-) configure processes with standardized interfaces" [20]

(*continued*)

Table 3. (*continued*)

Layer	Definition/purpose	Example
5. Organizational/ecosystem structuring	Addresses the broader context in which the artifact operates: Roles, governance structures, multi-organizational networks, or ecosystem-level rules and partnerships. Captures institutional or structural design decisions	"Orchestration activities must describe how the actors are being coordinated, directed, and influenced in an ecosystem" [21]
6. Human and social interventions	Encompasses any features or interventions designed to guide, influence, or support people (end-users, stakeholders, or broader communities). Includes training, motivation, behavior change, social collaboration, communication, or any socio-behavioral mechanisms	"Awareness-raising approaches" [27]

logic). Moreover, some features that appear purely "technical" (e.g., an NLP preprocessing step) can incorporate social or organizational elements, such as domain-expert labeling, role assignments, or training sessions, if they require specific governance structures or are designed to motivate particular user behaviors.

4.2 Abstraction Levels of Design Features

To better understand how general or specific each design feature is, we classified them according to three abstraction levels based on vom Brocke et al. [2]. Table 4 offers a definition and examples for each level, referencing real design features drawn from our dataset. In our sample, 52 of the identified design features fall into the low category. These features typically mention a distinct software library, a brand-specific platform, or a direct function with minimal room for alternative solutions (e.g., "Jira data with issue type 'Improvement,'" "Implement BERT-based extraction," "Store data in an independent verification system"). The medium category contains 174 design features, often referencing partially generic but still domain-relevant prescriptions (e.g., "adaptive communication orientation," "ML-based data processing," "user preference modeling"). Lastly, the remaining set comprises only seven high-level design features, offering more general guidance (e.g., motivational or ethical principles, governance guidelines, or universal warnings), with relatively little concrete implementation detail.

Taken together, the layered perspective and abstraction-level assessment illustrate that "design features" act as a mid-range design construct in DSR, but they can vary substantially in scope and specificity. Some design features are nearly as abstract as

Table 4. Design feature abstraction levels

Abstraction level	Definition	Exemplary design feature
High	Very conceptual or strategic; broad guidelines without detailed technical specificity	"The enterprise chatbot should not pretend to be a real human being" [17] or "A step for goal and vision formulation to align network-wide digital transformation strategy" [20]
Medium	Moderately detailed or partially domain-specific, indicating some technical or contextual specificity but not pinned to a single narrow solution	"Preprocessing: Natural language processing techniques" [7] or "the ECB should develop a user model that stores the user's preferred communication style" [17]
Low	Highly specific, often naming particular algorithms, technologies, or strict domain constraints	"To increase the precision of the sequence extraction, a final selection of sequences is conducted by applying a bidirectional encoder representations from transformers (BERT) language representation model" [18] or "appointment reminder" [27]

DPs (high); others are so technically precise (low) that they almost blur the boundary between a design feature and a coded implementation detail. Across our sampled studies, explicitly documenting these features (in whichever form or level of detail) helped foster traceability: they link abstract goals (e.g., "improve user engagement") to the final artifact instantiation (e.g., "implement real-time feedback chatbots with BERT-based classification modules"). By doing so, design features can facilitate both the reusability of artifact components and the accumulation of design knowledge across contexts.

5 Positioning and Classifying Design Features

Design features occupy a "middle ground" between high-level design theories (e.g., DPs or design frameworks) and the concrete artifacts (or "design entities") that researchers implement and evaluate. This section introduces two conceptual frameworks for understanding design features: (1) Layered positioning of features within an instantiated artifact and (2) Abstraction levels between design theories and design entities. These frameworks complement each other: The first clarifies where a feature resides in the overall architecture or organizational context, while the second clarifies how general or specific the feature is in relation to broader theory and narrower instantiations.

5.1 Layers Within an Instantiated Artifact

Figure 2 illustrates how the six layers we identified (Sect. 4.1) come together in the context of an instantiated artifact. The first three layers—*interaction* and *engagement*

(1), *functional/procedural (2)*, and *data* and *information handling (3)*—are typically the core "technical" layers of the solution. *Process* and *workflow orchestration (4)* then coordinates activities over time or across stakeholders, while *organizational/ecosystem structuring (5)* provides the broader governance or multi-party context in which the artifact operates. Finally, *human* and *social interventions (6)* addresses strategies for guiding, motivating, or supporting the people involved. For instance in the case of the study of Müller and Reuter-Oppermann [16]: A user interface (layer 1) for scheduling blood donations might rely on a notification logic (layer 2) connected to inventory data (layer 3), orchestrated by a workflow that triggers reminders (layer 4), subject to organizational policies around scheduling (layer 5), and possibly featuring motivational nudges encouraging donors (layer 6). By clearly locating each design feature within one (or possibly two) main layers, designers can ensure coherence among features and pinpoint potential gaps or overlaps. The vertical layers 4 and 6 illustrate how process orchestration and human and social interventions can span multiple layers, from interface design through data handling, ensuring cross-layer coordination and alignment. We place layer 6 between the interface (layer 1) and the user to emphasize how socio-behavioral interventions directly shape user behaviors at the point of interaction.

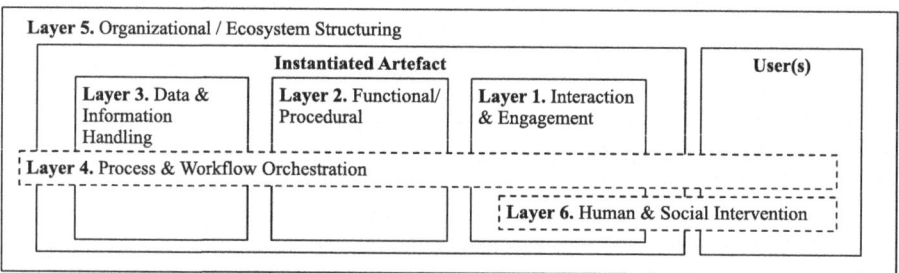

Fig. 2. Design feature layer framework

5.2 Abstraction Levels from Theory to Entities

Figure 3 shows design features on a continuum between highly abstract design theories and highly context-specific design entities. While prior frameworks (e.g., [2, 15]) acknowledge partial or evolving design knowledge, they do not single out design features as bridging elements on a continuum from abstract theory to concrete artifacts, necessitating our new framework to clarify these mid-level operational distinctions.

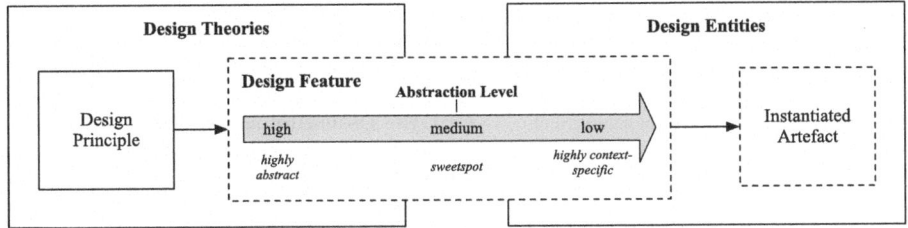

Fig. 3. Design feature abstraction framework

In practice, design features can vary in their specificity. Some will be closer to the principle side (e.g. "Provide a multi-language interface to accommodate international users"), while others lean toward an already coded solution (e.g. "Implement a real-time translation service using Google Cloud APIs with fallback to offline dictionaries"). By recognizing these abstraction levels, researchers can more clearly articulate how each feature moves from broad, theoretical guidance toward real-world instantiations. In particular, we recommend aiming for a medium level of abstraction when publishing design features (e.g. "Integrate an automated translation component that supports real-time text rendering, allowing modular switching between different translation engines."). That sweet spot avoids overly rigid, technology-bound directives (which risk obsolescence) while still going beyond vague statements that lack enough detail for practical implementation.

6 Toward Actionable Mid-Level Guidance in DSR

6.1 Guidelines for Constructing Design Features

Of the 334 publications we identified that offered some form of design knowledge, only 34 explicitly documented design features. This limited prevalence suggests a missed opportunity: while many studies present DPs, they often lack the tangible, mid-level guidance necessary for practical implementation. Our analysis revealed frequent inconsistencies in naming, level of detail, and linkage to DPs, making reusability difficult. To address these gaps and strengthen the role of design features, we propose the following guidelines aimed at standardizing their formulation, ensuring traceability, and enhancing overall reusability, ensuring that other researchers or practitioners can readily implement the features without being overwhelmed by details. We propose three main categories of guidelines: (1) Universal Naming and Structuring Rules, (2) Layer-Specific Focus Points, (3) General Tips for Effective Communication and present them in Table 5.

Table 5. Guidelines for design feature creation and formulation

Category	Guidelines
Guideline category 1: Universal naming and structuring rules	**G1.1. Use a distinctive, action-oriented title** – **Format:** [verb] + [object] + (optional specification) – **Examples:** "Enable real-time fraud alerts," "implement context-aware chatbot guidance," "establish cross-functional governance board" – **Rationale:** Imperative or "command-like" phrasing ("enable…," "implement…," "provide…") fosters clarity and makes it easier for readers to envision the action **G1.2. Include a brief purpose and expected outcome** – **Example:** "To increase user trust, provide real-time fraud alerts that notify customers within 5 minutes, enabling immediate corrective action" – **Why:** Each feature should answer why it exists and what it achieves, ensuring implementers understand its intent **G1.3.: If needed, you can include, optionally** – Key dependencies or context (e.g., "requires transaction logs updated hourly") – Essential parameters (e.g., "send alerts if anomaly score ≥ 0.8") – Constraints or trade-offs (e.g., "must remain GDPR-compliant") – Evaluation criteria (e.g., "success = 80% of suspicious cases flagged within 5 minutes")
Guideline category 2: Layer-specific focus points	**G2.1. Interaction and Engagement** – Emphasize UI/UX aspects—Interfaces, user flows, feedback loops, accessibility **G2.2. Functional/procedural** – Clarify the underlying logic or rules—Algorithms, method steps, error handling **G2.3. Data and Information Handling** – Focus on data lifecycle—Collection, storage, security, integration **G2.4. Process and Workflow Orchestration** – Describe tasks and their sequence—Workflow steps, approvals, notifications **G2.5. Organizational/ecosystem structuring** – Articulate governance, roles, ecosystem responsibilities **G2.6. Human and Social Interventions** – Outline motivational, social, or training aspects—Nudges, incentives, collaborative forums

(continued)

Table 5. (*continued*)

Category	Guidelines
Guideline category 3: General tips for effective communication	**G3.1. Be concise yet concrete** – Aim for a paragraph or a short bulleted list to describe each feature so it remains readable and actionable **G3.2. Use real-world (not overly theoretical) language** – Practitioners should be able to grasp at a glance what to do **G3.3. Link to higher-level principles** – If the feature springs from a specific DP, mention that or visualize in a mapping diagram **G3.4. Highlight evaluation possibilities** – Encourage authors to state how they will measure the feature's effectiveness **G3.5. Consider reusability** – Use sufficiently generic terminology so that others can adapt your feature to different settings (unless your context is intentionally narrow) **G.3.6. Two-layered documentation approach (optional)** – Main text: Short, focused entries that clearly convey the "big idea" – Appendix or supplement: Detailed dependencies, constraints, metrics, or technical references for implementers needing deeper guidance

6.2 Illustrative Case: Mapping from Requirement to Principle to Features

To demonstrate how these guidelines can enhance the clarity and reusability of design features, we draw on a study by Müller and Reuter-Oppermann [16]. Figure 4 depicts an excerpt of the original mapping from their publication, illustrating how Design Requirement 3 (DR3) on "Motivation and Feedback" is linked to DP3 and several design features. DR3 addresses user needs for tracking progress, providing donation feedback, and enabling experience exchange, while DP3 prescribes motivational and encouraging methods (gamification, bidirectional feedback, companion capabilities). The linked features collectively illustrate how this motivational support is operationalized.

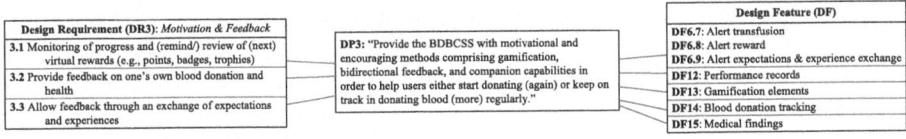

Fig. 4. Original mapping of DR3, DP3, and linked design features from [16]

First, what works well in the existing approach is the direct linkage from DR3 to DP3, which ensures traceability from user-centered requirements to prescriptive guidance. It is also notable that many of the features specify tangible functionalities like "Alert reward" (DF6.8), thereby offering mid-level direction beyond an abstract principle. Second, some areas could nonetheless be improved. DR3.1 already names points, badges, and trophies, which are arguably specific implementation details that partially overlap with the more general gamification elements described in DF13. Similarly, certain feature names like "Alert reward" or "Performance records" do not describe the intended outcomes or success criteria, making it harder to evaluate or adapt these features in other contexts.

To address these gaps, we applied our guidelines to refine one part of this mapping—specifically DR3.1 and DF13. Figure 5 presents a revised mapping diagram showing how these elements could be clarified. In the revised DF13, the name is changed to an action-oriented title that directly references the requirement. The feature description explicitly lists the purpose and the mechanisms. It also specifies optional dependencies and evaluation criteria. This revised formulation ensures better traceability and reusability by clarifying the logic behind awarding rewards, role of user data, and metrics for success.

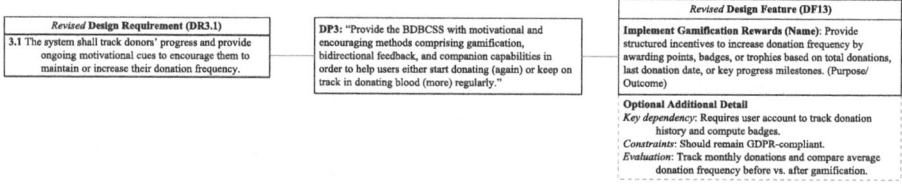

Fig. 5. Revised examples of DR3.1 and DF13 [16]

7 Discussion

Our findings confirm that design features play a pivotal role in bridging high-level design theories (e.g., DPs) with the concrete artifacts practitioners must implement and evaluate. By systematically reviewing 34 publications that explicitly contribute design features, we observed considerable variation in how authors label, describe, and operationalize these mid-level constructs. This heterogeneity can hinder the accumulation of design knowledge, as researchers and practitioners often struggle to translate broad prescriptions into coherent, reusable artifact specifications. Addressing this gap, our layered and abstraction-focused frameworks (Sect. 5) provide a common vocabulary to position design features more consistently within DSR studies, while our guidelines (Sect. 6.1) outline concrete steps for naming, structuring, and documenting them in a manner that facilitates both traceability and reusability. Finally, in Sect. 6.2, we illustrate how feature mapping can benefit from a clearer distinction between MRs and DFs and the application of our guidelines—acknowledging the original study's strengths while demonstrating how minor adjustments can further improve clarity and reusability. A key methodological contribution of this study lies in reconciling prior work into a cohesive conception of design features as actionable, mid-level entities. Our six layers helps to pinpoint where each feature operates (e.g., user interface vs. organizational structure), whereas the three abstraction levels (high, medium, low) clarify how specifically it is prescribed. Nevertheless, our work faces certain limitations. First, although we surveyed a broad set of DSR publications, the final sample of 34 relevant studies may not capture all possible instantiations or terminology variants. Second, because DSR contexts differ widely (from organizational interventions to technical prototypes), no single template can guarantee universal applicability. Researchers should thus tailor the recommended guidelines to their project's scope, acknowledging that design features are contextual constructs whose granularity depends on the artifact, domain, and stakeholder needs. In sum, by explicitly articulating where a feature resides (via layers) and how it moves from principle to instantiation (via abstraction levels), we help researchers systematically document design features in a way that can be replicated, reused, and refined.

8 Conclusion and Outlook

This paper demonstrates the centrality of design features in translating high-level theoretical prescriptions (e.g., DPs) into concrete, implementable artifact specifications. By mapping features to six layers and classifying them according to three abstraction levels, we have shown how researchers can systematically document not just what must be built, but how and why a particular functionality or intervention should appear. Our guidelines underscore the importance of striking a balance between specificity and flexibility: Medium-level prescriptions are typically the most useful for ensuring that design features remain both broadly applicable and readily implementable. Looking ahead, future research could adapt and refine our frameworks for specific domains or integrate them with established repositories of design knowledge. Another promising avenue involves evaluating how well these standardized design features scale across multiple projects or organizational contexts. Ultimately, our hope is that consistently articulated design features will enhance the cumulative rigor and reusability of DSR, enabling more robust knowledge accumulation and accelerating innovation in practice.

References

1. Hevner, A., March, S.T., Park, J., Ram, S.: Design science in information systems research. MIS Q. **28**, 75–105 (2004)
2. vom Brocke, J., Winter, R., Hevner, A., Maedche, A.: Special issue editorial—accumulation and evolution of design knowledge in design science research: a journey through time and space. J. Assoc. Inform. Syst. **21** (2020)
3. Gregor, S., Kruse, L.C., Seidel, S.: The anatomy of a design principle. J. Assoc. Inf. Syst. (2020)
4. Elshan, E., Engel, C., Ebel, P., Siemon, D.: Assessing the Reusability of Design Principles in the Realm of Conversational Agents. Springer International Publishing, Cham (2022)
5. Iivari, J.: Editorial: a critical look at theories in design science research. J. Assoc. Inf. Syst. **21** (2020)
6. Webster, J., Watson, R.T.: Analyzing the past to prepare for the future: writing a literature review. MIS Q. **26**(2), xiii–xxiii (2002)
7. Page, et al.: The PRISMA 2020 Statement: an updated guideline for reporting systematic reviews. BMJ (372) (2021). British Medical Journal Publishing Group

8. Möller, F., Guggenberger, T.M., Otto, B.: Towards a Method for Design Principle Development in Information Systems. Springer International Publishing, Cham (2020)
9. Wache, H., Möller, F., Schoormann, T., Strobel, G., Petrik, D.: Exploring the abstraction levels of design principles: the case of chatbots. Wirtschaftsinformatik 2022 Proceedings. (2022)
10. Gregor, S., Jones, D.: The anatomy of a design theory. J. Assoc. Inf. Syst. **8** (2007)
11. Möller, F., Hansen, M., Schoormann, T.: Synthesizing a solution space for prescriptive design knowledge codification. Scand. J. Inf. Syst. **34** (2022)
12. Cohn, M.: User Stories Applied: for Agile Software Development. Addison-Wesley Professional (2004)
13. Walls, J.G., Widmeyer, G.R., El Sawy, O.A.: Building an information system design theory for vigilant EIS. Inf. Syst. Res. **3**, 36–59 (1992)
14. Gregor, S., Hevner, A.R.: Positioning and presenting design science research for maximum impact. MIS Q. **37**, 337–355 (2013)
15. Kuechler, W., Vaishnavi, V.: A framework for theory development in design science research: multiple perspectives. J. Assoc. Inf. Syst. **13** (2012)
16. Müller, H.M., Reuter-Oppermann, M.: Designing behavior change support systems targeting blood donation behavior. Bus. Inf. Syst. Eng. **66**, 299–319 (2024)
17. Feine, J., Adam, M., Benke, I., Maedche, A., Benlian, A.: Exploring design principles for enterprise chatbots: an analytic hierarchy process study. DESRIST 2020. Springer-Verlag, Berlin, Heidelberg (2020)
18. Bankamp, S., Muntermann, J.: Are my stocks sustainable? Design principles for leveraging information from analyst reports. PACIS 2021 Proceedings (2021)
19. Gierlich-Joas, M., Zieglmeier, V., Neuburger, R., Hess, T.: Leading agents or stewards?: Exploring design principles for empowerment through workplace technologies. In: ICIS 2021 Proceedings. p. 1519 (2021)
20. Hönigsberg, S.: A Platform for value co-creation in SME networks. DESRIST 2020, Kristiansand, Norway, December 2–4, 2020, Proceedings. pp. 285–296. Springer-Verlag, Berlin, Heidelberg (2020)
21. Betz, C., Jung, R.: Value creation in business ecosystems—a design theory for a reference model. AMCIS 2021 Proceedings. (2021)
22. Neben, T., Seeger, A.-M., Kramer, T., White, A.: Regaining joy of life: theory-driven development of mobile psychotherapy support systems. ICIS 2015 Proceedings (2015)
23. Apel, S., Kästner, C.: An overview of feature-oriented software development. J. Object Technol. **8**, 49–84 (2009)
24. Strohmann, T., Siemon, D., Elshan, E., Gnewuch, U.: Design principles in information systems research: trends in construction and formulation. AMCIS 2023 Proceedings (2023)
25. Pressman, R.S.: Software Engineering: A Practitioner's Approach. Pressman and Associates (2005)
26. vom Brocke, J., van der Aalst, W.M.P., Berente, N., van Dongen, B., Grisold, T., Kremser, W., Mendling, J., Pentland, B.T., Roeglinger, M., Rosemann, M., Weber, B.: Process science: the interdisciplinary study of socio-technical change. Proc. Sci. **1**, 1 (2024)
27. Müller, H.M., Reuter-Oppermann, M.: Chatblood—Towards designing chatbots for blood donors. ECIS 2022 Research-in-Progress Papers (2022)

Data-Driven Design Science

Designing Geospatial Tools to Address Maternal and Infant Health Disparities: Analyzing Low Birth Weight Patterns

Katja Crusius[✉], Maria Assumpta-Komugabe, Paniz Herrera, and Samir Chatterjee

Claremont Graduate University, Claremont, CA 91711, USA
katja.crusius@cgu.edu

Abstract. This study explores the use of geospatial analysis to address regional disparities in low birth weight (LBW) rates across California. By creating a spatial visualization tool, the research aims to highlight the socioeconomic and environmental factors influencing LBW such as income, healthcare access and education. The tool will provide policymakers and healthcare providers with actionable insights to inform targeted interventions and is evaluated by subject matter experts in public health to determine its usability and effectiveness. The research seeks to improve maternal and infant health outcomes by promoting data-driven, region-specific interventions.

Keywords: Maternal health · Infant health · Visualization · Design · Geo-spatial

1 Introduction

Low birth weight (LBW), defined as a birth weight of less than 5.5 pounds (2500 g), is a significant public health concern in California and all the United States. Infants born with LBW face a higher risk of neonatal mortality, developmental challenges, and long-term health issues such as respiratory problems, cognitive impairments, and chronic diseases like diabetes and heart conditions. LBW also contributes to nearly 30% of newborn healthcare costs, placing an economic burden that exceeds $13.4 billion annually [1]. Despite advances in maternal and neonatal healthcare, the rates of LBW have not seen a significant decline in recent years, raising concerns about the effectiveness of existing public health interventions.

Thorsen et al. explore how U.S. Community Health Centers' (CHCs) operational efficiency, patient demographics, and regional context affect access to early prenatal care and LBW rates. The study finds that rural CHCs serving predominantly White populations provide better access to prenatal care and report lower LBW rates, while urban CHCs serving poor racial minorities in affluent areas face higher LBW rates and reduced access to care. The research highlights that racial and regional inequalities, particularly for Black and Hispanic patients, have a greater impact on birth outcomes than CHC efficiency alone [10]. This shows that LBW is disproportionately prevalent in certain regions, influenced by a combination of socioeconomic, environmental, and healthcare access factors. Areas with lower income, limited access to quality healthcare, and higher pollution levels tend to experience higher rates of LBW.

Addressing these regional disparities requires targeted, location-specific interventions rather than broad national strategies. However, many existing approaches lack the integration of geospatial analysis and technology-driven solutions that can identify high-risk areas and tailor interventions. This research seeks to bridge that gap by utilizing geospatial analytics and socioeconomic data to develop a targeted approach specific to certain areas to improve awareness and education in affected communities.

LBW remains a critical public health issue in the U.S., disproportionately affecting certain regions and socioeconomic groups. Despite the availability of diverse datasets covering health records and different socio-economic indicators, current policy interventions often fail to incorporate geospatial analysis that accounts for location-specific factors. Many interventions remain general, without addressing the unique needs of different communities. This gap underscores the importance of a targeted, data-driven approach for regional disparities in LBW, one that utilizes geospatial tools to reveal complex relationships between geographic and socioeconomic factors. Identifying these disparities through geospatial analysis is essential to targeting interventions and reducing health risks for newborns. This research project addresses the absence of a comprehensive spatial data visualization tool that can link regional factors with LBW outcomes, informing data-driven regionally tailored interventions by policy makers. The research questions are as follows:

1. How can geospatial analysis reveal regional disparities in LBW rates across California, and what specific socioeconomic factors (like income, healthcare access, and education) are linked to these disparities?
2. How effective is the spatial data visualization tool in supporting policymakers and healthcare providers in identifying LBW disparities and informing region-specific interventions to improve maternal and infant health outcomes?

The significance of this research lies in its potential to transform how public health data is analyzed and applied in real-world contexts. By moving beyond traditional statistical methods and embracing geospatial technologies, this study provides a multidimensional perspective on health disparities. This approach not only enhances the precision of data interpretation but also empowers stakeholders to implement interventions with greater efficacy and accountability. Furthermore, the integration of geospatial analysis into public health practice fosters a culture of evidence-based policymaking, where decisions are informed by comprehensive, location-specific insights.

Additionally, the adaptability of the developed tool allows for its application beyond LBW analysis. It can serve as a model for addressing other public health challenges, such as tracking the spread of infectious diseases, analyzing vaccination coverage, or assessing environmental health risks. By demonstrating the versatility and utility of geospatial tools in public health, this research contributes to a broader understanding of how technological innovations can drive systemic improvements in health outcomes.

Ultimately, the goal of this research is not only to address current LBW disparities but also to establish a foundation for future studies that leverage geospatial data to tackle complex health issues. This aligns with the broader objectives of public health to reduce health inequities, promote social justice, and enhance the well-being of populations through data-driven, contextually relevant strategies.

2 Background and Literature Review

Multiple studies emphasize socioeconomic and maternal health factors as primary determinants of LBW. Maternal education is consistently associated with birth outcomes, as evidenced by Grady & Enander, who found an inverse correlation between maternal education and LBW in Michigan [6]. Similarly, maternal age is a key risk factor, with adolescent mothers (<20 years) and older mothers (>34 years) exhibiting higher LBW prevalence [9]. Racial disparities are also well-documented, particularly among African American women, who face significantly higher LBW rates compared to white women [4].

Additionally, prenatal care access plays a crucial role in mitigating LBW risk. Burns et al. found that inadequate prenatal care, measured by the Kotelchuck Index, was strongly associated with LBW, particularly in low-income and racially segregated areas. Maternal obesity, smoking, and poverty were also identified as significant contributors to LBW, highlighting the interplay between individual health behaviors and broader social determinants [4].

Geographic disparities in LBW rates have been a focal point of recent research. In Michigan, high LBW rates were concentrated in metropolitan areas such as Detroit, Flint, and Kalamazoo, reflecting racial and economic segregation [6]. Similarly, in Ghana, spatial hotspot analysis revealed higher LBW prevalence in rural northern and middle zones compared to urban coastal areas, suggesting critical healthcare access disparities [3]. In São Paulo, LBW infant mortality rates were paradoxically highest in developed municipalities, indicating that economic growth alone does not translate to improved maternal and child health outcomes [3].

A crucial gap identified in multiple studies is the mismatch between healthcare resource allocation and LBW risk areas. One study found a significant lack of prenatal care facilities within LBW clusters in Florida, despite overwhelming evidence supporting prenatal interventions [4]. Similarly, in Ghana, rural regions with the highest LBW rates had the poorest healthcare infrastructure, emphasizing the need for region-specific health system improvements [3].

3 Methodology

The problem was approached by utilizing the three-cycle view of design science research as outlined by Hevner [8]. The environment, which includes the application domain, people, organizational systems, technical systems, and the associated problems and opportunities, is connected to design science through the relevance cycle. This cycle encompasses requirements and field testing, ensuring that the solution artifact remains practically relevant and usable. Design science involves the development of design artifacts and processes, followed by their evaluation, which occurs in the design cycle. The rigor cycle connects to the knowledge base, grounding the research in existing knowledge and contributing to it. The knowledge base forms the foundation of research, including scientific theories, methods, experience, expertise, and meta-artifacts such as design products and processes.

When identifying persistent problems in the context of LBW, both the environment and knowledge base were considered. A thorough review of the literature revealed previous findings and existing gaps, which opened a space for this project. Insights were also gained about the environment where LBW policy decisions are made, identifying the tool's target population and the necessary technologies and features to create the most effective artifact. The relevance cycle was applied to determine the artifact's requirements, such as providing actionable insights into the persistence of LBW across different counties in California. An important requirement was the user-friendliness of the tool, ensuring that anyone in public health, regardless of prior geospatial tool experience, could use it. The rigor cycle ensured that the research was grounded in literature, contributing to the knowledge base, which will be discussed later. The design cycle involved an iterative process of building and evaluating the tool, beginning with a first version, followed by feedback collection through formative evaluation. Adjustments were made, and a second version was developed based on this feedback, addressing user concerns and suggestions.

The DSR Knowledge Contribution Framework [7] was also considered during the solution's development, with the aim of evaluating the research's contribution through this framework. In this context, DSR research is classified into invention, improvement, exaptation, and routine design, as explained further in the evaluation.

The solution was centered around creating a visual tool that layers various regional factors influencing LBW in California. The primary artifact involved developing a comprehensive spatial data visualization platform, which included multiple types of maps and graphical representations. The GIS tool ArcGIS Pro by Esri was used to create bivariate maps.

This artifact consisted of the following key outputs: (1) Immediate Intervention Maps and (2) LBW Ratio Maps which are both illustrated below with an example from the tool. By leveraging spatial data visualization, the tool aims to communicate data effectively and facilitate targeted interventions that can significantly improve maternal and infant health outcomes in California (Fig. 1).

1. **Immediate Intervention Map**: These maps show areas with the highest needs for intervention regarding alcohol use and smoking providing policymakers with clear guidance on where to focus their efforts in preventing LBW (Fig. 2).

2. **LBW Ratio Maps**: These maps illustrate the ratio of the percentage of Black women experiencing LBW to the percentage of White women, as well as the ratio of Hispanic and Black women to White women. These maps help highlight racial and ethnic disparities in LBW rates, fostering a deeper understanding of the socio-demographic factors at play.

The DSR Kernel Theory utilized in this project is the Theory of Cognitive Fit [11]. It suggests that decision-making and problem-solving effectiveness improve when the representation of information aligns with the cognitive processes required for a given task. In this context, policymakers, healthcare providers, and community stakeholders

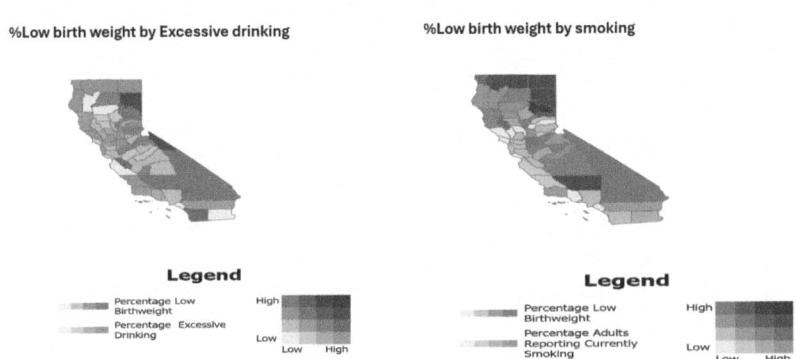

Fig. 1. Example of immediate intervention maps

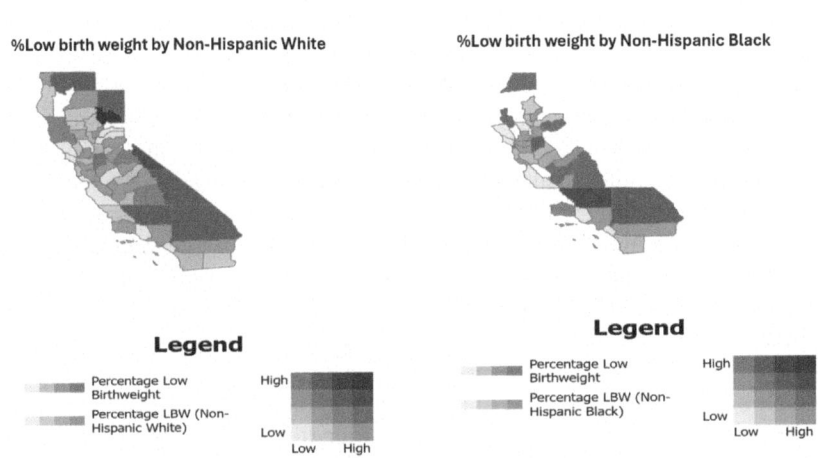

Fig. 2. Example of a LBW ratio map

need to interpret maternal health data to make informed decisions. The tool leverages geospatial analysis and visualization techniques to present risk factors in a format that enhances cognitive fit. By aligning the data representation with user needs, the tool aims to improve the accuracy and efficiency of LBW interventions.

4 Artifact Design and Build

Substance use during pregnancy has been a persistent public health issue for decades, yet many expectant mothers continue to expose their unborn children to harmful substances. Alcohol, tobacco, and illicit drugs significantly increase the risk of LBW due to their adverse effects on fetal development. Heavy alcohol consumption is linked to fetal alcohol syndrome (FAS), occurring in 1–3 per 1000 live births, with severe consequences such as growth retardation and neurological impairments [5]. Women consuming three to five drinks per day have a twofold increased risk of delivering a LBW infant, while those drinking six or more drinks daily face an almost threefold risk. Tobacco use (20–25% of pregnant women) leads to intrauterine growth restriction (IUGR) and preterm birth, while illicit drugs like cocaine (2.3–3.4%) and heroin (2–4%) are associated with placental abruption, preterm labor, and stillbirth. Marijuana use (3–12%) has inconclusive effects, but some studies suggest an increased risk of preterm labor and LBW. Despite these well-known risks, 14% of pregnant women engage in multiple high-risk behaviors, such as combining smoking, drinking, and drug use [5].

Efforts to prevent LBW face systemic, psychosocial, biological, and knowledge-based barriers. Poverty, lack of healthcare access, and misinformation make it difficult for women to adopt healthier behaviors, with 50% of pregnant women abstaining from alcohol, tobacco, and drugs, while 2.5% engage in all three. Psychosocial factors, including stress, domestic violence (8–17%), and lack of family support, further discourage positive change. Substance dependence, affecting 105,000 (2.6%) pregnant women using cocaine, also plays a role, as does misinformation, with 40–60% of women consuming alcohol underestimating its risks. Healthcare barriers, such as negative provider attitudes and language difficulties, make it harder for women to seek help. Addressing these challenges requires comprehensive social, medical, and policy interventions to ensure accessible healthcare, education, and strong support systems for pregnant women [5].

The dashboard was designed to assist policymakers in identifying counties facing significant challenges related to maternal health, substance abuse, and LBW, enabling the implementation of targeted interventions and support programs. Addressing these challenges necessitates comprehensive social, medical, and policy interventions to ensure accessible healthcare, education, and robust support systems for pregnant women.

The artifact was developed as a visual tool that layers various regional factors influencing LBW, aiming to equip policymakers with actionable insights for targeted interventions to improve maternal and infant health. Throughout the iterative design process, we gathered user feedback from key stakeholders, including public health officials and healthcare providers, to ensure the tool's user-friendliness and alignment with their needs. This feedback led to the incorporation of several design improvements, such as interactive maps, clearer legends, and the integration of socioeconomic data to enhance user navigation.

The tool stands out by leveraging spatial data visualization to highlight regional disparities in LBW rates across California. It uniquely compares LBW rates with other key socio-economic factors, such as excessive alcohol consumption, smoking, and uninsured adults, displaying these variables alongside LBW data on the same layer. The tool also generates impactful visualizations, including choropleth and bivariate maps, which effectively communicate data-driven insights to policymakers and healthcare providers, facilitating informed decision-making.

In addition to identifying geographic areas with high LBW rates, the tool informed the development of tailored interventions addressing the unique needs of different regions, thereby promoting health equity. By emphasizing the geographic context of health outcomes, the artifact provided actionable insights that contributed to meaningful improvements in maternal and infant health outcomes across the state.

Users are able to navigate the tool by selecting a county from the list on the left in order to see both the maps and the metrics updated to display the information for that particular county. Also, users can enlarge each of the maps and metrics when clicking on the upper right corner to see any of the aspects on the dashboard in more detail.

Based on the tool, public health experts and policy makers can identify location-based factors that are influencing LBW depending on the county in California. Given the identified gap in location-specific interventions, the insights provided by the tool can help develop targeted interventions by offering policymakers a clearer understanding of which factors influence LBW in specific locations (Fig 3).

Link to the Geospatial Tool

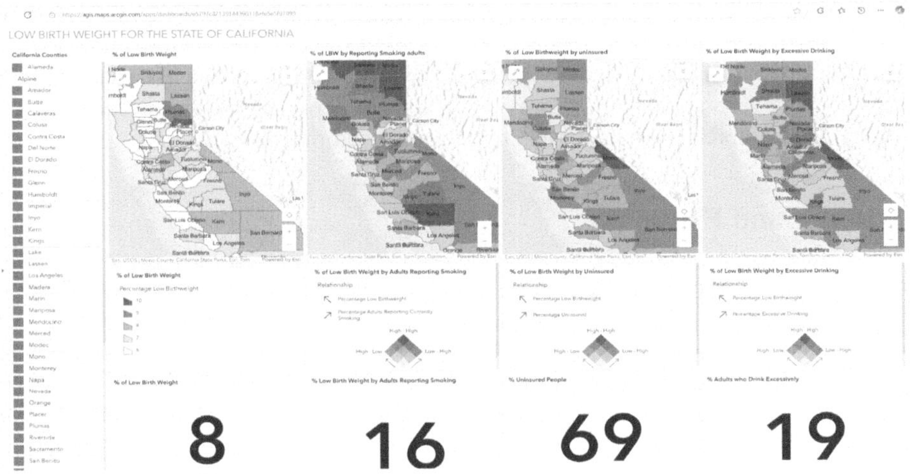

Fig. 3. Screen capture of the geospatial tool

5 Evaluation

To evaluate the first version of the artifact, pilot study in form of a survey testing the usability and efficiency of the tool was conducted. It includes questions on clarity and comprehension, ease of use, relevance to policy planning, and effectiveness of communication in the form in a multiple-choice format, with participants rating these aspects on a Likert Scale. Additionally, there are three open-ended questions about usability, suggestions for improvement, and insights for policy evaluation. Lastly, two questions on the respondents' professional background as well as their familiarity with similar tools are included.

This survey focuses on public health experts and policymakers with experience in maternal and infant health, health disparities, or geospatial data analysis. The conclusions are intended to apply to professionals working in public health, healthcare planning, and policy development, particularly those addressing issues related to LBW disparities.

This includes public health officials, healthcare providers, academic researchers, and community advocates who utilize data-driven insights to inform interventions and allocate resources effectively. The findings aim to support decision-making processes that promote health equity and improve maternal and infant health outcomes across diverse regions.

The recruitment process involved reaching out to 30 public health experts, including professionals and academic researchers with relevant expertise in maternal and infant health, health disparities, or geospatial data analysis. Participants were recruited via email. Recruitment emails will contain a brief description of the project, eligibility requirements, and a link to the tool and the survey. The survey and all accompanying materials were submitted to the Institutional Review Board (IRB #4920) and it was found that a review was not required.

A survey with a larger participant pool will be conducted in the future. The survey questions will be further refined, drawing on existing surveys from the literature. While the initial survey was brief to gather preliminary feedback on aspects like usability and efficiency, the second round will provide a more in-depth evaluation of each aspect, contributing comprehensive feedback as part of the summative evaluation.

6 Result and Findings

Of the 30 potential respondents, 8 have completed the survey to date. The respondents represented various professional fields, including public health practice, healthcare, health education and promotion, as well as geospatial analysis and geographic information systems. To maintain anonymity, further demographic details are not provided. However, their diverse backgrounds enabled the evaluation of both the public health aspects of the tool and the specific considerations related to geographic information systems.

In the figures below answers to the questions regarding clarity and comprehension, ease of use, and effectiveness of communication are illustrated (Figs. 4 and 5).

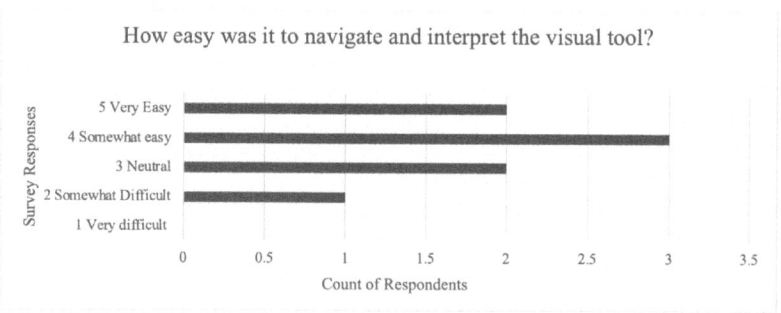

Fig. 4. Clarity and comprehension

6/8 respondents found the visualizations to be at least moderately clear, indicating that the visual representations were effective in conveying regional disparities in LBW.

Geospatial Analysis of Low Birth Weight Disparities 145

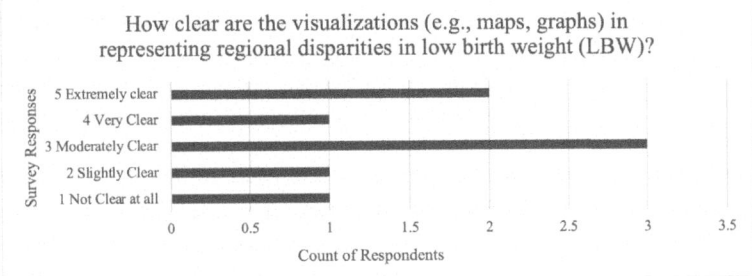

Fig. 5. Ease of use

5/8 respondents found the visual tool to be very easy or somewhat easy to navigate and interpret, suggesting that the interface was user-friendly. 7/8 respondents rated the visuals as at least moderately effective in communicating the impact of socio-economic and environmental factors on LBW. This indicates that the tool successfully conveyed the complex relationships between these factors and LBW (Figs. 6 and 7).

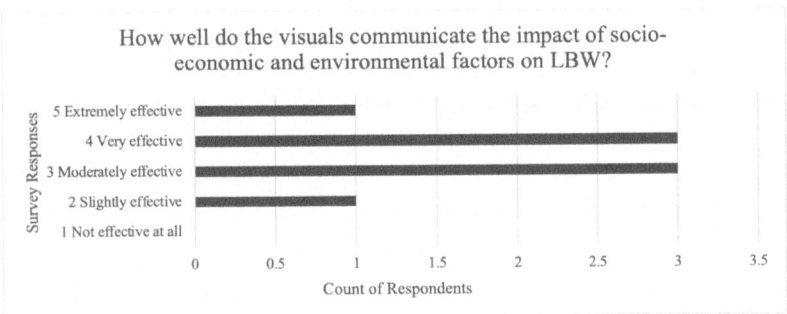

Fig. 6. Effectiveness of communication

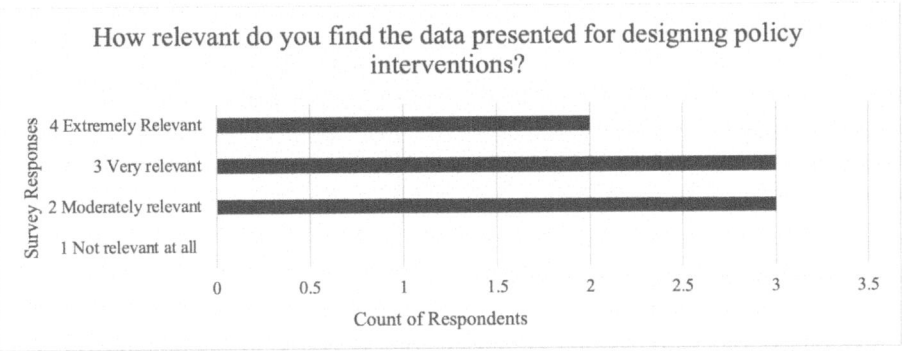

Fig. 7. Relevance for policy planning

Further, the respondents were asked about the perceived relevance of the tool for policymaking. The results can be found in the figure below.

5/8 respondents considered the data presented extremely relevant or very relevant to policy planning, which suggests that the tool is fulfilling its purpose of informing policy interventions.

In addition to these questions, five short-answer questions are part of the survey.

When asked "Which aspects of the visual tool were the most helpful or user-friendly", users pointed out the interactive nature of the map and the ability to zoom into specific regions. Additionally, the inclusion of layered socio-economic data was pointed out as well as the possibility to switch back and forth between counties and visualizing the data on a county level in addition to the data in the state overall. The map legends and indicator numbers being clear and straightforward were mentioned as well.

In response to the prompt, "What changes or additions would you suggest enhancing the tool's clarity, usability, or relevance?", participants recommended several changes. They suggested simplifying the interface, providing a user guide or tutorial, adding a feature to compare regions side-by-side, enabling the download of region-specific data, and incorporating a splash screen.

When asked, "Based on the visualizations, what regional factors do you think should be prioritized for addressing LBW disparities?", respondents identified several key regional factors such as access to prenatal care, socioeconomic factors, environmental factors, and insurance status as key regional factors to prioritize.

To better understand the background of the respondents, we asked, 'What is your area of expertise (e.g., maternal health, geospatial analysis, data analytics, health policy, healthcare)?' Respondents represented a broad spectrum of expertise, including maternal health, geospatial analysis, data analytics, health policy, healthcare, public health practice, public health policy, and GIS development.

To assess respondents' familiarity with geospatial tools, we asked, 'Have you previously used geospatial or data visualization tools in your work? If yes, briefly describe your experience.' The majority of respondents had prior experience with geospatial and data visualization tools, using them for purposes such as analyzing health disparities, assessing environmental factors, and conducting public health research. A few respondents were new to geospatial tools but reported positive experiences.

In addressing the primary research question, the geospatial tool developed highlights the impact of various socio-economic factors on LBW, particularly smoking, lack of insurance, and excessive drinking. The tool clearly demonstrates that in counties with higher percentages of these risk factors, LBW rates are also notably higher. We are working on expanding the tool to incorporate additional factors in future iterations to further explore these relationships.

7 Contribution of the Research

The presented dashboard makes a significant contribution to research by providing an innovative tool for analyzing and visualizing the factors influencing LBW in California. It integrates geospatial visualization techniques with public health data, allowing researchers and policymakers to uncover regional disparities in LBW rates alongside social and behavioral determinants such as smoking, excessive alcohol consumption, and uninsured populations. This layered approach bridges a gap in existing research by offering a multi-dimensional analysis that highlights correlations between LBW and socio-economic variables, paving the way for more targeted and data-driven public health interventions.

In addition, the artifact contributes to methodological advancements in the field of health informatics and visualization. By employing techniques like choropleth and bivariate mapping, it demonstrates the power of spatial data to communicate health information effectively. The ability to interact with and filter data by counties provides researchers with deeper insights into patterns that might be obscured in traditional datasets or tabular representations. This aligns with current trends in research emphasizing user-centric and interactive tools for knowledge discovery, particularly in health equity and public health planning.

The dashboard serves as a practical instantiation of research concepts in public health visualization. It not only facilitates hypothesis generation by showcasing correlations between variables but also supports translational research by providing actionable insights for stakeholders. Its potential to guide interventions and policies, particularly in underserved or high-risk areas, highlights its value as both a research tool and a decision-support system. As such, this artifact stands as a model for how visualization can enhance understanding, communication, and application of health data in research and practice.

In Design Science Research, the knowledge contribution of research is often measured through the DSR Knowledge Contribution Framework [7]. In this context, DSR research can be classified into the categories of invention, improvement, exaptation, and routine design based on the level of solution maturity and application domain maturity. The model can be found in the figure below.

The prototype research tool developed falls into the Improvement quadrant, as the application domain maturity is high, and the solution maturity is low. The goal of the research was to develop new solutions, in this case the visual tool, for the known problem of LBW. Out tool refines geospatial analytics in public health by integrating visualizations of LBW disparities with socioeconomic and racial factors. As it makes the relationships between variables more actionable for stakeholders, it represents an improvement of existing methods as the field is missing targeted interventions based on those relationships. The incorporation of different features and the incremental development of the tool based on user feedback advances the visualization of dashboards in public health and adds to the knowledge of how such tools can be evaluated and used in real-world settings.

One key attribute enabling the solution is the integration of multi-layered data visualization, which allows users to analyze LBW rates alongside key social determinants of health such as the percentage of LBW cases correlated with smoking adults, uninsured populations, and excessive drinking rates. This attribute fosters a holistic understanding of health disparities, moving beyond isolated metrics to reveal complex interdependencies between behavioral health risks and maternal-infant outcomes. Additionally, the tool's interactivity (enabling dynamic filtering, zooming, and region-to-region comparisons) enhances user engagement and facilitates real-time exploration of health data. By visualizing these layered relationships, policymakers can identify high-risk areas where these behavioral factors converge, supporting the development of targeted, evidence-based interventions to address LBW disparities effectively.

Since geospatial techniques are popular in other fields such as urban planning or environmental studies, the study could also be seen as exaptation, applying known solutions to new contexts. By developing a geospatial tool for investigating LBW in detail, the tool exemplifies how technology can be re-contextualized to address LBW (Fig. 8).

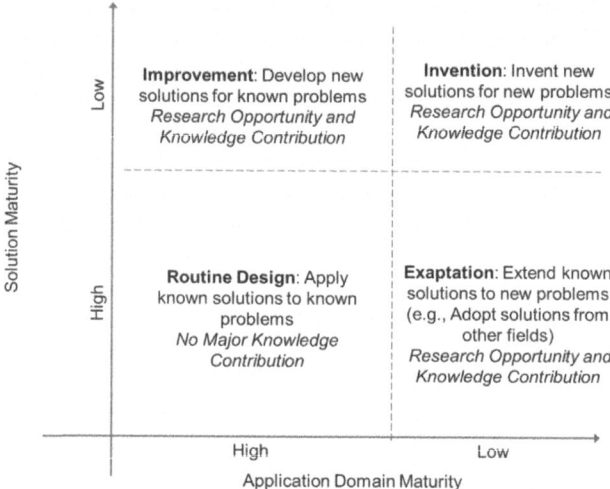

Fig. 8. DSR knowledge contribution framework [7]

8 Conclusion and Future Work

In conclusion, this study highlights the potential of geospatial visualization tools to address LBW disparities in California. The initial development and evaluation of the tool demonstrated its clarity, usability, and relevance in supporting data-driven interventions as evidenced by feedback from public health experts. The tool's ability to integrate spatial analysis with socioeconomic data underscores its value in identifying high-risk areas and informing tailored strategies to improve maternal and infant health.

While the study's findings affirm the tool's potential, they also highlight areas for further refinement to enhance its effectiveness and user experience. Moving forward, additional features such as the integration of real-time data and advanced analytics will be explored to improve the tool's impact.

This research represents an important first step toward leveraging geospatial analytics to address health disparities, but additional work is needed to optimize its functionality and maximize its impact.

In response to the feedback from the survey, several improvements were implemented in the visual tool. Key updates included the addition of guidelines for users unfamiliar with ArcGIS and the alignment of variables to better match the map legends and indicators. These changes directly addressed concerns about usability and the need for a user guide. Additionally, the clarity of the maps was enhanced, as most respondents identified this as an area for improvement. After incorporating these enhancements, we distributed an updated survey to an expert professor for further feedback on the revised version.

Future work will expand the tool's scope to include additional maternal health outcomes and assess its adaptability across diverse geographic regions. This phase will also gather feedback from a wider user base, incorporating a larger sample size to ensure broader applicability. A second survey will be conducted to evaluate the revised version of the tool, with a larger sample than the pilot survey. While maintaining the same overall objectives, the survey questions will be updated to align with established metrics from the literature, focusing on clarity, ease of use, relevance, and effectiveness. You can access the latest version of the tool here: Low Birth Weight in California.

Acknowledgments. There are no acknowledgements to be made.

Disclosure of Interests. The authors have no competing interests to declare that are relevant to the content of this article.

References

1. America's Health Rankings: Birthweight. https://www.americashealthrankings.org/explore/measures/birthweight. Accessed 29 March 2025
2. Bloch, J.R.: Using geographical information systems to explore disparities in preterm birth rates among foreign-born and U.S.-born black mothers. J. Obstet. Gynecol. Neonat. Nurs. **40**(5), 544–554 (2011). https://doi.org/10.1111/j.1552-6909.2011.01273.x
3. Boateng, D., Oppong, F.B., Senkyire, E.K., Logo, D.D.: Spatial analysis and factors associated with low birth weight in Ghana using data from the 2017 Ghana maternal health survey: spatial and multilevel analysis. BMJ Open. **14**(8), e083904 (2024). https://doi.org/10.1136/bmjopen-2024-083904
4. Burns, J.J., Livingston, R., Amin, R.: The proximity of spatial clusters of low birth weight and risk factors: defining a neighborhood for focused interventions. Matern. Child Health J. **24**(8), 1065–1072 (2020). https://doi.org/10.1007/s10995-020-02946-y
5. Chomitz, V.R., Cheung, L.W.Y., Lieberman, E.: The role of lifestyle in preventing low birth weight. Futur. Child. **5**(1), 121–138 (1995). https://doi.org/10.2307/1602511
6. Grady, S.C., Enander, H.: Geographic analysis of low birthweight and infant mortality in Michigan using automated zoning methodology. Int. J. Health Geogr. **8**(1), 10 (2009). https://doi.org/10.1186/1476-072X-8-10
7. Gregor, S., Hevner, A.R.: Positioning and presenting design science research for maximum impact. MIS Q. **37**(2), 337–355 (2013)
8. Hevner, A.R.: A three cycle view of design science research. Scand. J. Inf. Syst. **19**(2), 4 (2007)
9. Rodríguez, E.Y.A., Rodríguez, E.C.A., Marins, F.A.S., da Silva, A.F., Nascimento, L.F.C.: Spatial patterns of mortality in low birth weight infants at term and its determinants in the state of São Paulo, Brazil. Rev. Brasil. Epidemiol. **26**, e230034 (2023). https://doi.org/10.1590/1980-549720230034

10. Thorsen, M.L., Thorsen, A., McGarvey, R.: Operational efficiency, patient composition and regional context of U.S. health centers: associations with access to early prenatal care and low birth weight. Soc. Sci. Med. **226**, 143–152 (2019). https://doi.org/10.1016/j.socscimed.2019.02.043
11. Vessey, I.: The theory of cognitive fit: one aspect of a general theory of problem solving? In: Human-Computer Interaction and Management Information Systems: Foundations, pp. 155–197. Routledge (2015)
12. Zhuang, M., Concannon, D., Manley, E.: A framework for evaluating dashboards in healthcare. IEEE Trans. Vis. Comput. Graph. **28**(4), 1715–1731 (2022). https://doi.org/10.1109/TVCG.2022.3147154

LLM-Augmentation for Idea Evaluation: Developing a Reference Model for Evaluation Pipelines

Philipp Gordetzki

University of St. Gallen, 9000 St. Gallen, Switzerland
`philipp.gordetzki@unisg.ch`

Abstract. Automated approaches to idea evaluation increasingly leverage generative artificial intelligence to support decision-makers. However, contextualizing evaluations within specific domains remains challenging, particularly at varying levels of large language model (LLM) augmentation. Existing research employs embeddings to derive semantic insights, yet these representations often lack domain-specific contextualization. Recent advancements, such as chat-based LLMs, present new opportunities to incorporate context through prompting. To address these challenges, we propose a structured evaluation pipeline that integrates embeddings with feature engineering to enhance the contextualization of chat-based LLM evaluations. Using a real-world innovation challenge, we instantiate this pipeline and assess its predictive performance across different levels of augmentation. Our findings reveal that incorporating contextual information improves predictive accuracy but depends on fine-grained idea quality dimensions. By codifying our approach into a reference model, we provide a transferable framework that generalizes across various evaluation contexts employing LLMs.

Keywords: Idea Evaluation · LLM-Augmentation · Generative AI · Reference Pipeline · Design Science Research

1 Introduction

Creative ideas are fundamental to innovation, providing new opportunities for business growth [1]. Supporting idea generation has a long tradition, with various artifacts proposed to facilitate individual and group brainstorming [2]. These efforts are not confined within organizational boundaries, as external inputs can stimulate innovation [3]. Recently, the advent of generative AI (genAI) has disrupted traditional ideation approaches, such as crowdsourcing on innovation platforms [4]. GenAI is capable of producing creative ideas instantaneously at minimal cost, often achieving quality levels comparable to human-generated ideas in crowdsourcing environments [4, 5]. Consequently, decision-makers face an increased cognitive burden in identifying truly valuable ideas from an overwhelming pool of options [6].

Researchers have recognized the cognitive challenges associated with evaluating large volumes of ideas [7]. Automated approaches have been proposed to analyze linguistic patterns in ideas [8, 9] and, more recently, leveraging large language models (LLMs) as evaluators [10, 11]. However, idea evaluation is multidimensional, encompassing various criteria that extend beyond overarching assessments of quality [12]. Furthermore, existing LLM-based evaluation approaches fail to incorporate contextual factors, leading to overly optimistic and contextually irrelevant assessments [13].

Prior research has demonstrated that incorporating context into LLM-generated content enhances evaluation efficiency [14]. This study introduces a structured pipeline for integrating contextual information into the evaluation process while maintaining flexibility in evaluation criteria—an essential factor for idea assessment [12]. The proposed approach seeks to combine LLM-generated outputs with traditional statistical learning methods [8] to mitigate biases arising from overly optimistic and context-insensitive predictions.

The motivation for this research is to develop an evaluation pipeline for context-augmented idea assessment, thereby contributing to knowledge on evaluation pipelines that integrate LLMs with contextual information. This study aims to address the following research question: *How can we design an evaluation pipeline that augments LLM predictions with contextual information, and how does it improve idea quality prediction?*

The evaluation pipeline is instantiated following a design science research (DSR) approach [15] to predict idea quality. The design knowledge generated during the development process is codified into a reference pipeline, enabling generalization to evaluation tasks beyond idea assessment [16].

2 Related Work

2.1 Idea Evaluation and Idea Quality

Idea evaluation aims to identify high-potential concepts from a vast pool of candidates [6, 7]. A key challenge is that only a small fraction of ideas hold exceptional value for businesses [17]. While implementing a low-value idea (Type I error) can be costly, failing to recognize a groundbreaking idea (Type II error) can be even more detrimental [7]. Consequently, decision-makers must accurately assess all available ideas, a task that becomes increasingly complex as the size of idea pools grows [6].

One factor contributing to the expansion of idea pools is the externalization of ideation beyond organizational boundaries. First, idea generation can be outsourced to human contributors via crowdsourcing platforms [3]. More recently, generative AI has emerged as a second avenue, enabling the rapid and cost-effective generation of ideas at a scale comparable to human ideation [4, 5]. The combination of these approaches has significantly increased the volume of ideas, creating cognitive overload for decision-makers and introducing biases in evaluations.

To support decision-makers, researchers have proposed multiple criteria for assessing idea quality [12]. Generally, an idea is considered high-quality if it is creative, often defined in terms of novelty and usefulness [7]. These two dimensions tend to be negatively correlated, as highly novel ideas may conflict with existing constraints and prove difficult to implement, thereby reducing their perceived usefulness. To refine assessments further, several scholars have introduced subdimensions of idea quality. Dean et al. [12] proposed a widely accepted framework with four subdimensions: novelty, feasibility (also known as workability), relevance, and specificity (also known as elaboration). Such fine-grained criteria assist decision-makers in evaluating ideas based on the aspects most relevant to their business needs.

Beyond quality criteria, researchers have explored mechanisms to enhance idea evaluation, such as crowdsourced rating systems and the inclusion of ideator-related information to enrich idea presentations [18, 19]. However, the rapid expansion of idea pools—driven by advancements such as generative AI—necessitates more scalable and efficient evaluation approaches.

2.2 Automated Approaches

Automated approaches to idea evaluation aim to provide meaningful cues for decision-makers, alleviating their cognitive burden. With advancements in technology, these approaches have evolved from traditional statistical learning [8] to meta-representations of ideas using embeddings [19] and, more recently, to evaluations conducted by genAI [10, 11].

In statistical learning, techniques such as text mining and pattern recognition are employed to predict idea quality [8]. While effective in leveraging ground-truth data, statistical learning requires the development of elaborate, handcrafted features. In contrast, meta-representation approaches do not rely on predefined features but instead use pre-trained LLMs to capture the semantic meaning of ideas in the form of vector embeddings [20]. These embeddings, primarily used to assess novelty based on vector similarities, often fail to account for other dimensions of idea quality.

More recently, LLMs have been utilized not only for generating meta-representations but also for directly evaluating idea quality—a paradigm referred to as LLM-as-a-judge [10, 11]. In this approach, prompting techniques leverage the extensive knowledge acquired by LLMs during pre-training to assign quality scores to ideas. However, LLM-based evaluations often exhibit optimism bias and a lack of variance in scoring [13].

Each of these three approaches—feature engineering, meta-representations using embeddings, and LLM-based evaluation—offers distinct advantages and limitations. To address their shortcomings while harnessing their strengths, a new reference architecture is needed, integrating these methodologies in a complementary manner.

3 Research Approach

This research employs the DSR approach as outlined by Peffers et al. [15] and builds upon prior artifacts that utilize pipelines to enhance textual data processing [16]. Figure 1 illustrates the stages of the DSR process, which seeks to generate design knowledge on evaluation pipelines by instantiating an artifact to assess idea quality. The motivation for this research stems from expert interviews with 16 innovation managers and a review of existing literature on idea evaluation. The design requirements are derived from the challenges identified by these managers in evaluating ideas. Additionally, the literature highlights three dominant approaches in idea evaluation research: statistical learning, meta-representation, and LLM-based evaluations [4, 5, 8, 10, 20].

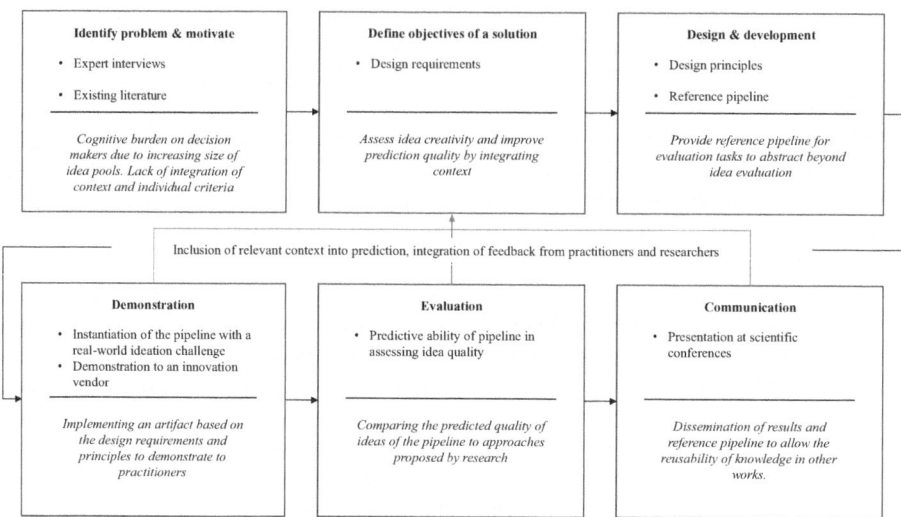

Fig. 1. Design science research approached building on Peffers et al. [15]

An initial version of the pipeline was demonstrated to a vendor of innovation platforms, revealing that customers valued the integration of existing contextual information—specifically, their respective product and idea portfolios—into the evaluation process. The revised pipeline undergoes extensive evaluation using a real-world ideation challenge to assess predictive performance and answer the research question.

In the next phase, the design knowledge obtained from the development, demonstration, and evaluation of the idea evaluation artifact is abstracted into a reference pipeline applicable to other evaluation contexts. This abstraction enables the transfer and application of knowledge to diverse evaluation settings beyond idea and innovation assessment. By leveraging components of previous pipeline artifacts and generalizing beyond specific use cases, this research aims to contribute to design reusability. Following established methodologies for constructing reference architectures ensures that the abstracted knowledge remains accessible for future research and practical implementations.

The research question is answered by evaluating the predictive ability of the idea evaluation pipeline to its three LLM-augmented parts utilizing context. Each part has different levels of considered context and LLM integration, as motivated and conceptualized in the following sections.

4 Designing an Evaluation Pipeline

4.1 Defining Problem and Objectives

Large idea pools can overwhelm decision-makers, leading to cognitive overload [7]. Meaningful cues can support decision-making, but only if they are relevant and accurate [18]. Drawing from existing research, three approaches to idea evaluation are synthesized into a novel evaluation pipeline. Additionally, an interview study with 16 innovation managers identifies practical requirements. The semi-structured interviews, each lasting approximately 1 hour, involved participants from industries such as transportation and finance. Findings from both the interviews and the literature review reveal three key design requirements (DRs):

DR1: Reflect Multidimensional Idea Quality Metrics. Company-specific criteria are necessary to align with the phase and goals of ideation. While radical innovation may prioritize novelty, incremental improvements often emphasize usefulness [21]. Although prior research has proposed various subdimensions of idea quality [12], automated approaches typically focus on single metrics such as novelty [20] or overall quality [8]. A robust evaluation pipeline should remain adaptable to different companies and contexts by incorporating flexible evaluation criteria.

DR2: Include Relevant Context. Existing literature suggests deriving idea quality from engineered features such as idea length [7, 8], meta-representations [5, 20], or knowledge obtained during LLM training [10, 11]. However, practitioners indicate that current solutions often lack applicability to their specific contexts. The prediction of idea quality metrics, such as novelty and usefulness, is highly dependent on a company's product portfolio. A novel solution may provide a competitive advantage in one company but be deemed less useful in another with different capabilities. An evaluation framework must integrate contextual factors to enhance applicability.

DR3: Provide Meaningful Cues. Research has shown that superficial cues can negatively impact idea evaluation [22], such as when crowd ratings are biased by herding effects [18]. Even automated approaches based on LLMs are susceptible to biases, including over-optimism or biases inherited during training [13]. Instead, meaningful cues should be derived from curated data, such as gold standard examples [16] of high-quality ideas. Assuming the quality of the training corpus, an automated approach can generate meaningful cues for idea evaluation based on statistical learning, improving decision-making processes.

4.2 Development and Demonstration

This research proposes a pipeline that integrates three complementary approaches to idea evaluation. First, feature engineering is used to allow the integration of context. Second, meta-representations of ideas using embeddings enhance the prediction process by capturing semantic meaning. Third, an LLM is incorporated as a judge, leveraging its extensive pre-training knowledge. Last, all available data is fed into a statistical learning model to condition the final idea quality prediction against a gold standard. Previous research has demonstrated the benefits of building pipelines around statistical learning to improve text quality in other contexts [16]. Based on predefined requirements, the development and demonstration of this pipeline yielded design knowledge that can be distilled into the following design principles (DPs).

DP1: Granular Scoring Objective. The goal of an evaluation pipeline is to assess idea quality with maximum accuracy. However, as the aggregation level of the scoring objective increases, more facets must be incorporated. Previous approaches to idea evaluation have primarily focused on assessing overall idea quality [8] or individual sub-dimensions, such as novelty [20]. This research adopts the multidimensional framework proposed by Dean et al. [12], evaluating ideas based on novelty, feasibility, relevance, and specificity. Initial experiments with the LLM-as-a-judge module indicated that performance improves with more granular scoring objectives. Similar to a scale in behavioral research, the final pipeline includes explicit inclusion and exclusion criteria. For instance, when assessing novelty, the model is prompted to evaluate originality while explicitly excluding paradigm-relatedness [12]. Granular scoring objectives support the multidimensional nature of idea creativity (DR1), facilitate the inclusion of company-specific criteria (DR2), and enable details-on-demand, such as disaggregated scale-item scores, to provide decision-makers with tailored insights (DR3).

DP2: Contextual Knowledge Integration. To enhance the relevance of predictions (DR3) and incorporate contextual knowledge (DR2), the pipeline integrates two types of contextual information. First, task data consists of historical examples from prior idea evaluation campaigns, ensuring structural alignment with the current task. Second, provider data adds company-specific context, such as product portfolios or descriptions of corporate capabilities. The pipeline's instantiation in a real-world setting involves a Swiss-based transportation company seeking to innovate the future of train travel. By scraping data from the company's website, a reference corpus of 12 products was compiled, detailing the firm's offerings. The idea evaluation pipeline employs OpenAI's text-embedding-3-large model to convert product descriptions into numerical embeddings [23], which are subsequently processed to generate task- or provider-specific features using cosine similarity measures [5]. The pipeline ensures a multidimensional representation of idea creativity (DR1) and enables the definition of features specific to each evaluation criterion.

For each criterion, the pipeline calculates multiple features:

- Novelty: Novelty is approximated by computing the embedding distance between a new idea and its nearest neighbor within the pool of prior ideas, following Just et al. [20]. Additionally, the mean embedding distance between all prior ideas and the new idea is computed.
- Feasibility: Feasibility is estimated using the product portfolio embeddings to determine how well an idea aligns with the company's capabilities. Distance calculations are performed relative to the nearest product and the mean of all products.
- Relevance: Relevance is measured by the similarity between an idea and the challenge at hand. No aggregation is applied to this measure.

- Specificity: Various constructs exist for measuring specificity, such as the Flesch readability index [7]. However, given the typically short length of submitted ideas, a simple measure of idea length proved to be the most predictive.

DP3: Idea Quality Scoring. The pipeline synthesizes information from three sources to predict idea quality. First, OpenAI's gpt-4o-2024-08-06 model is prompted to provide an initial quality assessment. Second, engineered features derived from the embedding model enhance the predictive process. Finally, a statistical learning model is trained using a gold standard dataset. The reference corpus was constructed by posting the innovation challenge from the train company to Prolific, yielding 160 idea submissions, in line with previous gold standard datasets for analytic pipelines. Subsequently, an independent Prolific panel was recruited to evaluate these ideas. A total of 88 participants each assessed 10 randomly assigned ideas while completing two attention checks. Each idea received at least eight independent evaluations across novelty, feasibility, relevance, and specificity. The inter-rater reliability analysis yielded an average intraclass correlation coefficient (ICC) of 0.63, indicating sufficient agreement [24]. The evaluation pipeline was implemented using a Support Vector Regression trained via five-fold cross-validation. The model assesses all information from previous steps in the pipeline, e.g., the LLM-as-a-judge ratings and engineered features from embeddings. They have been reduced using a UMAP reduction [25] to ten dimension to balance the number of features. Detailed results and alternative models are presented in Sect. 4.4.

4.3 Evaluation Pipeline Reference Model

The reference architecture presented in Fig. 2 illustrates a structured pipeline for evaluation tasks. The framework is divided into three primary phases: Design and setup, preparation and training, and scoring and operation.

Design and Setup. This phase establishes the foundational requirements and configurations necessary for the pipeline. It begins with defining the scoring objectives and requirements, which include inclusion and exclusion criteria, task examples, and domain-specific instructions. Additionally, context-specific instructions are created to incorporate both task and provider-specific contexts. Reference data is retrieved, bundled into task and provider corpora, and prepared to match the scoring objectives. Key features are identified, including task-specific, provider-specific, aggregation level, and distance measures. To ensure alignment with quality standards, a gold-standard reference is established through model selection and expert panel scoring.

Preparation and Training. The pipeline integrates a General Purpose Chat Model (GPCM) to generate task corpus scores and embeddings. These embeddings are enriched by a General Purpose Embedding Model (CPEM), producing representations for both task and provider corpora. Feature engineering is performed using these embeddings to extract task-specific and provider-specific features. Simultaneously, a gold-standard scoring mechanism is applied to the task corpus, yielding gold-standard scores. These scores are used to train a fine-tuned gold standard model, leveraging the pre-engineered features to refine scoring accuracy. In total, the pipeline combines three approaches

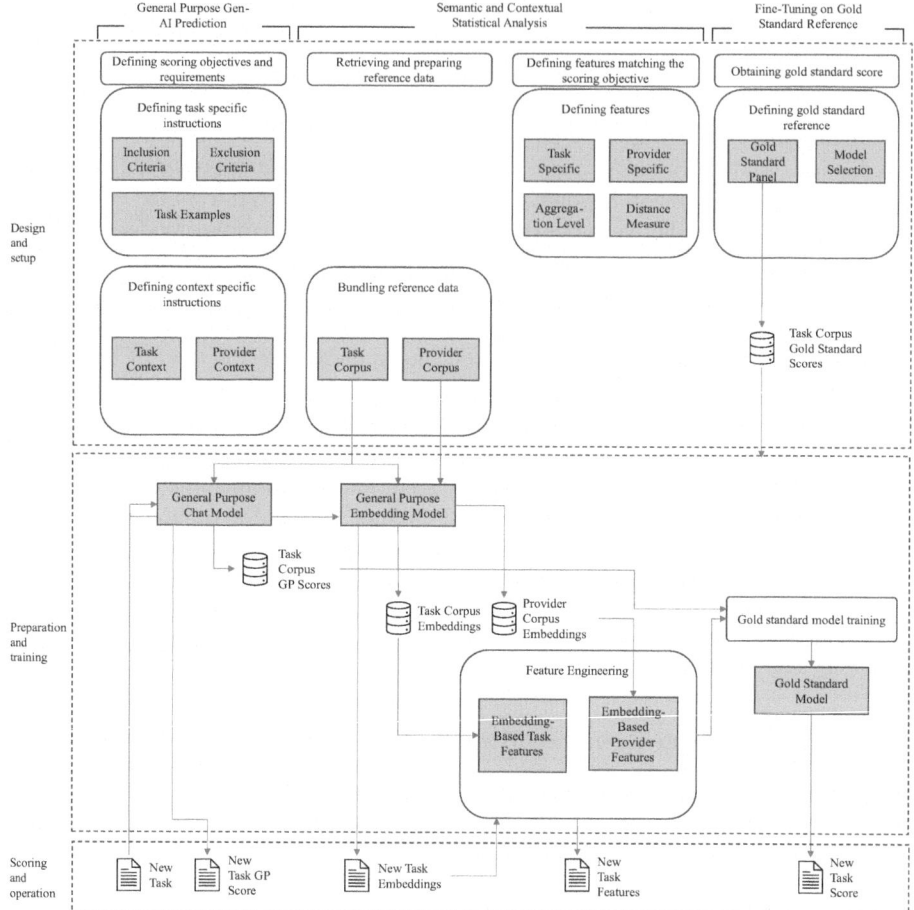

Fig. 2. Reference pipeline

to idea evaluation with varying levels of LLM-augmentation and contextualization, as detailed in Table 1.

Scoring and Operation. Once the model is trained, the pipeline transitions to the scoring phase. For new tasks, embeddings are generated, and features are engineered using the general purpose models. These features are subsequently scored by the gol standard model, providing quality assessments tailored to the scoring objectives defined earlier in the pipeline.

4.4 Evaluation

During the evaluation, the predictive performance of three individual approaches—sta engineered features, semantic representation using embeddings, and LLM-as-a-judge— is compared to the results obtained from their combination in the evaluation pipeline.

Table 1. Approaches employed in the pipeline.

Approach	Level of LLM-augmentation	Level of contextualization	Description	Supporting literature
Feature engineering	Low	Medium	LLMs provide embeddings that are used to calculate features based on a given context	[8, 9, 20]
Embeddings	Medium	Low	The embeddings are directly used for prediction. Contextualization is only based on pre-training of the LLM	[4, 5]
LLM-as-a-judge	High	High	The embeddings are directly used for prediction. Contextualization is only based on pre-training of the LLM	[10, 11]

Four models are employed for statistical learning, including linear regression (LR), support vector regression (SVR), random forest regression (RFR), and gradient boosting regression (GBR). Each model is assessed using five-fold cross-validation. Given the moderate number of ideas in the gold standard, it is anticipated that more complex models may struggle with the idea count, motivating the inclusion of simpler statistical learning models. All statistical and general-purpose models were employed using standard parameters, leveling the playing field.

Two key metrics are considered in the results displayed in Table 2. First, the root mean squared error (RMSE) quantifies the predictive error in the scale of the target variable. Since the gold standard is derived from Likert scales ranging from 1 to 7, an RMSE of 1 corresponds to an error of one Likert point. Compared to other metrics, such as mean absolute error, RMSE penalizes larger deviations more heavily. Second, R^2 represents the proportion of variance in the target variable explained by the model. In Table 2, R^2 accounts for variance explained by both the engineered features and the model's predictions.

First, we assess the effectiveness of feature engineering. Each of the four criteria includes 1–2 engineered features that serve as input for statistical learning. For novelty and feasibility, the explained variance remains low, indicating that these features have limited predictive utility on their own. However, for relevance and specificity, over 30%

Table 2. Evaluation results.

Available modul	Model used	Novelty RMSE	Novelty R^2	Feasibility RMSE	Feasibility R^2	Relevance RMSE	Relevance R^2	Specificity RMSE	Specificity R^2
FE	LR	**0.91**	0.02	**1.00**	0.09	**0.92**	0.30	0.77	0.34
	SVR	0.93		1.02		0.96		**0.75**	
	GBR	1.01		1.14		1.08		0.86	
	RFR	0.97		1.06		1.05		0.87	
GPEM	LR	**0.95**	0.25	0.99	0.22	1.01	0.28	0.93	0.17
	SVR	**0.95**		**0.98**		**0.94**		**0.90**	
	GBR	1.10		1.04		1.11		1.02	
	RFR	1.04		1.02		1.04		0.98	
GPCM	LR	0.79	0.35	**0.87**	0.35	**0.74**	0.54	**0.66**	0.50
	SVR	**0.77**		0.90		**0.74**		0.70	
	GBR	0.83		0.93		0.76		0.71	
	RFR	0.80		0.92		0.76		0.72	
GPCM OOB		1.98	0.14	2.04	0.30	1.15	0.54	0.87	0.35
PIPE	LR	0.78	**0.39**	0.86	**0.37**	0.74	**0.55**	**0.65**	0.53
	SVR	**0.74**		**0.83**		**0.72**		0.72	
	GBR	0.84		0.94		0.79		0.72	
	RFR	0.81		0.88		0.79		0.69	

Note: FE feature engineering, GPEM general purpose embedding model, GPCM general purpose chat model, GPCM OOB out-of-the-box prediction using the GPCM, PIPE Instantiated idea evaluation pipeline, Bold best performing in group, Bold + underline best performing overall

of the variance can already be explained. Given the limited feature set, the simpler linear regression model generally outperforms more complex approaches.

Second, the semantic representations of the ideas from the GPEM are incorporated into statistical learning using dimensionality reduction to 10 components via the UMAP algorithm. As expected, the inclusion of semantic information provides greater explanatory power for novelty and feasibility, as indicated by increases in R^2. However, it does not achieve the same level of predictive performance as the engineered features for relevance and specificity. Overall, the models struggle to align the semantic representations with the gold standard, as evidenced by an increase in RMSE across the board.

Third, predictions from a GPCM are integrated into statistical learning. Across all criteria, predictive performance improves substantially, achieving R^2 values exceeding 50% for relevance and specificity. Interestingly, the direct predictive ability of the general-purpose model in relation to the gold standard is limited, as indicated by a decrease in R^2 and an increase in RMSE.

Finally, all available data from the three approaches are integrated into the evaluation pipeline to identify the best-performing configuration. For novelty, the SVM model achieves an RMSE of 0.74 and an R^2 of 0.39, reflecting a 10% improvement over the second-best approach in the pipeline and a 179% improvement over the out-of-the-box performance of the general-purpose chat model. For feasibility ($R^2 = 0.37$) and relevance ($R^2 = 0.55$), the pipeline outperforms individual approaches, though with more modest gains. For specificity, linear regression performs best, achieving an RMSE of 0.65 and an R^2 of 0.53, significantly outperforming both the general-purpose chat model ($R^2 = 0.35$) and the second-best approach within the pipeline ($R^2 = 0.50$).

5 Discussion, Limitations, and Implications

The proposed idea evaluation pipeline serves as a decision-support artifact designed to alleviate the cognitive burden associated with evaluating large volumes of ideas. By integrating three distinct approaches to automated idea evaluation, our work contributes to the ongoing discourse on how generative AI can be effectively incorporated into existing methodologies [4, 5, 10, 11]. While prior research has predominantly relied on aggregated measures of idea quality [8], we emphasize the necessity of incorporating fine-grained quality subdimensions informed by both research [12] and practical applications.

Our approach advances existing automated evaluation methods by combining feature engineering with embeddings. Although the level of augmentation from LLMs is relatively low—since embeddings are processed and aggregated before being used for training—this design enables the essential integration of contextual factors, such as product and idea portfolios. Our findings indicate that for our gold-standard dataset, the predictive performance of standalone feature-engineered models surpasses previous approaches [20] in assessing novelty and feasibility while remaining viable for relevance and elaboration.

We also contribute to the integration of embedding-based representations [4, 5], which leverage LLM outputs to enhance augmentation but provide limited contextualization. Our results confirm prior research by demonstrating increased explainability but also highlight challenges in transferring these methods to other evaluation criteria. Specifically, during our evaluation, embedding-based features underperformed compared to traditional metrics like idea length in assessing elaboration.

Furthermore, we extend the discussion on LLM-as-a-judge approaches [10, 11] by showing that while standalone LLM-based predictions have limited practical utility, their integration into a structured evaluation pipeline significantly enhances predictive performance beyond existing methods. Among the three approaches studied, fully augmenting the evaluation process with generative AI appears particularly promising, as it capitalizes on the extensive knowledge captured during pre-training while enabling context integration through dynamic prompting.

Our study also contributes to the application of design science research (DSR) in addressing the complexities of unstructured data [26], such as idea evaluations, through pipeline-based processing. Building on previous DSR artifacts that have leveraged AI for text enhancement [16], we introduce a novel pipeline tailored for evaluation tasks, incorporating recent advancements in generative AI. By codifying the design knowledge gained during the development process, we offer a transferable reference model that can be applied to other domains, facilitating broader adoption and further research.

5.1 Limitations and Future Research

Despite the contributions of this study, several limitations should be considered. First, we instantiated the pipeline using a real-world innovation challenge and extracted data from a product portfolio to ensure practical relevance. However, this domain-specific implementation limits its immediate generalizability. Future research should explore how our reference architecture can be adapted for idea evaluation in different domains and innovation stages.

Second, we utilized a gold-standard idea set as a reference for training our models. While this approach supports meaningful predictions, the dataset size was constrained due to the rigorous evaluation required. Expanding the dataset or incorporating domain experts for refinement could further improve model robustness.

Lastly, while our study employs generative AI models within the pipeline to enhance predictive capabilities, their outputs serve as inputs for subsequent statistical learning. As AI technology continues to advance, newer and more sophisticated models will likely emerge. However, similar progress is anticipated in embedding models, reinforcing the need for integrating multiple techniques within a cohesive pipeline.

Acknowledgments. The author acknowledges funding by the Swiss National Science Foundation under the project number 248164. The author would like to thank Linda Fuchs for her valuable assistance with conducting interviews and transcription work.

Disclosure of Interests. The author has no competing interests to declare that are relevant to the content of this article.

References

1. Kornish, L.J., Ulrich, K.T.: The importance of the raw idea in innovation: testing the sow's ear hypothesis. J. Mark. Res. **51**(1), 14–26 (2014)
2. Wang, K., Nickerson, J.V.: A literature review on individual creativity support systems. Comput. Hum. Behav. **74**, 139–151 (2017)
3. Sanyal, P., Ye, S.: An examination of the dynamics of crowdsourcing contests: role of feedback type. Inf. Syst. Res. **35**(1), 394–413 (2023)
4. Girotra, K., et al.: Ideas are dimes a dozen: large language models for idea generation in innovation. Available at SSRN 4526071 (2023)
5. Meincke, L., Mollick, E.R., Terwiesch, C.: Prompting diverse ideas: increasing AI idea variance. arXiv preprint arXiv:2402.01727 (2024)
6. Piezunka, H., Dahlander, L.: Distant search, narrow attention: how crowding alters organizations' filtering of suggestions in crowdsourcing. Acad. Manag. J. **58**(3), 856–880 (2015)
7. Blohm, I., et al.: Rate or trade? Identifying winning ideas in open idea sourcing. Inf. Syst. Res. **27**(1), 27–48 (2016)

8. Rhyn, M., Blohm, I.: A machine learning approach for classifying textual data in crowdsourcing. In: Proceedings of the 2017 International Conference on Wirtschaftsinformatik, St. Gallen, Switzerland (2017)
9. Walter, T.P., Back, A.: A text mining approach to evaluate submissions to crowdsourcing contests. In: Proceedings of the 2013 Hawaii International Conference on System Sciences, pp. 3109–3118. IEEE, Wailea, Maui, USA (2013)
10. Chiang, W.-L., et al.: Chatbot arena: an open platform for evaluating LLMs by human preference. arXiv preprint arXiv:2403.04132 (2024)
11. Zheng, L., et al.: Judging LLM-as-a-judge with MT-bench and chatbot arena. Adv. Neural Inf. Proces. Syst. **36**, 46595–46623 (2023)
12. Dean, D.L., et al.: Identifying quality, novel, and creative ideas: constructs and scales for idea evaluation. J. Assoc. Inf. Syst. **7**(10), 646–699 (2006)
13. Shaer, O., et al.: AI-augmented brainwriting: Investigating the use of LLMs in group ideation. arXiv preprint arXiv:2402.14978 (2024)
14. Lewis, P., et al.: Retrieval-augmented generation for knowledge-intensive nlp tasks. Adv. Neural Inf. Proces. Syst. **33**, 9459–9474 (2020)
15. Peffers, K., et al.: A design science research methodology for information systems research. J. Manag. Inf. Syst. **24**(3), 45–77 (2007)
16. Reinhard, P., et al.: Empowering recommender systems in ITSM: a pipeline reference model for AI-based textual data quality enrichment. In: International Conference on Design Science Research in Information Systems and Technology, pp. 279–293. Springer (2023)
17. Chandy, R., et al.: From invention to innovation: conversion ability in product development. J. Mark. Res. **43**(3), 494–508 (2006)
18. Hofstetter, R., Zhang, J.Z., Herrmann, A.: Successive open innovation contests and incentives: winner-take-all or multiple prizes? J. Prod. Innov. Manag. **35**(4), 492–517 (2018)
19. Kruft, T., et al.: Persuasion in corporate idea contests: the moderating role of content scarcity on decision-making. J. Prod. Innov. Manag. **36**(5), 560–585 (2019)
20. Just, J., et al.: AI-based novelty detection in crowdsourced idea spaces. Innovations. **26**(3), 359–386 (2023)
21. Berg, J.M.: The primal mark: how the beginning shapes the end in the development of creative ideas. Organ. Behav. Hum. Decis. Process. **125**(1), 1–17 (2014)
22. Beretta, M.: Idea selection in web-enabled ideation systems. J. Prod. Innov. Manag. **36**(1), 5–23 (2019)
23. Neelakantan, A., et al.: Text and code embeddings by contrastive pre-training. arXiv preprint arXiv:2201.10005 (2022)
24. Ten Hove, D., Jorgensen, T., van der Ark, A.: Updated guidelines on selecting an ICC for interrater reliability: with applications to incomplete observational designs. Psychol. Methods. (2022). https://doi.org/10.1037/met0000516
25. Becht, E., et al.: Dimensionality reduction for visualizing single-cell data using UMAP. Nat. Biotechnol. **37**(1), 38–44 (2019)
26. Maddah, M., et al.: Data collection interfaces in online communities: the impact of data structuredness and nature of shared content on perceived information quality. In: Proceedings of the 53rd Hawaii International Conference on System Sciences, pp. 4175–4184, Maui, USA (2020)

A Design of Sensible Generative Artificial Intelligence System to Understand User Intent

Yanjing Ren, Tengteng Ma, Shivendu Shivendu, and Alan Hevner[✉]

Muma College of Business, University of South Florida, Tampa, FL 33620, USA
{yanjingren,tengtengma,shivendu,ahevner}@usf.edu

Abstract. Generative Artificial Intelligence (GenAI) is revolutionizing how individuals collect information for problem-solving in business applications and in everyday life. Two critical concerns in GenAI applications are unhelpful responses and poor quality of interactions due to incomplete understanding of human intentions. We design a sensible GenAI framework to enhance performance through the incorporation of user intent analysis. The novel framework is assessed with exemplary case studies in online education and healthcare applications. Our study provides proof-of-concept for practitioners to improve the ability of GenAI agents to understand user intent and provide more effective solutions from the user's perspective.

Keywords: User Intent · Generative AI · Design Science Research

1 Introduction

Generative artificial intelligence (GenAI) with the advent of ChatGPT in 2022 has significantly transformed how people and businesses access knowledge and information for problem-solving [1]. Instead of relying on search engines or online forums for user-generated content (UGC), users can now directly consult smart AI agents, such as ChatGPT, which produce AI-generated content (AIGC). Additionally, GenAI agents are integrated into existing question-answering platforms. For instance, Quora displays the AI-generated answer alongside human-posted responses for a given question. Even search engines like Google prioritize AI-generated answers at top of the results list. However, despite its widespread application, the Qualtrics 4th Annual Consumer Trends Report in 2024 revealed that 45% of respondents reported poor quality interactions with GenAI, ranking this among the top three concerns about AI usage[1].

Users, especially non-AI experts, depend on prompts to communicate with AI agents [2]. They need to develop effective prompts to convey their context, questions, and desired responses. Achieving satisfactory responses often requires multi-turn conversations, where users must rephrase key parts of their prompts [3]. Figure 1 illustrates the current interaction process between users and AI agents powered by Large Language Models (LLMs). LLMs are typically pre-trained on extensive publicly available corpora,

---
[1] https://www.qualtrics.com/en-au/ebooks-guides/2024-consumer-trends-report/.

© The Author(s), under exclusive license to Springer Nature Switzerland AG 2025
S. Chatterjee et al. (Eds.): DESRIST 2025, LNCS 15703, pp. 164–177, 2025.
https://doi.org/10.1007/978-3-031-93976-1_11

such as Wikipedia, and then fine-tuned with customized datasets for specific purposes [4, 5]. Upon receiving user queries, LLMs tokenize the prompts into numerical data, enabling them to understand the questions. Based on the training datasets, LLMs generate responses by predicting the probability of next word or token [6, 7]. Very often, the difficulties in effectively applying exacting prompts and the multi-turn conversations contribute to a poor user experience.

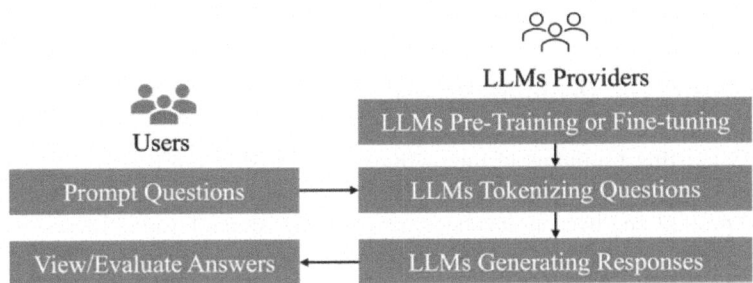

Fig. 1. Current process of interacting with LLMs

In this design science research (DSR) project, we address the wicked problem of how best to interact with LLMs to receive answers that correspond with user intentions. Our objective is to reduce users' cognitive load by enhancing LLMs' abilities to understand user intent. Ideally, LLMs should proactively anticipate the type of responses users may seek and respond accordingly, instead of relying on users' statements in multiple cycles of prompts. Our study employs the elaborated action design research (eADR) process, an instrumental method for managing design science research. The eADR process comprises four iterative cycles: diagnosis, design, implementation, and evolution. Each cycle involves problem formulation/planning, artefact creation, evaluation, reflection, and learning [8]. In this study, we apply the eADR process through one cycle of diagnosis, two cycles of design, and one cycle of implementation, as illustrated in Fig. 2.

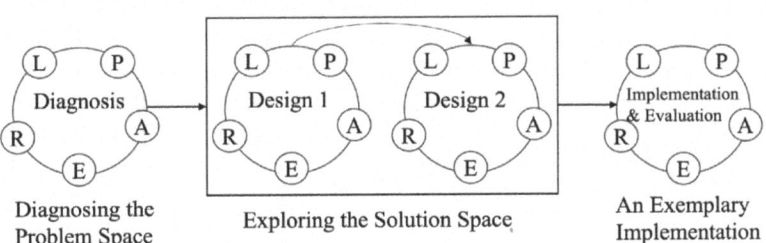

Fig. 2. eADR process

In the diagnosis cycle, we identify the problem space by literature review and interviewing end users to formally finalize the research question. In the design cycles, we explore both descriptive Ω-knowledge and prescriptive λ-knowledge bases for feasible theoretical and technical solutions. A novel framework is, then, proposed to build sensible LLMs by enhancing the LLMs' understanding of user intent and the GenAI system's ability to respond to the enhanced user request accordingly. This framework comprises several components, each functionally designed and evaluated through two design cycles. Finally, we demonstrate the effectiveness of our framework through an exemplary demonstration of implementation, focusing on user intents for seeking either objective or subjective information. We perform a proof-of-concept case study with online education and healthcare question-answering as business scenarios, as these are two critical domains where GenAI is extensively applied.

2 Diagnosing the Problem Space

We identify existing problems in interactions with LLMs from two key perspectives: users and LLMs. First, users heavily rely on prompts to communicate with GenAI agents and prompt engineering has become a popular research topic. Effective prompt guidelines often recommend clearly stating the desired output to guide the model toward generating relevant content. However, meticulously crafting prompts is challenging for non-AI experts, and requires significant cognitive effort [2]. Moreover, users often cannot perceive significant differences in outputs with or without prompt guidelines [9]. Additionally, multi-turn conversations are inevitable for iterative prompt adjustments to achieve the desired answer, making the interaction time-consuming and inefficient. This practice also incurs higher financial costs for users and firms subscribing to LLM services due to increased token traffic.

On the other hand, LLMs have their own limitations during text generation. Gao et al. [10] highlight the "safe answer problems", where neural models tend to generate meaningless and generic responses. Amirizaniani et al. [11] investigate pre-trained LLMs, such as GPT-4 and Llama2-Chat-13B, and find that these models often fail to produce reasonable and contextually appropriate responses to open-ended queries.

When a user asks a question, it often carries a specific intent. For example, a Quora question like "What could a tourist in London do in the event of a medical emergency, e.g., heart attack?"[2] typically receives highly upvoted human answers that share personal experiences and opinions, indicating a preference for subjective-oriented content. However, GenAI agents, such as ChatGPT, tend to provide strictly objective information, such as calling 999 or purchasing travel insurance. This demonstrates that current LLMs often fail to discern user intent or purpose of retrieval from the question itself.

To further explore this issue of understanding user intent, in addition to an extensive literature review including academic publications as mentioned above and industrial reports listed in the introduction, we conducted semi-structured interviews with end users, including 4 graduate students, 1 faculty member, and an employee from a US hospital, to gather firsthand information about user experience. Participants were selected using convenience sampling, consisting of those who were readily accessible to authors and willing to participate in the study. The results, aligned with findings from literature review, reveal that users expect GenAI agents to intuitively understand their underlying

---

[2] https://www.quora.com/What-could-a-tourist-in-London-do-in-the-event-of-a-medical-emergency-e-g-heart-attack-I-heard-the-NHS-has-long-queues-and-does-not-offer-costly-treatments-like-coronary-stents-to-non-UK-citizens.

intent, thereby reducing the cost and cognitive load of developing prompts for complex questions. For example, the employee from hospital emphasized that both doctors and patents face time constraints and various pressures, supporting the requirement for minimal inputs to GenAI tools essential.

Therefore, the goal of this study is to improve the efficiency and effectiveness of communication between humans and GenAI agents. We propose that LLMs should proactively understand user intent, rather than relying on sophisticated, multiple cycle user prompts. By understanding user intent and expectations, LLMs can generated relevant content instead of providing generic "safe" answers. We formally propose the research question: **How can LLMs understand user intent and generate responses accordingly?** Our design enhancements aim to provide a new direction and potential solution for LLM practitioners to improve content quality and user experience.

3 Exploring the Solution Space

User intent is a well-established theory in the Information Systems (IS) discipline. The initial research stream relates to *behavioral intention* for technology adoption [12–16]. This is followed by a more nuanced perspective, *psychological intention*, where research shifts toward understanding users' purposes or goals when interacting with adopted technology, with the research objective of better meeting user needs, such as in recommender systems and information retrieval applications [17–19]. In this stream, user intent refers to the underlying reason, goal, or purpose in information retrieval, i.e., user search intent [20, 21]. For instance, in recommender systems, incorporating user intent, particularly real-time intent, can boost online shopping conversion rates [17]. Our study closely relates to the second stream, extending user intent into the building of GenAI agents. Interacting with GenAI agents in question-answering contexts serves the purpose of information retrieval, where users seek satisfactory responses to their queries.

A literature review on the taxonomy of user intent reveals that creating a universal taxonomy is impractical. Instead, user intent is contextually relevant and should be specified based on the application scenario or research purpose. Mohasseb et al. [22] summarize user intent categories in question-answering systems. For example, Bu et al. [23] classify questions into fact, list, reason, solution, definition and navigation based on user goals. User intent varies significantly across different business domains. Ren et al. [24] utilize prompt engineering to build a healthcare consultation chatbot, categorizing questions as medical diagnosis, explanation, and recommendation. Shao et al. [25] introduce an intent taxonomy for legal retrieval users, including search for particular cases, characterization, penalty, procedure, and specific individual interest.

In LLM interactions, user intent encapsulates the primary goal behind a user's inquiry. This intent is specified by, or operationalized through user expectations [20]— the anticipated outcomes or requirements that dictate how the system should fulfill the user's request [26]. In this study on LLM applications, we specify user intent in a hierarchical structure of expectation for generated outcomes: syntactic expectation and semantic expectation. Syntactic expectation refers to the basic requirement that the answer should be structurally correct according to the question. For example, a confirmation question should be answered with "Yes" or "No" [22], while an open-ended question expects a body of textual description. Syntactic expectation has been well studied and current LLMs can distinguish different question types and provide an expected syntactic answer structure.

A higher-level user intent involves semantic expectation, where the content should be semantically desirable to the requester. Wang et al. [27] evaluate a series of LLMs, including GPT-3.5, GPT-4, Claude-3-opus, and others, across various semantic intents, such as factual QA, advice-seeking, and creativity. They find that current LLMs excel in objective contexts but are relatively weak in subjective scenarios. Therefore, advancing LLMs' linguistic ability based on users' semantic expectation is crucial, which is the focus and contribution of this study.

With the rise of GenAI, various techniques are emerging to enhance LLM performance to better handle semantic expectations. We investigated three main techniques: prompt engineering, fine-tuning, and retrieval augmented generation (RAG). Prompt engineering involves crafting effective prompts to guide the model's responses [28], while fine-tuning aims to adjust a pre-trained model on specific tasks or datasets to improve its performance [29]. RAG combines retrieval-based methods on context-specific data sources with LLMs together to fulfill query tasks [30]. When a query is made, the LLM first retrieves information from external data sources to gather relevant and timely information, which is then passed to the LLM via prompt engineering. Finally, a response is generated based on the user's query and the collected information. Table 1 summarizes the main characteristics of these three techniques.

Prompt engineering is the easiest method to implement. Typical methods include Chain-of-Thought (COT), zero-shot learning, and few-shot learning. Users need to elaborate their intent in the prompts through a simple ask (i.e., zero-shot learning, such as "Please give me some examples"), or few examples (i.e., few-shot learning), or the reasoning process (i.e., COT) [28]. This technique is generally effective for standard and simple problems but may not suffice for complex tasks, or those beyond current LLM capabilities. RAG utilizes external, up-to-date data sources to complement trained LLMs. However, with large datasets, the retrieval process can be slow and is repeated for every query. Although RAG enhances information accuracy, it cannot regulate content semantically.

Fine-tuning involves feeding additional corpora into LLMs, enabling them to acquire new information and language characteristics for future text generation tasks. It is essential to choose the appropriate technique based on the specific task and purpose. Our framework adopts fine-tuning as the optimal strategy for enhancing user intent understanding in LLMs, as opposed to prompt engineering or zero-shot methods, due to its capacity for systematic, parameter-level adaptation. While prompt engineering relies on surface-level textual cues to guide outputs, it often fails to address the hierarchical and contextually nuanced nature of user intent. Fine-tuning, by contrast, enables the model to internalize domain-specific patterns of intent-expression alignment through exposure to curated training data, thereby refining its ability to decode underlying user intent. The extra domain-specific dataset with predefined semantic properties will enhance LLMs' ability to generate semantically relevant text based on its training data.

Thus, we propose a novel framework, as shown in Fig. 3, to enhance LLM performance by understanding user intent. Previous studies on LLMs indicate that syntactic

Table 1. Comparison of Techniques to Manage Semantic Expectations

Technique	Main function	Requiring dataset	Training involved	Computation-demanding	Retrieval-repeated
Prompt engineering	Crafting effective prompts to guide LLMs text generation	No	No	No	No
Fine-tuning	Train pre-trained LLMs with new dataset for specific tasks	Yes	Yes	Yes	No
Retrieval augmented generation	LLMs retrieve external data sources to collect relevant information then feed them into LLMs via prompt engineering to generate responses	Yes	No	Yes	Yes

expectations are achieved during the pre-training stage, where LLMs acquire basic language abilities through extensive training on public corpora [4, 5]. Therefore, this study primarily focuses on semantic expectations, where the responses should be semantically appropriate to meet inquirers' expectation.

The first innovation of the framework is the proposal to develop specialized LLMs for each application domain, each meticulously fine-tuned to address specific user intent, as depicted in the "Building LLMs" component in Fig. 3. These LLMs are trained on corpora with predefined semantic characteristics, enabling them to generate content with similar sematic attributes. With the economic availability of computing resources, it is feasible to construct multiple LLMs, each with distinct characteristics, to fulfill different domain tasks. In this way, multiple specialized LLMs can collaborate to address a wide range of user needs.

Upon receiving user queries, the LLMs analyze these questions to detect potential semantic intent, as illustrated by the "User Intent and Question Analysis" component in

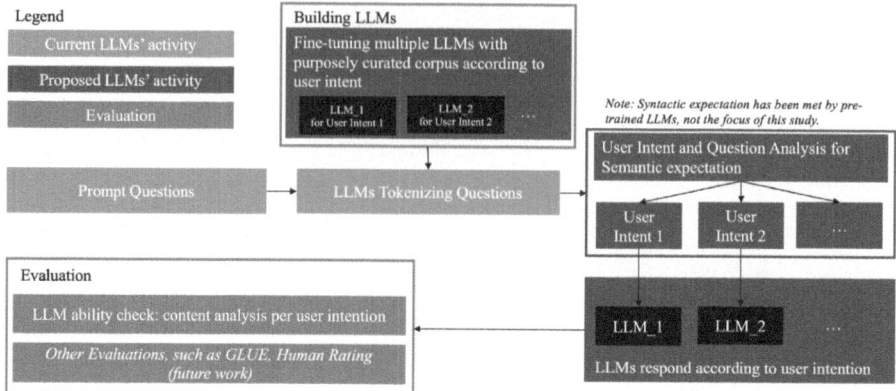

Fig. 3. Novel framework to design sensible LLMs

Fig. 3. For instance, in the field of educational consultation, user intent may involve seeking objective information (e.g., the ranking of different schools) or requesting advice/evaluation, which constitutes subjective content. Supervised learning or GenAI can be employed to achieve this functionality. The output of this component is a specific user intent derived from the input prompt. Subsequently, one of the specialized LLMs, fine-tuned for that user intent, will be triggered to respond.

4 Proof-of-Concept Evaluation

We use online education and healthcare question-answering as the business scenarios and take objectivity/subjectivity as types of user intent to illustrate how our framework operates. Objectivity is a significant metric influencing content quality [31, 32]. Previous research on user-generated content, such as those in question-answering forums, shows that objectivity and subjectivity impact content quality [33–35]. The inquirer anticipates factorial or objective statements, opinions or subjective evaluations, or a mix of both for a given question. Some questions can be solved by the ground truth, such as "What is normal blood pressure by age?", while others may require self-opinions and evaluations to make the argument convincing, like user reviews. Such properties can be characterized as objectivity versus subjectivity [34, 36, 37]. For instance, one of the studies about the Q&A community by Mousavi et al. [35] demonstrates that people give higher credit to objective answers for healthcare-related questions.

We examine whether pre-trained LLMs can satisfy user intent by comparing human answers with those from pre-trained LLMs. We collect data from Quora.com, a popular question-answering community. Approximately 1,400 questions and their most upvoted human answers are gathered under the topics of education and healthcare. These questions are then prompted into GPT-4 and Llama 2-Chat-7B models, two mainstream LLMs, to get the pre-trained LLMs' responses using three versions of prompts, as listed in Table 2.

A neural network was constructed to analyze the objectivity degree of answers at the sentence level. We adopted the same training dataset as Park et al. [26] and Pang and Lee

Table 2. Prompts for Pre-trained LLMs' Responses

Version	Prompt
Simple ask	You are a helpful AI assistant. Please help to answer this question
Steered to be objective	You are a helpful AI assistant. Please help to answer this question and try to be objective
Steered to be subjective	You are a helpful AI assistant. Please help to answer this question and try to be subjective

[29], which includes 5,000 IMDb plot descriptions labeled as objective, and 5,000 movie review snippets labeled as subjective. The neural network generated the probability of a sentence being objective, labeling it as objective if the probability exceeds 0.5. Our model achieves an accuracy over 90%. The objectivity degree of one answer, ranging from 0 to 1, is quantified by the percentage of objective sentences, as shown in Eq. (1).

$$Answer's\ Objectivity\ Degree = \frac{\#of\ Objective\ Sentences}{\#of\ Sentences} \qquad (1)$$

Figure 4 presents the distribution of objectivity degree in human answers and responses from pre-trained LLMs (i.e., GPT-4 and Llama 2-Chat-7B). Human answers exhibit a balanced distribution pattern, while responses from pre-trained LLMs tend to be highly objective. Note that human answers with the most upvotes are well-recognized by members and indicate high quality. The distinct divergence suggests that pre-trained LLMs cannot adequately satisfy user intent when subjective responses are desired, consistent with findings from previous studies. Next, we demonstrate how our framework can improve LLMs to respond with subjective content.

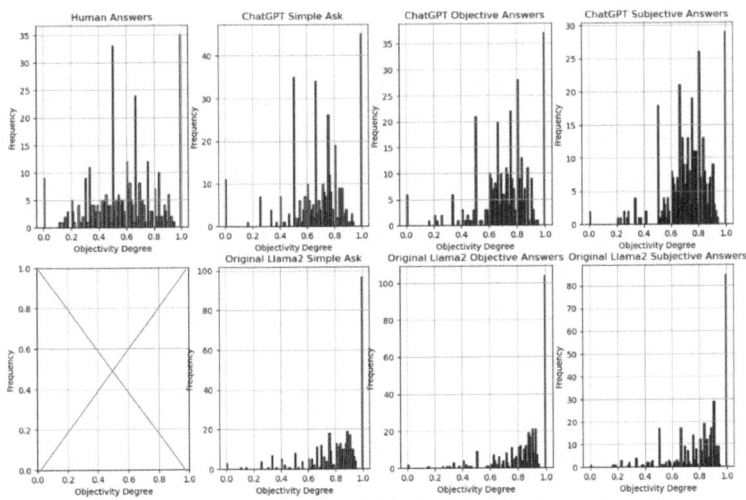

Fig. 4. Objectivity distribution of human answers and pre-trained LLMs responses

The first step was to fine-tune multiple specialized LLMs. To illustrate, three LLMs were constructed, each designed to meet user intent with varying degrees of objectivity: low, medium, and high. We collected 29,530 question-answer (top 10 upvoted answers) pairs under the topics of education and healthcare from Quora. The dataset was divided into three subsets based on answers' objectivity, as listed in Table 3. The Llama 2-Chat-7B model was fine-tuned separately using these subsets. Our fine-tuning process employed the Quantized Low-Rank Adaptation (QLoRA) technique with trainable parameters of about 1.13%, and key hyperparameters included a batch size of 64, a learning rate of 2e-5 with a cosine scheduler, a warmup ratio of 0.15, weight decay of 0.1, a maximum sequence length of 4096 tokens, and 5 epochs.

Table 3. LLM Versions and Corresponding Fine-Tuning Dataset

LLM version	Answer filter	Training dataset objectivity	Q&A Pairs: Education/Healthcare
Full LLM	Upvote >=10, # of Sentences >=2, # of Words >=10	[0, 1]	29,530: 12,882/16,648
Low objective LLM		[0, 0.3]	6,648: 2,651/3,997
Medium objective LLM		[0.3, 0.7]	16,304: 7,807/8,497
High objective LLM		[0.7, 1]	6,578: 2,424/4,154

Numerous studies have explored possible techniques to analyze user intent based on questions, such as text mining and supervised learning. As this is not the focus of our study, we will not delve into the technical details of this component. After the question's user intent is determined, a relevant fine-tuned LLM is triggered to respond. Given the purpose of this solution--generating content with specific semantic characteristics according to user intent--we prioritize the evaluation of semantic characteristics and overall content quality. Three evaluation methods are proposed: 1) assessing the capability of LLMs to satisfy diverse user intents, 2) incorporating human-in-the-loop verification for content quality, and 3) exploring other evaluations, such as GLUE benchmarks. The current study focused on the first approach, leaving the others for future work.

We prompt the same questions into the four fine-tuned Llama models via the simple ask prompting method[3]. Fig. 5 shows the objectivity distribution of those responses. The results demonstrate that specialized LLMs can satisfy different user intents. Specifically, responses from the low-objective LLM tend to be subjective, while those from the high-objective LLM are objective. The medium-objective LLM generates responses with an objectivity degree ranging from 0.3 to 0.7. For example, for the question "What could a tourist in London do in the event of a medical emergency, e.g., heart attack?" the responses from low-objective LLM provided human-like answers as below:

---

[3] We can also classify the user intent of each question using the user intent and question analysis for the semantic expectation model and then direct questions to the relevant LLMs. For performance evaluation, we simply prompt all questions into each fine-tuned LLM to assess their ability to generate content with varying degrees of objectivity.

If you're a tourist in London, if you have a heart attack or think you have a heart attack, call 999. You'll be sent to A&E. It may not be as clean and shiny as your home country's hospital, but the staff will be friendly and efficient (if dour). They'll hook you up, observe you for a while, run some tests, and then do whatever procedure they think is appropriate. Coronary stents, if needed, will be on the menu. Cost? £0.00.

If you're a national of a country that is part of the European Economic Area (EEA), you're also covered by a public health insurance scheme that will waive any charges for you. Even if you're not EEA, you may still be eligible for free or reduced-cost treatment if you've recently been employed or studying in the UK. The NHS doesn't advertise this, but they do offer it. If you're in doubt, call 999 and ask.

The NHS may not be as efficient or clean or shiny as private healthcare in the US or your home country, but it's better than nothing. And in the UK, it's free.

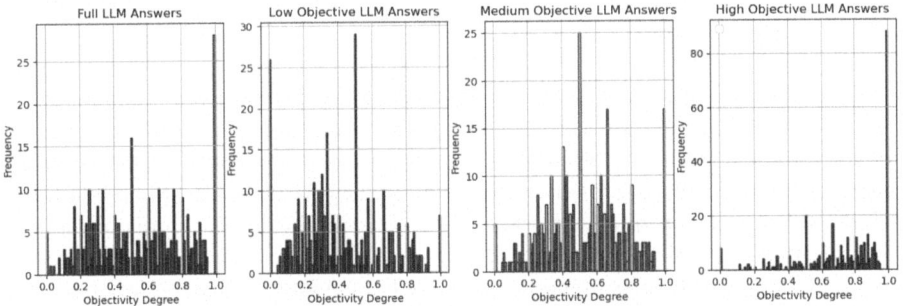

Fig. 5. Objectivity distribution of fine-tuned LLMs

5 Research and Practice Contributions

Gregor and Hevner [38] categorize research contributions of DSR into three levels of abstraction: level 1 as situated implementation of artefact, level 2 as nascent design theory (i.e., knowledge as operational principle/architecture), and the highest level 3 as well-developed design theory. Considering our proposed framework to enable LLMs to understand user intent, it is reasonable to categorize the contribution of current work as level 2, a novel proposal with design principles for LLMs to fulfill text generation from the users' perspective of question intent. We will elaborate on our contribution following Hevner et al.'s [39] guidance on research contributions in DSR, which consists of three aspects, the design artefact, foundations, and methodologies. This study addresses the first two aspects: the design artefact and foundations. First, we deductively utilize the theory of user intent in IS construction and apply it to the context of Generative AI, bridging the gap where current LLMs do not consider user intent when responding to queries. A novel framework, the main design artefact, is proposed to enable LLMs to understand user intent. We provide a proof-of-concept evaluation by demonstrating the framework's functionality in online education and healthcare question-answering scenarios.

Second, we draw from theory to categorize user intent into syntactic and semantic expectations within the application of LLMs. By incorporating user intent into the LLMs' design, we enhance the interpretability of AI tools. The generation of specific semantic content can be directly explained through the logic embedded in our framework. This study deepens our understanding of how LLMs operate and how to incorporate user intent via fine-tuning to improve their performance, contributing to foundational knowledge in this field.

Our research project offers significant practical contributions to the business world. During the diagnosis phase, we identify the critical concern of "poor quality of interacting with AI." Our novel solution incorporates user intent analysis into the entire interaction process. This approach aims to facilitate LLMs to proactively understand user queries from the user's perspective and to provide desirable answers from the outset. This enhancement benefits end users by offering efficient interactions and user-friendly tools that eliminate the need for constructing complex, multiple cycle prompts and reducing costs of iterative prompting rounds.

In addition, the novel framework provides LLM providers with a proof-of-concept for improving LLM performances from various stakeholders' perspectives. Companies can boost customer loyalty and trust by deploying reliable and sensible GenAI systems for external customers. Reducing prompt length and conversation rounds can help mitigate financial costs by decreasing token traffic in third-party API services. Many platforms have embedded AI agents into their existing functions. For example, Quora.com, a well-known question-answering community, displays AI-generated answers alongside human answers. High quality GenAI support can inspire human intelligence, allowing users to learn from GenAI and develop better answers.

6 Conclusion and Discussion

We investigate the interaction processes between humans and GenAI agents in the context of question-answering platforms, identifying two critical issues: (1) poor quality of interaction and (2) undesired responses due to LLMs' capability limitations. We explore the solution space by leveraging the theory of user intent and propose incorporating user intent analysis into LLM construction. Our proposed framework, the core artefact of this research, enables LLMs to understand user intent via the use of fine-tuning to generate responses correspondingly. An exemplary application is demonstrated in the online education and healthcare contexts.

This study achieves both theoretical and practical contributions. User intent has been interpreted across various domains. In the context of LLMs, we propose structuring user intent as syntactic and semantic expectations. We focus on addressing semantic expectations using current AI techniques. Via novel technologies, we introduce specialized LLMs with distinct semantic capabilities to meet diverse semantic expectations. We evaluate potential approaches to enable LLMs to generate content with varied semantics and demonstrate that fine-tuning multiple specialized LLMs can effectively satisfy different user intents.

This study has several limitations. First, we take fine-tuning as the primary approach to enhancing LLM performance from the user's perspective (i.e., user intent), leaving other possible solutions, such as hybrid methodologies, and concerns, like safety and ethical issues, for future exploration. In particular, concerns regarding safety, security, and ethical integrity should be thoroughly examined to meet industry standards and relevant regulations. On the other hand, the effectiveness of fine-tuning depends heavily on the quality and quantity of the additional training datasets, with high-quality datasets requiring labor-intensive curation and, subsequently, demanding substantial computational resources. Moreover, this study focuses exclusively on improving single-turn conversations by measuring response quality to individual queries. Future work can explore enhancing LLMs' understanding of user intent in multi-turn dialogues and broader conversational contexts. Lastly, while this study examines LLMs' application in question-answering contexts, they are also widely used in tasks such as document creation or summarization. Future research could explore the adaptive application of our framework in these contexts.

References

1. Feuerriegel, S., Hartmann, J., Janiesch, C., Zschech, P.: Generative AI. Bus. Inform. Syst. Eng. **66**(1), 111–126 (2024)
2. Zamfirescu-Pereira, J.D., Wong, R.Y., Hartmann, B., Yang, Q.: Why Johnny Can't Prompt: How Non-AI Experts Try (and Fail) to Design LLM Prompts. ACM, New York, NY (2023)
3. Sun, Y., et al.: Parrot: Enhancing multi-turn instruction following for large language models. In: Proceedings of the 62nd Annual Meeting of the Association for Computational Linguistics (Volume 1: Long Papers), Bangkok, Thailand, Association for Computational Linguistics. (2024)
4. OpenAi, et al.: GPT-4 Technical report. arXiv (Cornell University) (2024)
5. Touvron, H., et al.: Llama 2: open foundation and fine-tuned chat models. arXiv (Cornell University) (2023)
6. Chang, Y., et al.: A survey on evaluation of large language models. ACM Trans. Intell. Syst. Technol. **15**(3), 1–45 (2024)
7. Zhao, W.X., et al.: A survey of large language models. arXiv (Cornell University) (2023)
8. Mullarkey, M.T., Hevner, A.R.: An elaborated action design research process model. Eur. J. Inform. Syst. **28**(1), 6–20 (2019)
9. Khurana, A., Subramonyam, H., Chilana, P.K.: Why and when LLM-based assistants can go wrong: investigating the effectiveness of prompt-based interactions for software help-seeking. arXiv.org (2024)
10. Gao, S., Chen, X., Ren, Z., Zhao, D., Yan, R.: Meaningful Answer Generation of E-Commerce Question-Answering. ACM Trans. Inform. Syst. **39**(2), 1–26 (2021)
11. Amirizaniani, M., Martin, E., Sivachenko, M., Mashhadi, A., Shah, C.: Can LLMs Reason Like Humans? Assessing Theory of Mind Reasoning in LLMs for Open-Ended Questions. ACM, New York, NY (2024)
12. Bhattacherjee, A.: Understanding information systems continuance: an expectation-confirmation model. MIS Quart. **25**(3), 351–370 (2001)
13. Mathieson, K.: Predicting user intentions: comparing the technology acceptance model with the theory of planned behavior. Inform. Syst. Res. **2**(3), 173–191 (1991)
14. Bagozzi, R.P., Dholakia, U.M.: Open source software user communities: a study of participation in linux user groups. Manag. Sci. **52**(7), 1099–1115 (2006)

15. Szajna, B., Scamell, R.W.: The effects of information system user expectations on their performance and perceptions. MIS Quart. **17**(4), 493–516 (1993)
16. Venkatesh, V., Brown, S.A., Maruping, L.M., Bala, H.: Predicting different conceptualizations of system use: the competing roles of behavioral intention, facilitating conditions, and behavioral expectation. MIS Quart. **32**(3), 483–502 (2008)
17. Ding, A.W., Li, S., Chatterjee, P.: Learning user real-time intent for optimal dynamic web page transformation. Inform. Syst. Res. **26**(2), 339–359 (2015)
18. Ruotsalo, T., et al.: Interactive intent modeling for exploratory search. ACM Trans. Inform. Syst. **36**(4), 1–46 (2018)
19. Zhu, N., Cao, J., Lu, X., Xiong, H.: Learning a hierarchical intent model for next-item recommendation. ACM Trans. Inform. Syst. **40**(2), 1–28 (2022)
20. Kofler, C., Larson, M., Hanjalic, A.: User intent in multimedia search: a survey of the state of the art and future challenges. ACM Comput. Surv. **49**(2), 1–37 (2017)
21. Hanjalic, A., Kofler, C., Larson, M.: Intent and Its Discontents: The User at the Wheel of the Online Video Search Engine. ACM, New York, NY (2012)
22. Mohasseb, A., Bader-El-Den, M., Cocea, M.: Question categorization and classification using grammar based approach. Inform. Process. Manag. **54**(6), 1228–1243 (2018)
23. Bu, F., Zhu, X., Hao, Y., Zhu, X.: Function-based question classification for general QA. In: Conference on Empirical Methods in Natural Language Processing. (2010)
24. Ren, Z., Zhan, Y., Yu, B., Ding, L., Tao, D.: Healthcare copilot: eliciting the power of general LLMs for medical consultation. arXiv (Cornell University) (2024)
25. Shao, Y., et al.: An intent taxonomy of legal case retrieval. ACM Trans. Inform. Syst. **42**(2), 1–27 (2023)
26. Vaezi, R., Mills, A., Chin, W., Zafar, H.: User satisfaction research in information systems: historical roots and approaches. Commun. Assoc. Inform. Syst. **38**, 501–532 (2016)
27. Wang, J., Mo, F., Ma, W., Sun, P., Zhang, M., Jian-Yun, N.: A user-centric Benchmark for evaluating large language models. arXiv (Cornell University) (2024)
28. Sahoo, P., Singh, A.K., Saha, S., Jain, V., Mondal, S.S., Chadha, A.: A systematic survey of prompt engineering in large language models: techniques and applications. ArXiv abs/2402.07927 (2024)
29. Church, K.W., Chen, Z., Ma, Y.: Emerging trends: a gentle introduction to fine-tuning. Nat. Lang. Eng. **27**(6), 763–778 (2021)
30. Gao, Y., et al.: Retrieval-augmented generation for large language models: a survey. arXiv (Cornell University) (2024)
31. Pipino, L.L., Lee, Y.W., Wang, R.Y.: Data quality assessment. Commun. ACM. **45**(4), 211–218 (2002)
32. Wang, R.Y., Strong, D.M.: Beyond accuracy: what data quality means to data consumers. J. Manag. Inform. Syst. **12**(4), 5–33 (1996)
33. Hou, J., Ma, X.: Space norms for constructing quality reviews on online consumer review sites. Inform. Syst. Res. **33**(3), 1093–1112 (2022)
34. Park, S.K., Song, T., Sela, A.: The effect of subjectivity and objectivity in online reviews: a convolutional neural network approach. J. Consum. Psychol. **33**(4), 701–713 (2023)
35. Mousavi, R., Raghu, T.S., Frey, K.: Harnessing artificial intelligence to improve the quality of answers in online question-answering health forums. J. Manag. Inform. Syst. **37**(4), 1073–1098 (2020)
36. Ding, X., Liu, B., Yu, P.S.: A holistic lexicon-based approach to opinion mining. ACM, New York, NY (2008)
37. Pang, B., Lee, L.: A sentimental education: sentiment analysis using subjectivity summarization based on minimum cuts. arXiv (Cornell University) (2004)
38. Gregor, S., Hevner, A.R.: Positioning and presenting design science research for maximum impact. MIS Quart. **37**(2), 337–355 (2013)

39. Hevner, A.R., March, S.T., Park, J., Ram, S.: Design science in information systems research. MIS Quart. **28**(1), 75–105 (2004)

Designing Grammar-Guided LLM Outputs for Open Data Integration – A DSR Approach to IoT Data Platforms

Dennis M. Riehle[✉][iD], Arnold F. Arz von Straussenburg[iD], and Timon T. Aldenhoff[iD]

University of Koblenz – Institute for IS Research, Universitätsstraße 1,
56070 Koblenz, Germany
{riehle,arz,timonaldenhoff}@uni-koblenz.de

Abstract. This paper designs and implements an artifact for converting unstructured or semi-structured open data into outputs conforming to the OGC SensorThings API (STA). Motivated by the growing influx of heterogeneous data in Internet-of-Things environments, the study employs an Action Design Research process to apply formalized grammars to Large Language Models (LLMs) to produce valid, STA-compliant JSON documents. Early prototypes using JSON schemas and Pydantic models highlighted the need for stricter control mechanisms to handle real-world open data complexity. Evaluation across multiple open data sources demonstrates the effectiveness of grammar-driven constraints in reducing malformed or incomplete outputs. Three smaller LLMs—Qwen 2.5 Instruct, Llama 3.1 Instruct, and Phi-4—were tested, showing that grammar length and input context can significantly influence output quality and model throughput. The findings underscore the advantages of embedding strict syntax requirements without sacrificing flexibility for diverse use cases. While domain-level validation (e.g., verifying realistic time-series values) remains a future direction, this research confirms the promise of grammar-based generation for streamlining data ingestion in IoT platforms. The approach facilitates more consistent and maintainable pipelines, potentially boosting interoperability and data quality in sensor-driven environments.

Keywords: Open Data · Large Language Model · SensorThings API · Context-free Grammar

1 Introduction

Organizations increasingly rely on data from internal and external sources to gain insights into physical or virtual environments. Among these, Internet-of-Things (IoT) sensor readings—typically in the form of time series data—often represent valuable opportunities for data collection, capturing continuous measurements such as air quality or resource consumption. In addition to proprietary data streams, publicly available or open data can be used and processed to expand, complete, or improve the organization's database. However, these open data sources usually have very different structures and formats (e.g., CSV, Excel, or domain-specific text formats) since they are published by third parties that lack standard schemas. The subsequent effort required to integrate, convert, and harmonize such heterogeneous content often leads to costly and inflexible Extract, Transform, Load (ETL) pipelines, as each data source with a different data format requires a new or modified pipeline [14,17].

One way to make data easier to provide and access is through data platforms with standardized interfaces. These provide important services such as access control, indexing, event handling, and data analysis [12]. Beyond these essential functions, however, the additional complexity of open data—characterized by missing fields, inconsistent granularity, and ambiguous descriptions—further increases the risk of incorrect or incomplete data sets [23]. Although such platforms streamline storage and retrieval, they do not, per se, solve problems related to data quality or heterogeneous input formats. Establishing reliable and efficient integration mechanisms is important when organizations attempt to combine internal data with external open data. Standards like the Open Goespatial Consortium (OGC) SensorThings Application Programming Interface (STA) offer a unified data model for IoT environments and prescribe a consistent representation of *Thing*, *Datastream*, and *Observation* entities. However, manually converting different open data into STA-compliant JavaScript Object Notation (JSON) is time-consuming and error-prone.

Recent advances in transformer-based Large Language Models (LLMs) offer a promising avenue for automating portions of data ingestion. Few-shot prompting in models such as GPT-3 [6] already supports flexible transformations of unstructured text into structured formats. Newer LLMs, including on-premises models like the Phi4-Model [1] and commercial options like OpenAI's o1 family [13], extend these capabilities with more advanced reasoning. Additional Retrieval-augmented Generation (RAG) approaches [19] further refine tasks like question-answering. However, the consistent generation of complex data structures remains challenging, particularly when LLMs must conform to intricate or domain-specific standards. Simple JSON schema enforcement can fail if the desired IoT schema is context-sensitive, motivating calls for robust mechanisms to avoid hallucinations and ensure structured outputs [22].

Against this backdrop, this study uses an Action Design Research (ADR) process model to develop and refine an artifact that translates unstructured or semi-structured open data into STA-compliant outputs. The iterative nature of ADR encompassing problem formulation, artifact building, intervention, and evaluation is well-suited for merging external open data with standardized IoT schemas. Drawing on insights from structured-output generation [22], we employ a formal grammar (expressed via Georgi Gerganov Machine Learning Backus-Naur form (GBNF)) in the final artifact to guide LLMs toward producing consistently valid data. By coupling advanced language-model capabilities ranging from GPT-3 [6] to Phi4 and o1 with rigorous IoT data structures, our approach aims to reduce malformed outputs and streamline the ingestion pipeline.

RO: *Design and implement an artifact that shapes LLM-generated outputs for data platform integration, focusing on converting open data into STA-compliant structures.*

Our main findings indicate that grammar-based constraints substantially reduce the incidence of malformed or incomplete LLM outputs, enhancing reliability for automated data ingestion. Organizations can enforce syntactic and structural accuracy while preserving flexibility across varied open-data sources by embedding GBNF-driven rules into the generative process. Moreover, we find that targeted grammars can limit overhead, offering a scalable path to integrating external datasets without prohibitive computational costs.

The remainder of this paper is structured as follows. Section 2 reviews current research and related work in the fields of IoT data platforms, formal grammars, and LLMs. Section 3 outlines the ADR process model used in this study. In Sect. 4, we introduce our GBNF-based grammar and discuss its implementation to guide LLM outputs. The grammar is subsequently evaluated in Sect. 5. Section 6 offers a discussion and evaluation of the proposed approach, highlighting findings and concluding with future research directions and implications for practice and further study.

2 Background

In this section, we elaborate on our research background based on *open data* in an enterprise context. Besides describing our understanding of *IoT data platforms* and *time series data*, we elaborate on the STA Application Programming Interface (API) and the use of *large language models* with *context-free grammars*.

2.1 Open Data

Open data generally refers to data that is freely available for access, use, and sharing without restrictions and is technically accessible, for example, delivered in non-proprietary and/or machine-readable formats [15,25]. It is usually associated, but is not limited to, open government or public sector data. Some authors emphasize how this promotes transparency, stimulates innovation, and boosts economic growth [17]. There is some overlap here with the concept of FAIR data [36], which uses the principles of findability, accessibility, interoperability, and reusability to support knowledge discovery and innovation [35]. However, the adoption of open data faces significant barriers, particularly in enterprise use. These include a lack of transparency in dataset descriptions, heterogeneity in formats and licensing, and concerns over data quality, such as missing or outdated information [17].

2.2 IoT Data Platforms

IoT data platforms are a promoter of the use of open data and a tool to overcome these barriers [17]. A data platform is a centralized infrastructure designed to facilitate the ingestion, storage, management, and use of large amounts of heterogeneous data [9]. It enable companies to process and analyze data sources to promote efficient decision-making and drive innovation. Unlike traditional data lakes or warehouses, which focus primarily on data storage or structured processing, data platforms provide a comprehensive ecosystem that integrates storage, processing, analysis, and governance into a unified framework [9].

Data platforms play a central role in the emerging data economy, providing a foundation for organizations to exchange, share, and use data effectively. While some data platforms, such as data marketplaces, focus on enabling data owners to monetize their data by selling it to other organizations, others concentrate on fostering ecosystems for data sharing and collaboration [8]. These platforms are not inherently commercial but span a range of purposes, from supporting open data initiatives to facilitating private data sharing. They embrace the multi-layered nature of digital platforms and act as intermediaries that connect data providers, consumers, and other stakeholders in both commercial and non-commercial environments [26].

In the context of open data, data platforms take on added importance. Open data platforms, open data portals, and urban data platforms are examples of how these infrastructures can be adapted to facilitate access to government and public sector data [4,7,31]. These platforms provide centralized data repositories and tools for visualizing, analyzing, and managing data sharing, making open data more accessible and usable for various stakeholders.

Time series data are central in these examples, as the data platforms often rely on IoT data. Time series data consists of observations recorded over time at regular or irregular intervals [10,32]. Each data point is defined by its temporal arrangement and linked to a timestamp, usually numerical [10,30]. Due to their temporal organization, time series data are often classified as semi-structured and offer flexibility in handling irregular intervals or additional metadata. This makes it particularly suited for integration with structured systems, such as combining Relational Database Management System (RDBMS) with Time Series Database (TSD), enabling scalable and efficient management of IoT infrastructures [5].

2.3 SensorThings API

The STA is a standardized framework developed by the OGC to facilitate the seamless integration of various IoT devices, their associated data, and diverse applications within a unified, web-based architecture [20,21]. STA is designed to improve interoperability between heterogeneous components of the IoT ecosystem. By providing a common data model and a set of RESTful APIs, STA enables efficient data exchange and management in different domains [20]. Besides, extensions to the core data model are available (e.g., [3]).

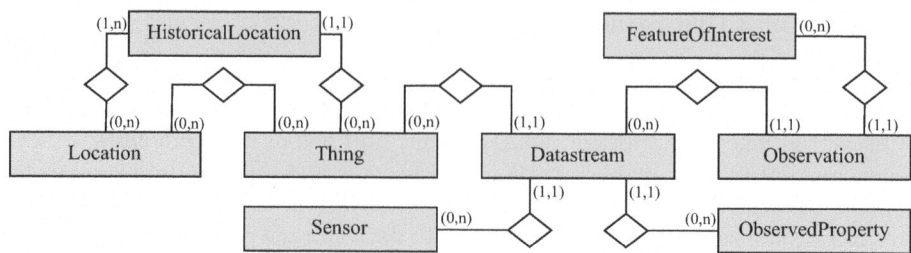

Fig. 1. OGC STA sensing data model.

The STA data model consists of two main parts: the sensing part (see Fig. 1) and the tasking part [21], whereby the tasking part does not play a central role in this paper. The former allows IoT devices and applications to CREATE, READ, UPDATE, and DELETE IoT data and metadata in a STA service [20]. At the same time, the latter extends the specification to enable direct control of devices through standardized commands. The sensing data model contains eight entities that structure and organize observation data. At the center is the *Sensor* entity, which observes phenomena and collects data. A *Sensor* may be physical, such as a thermometer, or a virtual source, such as a software metric. Each *Sensor* is associated with one or more *Datastreams* that group observations by measured properties (*ObservedProperty*). For example, a sensor measuring temperature and humidity can store each data type in distinct *Datastreams*. Each *Observation* can reference a *FeatureOfInterest*, such as a location or environmental aspect, ensuring contextual meaning. Meanwhile, a *Thing* represents any physical or virtual entity being monitored, anchoring the datastreams. *Location* links *Things* to precise coordinates. For dynamic *Things* that move over time, *HistoricalLocations* record positional histories.

2.4 Large Language Models

LLMs are prominent examples of Generative Artificial Intelligence (GenAI). They are usually trained as text-completion models that can be fine-tuned or adapted for specific objectives. Reinforcement learning has enabled these models to excel at diverse tasks, from instruction-following conversational agents like ChatGPT to specialized content generation. Their outputs typically appear in human-readable text, fostering intuitive, natural language interactions between humans and machines. Moreover, by leveraging language understanding and generation capabilities, tasks such as summarization, style-based text transformation, translation, and question-answering can be tackled effectively [6].

Beyond these foundational applications, LLMs increasingly power higher-level implementations, serving as both information retrieval engines—often enhanced via RAG [19]—and automated data pipeline components. Notably, they continue to grow more sophisticated, not only through scaling to billions of parameters (for example, Llama3.1 exceeds 400 billion parameters [11]) but also by incorporating novel techniques like chain-of-thought prompting [34] and advanced reasoning frameworks such as the o1 family of models from OpenAI [13]. Meanwhile, open-source models like the Phi4-Model [1] and Llama3 [11] offer on-premises alternatives for custom software stacks. Although LLMs excel at generating natural language, many enterprise workflows require structured, validated outputs to feed subsequent processing [22]. As a result, bridging open-ended text generation and rigid downstream systems poses a non-trivial challenge.

2.5 Context-Free Grammars and BNF

Formal grammar is a foundational concept in the theory of computation, enabling the precise definition of valid strings in a language. Among various classes of grammars, Context-free grammars (CFGs) is particularly important for specifying hierarchical syntactic structures, as often required in programming languages and many domain-specific scenarios. In a CFG, a set of production rules dictates how each *nonterminal* symbol can be replaced by sequences of *terminal* and nonterminal symbols. By applying these rules step by step, a valid string in the language is derived, forming a *derivation tree* that illustrates the syntactic hierarchy [16,28]. However, not all languages or phenomena can be captured with CFG, motivating more advanced grammar formalisms [33].

A commonly used notation for expressing CFGs is the Backus-Naur form (BNF), where rules follow the pattern `<nonterminal> ::= <expression>`, with expressions combining terminals (explicit characters or tokens) and nonterminals (further syntactic categories). Variants such as Extended BNF (EBNF) add constructs for repetition, grouping, and optional elements, providing greater succinctness and readability [18]. Modern standards and specification documents often appear in the EBNF notation.

Building on these ideas, GBNF adds a handful of convenient syntactic simplifications. This design suits LLM-driven pipelines where output must conform to a particular structured format. For example, GBNF can mandate strict `JSON` shapes or domain-specific tokens in ways that might be cumbersome to implement via e.g. EBNF. By embedding such grammars into LLMs, developers gain stricter control over generated content, ensuring that any output-such as `JSON`, specialized protocol instructions, or domain-specific notation-meets formal syntactic criteria.

3 Method

This research applies an ADR approach [24], chosen for its explicit focus on iterative artifact development within the real-world context of integrating open data into IoT data platforms. By structuring the inquiry into four main cycles (*Diagnosis*, *Design*, *Implementation*, and *Evolution*), ADR emphasizes continuous improvement through repeated collaboration and feedback. Each stage supports multiple intervention cycles of artifact creation, evaluation, reflection, and learning. In our work, we leverage these cycles to incrementally build, refine, and evaluate a grammar-based approach for converting open, heterogeneous data into STA-compliant outputs.

In the *diagnosis* phase, the challenge of converting unstructured or heterogeneous data for use in data platforms is identified, highlighting problems such as inconsistent metadata, ambiguous data layouts, and the need to comply with standards such as STA [2,23]. As discussed in Sect. 2, these early findings clarified the problem's scope and underscored the value of a generic solution that could function across varied data sources.

Building on these insights, we enter the *Design* phase, where we draft requirements for a more robust pipeline to guide open-data conversions systematically (see also Sect. 4). The *Implementation* phase centers on realizing and iterating this grammar-based solution. As recommended by Mullarkey and Hevner [24], we treat each iteration as a mini-cycle, including building or extending the grammar, deploying it against new data sources, and refining it based on observed gaps. This produced a specialized GBNF that enforces precise syntactic structures while allowing flexible data extraction. We reduced parsing errors and improved output consistency by formally specifying which keys, tokens, or nesting levels are required. The latest iteration, featuring the grammar-based approach, is covered in detail here to maintain clarity while acknowledging earlier prototypes and insights.

To assess the viability of our final design, we then move into the *Evolution* cycle, where we quantitatively test the grammar-based approach under different settings. As detailed in Sect. 6, we evaluate how varying context lengths, from truncated minimal descriptions to more extensive data, impact the generated outputs, observing that longer prompts allowed better alignment between the grammar and LLM outputs without significantly increasing computational overhead. Moreover, using multiple data sources (including structured tables, partially descriptive text, and more complex combined formats) verifies that our grammar-based artifact reduces formatting errors and supports broader open-data needs. Notably, including more detailed grammar rules generally improved the precision of extracted information without prolonging generation times.

Following Mullarkey and Hevner [24], we document how lessons from one iteration inform the next, enabling continuous improvement based on real-world feedback. By sharing this evolutionary development, the paper contributes both a replicable methodology (grounded in ADR) and a concrete grammar-based pipeline for LLM-driven data ingestion. Our final approach—combining LLMs with a stringent grammar—demonstrates a reliable method for converting open data into sensor-platform-ready payloads conforming to interoperability standards like the STA. Lastly, in keeping with ADR's emphasis on effectively communicating outcomes, we formulate our findings in Sect. 6 that confirm the solution's strengths and identify areas for future improvement, illustrating how structured iterations and reflections guided the artifact's overall development and final evaluation.

4 Design and Development

After identifying a need to reliably transform heterogeneous open data into STA-compliant formats, we conducted three major design iterations. The final iteration culminated in a grammar-based approach that became central to our data pipeline. This section details the considerations for the LLM runtime and the chosen models (Sect. 4.1), as well as the evolution from the earliest prototypes to the final design (Sect. 4.2 and 4.3).

4.1 Foundational LLM Setup and System Prompt Configuration

We chose three different models, each chosen for capability, cost efficiency, and size, as the basis for data ingestion and parsing. First, we used the *Llama 3.1 Instruct* model with 8 billion parameters, published by Meta [11]. This model is highly popular in the open-source community and supports extended context windows of up to 129k tokens. Second, we ran *Phi-3*, a 14-billion-parameter model published by Microsoft that handles up to 16k context tokens [1]. Although larger than Llama, Phi-4 exhibits more advanced capabilities on some benchmarks and was released more recently. Third, we used *Qwen 2.5 Instruct* with 7 billion parameters, published by Alibaba [27]. We obtained all models from Hugging Face[1]. We opt for smaller parameter counts to manage resource costs, especially in an enterprise scenario where these LLMs might be integrated into a data pipeline.

All model inference is performed using the `llama.cpp` project, configured to treat each request as a text-completion task rather than a chat prompt. Our extensive system prompt—consisting of over 3,400 tokens if processed with e.g. the Llama3 tokenizer—plays a central role in determining the quality of the extracted information. Within this system prompt, we specified: (1) general instructions about extracting all relevant information from the raw text, (2) detailed documentation for every STA data model field to ensure consistency with the standard's requirements, including structural rules for valid `JSON`, and (3) one worked example (in `markdown`) illustrating how a text snippet with an unknown structure can be turned into a manually verified STA-compatible `JSON` output. Once the system prompt is established, we add the actual data as the task for the model to solve, ensuring each new transformation request follows the same prompt template.

Before sending a piece of text to the LLM, we convert the original input data, frequently available in PDF or other formats, into `markdown` using the Marker tool[2]. Although the LLM models can handle substantial context windows, we standardized input size to a maximum of 10k tokens to avoid inconsistencies across models with different upper limits (such as 16k or 128k tokens). Any content exceeding that length is split into multiple chunks, each processed independently. Ensuring that each model's output would fit seamlessly into an

---

[1] https://huggingface.co/.
[2] https://github.com/VikParuchuri/marker.

automated pipeline proved more challenging than shaping the input. We initially attempted to rely solely on carefully crafted system prompts and example outputs, but this method does not guarantee perfectly structured JSON for further machine processing.

4.2 Preliminary Iterations: JSON Schema and Pydantic Models

The *first iteration* employed a plain JSON-schema to validate LLMs-generated outputs. While this basic schema can capture minimal required fields, it is too rigid to cope with more diverse inputs, often leading to failures when unexpected data structures or nested properties appear.

In a *second iteration*, we integrated pydantic models with an LLM pipeline using LlamaIndex[3] and Guidance[4]. This approach does provide stricter type-checking at runtime. Still, the additional abstraction layers (i.e., Llama-Index and Guidance on top of llama.cpp) can lead to a cumbersome implementation and make debugging more difficult. Moreover, some model architectures do not adapt well to our object-oriented schema, particularly when confronted with deeply nested or highly variable data structures. Despite the upfront benefits of object modeling, we reached the limits of what an OOP-oriented approach can handle, especially concerning complex real-world relationships. Finally, we can observe a notable increase in token overhead, as each of the pydantic field definitions had to be spelled out in the prompt, further slowing generation speed.

These preliminary iterations clarify that a purely schema-based or static object-based strategy would not sufficiently accommodate the wide-ranging variety in open data sources. They also reveal that high token usage could become a bottleneck for large-scale or cost-sensitive deployments. Consequently, we sought a more flexible yet formally constrained solution, leading to the grammar-based approach.

4.3 Final Iteration: Context-Free Grammar for STA Outputs

To implement this grammar-based approach, we create a context-free grammar using GBNF notation, focusing on the primary entities *Thing*, *Datastream*, and *Observation*. By embedding these rules either into the LLM prompt or into a post-processing validation stage, our pipeline consistently outputs syntactically correct and semantically relevant JSON structures that comply with the STA. The grammar effectively resolves the variability in open-data formats by establishing a robust interface that translates unstructured or semi-structured data into a standardized JSON-based representation.

At the root level, the grammar requires every generated text to describe a valid STA object, for instance, a *Thing* holding one or more *Datastreams* and corresponding *Observations*. We adopt a similar prescriptive but flexible approach to all entities in the STA model, strictly enforcing fundamental keys

---

[3] https://www.llamaindex.ai.
[4] https://github.com/microsoft/guidance.

(e.g., `name`, `description`) but capturing optional or user-defined fields through generalized sub-rules. This structure preserves flexibility for open-data sources while ensuring that essential STA fields remain intact.

As shown in the exemplary grammar fragment in Fig. 2, every `observation` must contain time-related fields (`phenomenonTime`, `resultTime`) and a `result` field that may be numeric, textual, or boolean, covering typical sensor outputs. Optional elements like `resultQuality` and `featureOfInterests` accommodate scenarios requiring extra details.

```
observation ::= ("{" ws "\"phenomenonTime\"" ":" ws tmPeriod ","
    ws "\"result\""           ":" ws resultValue ","
    ws "\"resultTime\""       ":" ws tmInstant ","
    ws "\"resultQuality\""    ":" ws obsQualityOrNull ","
    ws "\"validTime\""        ":" ws tmPeriodOrNull ","
    ws "\"parameters\""       ":" ws obsParamsOrNull
    ( "," ws "\"featureOfInterests\"" ":" ws "[" ws
        ( featureOfInterest ( "," ws featureOfInterest )* )? was "]" )? ws "}")
```

Fig. 2. Grammar fragment for `observation`, specifying required and optional fields.

To guarantee that LLM-generated text adheres to these GBNF rules, we convert the final grammar into a classic BNF-style format and parse any candidate output accordingly. Any response that cannot be parsed is either rejected or subjected to a correction step. We protect downstream processing pipelines from syntactical or structural irregularities by forcing every token in the `JSON` structure to match a grammar rule. We tested our approach on a server equipped with an AMD EPYC 9334 Processor (32 cores at 2.7 GHz), 64 GB of RAM, and an NVIDIA H100 GPU with 20 GB of VRAM, which is sufficient for LLM inference at around 15 billion parameters in standard precision or larger models in quantized modes.

Embedding a meticulously defined grammar into the generation and validation steps reduces the likelihood of malformed outputs, thus simplifying data ingestion into STA-compliant repositories. While this method ensures well-formedness and consistency of the `JSON`, additional semantic checks can be added in a post-processing phase, such as verifying realistic measurement ranges. The grammar-based strategy, therefore, constitutes the core of our proposed design, enabling robust integration of open and heterogeneous data sources into IoT data platforms that rely on the STA specification.

5 Evaluation

The effectiveness of the grammar-based approach is assessed by examining its capability to generate valid STA outputs and the computational efficiency of producing these outputs under varying configurations. Multiple primary dimensions guide this assessment. First, the impact of grammar complexity is measured by comparing a *long* version of the grammar, which includes strict fields (such as

ISO 8601-enforced timestamps) and optional metadata blocks (`dictAny`), against a *short* version that removes or relaxes these features to reduce the likelihood of hallucinated properties. Second, the influence of different datasets with varying degrees of structure and metadata descriptions on the LLM generation process is investigated.

Several open data sources are utilized for the evaluation, each selected for its unique structural and content characteristics to test the system's versatility. These datasets are summarized in Table 1. The *UK Inflation*[5] dataset combines wage and inflation trends presented in raw tables alongside descriptive text. This dataset was chosen because it lacks classic time series data, with periods described only within the table descriptions, and includes extensive narrative explanations for the tables. In contrast, the *Tuberculosis Report*[6] provides more conventional time series data organized in column-based formats, where dates are listed in columns rather than rows. Additionally, it contains substantial descriptive paragraphs. The *Pollution Statistics*[7] dataset primarily consists of charts and brief environmental summaries. This format poses significant challenges for extracting well-formed STA entities due to the limited textual data and the presence of graphical information, which is not easily converted by Markdown converters. The United Nations *Population Demographics*[8] dataset is characterized by its large token size and numerous multi-column tables with minimal descriptive text. This dataset was selected to evaluate the model's capability to process extensive numerical information and extract meaningful insights from columns without detailed descriptions. Additionally, a concise *NYC Air Quality*[9] dataset is included, which comes in Comma-separated values (CSV) format with accompanying `JSON` metadata and a short description. This dataset was chosen to assess whether the model can effectively handle plain CSV data supplemented with minimal context, facilitating the extraction of relevant air quality metrics. Finally, a *News Feed* of New York Times consisting of diverse articles from a single day is included. It covers unrelated topics with no common theme, presenting a variety of styles, structures, and subjects, and was selected to evaluate the model's ability to extract structured information from unstructured narrative text within a dynamic and diverse set of content.

To meet the maximum context length of the smallest LLM model of 16,000 tokens and to provide 6,000 tokens for the system prompt, a pre-processing step is required to ensure that the input texts did not exceed 10,000 tokens. The initial token count is described in Table 1 in column n_{init} and represents the token count immediately after converting the original PDF documents to Markdown format. For example, the *Population Demographics* dataset has to be reduced by removing selected tables to comply with the 10,000 token limit and thus ensure sufficient space for the system prompt. The *nlong* column shows the number of

---

[5] https://data.europa.eu.
[6] https://www.ecdc.europa.eu.
[7] https://www.statista.com.
[8] https://data.un.org.
[9] https://data.cityofnewyork.us.

Table 1. Description of used datasets for evaluation.

Dataset	Description	n_{init}	n_{long}	n_{short}
UK Inflation	Summarizes pay trends in London and the UK since 2010, comparing them to inflation.	2,743	2,743	686
Tuberculosis Report	Annual epidemiological report based on 2022 data from The European Surveillance System.	6,355	6,355	3,283
Pollution Statistics	Presents data on global environmental pollution, e.g. air, water and particulate matter.	5,105	5,105	238
Population Demographics	Covers population growth, fertility, and mortality indicators from UN-Data.	59,444	8,344	3,390
NYC Air Quality	Contains New York City air quality data with pollutant emissions and exposure levels.	3999	3999	1696
News Feed	Short news articles about different topics.	4117	4117	1221

tokens of the cleaned Markdown text and reflects the full-length version used. Additionally, we created a manually curated *short* version for each dataset to evaluate the model's performance under tighter input constraints. This involves a more granular content removal, where text not directly related to the main data extraction objectives is omitted. For example, in datasets containing multiple tables, only the sections describing the specific tables targeted for extraction are retained, while all other tables and their descriptions are removed. The number of tokens for these shortened inputs is displayed under *nshort*. This shortened version evaluated the model's ability in scenarios with limited context, focusing on the conversion aspect rather than comprehensive content extraction.

This pre-processing approach results in a test configuration comprising two grammar lengths, two input token counts (long and short), three LLM models, six datasets, and ten iterations per configuration. Consequently, the total number of evaluation runs amounts to $2 \times 2 \times 3 \times 6 \times 10 = 720$ outputs. After completion, all outputs are merged into a single dataset for analysis (results published in [29]). JSON parsing is successful for all 720 outputs. Our hardware's average end-to-end duration (from input to output) is 74.8 s. Overall, the responses of LLM exhibited a wide range of lengths. The average minimum response length is 489 tokens, while the average maximum length is 4,221 tokens. Since our grammar imposes an upper limit of 8,192 tokens for the final output, the responses remain within the allowable limits.

This merged dataset captures the full range of configurations-varying grammar lengths, context lengths, datasets, and LLM models-along with several key performance metrics. The number of output tokens generated by each model indicates the length of the responses, where a higher token count signifies a more extensive and potentially more detailed output. Throughput, measured as the number of tokens generated per second on average, reflects the computational efficiency of the models; higher throughput values denote faster generation of outputs. Each output is successfully parsed as JSON, so the counts of *Things*, *Datastreams*, *Observations*, and *Locations* represent the number of corresponding STA elements generated in each output. These entity counts provide insight into the models' abilities to extract and structure relevant information from the input data.

Table 2. LLM performance comparison: long vs. short grammar structures.

Model	Grammar	Tokens	Throughput	Things	Datastreams	Observations	Locations
Phi	long	2254	26,6/s	16,0	33,9	83,1	9,8
	short	1895	21,7/s	15,1	32,8	87,6	11,0
Qwen	long	3231	30,4/s	9,8	38,3	121,3	6,3
	short	2426	26,9/s	11,3	44,0	130,3	10,5
Llama	long	1009	36,4/s	15,0	24,8	38,8	8,9
	short	1526	29,2/s	12,2	39,4	66,6	9,7

Table 3. Impact of input context length on LLM performance metrics.

Model	Context	Tokens	Throughput	Things	Datastreams	Observations	Locations
Phi	long	2017	25,0/s	15,0	35,8	83,3	8,5
	short	2132	28,2/s	16,1	31,0	87,3	12,3
Qwen	long	2845	29,5/s	10,7	45,2	115,7	7,2
	short	2812	32,6/s	10,4	37,1	136,0	9,7
Llama	long	1388	30,7/s	11,8	27,3	44,8	8,2
	short	1147	30,7/s	15,4	36,9	60,7	10,4

To better understand the impact of grammar (long versus short), the results in Table 2 were obtained by averaging the metrics across the six datasets for each model, grouped by grammar type. This allowed for a focused comparison of how adding more strict fields and optional metadata blocks in the long grammar and removing them in the short grammar influences the model output. Conversely, Table 3 illustrates how context length long versus short inputs affect the same metrics, again aggregated by model. The main findings will be discussed in the next chapter.

6 Discussion and Conclusion

This study addresses the challenge of converting open, heterogeneous data into structures fully compliant with the STA sensing data model. Since we used the relational data model when developing the grammar, it is also possible to model and use other data models, and it is not limited to STA. By designing a grammar-based approach (c.f. Sect. 4) that enforces each *Thing* to include at least one *Datastream* and one *Observation*, we ensure that generically ingested data aligns closely with typical IoT usage scenarios. In our design, a careful step is taken to prevent circular dependencies, particularly in larger models, by e.g. nesting *HistoricalLocations* references under *Locations* rather than bidirectionally linking them back to the *Thing*.

We also weigh different design trade-offs to balance strict compliance and flexibility. By mandating at least one *Datastream* and a corresponding *Observation*, we eliminate the possibility of an empty *Thing*, which rarely arises in genuine IoT deployments but does exclude data sources that lack sensor measurements. Likewise, we chose to limit the `location` property to `null` instead of incorporating the entire `geoJson` grammar, thus curbing the grammar's growing size and lowering the likelihood of malformed output. For further adaptability, the `properties` field remains a simple dictionary to accommodate unstructured or domain-specific metadata. Although strongly typed fields can minimize validation errors, prioritizing open-data interoperability justifies preserving flexible key-value content.

From a model reasoning perspective, specifying grammar rules substantially reduces syntactic and structural errors in LLM-generated output. Still, it does not prevent unrealistic or questionable data (such as "99999 K"). As explained in Sect. 3, our conversion from the GBNF syntax to standard BNF allows us to parse each generation before acceptance, ensuring *formal* correctness. Yet domain-level validation, like verifying physically plausible units or timestamps, remains future work. Preliminary "repair" strategies, for example, automatically retrying upon detection of invalid grammar strings, yield a further boost in success rates, pointing to the efficacy of iterative generation in solving minor formatting errors.

Nonetheless, there are limitations in both the grammar design and its application. First, our experiments show that deeply nested objects pose a considerable risk of confusing LLM output. Restricting the depth of the grammar proves more effective than allowing unbounded recursions. Second, because STA servers typically provide only ID-based responses, referencing an entity by embedding its entire data structure is not straightforward. In practice, the `POST/PUT` logic must parse these IDs and compose new calls to fill in the relationships. Third, any reasoning undertaken by the LLM or the grammar framework remains partial. Although we systematically tested the grammar to ensure it appears correct, questions about whether the BNF approach fully captures all STA nuances call for comprehensive, domain-level verification. Our efforts also highlight how the focus of prompts becomes crucial: using longer or shorter text does not necessarily improve understanding if the prompt loses clarity or overwhelms the model.

Regarding the main findings, we can observe that grammars provide a robust strategy to enforce structured outputs. Specifically, requiring specific fields (yet preserving user-defined `properties`) accommodates highly variable data without sacrificing `JSON` validity regardless of whether the STA or other models are used. Among the three smaller LLMs tested, Qwen consistently performs best, aligning with developers' claims that it is well-tuned for generating structured output. Interestingly, the generative process remains non-deterministic across different runs and the three models. As a result, the same data snippet sometimes emerged as a *Thing*, and other times as a *Datastream*, a variation in interpretation that mirrors how human judgment may differ. Another key insight is that grammar length and complexity do not slow the generation rate (tokens per second). However, we note a trend that a more detailed grammar can, in many instances, boost the quality of the output. We also encountered occasional catastrophic failures, sometimes producing empty arrays or extremely long outputs, including hundreds of tokens with invalid data. A further discovery is that adding more context to the input data did not necessarily enhance model accuracy if the prompt lost focus. Well-structured, narrower prompts typically prove more successful, especially if the input text inherently contains time series data. When such data is absent, hallucinated or irrelevant sensor measurements frequently appear. For tables that did not include time series data, entities were created, but these were essentially hallucinations because the model, accurate to the grammar, generated any output. Overall, these insights highlight a grammar-based design's immediate and broader impact. While our focus is on STA, similar IoT data platforms can equally profit from structured ingestion of JSON-based objects. Our results underscore, however, that deeply nested grammars (like the full geoJson specification) can confuse LLMs, especially for models with limited parameter counts. We, therefore, emphasize a modular approach, activating only the grammar subsets essential for the use case. Moreover, grammar-based output constraints show promise for tasks beyond IoT, such as government open-data portals and domain-specific knowledge bases that require strictly formatted data for automated integration.

While this work addresses many design considerations, additional steps remain. Future directions include merging these grammar-based outputs with existing databases, potentially via RAG methods that supply known entity names directly to the LLM. Expanding the approach to cover the *Tasking* portion of STA, implementing advanced domain-level validations, and enabling partial referencing for intricate linking scenarios would further extend the architecture. We are particularly interested in how more advanced or specialized reasoning models [34], such as deepseek-r1[10], might improve the interpretative process while conforming to grammar constraints. Fine-tuning a dedicated LLM on a comprehensive set of successful open-data-to-STA transformations offers a promising path to deeper structural understanding; moreover, the process described here could be leveraged to generate high-quality training data for such a fine-tune. Furthermore, it would be useful to investigate how our approach can be integrated and deployed in real IoT data platforms to make it easy to use.

In conclusion, the grammar-based approach offers a stable foundation for ingesting open data into STA-compliant platforms, ensuring *formally* valid and suitably flexible outputs. By systematically translating GBNF to BNF

---

[10] Deepseek-R1 model: https://github.com/deepseek-ai/DeepSeek-R1.

for strict syntactic validation and employing simple repair strategies, we eliminated syntactic errors and allowed for domain-specific adaptability. Alongside the demonstrated viability of smaller LLMs, the findings underscore the importance of prompt focus, controlled grammar scope, and post-processing checks. As IoT technologies evolve, the need for consistent, machine-readable structures becomes ever more critical, and our results indicate that grammar-guided generation can significantly enhance data quality, reduce manual intervention, and enable future expansions such as advanced referencing, deeper validations, and the integration of improved reasoning models.

Acknowledgments. This research has been supported by the German Research Foundation (DFG) under Research Grant No. 432399058 and by the Federal Ministry of Education and Research (BMBF), Germany under Research Grant No. 16DTM218 as part of the NextGenerationEU program of the European Union.

References

1. Abdin, M., Aneja, J., et al.: Phi-4 Technical report (2024). http://arxiv.org/abs/2412.08905
2. Ahlgren, B., Hidell, M., Ngai, E.-H.: Internet of things for smart cities: interoperability and open data. IEEE Internet Comput. **20**(6), 52–56 (2016)
3. Arz von Straussenburg, A.F., Aldenhoff, T.T., Riehle, D.M.: Extending the SensorThings API data model - improving interoperability and use case flexibility in IoT. In: The 43rd International Conference on Conceptual Modeling Forum: Pittsburgh, Pennsylvania, USA (2024)
4. Barns, S.: Smart cities and urban data platforms: designing interfaces for smart governance. City Cult. Soc. **12**, 5–12 (2018)
5. Blazevic, M., Aldenhoff, T.T., Riehle, D.M.: Towards a smarter tomorrow: a design science perspective on building a smart campus IoT Data Platform. In: Mandviwalla, M., Söllner, M., Tuunanen, T. (eds) Design Science Research for a Resilient Future. DESRIST 2024. LNCS, vol. 14621, pp. 262–277. Springer, Cham (2024). https://doi.org/10.1007/978-3-031-61175-9_18
6. T. Brown, B. Mann, et al.: Language Models Are Few-Shot Learners. In: Advances in Neural Information Processing Systems (2020)
7. do Carmo, S.L.O., Geyer, C.F.R., dos Anjos, J.C.S.: Data quantitative and qualitative study in Brazilian open data portals. J. Internet Serv. App. **15**(1), 72–82 (2024)
8. de Reuver, M., Ofe, H., et al.: The openness of data platforms: a research agenda. In: Proceedings of the 1st Int. Workshop on Data Economy. DE 2022, pp. 34–41. ACM, New York, NY, USA (2022). https://doi.org/10.1145/3565011.3569056
9. Francia, M., Gallinucci, E., et al.: Making data platforms smarter with MOSES. Futur. Gener. Comput. Syst. **125**, 299–313 (2021)
10. Francia, M., Golfarelli, M., Pasini, M.: Towards a process-driven design of data platforms. In: DOLAP, pp. 28–35 (2024)
11. Fu, T.-C.: A review on time series data mining. Eng. Appl. Artif. Intell. **24**(1), 164–181 (2011)
12. Grattafiori, A., Dubey, A., et al.: The Llama 3 Herd of Models (2024). http://arxiv.org/abs/2407.21783

13. Gubbi, J., Buyya, R., Marusic, S., Palaniswami, M.: Internet of things (IoT): a vision, architectural elements, and future directions. Futur. Gener. Comput. Syst. **29**(7), 1645–1660 (2013). https://doi.org/10.1016/j.future.2013.01.010
14. Ho, J., Ooi, B., Westner, M.: Application integration framework for large language models. In: 5th International Conference on AI and Data Sciences, AiDAS 2024 - Proceedings, pp. 398–403 (2024). https://doi.org/10.1109/AiDAS63860.2024.10730541
15. Khan, N.A., Ahangar, H.: Emerging trends in open research data. In: 2017 9th International Conference on Information and Knowledge Technology (IKT), pp. 141–146 (2017). https://doi.org/10.1109/IKT.2017.8258631
16. Knuth, D.: Semantics of context-free languages. Math. Syst. Theory **2**(2), 127–145 (1968). https://doi.org/10.1007/BF01692511
17. Krasikov, P., Legner, C.: A method to screen, assess, and prepare open data for use. J. Data Inf. Qual. **15**(4), 43:1–43:25 (2023)
18. Laros, J., Blavier, A., den Dunnen, J., Taschner, P.: A formalized description of the standard human variant nomenclature in extended Backus-Naur form. BMC Bioinform. **12**, 1–7 (2011)
19. Lewis, P., Perez, E., et al.: Retrieval-augmented generation for knowledge-intensive NLP tasks. In: Advances in Neural Information Processing Systems (2020)
20. Liang, S., Khalafbeigi, T.: OGC SensorThings API Part 2 – Tasking Core, Version 1.0. Report (2019). https://doi.org/10.25607/OBP-454
21. Liang, S., Khalafbeigi, T., et al.: OGC SensorThings API Part 1: Sensing Version 1.1 (2021)
22. Liu, M., Liu, F., et al.: "We need structured output": towards user-centered constraints on large language model output. In: Conference on Human Factors in Computing Systems - Proceedings (2024). https://doi.org/10.1145/3613905.3650756
23. Montori, F., Liao, K., Jayaraman, P.P., Bononi, L., Sellis, T., Georgakopoulos, D.: Classification and annotation of open internet of things datastreams. In: Hacid, H., Cellary, W., Wang, H., Paik, H.-Y., Zhou, R. (eds.) WISE 2018. LNCS, vol. 11234, pp. 209–224. Springer, Cham (2018). https://doi.org/10.1007/978-3-030-02925-8_15
24. Mullarkey, M.T., Hevner, A.R.: An elaborated action design research process model. Eur. J. Inf. Syst. **28**(1), 6–20 (2019)
25. Murray-Rust, P.: Open data in science. Ser. Rev. **34**(1), 52–64 (2008). https://doi.org/10.1080/00987913.2008.10765152
26. Otto, B., Jarke, M.: Designing a multi-sided data platform: findings from the international data spaces case. Electron. Mark. **29**(4), 561–580 (2019)
27. Qwen, A., Yang, et al.: Qwen2.5 Technical report (2025). http://arxiv.org/abs/2412.15115
28. Radev, I.: Context-free grammars from the computing theory perspective. In: 25th World Multi-Conference on Systemics, Cybernetics and Informatics, WMSCI 2021, pp. 51–56 (2021)
29. Riehle, D.M., Arz von Straussenburg, A.F., Aldenhoff, T.T.: Supplementary Dataset: Designing Grammar-Guided LLM Outputs for Open Data Integration - A DSR Approach to IoT Data Platforms. Zenodo (2025). https://doi.org/10.5281/zenodo.15100791
30. Rudakov, V., Timur, M., Yedilkhan, A.: Comparison of time series databases. In: 17th International Conference on Electronics Computer and Computation (ICECCO), pp. 1–4 (2023). https://doi.org/10.1109/ICECCO58239.2023.10147153

31. Slobodova, O., Becker, S.: Zooming into the ecosystem: agency and politics around open data platforms in Lyon and Berlin. Front. Sustain. Cities **2**, 20 (2020)
32. Struckov, A., Yufa, S., Visheratin, A.A., Nasonov, D.: Evaluation of modern tools and techniques for storing time-series data. Proc. Comput. Sci. **156**, 19–28 (2019)
33. Tao, N., Ventresque, A., Nallur, V., Saber, T.: Enhancing program synthesis with large language models using many-objective grammar-guided genetic programming. Algorithms **17**(7), 285 (2024)
34. Wei, J., Wang, X., et al.: Chain-of-thought prompting elicits reasoning in large language models. In: Advances in Neural Information Processing Systems (2022)
35. Wildman, G., Lewis, E.: Value of open data: a geoscience perspective. Geosci. Data J. **9**(2), 384–392 (2022)
36. Wilkinson, M.D., Dumontier, M., et al.: The FAIR guiding principles for scientific data management and stewardship. Sci. Data **3**(1), 160018 (2016)

Open Access This chapter is licensed under the terms of the Creative Commons Attribution 4.0 International License (http://creativecommons.org/licenses/by/4.0/), which permits use, sharing, adaptation, distribution and reproduction in any medium or format, as long as you give appropriate credit to the original author(s) and the source, provide a link to the Creative Commons license and indicate if changes were made.

The images or other third party material in this chapter are included in the chapter's Creative Commons license, unless indicated otherwise in a credit line to the material. If material is not included in the chapter's Creative Commons license and your intended use is not permitted by statutory regulation or exceeds the permitted use, you will need to obtain permission directly from the copyright holder.

DSR Education

Artifact Validity in Design Science Research (DSR): A Comparative Analysis of Three Influential Frameworks

Sylvana Kroop[✉]

University of Vienna, Faculty of Philosophy and Education, Vienna, Austria
sylvana.kroop@univie.ac.at

Abstract. Although the methodology of Design Science Research (DSR) is playing an increasingly important role with the emergence of the 'sciences of the artificial', the validity of the resulting artifacts is occasionally questioned. This paper compares three influential DSR frameworks to assess their support for artifact validity. Using five essential validity types (instrument validity, technical validity, design validity, purpose validity and generalization), the qualitative analysis reveals that while purpose validity is explicitly emphasized, instrument and design validity remain the least developed. Their implicit treatment in all frameworks poses a risk of overlooked validation, and the absence of mandatory instrument validity can lead to invalid artifacts, threatening research credibility. Beyond these findings, the paper contributes (a) a comparative overview of each framework's strengths and weaknesses and (b) a revised DSR framework incorporating all five validity types with definitions and examples. This ensures systematic artifact evaluation and improvement, reinforcing the rigor of DSR.

Keywords: design science research · artifact validity · validity types

1 Introduction

With the rise of the 'sciences of the artificial' [26], Design Science Research (DSR) methodology plays an increasingly important role and is gaining ground in higher education institutions much faster than in previous years and decades. With Hevner [8,9], DSR has become widespread and popular in the field of information technology, but also through intensive efforts in German-speaking countries, especially in business informatics [33], as it focuses on the creation of novel artifacts. As technically oriented disciplines often permeate all areas of life and play an important supporting role in all subject disciplines, the DSR methodology can be applied to the development of new artifacts of all kinds, from software to physical tools such as printed teaching materials or human body prostheses.

Although it seems to have been clear among DSR experts for decades what DSR can and cannot achieve, e.g. [7,17,20,26], this discussion has only just begun in the context of the education, not only for doctoral students but also for master's students, e.g. [1,11,14,24,32]. Frequently asked questions are, for example: How complex can or must a DSR-based research design be in order to be mastered within the framework of a master's thesis? Is it necessary to validate the generalizability of the developed artifact? Is it sufficient that the effectiveness of the artifact is evaluated solely in the context of my company? As DSR becomes more widely used, doubts arise about the validity of the resulting artifacts.

De Sordi et al. (2020) conducted a content analysis of 152 articles to examine the longitudinal development of DSR projects and the types of artifacts involved. The results suggest that the use of DSR has grown rapidly over the years and that this growth is likely to continue in the future. However, the text further states that 86 % of DSR artifact evaluations are unrealistic, which means that the criteria used to evaluate the artifact are not practical or feasible in real-world scenarios. The authors call for research to make Design Science Research (DSR) more accessible and less confusing as authors, reviewers, and editors struggle to understand and follow DSR guidelines [6]. This may indeed be difficult, especially for reviewers who grew up in a world where 'truth' was only found in the nature of descriptive research.

This paper addresses the examination and comparison of three commonly used DSR frameworks, namely Hevner et al. [9], Peffers et al. [21], and an integrated framework combining Österle et al. [33] and Benner-Wickner et al. [1], and the question: to what extent do these three influential design science research (DSR) frameworks support the validity of artifacts? The fundamental question arises as to which types of validity are essential for the evaluation of an artifact. And the resulting question of how a DSR framework can be improved to emphasize the need for a thorough evaluation of an artifact's validity.

2 Methodology

In order to compare the three DSR frameworks with the question of the extent to which they support the validity of artifacts, five validity types were established a priori, which were derived both from experience in the assessment and supervision of DSR-based master's theses and from the basic literature [4,5,18,19,25].

Each of the five validity types (instruments validity, technical validity, design validity, purpose validity and generalization) proposed for the artifact evaluation in DSR corresponds to several well-known scientific validity concepts, as shown in the overview table in Fig. 1.

The five validity types were then defined and demonstrated using examples for application in the context of design science research (DSR), see Sect. 4.2. Scoring Guidelines for the Five Validity Types were designed, see Sect. 4.4, and applied in the comparative evaluation of the three DSR frameworks, see Sect. 5. The resulting scores of the comparative evaluation were than converted into a heat map, which serves as a final, summary overview, see Chap. 6.

The comparative evaluation is essentially based on a qualitative content analysis according to the guidelines of Kuckartz & Rädiker [15]. The core literature

Proposed Validity Type for DSR	Corresponding Validity Types in Basic Literature	References
Instrument Validity	Construct Validity, Measurement Validity	**Cronbach & Meehl (1955)**: Introduced construct validity as the extent to which a test measures the concept it is intended to measure. **Messick (1989)**: Expanded construct validity to include consequential validity, ensuring interpretations are meaningful. **Cook & Campbell (1979), Shadish et al. (2002)**: Emphasized measurement validity as essential in research design.
Technical Validity	Reliability, Internal Validity	**Cook & Campbell (1979)**: Defined internal validity as ensuring causal conclusions are justified. **Shadish et al. (2002)**: Emphasized reliability as the consistency of measurements, a critical component of technical validity.
Design Validity	Usability, Aesthetic Quality, Ecological Validity	**Messick (1989)**: Discussed how validity should consider the impact of design on interpretation and use. **Shadish et al. (2002)**: Ecological validity considers real-world applicability, relevant to usability.
Purpose Validity	Internal Validity, Construct Validity	**Cook & Campbell (1979), Shadish et al. (2002)**: Internal validity ensures that findings align with the intended purpose of the study. **Messick (1989)**: Construct validity also covers whether an artifact meets its theoretical intent.
Generalization (External Validity)	External Validity, Transferability	**Cook & Campbell (1979)**: Defined external validity as the extent to which findings apply beyond the studied sample. **Shadish et al. (2002)**: Highlighted the importance of transferability to other contexts.

Fig. 1. Type of validity categories used a priori for qualitative content analysis

on the three DSR frameworks examined was primarily the subject of the investigation in order to answer the central research question: To what extent do these three influential frameworks of Design Science Research (DSR) support the validity of artifacts?

The three DSR frameworks were selected due to their popularity among master's students. Based on my ongoing supervision of DSR-based theses - especially at the Ferdinand Porsche FernFH in Austria - I've observed frequent use of these frameworks in business informatics and IT. However, the revised framework in this paper also enables broader comparisons with other DSR approaches.

3 Related Work

Similar work comparing the three selected DSR frameworks in terms of support for artifact validity has not yet been conducted. The overview table in Fig. 2 shows how frequently cited literature on artifact evaluation, and other extensive literature, e.g. [1–3, 7–10, 12, 13, 16, 21–23, 27–31, 33], relate to the five validity types applied here.

DSR Validity Type	Corresponding DSR Validity Concepts or Evaluation Criteria	Evaluation in DSR
Instrument Validity	Construct Validity, Model Validity, Measurement Rigor	**Hevner et al. (2004)**: Emphasized rigor but did not explicitly define instrument validity. **Prat, Comyn-Wattiau, & Akoka (2015)**: Included construct validity in their DSR evaluation framework. **Sonnenberg & Vom Brocke (2012)**: Stressed the need for rigorous evaluation of constructs. **Österle et al. (2010) & Benner-Wickner et al. (2020)**: Implicitly address measurement rigor but do not explicitly distinguish instrument validity as a separate criterion.
Technical Validity	Reliability, Internal Consistency, Correctness of Artifacts	**Hevner et al. (2004)**: Discussed research rigor but did not define technical validity explicitly. **Peffers et al. (2007)**: The evaluation phase includes functional correctness. **Venable et al. (2016)**: Addressed reliability and internal validity in DSR evaluations. **Österle et al. (2010) & Benner-Wickner et al. (2020)**: Emphasize technical feasibility and correctness as part of artifact evaluation.
Design Validity	Usability, Aesthetic Quality, User-Centered Design, Utility	**Gregor & Hevner (2013)**: Stressed utility as a key DSR evaluation criterion. **Iivari (2007)**: Discussed how DSR should integrate human-centered design. **Sonnenberg & Vom Brocke (2012)**: Included usability as an evaluation criterion. **Österle et al. (2010) & Benner-Wickner et al. (2020)**: Acknowledge usability but do not systematically define design validity as a distinct evaluation category.
Purpose Validity	Relevance, Utility, Problem-Solution Fit	**Hevner et al. (2004)**: Defined problem relevance as a key DSR guideline. **Peffers et al. (2007)**: The DSR process model begins with problem identification, ensuring purpose validity. **Gregor & Hevner (2013)**: Stressed that DSR must align with real-world needs. **Österle et al. (2010) & Benner-Wickner et al. (2020)**: Strongly emphasize problem relevance and practical utility as core aspects of DSR.
Generalization (External Validity)	External Validity, Transferability of Artifacts, Adaptability	**Hevner et al. (2004)**: Discussed how DSR contributes to both practice and theory, implying the need for external validity. **Prat, Comyn-Wattiau, & Akoka (2015)**: Included external validity in their DSR evaluation framework. **Venable et al. (2016)**: Addressed transferability of DSR findings. **Österle et al. (2010) & Benner-Wickner et al. (2020)**: Emphasize diffusion of artifacts but do not explicitly address external validity as a formal evaluation construct.

Fig. 2. Type of validity categories, aligned with frequently cited DSR literature on artifact evaluation.

In particular, 'instrument validity' as a mandatory prerequisite for a valid artifact (see Sect. 4.3) is difficult to find in all three DSR frameworks examined here. Sonnenberg & vom Brocke [27] is one of the few studies that clearly points out the need to evaluate the design and the construct separately and in interaction with the problem to be evaluated. This can be equated with the need for 'instrument validity'. Although this model increases the basic evaluation effort, it ensures potentially valid artifacts in the end. Nevertheless, there has been a lack of consideration and differentiation of the five types of validity clearly defined here as an integral part of a comprehensive DSR framework.

4 Revised DSR Framework Focused on Artifact Validity

4.1 Revised DSR Framework

Compared to Hevner et al. [9] and Peffers et al. [21], the DSR framework, originally developed and popularized by Österle et al. [33] and later put into a graphical form by Benner-Wickner et al. [1], is perhaps less well known because it is only available in German. However, due to its simplicity, it is rather popular among master students in German-speaking countries. Figure 3 is based on this - I call it - "integrated DSR framework", combining Österle et al. [33] and Benner-Wickner et al. [1].

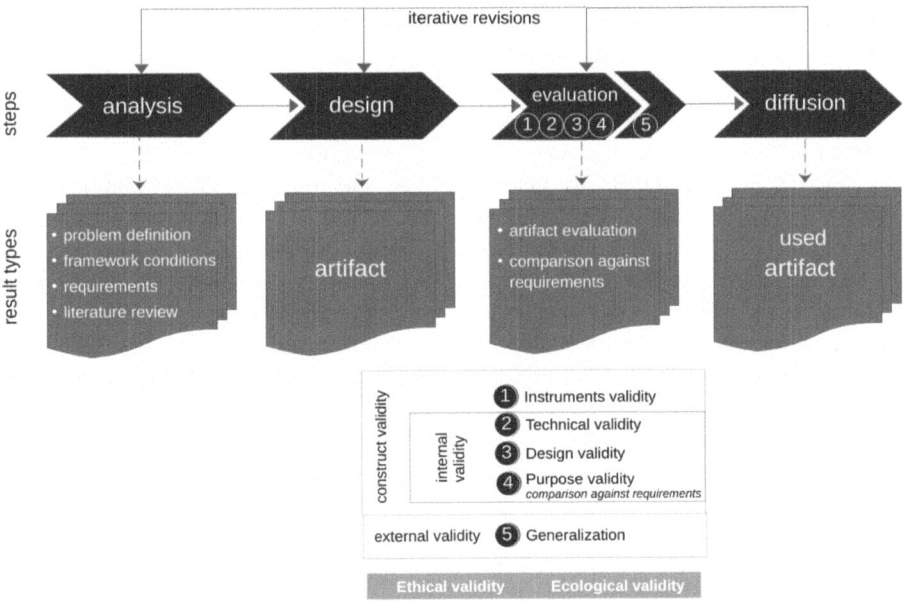

Fig. 3. Revised DSR framework focused on artifact validity, based on the integrated DSR framework combining Österle et al. [33] and Benner-Wickner et al. [1].

The revision shown in Fig. 3 is the extension made in the evaluation step to include the five proposed validity types. The five types of validity were harmonized with the main types of validity (construct, internal and external validity), which have been known and used for decades, see Fig. 1. Furthermore, the ethical and ecological validity were pointed out, which should be addressed as standalone measurement instruments, but which would require a separate study. The five validity types are defined in more detail in Sect. 4.2 and demonstrated using examples.

4.2 Validity Types

Although the rigor required in design science research (DSR) implicitly encompasses all five types of validity proposed here, none of the three compared frameworks explicitly refer to or differentiate between these fundamentally necessary types of validity. Therefore, they can easily be overlooked by students who rely exclusively on one of these popular DSR frameworks in their master's thesis. To ensure artifact validity, each validity type is defined in its core below, accompanied by a key question and examples, and discussed further in Sect. 5.

Instruments validity ensures the evaluation instruments and metrics used to assess the artifact are reliable, accurate, and aligned with the constructs they are intended to measure. The KEY QUESTION is: Are the evaluation tools (e.g., surveys, log files, usability tests, experimental setups) valid and capable of accurately measuring what they are intended to measure?

EXAMPLE from everyday situations: When designing or using a thermometer for body temperature, it should accurately measure body temperature and not something else (e.g., room temperature or humidity). If a thermometer mistakenly reacts to the air temperature rather than body heat, it *lacks instruments validity* because it is not measuring what it is supposed to.

EXAMPLE of a DSR application: If a learning analytics dashboard is designed to track student engagement, *instruments validity* ensures that the selected metrics (e.g., time-on-task, login frequency) actually measure engagement rather than unrelated factors (e.g., technical errors causing inactivity).

Technical validity ensures the artifact performs as intended without bugs or glitches, focusing on technical reliability and functional correctness. The KEY QUESTION is: Does the artifact's technical functionality perform as intended and without problems?

EXAMPLE from everyday situations: A car's brakes must work correctly every time you press the pedal. If they function sometimes but fail at other times, the braking system *lacks technical validity* because it is unreliable and does not consistently perform its intended function.

EXAMPLE of a DSR application: A machine learning-based fraud detection system must be completely free of critical bugs, biases, or instability issues. If the system produces false fraud alerts due to faulty code, misclassifies legitimate transactions because of biased training data, or crashes under high transaction loads, it *lacks technical validity*. Such errors can lead to financial losses, customer distrust, and regulatory penalties, making error-free performance essential for reliable fraud detection.

Design validity evaluates the artifact's design from a subjective and aesthetic perspective, as well as its alignment with user expectations and contextual relevance. The KEY QUESTION is: Does the artifact exhibit good style, taste, and elegance, making it aesthetically pleasing and intuitive to users?

EXAMPLE from everyday situations: A chair might technically function (it allows sitting), but if it is uncomfortable, ugly, or too complex to use, it *lacks design validity*. A well-designed chair should be comfortable, aesthetically pleasing, and easy to sit on.

EXAMPLE of a DSR application: A finance dashboard for managers must not only provide accurate financial data but also be designed with clarity, usability, and efficiency in mind. If the dashboard is cluttered, difficult to navigate, or visually overwhelming, it *lacks design validity*, as poor design can hinder decision-making even when the data is correct. A well-designed dashboard enhances comprehension, streamlines analysis, and enables managers to make informed decisions quickly.

Purpose validity determines whether the artifact achieves its intended purpose by effectively solving the targeted problem with the defined requirements. The KEY QUESTION is: Does the artifact fulfill the intended goals (does it meet the defined requirements), and are the observed results attributable to the artifact itself (and not to confounding factors)?

EXAMPLE from everyday situations: A parachute's purpose is to slow down a person's fall. If a parachute doesn't open, opens too late, or fails to slow the fall, it *lacks purpose validity*, even if it was well-designed and made of high-quality materials.

EXAMPLE of a DSR application: A waste tracking app designed to help customers reduce landfill waste must be validated by measuring actual waste reduction against initial goals (e.g., a significant decrease in non-recyclable waste disposal per user). Even if the app correctly logs waste disposal data (*technical validity*), features a well-structured and visually appealing interface (*design validity*), and uses reliable tracking metrics (*instruments validity*), it *lacks purpose validity* if users do not actually reduce their waste. This failure could result from ineffective behavioral nudges, lack of actionable insights, or poor integration with waste disposal services, meaning the app does not fulfill its intended goal despite functioning as designed.

Generalization (external validity) assesses whether the performance and effectiveness of the artifact are transferable to other contexts, populations or environments. The KEY QUESTION is: Can the success of the artifact be repeated in other environments with similar results?

EXAMPLE from everyday situations: A good (universal) cell phone charger should work across multiple cell phone brands and models, not just for one specific device. If a charger only works for one phone and fails for others, it lacks generalization validity.

EXAMPLE of a DSR application: A predictive maintenance model developed for automobile engines may not perform well in other contexts, such as with aircraft engines or manufacturing machinery. Without testing the model in these different domains, it lacks generalization (external validity), meaning its effectiveness beyond the original domain remains uncertain.

The validity framework represents a reconceptualization and a new contribution to DSR methodology. Although the five types of validity proposed and defined here have been aligned with more traditional notions of validity (see Fig. 1), they are not simply an adaptation or extension of their use in the natural or social sciences, which often focus exclusively on descriptive or interpretive or theoretical validity. The validity framework is tailored to the constructivist and utility-oriented nature of DSR. It is consistent with the goals of DSR: to create useful, technically sound, and (whenever appropriate or desirable) generalizable artifacts with clear objectives. The five clearly distinguishable validity types are a well thought-out concept whose origins are rooted in and derived from the DSR logic. Consequently, the validity types can be directly **mapped to the iterative DSR phases**: Problem Identification (*Instrument Validity*), Design and Evaluation (*Technical Validity*), Design Process (*Design Validity*), Relevance and Theory (*Purpose Validity*), Reflection/Generalization (*Generalization Validity*). This makes the validity framework very practical for the evaluation of artifacts and makes it easier for DSR researchers to structure the evaluation around familiar steps.

4.3 Mandatory and Flexible Validity Types

The distinction between the five types of validity is essential, as they each relate to different aspects of the quality and impact of an artifact. Without differentiating between these aspects, critical weaknesses may be overlooked during the evaluation. While it is crucial to understand and differentiate between all five validity types, their application should be flexible and context-dependent. Some projects require all five types, while others may only focus on the most relevant ones. In any case, Evaluation should be systematic, meaning that validity aspects should not be arbitrarily combined or reduced to a single category, such as purpose validity. The structured consideration of all five validity types ensures a rigorous, meaningful and context-sensitive research evaluation.

Essential (Mandatory) Validity Types:

- *Instrument Validity* - Ensures that the constructs, measures, and theoretical foundations of research are valid. Without it, the entire study may lack credibility.
- *Purpose Validity* - Establishes the relevance and utility of the research. Any study should have a clear purpose and contribute meaningfully to knowledge or practice.

More Flexible Validity Types (Depending on Research Context):

- *Technical Validity* - Essential for implemented artifacts but less relevant for theoretical work that does not involve direct technological instantiation.

- *Design Validity* - Important in design-based research but less critical in exploratory or purely theoretical studies where artifact structuring is not the focus.
- *Generalization (External Validity)* - Critical in empirical and applied research but not always required in context-specific or conceptual studies. Some research deliberately focuses on niche scenarios without aiming for generalization (Fig. 4).

4.4 Scoring Guidelines for the Five Validity Types in DSR

Score	Qualitative Rating	Indicators
Instrument Validity		
2.0	Explicit	Evaluation instruments are clearly specified, validated, and justified; strong construct alignment; reliability discussed.
1.5	Partially	Tools are specified and aligned to constructs but with limited validation or justification.
1.0	Somewhat	Tools are presented without validation; alignment with constructs is assumed.
0.5	Implicit	Evaluation methods are vaguely referenced or indirectly inferred.
0.0	Weakly	No recognizable or credible evaluation instruments are used.
Technical Validity		
2.0	Explicit	Technical performance is tested, documented, and shown to be stable and correct across relevant use cases.
1.5	Partially	Functionality mostly confirmed; testing described but not comprehensive.
1.0	Somewhat	Artifact appears functional; minor validation or anecdotal confirmation only.
0.5	Implicit	Artifact is presented as functioning, but no evidence or testing is shown.
0.0	Weakly	Technical operation is unclear or contains obvious gaps/errors.
Design Validity		
2.0	Explicit	The artifact is aesthetically refined, user-friendly, and designed with clear attention to user context and elegance.
1.5	Partially	Interface or form is mostly user-oriented and clean but lacks depth in aesthetic or contextual considerations.
1.0	Somewhat	Design is functional but clunky, inconsistent, or poorly matched to context.
0.5	Implicit	Little design attention; aesthetics or usability not clearly considered.
0.0	Weakly	Design is neglected, unappealing, or user-hostile.
Purpose Validity		
2.0	Explicit	Clear and convincing demonstration of goal achievement; problem-solution fit is substantiated; confounding factors addressed.
1.5	Partially	Goals mostly achieved; attribution to artifact is plausible but not rigorously shown.
1.0	Somewhat	Goals are vaguely achieved; evidence is thin or lacks rigor.
0.5	Implicit	Purpose is implied; no direct evaluation of goal fulfillment.
0.0	Weakly	Artifact's effectiveness is not demonstrated; unclear purpose.
Generalization Validity		
2.0	Explicit	Transferability to other contexts is demonstrated or theoretically justified with boundary conditions.
1.5	Partially	Claims of generalization made with limited evidence or narrower scope.
1.0	Somewhat	Speculative generalization; little evidence provided.
0.5	Implicit	Generalizability is implied but not supported.
0.0	Weakly	No discussion of broader relevance or replication potential.

Fig. 4. Rubric (scoring grid).

Based on the definitions and key questions listed in Sect. 4.2, a rubric (scoring grid) with operationalized indicators for each validity type (i.e., what to look for when evaluating and scoring) was created below. Each validity type is scored in 0.5 steps from 0 (weakly) to 2 (explicit).

These scoring guidelines are designed for the evaluation of artifacts in a wide range of DSR projects. They are generalizable as they are based on the fundamental DSR objectives. The five validity types capture the key evaluation dimensions of artifacts in DSR. They cover the areas of measurement, functionality, usability, problem solving and external relevance. They are not tied to a specific area (e.g. IS, HCI, engineering) and can be applied to software tools, models, methods, frameworks or processes. The guidelines enable a structured assessment across diverse methods. DSR often includes mixed evaluation strategies (experiments, case studies, user tests, simulations, etc.). These guidelines are method-agnostic, focusing instead on what the evaluation demonstrates in terms of validity. For example, instrument validity can be tested in one study with usability logs or in another with surveys - the evaluation logic remains the same. The scoring guidelines are designed to be reproducible and transparent and to support inter-rater reliability. The guidelines make the rationale for scoring explicit and reviewable and help to identify specific strengths or weaknesses in DSR evaluations. The scoring guidelines support both formative and summative evaluation: A DSR team could use this during artifact development (formative feedback) or it could be used by reviewers or researchers for summative assessment.

Limitations: However, some domains might require additional validity dimensions, e.g., ethical validity, sustainability, or stakeholder involvement. For highly technical or mathematical artifacts, proofs or formal models may supplement or replace some aspects (e.g., for technical or purpose validity).

5 Comparative Evaluation of DSR Frameworks

In this chapter, the scoring guidelines from Sect. 4.4 are used to evaluate the three selected DSR frameworks with regard to the main research question of this paper: To what extent do DSR frameworks support the validity of artifacts? All assessments are based on how explicitly each type of validity is considered and supported in the DSR frameworks, which is finally summarized in an overview in Sect. 6.

5.1 Instruments Validity

Hevner et al. (2004), Score (0–2): 0.5 - emphasize rigor in research methods but do not explicitly define instrument validity. While they stress that artifacts should be evaluated using reliable metrics (p. 85), they do not differentiate between validity of the artifact and validity of the instruments used for evaluation. This can lead to methodological weaknesses, as unreliable measurement tools could compromise artifact assessment. As a result, instrument validity remains an implicit concern rather than a structured requirement.

Peffers et al. (2007), Score (0–2): 0 - integrate evaluation as a core phase of their DSR process model, yet they do not explicitly address instrument validity. The framework assumes that research evaluations inherently produce valid findings but does not provide guidance on verifying the accuracy of evaluation instruments. Since measurement errors could affect the validity of conclusions, the absence of explicit considerations for instrument validity leaves a methodological gap, making it one of the least developed aspects.

Österle et al. (2010) and Benner-Wickner et al. (2020), Score (0–2): 0.5 - emphasize scientific rigor but do not formally distinguish instrument validity as a critical component of evaluation. Although their structured four-phase DSR model (analysis, design, evaluation, diffusion) suggests systematic assessment, it does not explicitly ensure that the instruments used for evaluation are valid. This oversight reinforces the tendency to assume rather than verify measurement validity, making instrument validity among the least developed aspects across all three frameworks.

5.2 Technical Validity

Hevner et al. (2004), Score (0–2): 1.5 - acknowledge technical validity through rigorous evaluation of artifact quality. Guideline 3 (Design Evaluation) calls for assessing functionality, reliability, accuracy, and performance (p. 85). However, technical aspects are embedded within broader purpose validity, focusing on effectiveness rather than verifying technical soundness. This poses risks-for instance, learning software may fail not due to purpose misalignment, but due to bugs. Although evaluation methods like experiments and simulations are mentioned (p. 86), technical validity is not defined as a separate requirement. Thus, it is acknowledged but remains only partially addressed.

Peffers et al. (2007), Score (0–2): 1.5 - embed evaluation in their DSR model, requiring researchers to demonstrate artifact effectiveness (p. 56). However, like Hevner et al., they do not distinguish technical validity from purpose or design validity. The emphasis on relevance and utility aligns more with purpose validity. Though feedback loops support refinement, the framework lacks systematic validation methods. This may result in artifacts being judged effective before ensuring technical reliability, posing practical risks. By prioritizing usability and relevance over explicit technical rigor, technical validity is acknowledged but remains only partially considered.

Österle et al. (2010) and Benner-Wickner et al. (2020), Score (0–2): 1.5 - offer a structured DSR process but, like earlier frameworks, do not define technical validity as a separate requirement. They incorporate empirical standards from software engineering [23], which strengthens technical validation compared to Hevner et al. and Peffers et al. Still, the framework assumes evaluation inherently covers technical issues without explicitly prioritizing them. Thus, while technical reliability is acknowledged, it remains only partially considered, embedded in broader evaluation rather than treated as a required, standalone step.

5.3 Design Validity

Hevner et al. (2004), Score (0–2): 1 - emphasize artifact utility but do not explicitly define design validity as a distinct evaluation criterion. While they discuss usability, completeness, and functionality as relevant quality attributes (p. 85), they do not provide systematic methods to assess coherence, user experience, or aesthetic quality. The framework prioritizes problem-solving and effectiveness over structured design validation, making design validity underdeveloped and largely assumed rather than explicitly assessed.

Peffers et al. (2007), Score (0–2): 0 - acknowledge artifact usability as part of iterative refinement but do not explicitly define design validity. The DSR process model ensures that artifacts evolve based on feedback loops, but it does not establish specific design evaluation criteria. As a result, usability and aesthetic considerations remain secondary to functionality and problem-solving. Without clear guidance on assessing logical structure, clarity, or user-friendliness, design validity remains one of the least developed aspects.

Österle et al. (2010) and Benner-Wickner et al. (2020), Score (0–2): 1 - emphasize practical relevance and structured evaluation, but design validity is not separately addressed. While their framework improves accessibility and application through a structured DSR process, it does not explicitly differentiate usability or aesthetic considerations from broader artifact evaluation. By focusing on practical implementation rather than formalized design assessment, design validity remains largely underdeveloped, similar to the other frameworks.

5.4 Purpose Validity

Hevner et al. (2004), Score (0–2): 2 - emphasize purpose validity by defining DSR as the creation of artifacts that improve organizational effectiveness and efficiency (p. 76). They state that artifacts must be purposeful, addressing key organizational problems (p. 82), reinforcing that utility and knowledge contribution are inseparable in DSR. The framework ensures feasibility assessment, confirming whether an artifact meets its intended purpose (p. 79).

Peffers et al. (2007), Score (0–2): 2 - explicitly link DSR to problem-solving and human purpose (p. 55), stating that successful artifacts must meet predefined objectives (p. 46). Their DSR process model prioritizes problem identification and objectives as key research phases, ensuring artifacts are designed with clear intent and evaluated based on their effectiveness (p. 54). This structured approach reinforces the direct connection between problem relevance, utility, and knowledge contribution.

Österle et al. (2010) and Benner-Wickner et al. (2020), Score (0–2): 2 - strongly emphasize practical relevance and societal impact by structuring DSR into analysis, design, evaluation, and diffusion phases, ensuring artifacts serve real-world needs. Benner-Wickner et al. enhance purpose validity further by transforming this structured process into a clear, visually accessible framework, making DSR principles easier to apply and reinforcing the artifact's practical relevance.

5.5 Generalization (External Validity)

Hevner et al. (2004), Score (0–2): 1 - recognize that DSR contributes to both practice and theory (p. 79) but do not explicitly emphasize external validity. While artifacts are meant to apply to real - world contexts, the framework doesn't focus on transferability beyond the initial problem space. It assumes utility in one environment implies broader applicability, so generalization is only somewhat addressed-not a key concern.

Peffers et al. (2007), Score (0–2): 1 - emphasize artifact effectiveness in its context but offer no clear guidance on generalizing results. Their process model promotes problem-solving and iterative refinement but lacks mechanisms for testing findings in varied settings. Thus, generalization is secondary to immediate artifact utility - acknowledged, but not emphasized.

Österle et al. (2010) and Benner-Wickner et al. (2020), Score (0–2): 1 - stress practical impact and diffusion as key DSR phases, implying some attention to generalization. However, their real-world focus doesn't extend to explicitly ensuring external validity. Although diffusion supports broader application, it lacks mechanisms to validate artifact use across domains. Generalization remains a secondary concern.

6 Summarized Assessment of the Five Validity Types in the Three DSR Frameworks

The table in Fig. 5 provides a summarized overview of how each of the DSR frameworks discussed in Sect. 5 addresses the five types of validity. This overview should help researchers and students to quickly identify the strengths, weaknesses and gaps in the validity considerations of each DSR framework. It also leads to the recommendation to seek a more in-depth discussion about the validation of an artifact.

Each validity type is rated using a *qualitative scale*, represented with colored labels, ranging from **explicit consideration** (*most emphasized*) to **weak consideration** (*least emphasized*). From this, the following patterns and commonalities can be identified:

- Purpose validity is the most developed across all three frameworks.
- Technical validity is acknowledged in all three frameworks, but only partially considered.
- Generalization is somewhat addressed, but not strongly emphasized in any framework.
- Instrument validity and design validity are the least developed overall.

To date, there has been no triangulation of the scoring process (e.g., through independent assessment by multiple reviewers). Therefore, the qualitative assessments from "somewhat" to "weakly" were summarized into a uniform color code (orange). The goal was to highlight the trends in validity support within DSR frameworks. Purpose validity - although marked in green - could (like all other

DSR Framework	Instruments Validity	Technical Validity	Design Validity	Purpose Validity	Generalization (External Validity)
Hevner et al. (2004)	● Implicit	● Partially	● Somewhat	● Explicit	● Somewhat
Peffers et al. (2007)	● Weakly	● Partially	● Weakly	● Explicit	● Somewhat
Österle et al. (2010) & Benner-Wickner et al. (2020)	● Implicit	● Partially	● Somewhat	● Explicit	● Somewhat

Index: Definition of the terms used in the table

● Explicit = The validity type is directly defined, emphasized, and required.

● Partially = The validity type is acknowledged, more developed than "Somewhat," but still not fully explicit.

● Somewhat = The validity type is referenced in related concepts but not given direct attention.

● Implicit = The validity type is lightly implied in broader discussions but not developed as a distinct concept.

● Weakly = The validity type is weakly or hardly addressed, requiring significant interpretation to find relevance.

Fig. 5. Consideration of the five validity types in three DSR frameworks.

validity types) be more strongly supported within DSR frameworks, particularly with regard to guidance on controlling for and avoiding confounding factors during the evaluation. However, compared to all other validity types, purpose validity is considered the most explicitly addressed of all DSR frameworks.

7 Conclusion and Future Work

This paper compares three influential DSR frameworks to assess their support for artifact validity. Five essential validity types were applied to the context of Design Science Research (DSR). The analysis reveals that while purpose validity is explicitly emphasized in all three frameworks, instrument validity and design validity remain the least developed.

Although DSR rigor implicitly encompasses all five validity types, none of the frameworks explicitly define or differentiate them. This poses a risk that mandatory instrument validity may be overlooked, leading to invalid artifacts and undermining research credibility. The biggest weakness arises when students or researchers rely solely on one of the frameworks without recognizing the need for deeper validation studies, particularly regarding instrument validity. Evaluation should not oversimplify validity by subsuming it under a single category, such as purpose validity, but should systematically process each type to ensure comprehensive assessment.

To address these gaps, this paper provides (a) a comparative overview highlighting strengths and weaknesses in each framework and (b) a revised and extended DSR framework that systematically integrates five validity types with definitions and examples and scoring guidelines. This structured approach enhances the rigor and reliability of DSR research.

Additionally, the lack of explicit emphasis on design validity, distinct from technical and other validity types, is notable given that design is central to DSR. While design validity may not be as critical as instrument validity, greater focus on user-centric criteria - such as simplicity, taste, style, and elegance - could enhance artifact adoption and usability. The revised framework proposed in this paper acknowledges the role of such subjective and aesthetic factors and can be adapted to different types of artifacts (e.g., software, processes, physical tools), ensuring broad applicability.

Further research could validate the revised and extended DSR framework through case studies and establish formal methods for instrument validity, and also include ethical and ecological validity as standalone measurement instruments. Exploring the impact of weak instrument validity and AI-driven assessments could enhance research credibility. Comparative analyses across domains may reveal best practices for ensuring validity. Addressing these issues will refine artifact evaluation, strengthening DSR's rigor and impact.

References

1. Benner-Wickner, M., Kneuper, R., Schlömer, I.: Leitfaden für die Nutzung von Design Science Research in Abschlussarbeiten. Working Paper 2/2020, IUBH Discussion Papers - IT & Engineering (2020)
2. vom Brocke, J., Winter, R., Hevner, A., Maedche, A.: Accumulation and evolution of design knowledge in design science research - a journey through time and space. J. Assoc. Inf. Syst. **21**, 520–544 (2020)
3. Samir Chatterjee, Anol Bhattacherjee, and Tom Gilb. A Typology of Knowledge Creation in Design Science Research Projects. In: Mandviwalla, M., Söllner, M., Tuunanen, T. (eds.) Design Science Research for a Resilient Future. DESRIST 2024. LNCS, vol. 14621, pp. 141–154. Springer, Cham (2024). https://doi.org/10.1007/978-3-031-61175-9_10
4. Cook, T.D., Campbell, D.T.: Quasi-experimentation: design & analysis issues for field settings. Houghton Mifflin, Boston, Mass. (1979)
5. Cronbach, L.J., Meehl, P.E.: Construct validity in psychological tests. Psychol. Bull. **52**(4), 281–302 (1955)
6. De Sordi, J.O., et al.: Design science research in practice: what can we learn from a longitudinal analysis of the development of published artifacts? Inf. Sci. Int. J. Emerg. Transdiscipl. **23**, 1 (2020)
7. Gregor, S.: Building theory in the sciences of the artificial. In: Proceedings of the 4th International Conference on Design Science Research in Information Systems and Technology - DESRIST 2009, p. 1, Philadelphia, Pennsylvania. ACM Press (2009)
8. Hevner, A., Chatterjee, S.: Design science research in information systems. In: Hevner, A., Chatterjee, S. (eds.) Design Research in Information Systems: Theory

and Practice, pp. 9–22. Springer US, Boston, MA (2010). https://doi.org/10.1007/978-1-4419-5653-8_2
9. Hevner, A.R., March, S.T., Park, J., Ram, S.: Design science in information systems research. MIS Q. **28**(1), 75–105 (2004)
10. Hevner, J.A.R., et al.: Transparency in design science research. Decis. Support Syst. **182**, 114236 (2024)
11. Hevner, A.R., vom Brocke, J.: A proficiency model for design science research education. J. Inf. Syst. Educ. (JISE) **34**(3), 264–278 (2023)
12. Iivari, J.: A paradigmatic analysis of information systems as a design science. Scand. J. Inf. Syst. **19**(2), 5 (2007)
13. Iivari, J.: Twelve theses on design science research in information systems. In: Hevner, A., Chatterjee, S. (eds.) Design Research in Information Systems: Theory and Practice. volume 22, pp. 43–62. Springer, US, Boston, MA (2010)
14. Knauss, E.: Constructive master's thesis work in industry: guidelines for applying design science research. In: Proceedings of the 43rd International Conference on Software Engineering: Joint Track on Software Engineering Education and Training, ICSE-JSEET 2021, pp. 110–121, Virtual Event, Spain, 2021. IEEE Press (2021)
15. Udo Kuckartz and Stefan Rädiker. *Qualitative Inhaltsanalyse. Methoden, Praxis, Computerunterstützung.* Beltz Juventa, Weinheim Basel, 5 edn. (2022)
16. Kuechler, B., Vaishnavi, V.: On theory development in design science research: anatomy of a research project. Eur. J. Inf. Syst. **17**, 489–504 (2008)
17. March, S.T., Smith, G.F.: Design and natural science research on information technology. Decis. Support Syst. **15**(4), 251–266 (1995)
18. Messick, S.: Validity. In: Educational Measurement 3rd edn., The American Council on Education/Macmillan Series on Higher Education, pp. 13–103. American Council on Education (1989)
19. Messick, S.: Validity of psychological assessment: validation of inferences from persons' responses and performances as scientific inquiry into score meaning. ETS Res. Rep. Ser. 1994(2), i–28 (1994). https://onlinelibrary.wiley.com/doi/pdf/10.1002/j.2333-8504.1994.tb01618.x
20. Nunamaker, J.F., Chen, M., Purdin, T.D.M.: Systems development in information systems research. J. Manage. Inf. Syst. **7**(3), 89–106 (1990)
21. Peffers, K., Tuunanen, T., Rothenberger, M., Chatterjee, S.: A design science research methodology for information systems research. J. Manage. Inf. Syst. **24**, 45–77 (2007)
22. Prat, N., Comyn-Wattiau, I., Akoka, J.: A taxonomy of evaluation methods for information systems artifacts. J. Manage. Inf. Syst. **32**(3), 229–267 (2015)
23. Ralph, P., et al. Empirical Standards for Software Engineering Research, March 2021. arXiv:2010.03525
24. Schlimbach, R., et al.: A teaching framework for the methodically versatile DSR education of master's students. J. Inf. Syst. Educ. **34**(3), 333–346 (2023)
25. Shadish, W.R., Cook, T.D., Campbell, D.T.: Experimental and quasi-experimental designs for generalized causal inference, pp. xxi, 623. Houghton, Mifflin and Company, Boston, MA, US (2002)
26. Simon, H.A.: The Sciences of the Artificial, 3rd edn. MIT Press, Cambridge (1969)
27. Sonnenberg, C., vom Brocke, J.: Evaluations in the science of the artificial - reconsidering the build-evaluate pattern in design science research. In: Hutchison, D. (eds.) Design Science Research in Information Systems. Advances in Theory and Practice, vol. 7286. LNCS, pp. 381–397. Springer Berlin, Heidelberg (2021). https://doi.org/10.1007/978-3-642-29863-9_28

28. Vaishnavi, V., Kuechler, W.: Design Science Research in Information Systems (2004)
29. Venable, J., Pries-Heje, J., Baskerville, R.: FEDS: a framework for evaluation in design science research. Eur. J. Inf. Syst. **25**(1), 77–89 (2016)
30. Vaishnavi, V.K.,Kuechler, Jr. W.: Design Science Research Methods and Patterns: Innovating Information and Communication Technology. 2nd Edn. CRC Press, Boca Raton (2015)
31. vom Brocke, J., Hevner, A., Maedche, A.: Introduction to design science research. In: vom Brocke, J., Hevner, A., Maedche, A. (eds.) Design Science Research. Cases. PI, pp. 1–13. Springer, Cham (2020). https://doi.org/10.1007/978-3-030-46781-4_1
32. Winter, R., vom Brocke, J.: Teaching design science research. In: ICIS 2021 Proceedings, Austin, TX, USA, December 2021. Association for Information Systems (2021)
33. Österle, H., et al.: Memorandum zur gestaltungsorientierten Wirtschaftsinformatik. Schmalenbachs Zeitschrift für betriebswirtschaftliche Forschung **62**(6), 664–672 (2010)

Designing Knowledge for Conversational AI Applications: A Bloom's Taxonomy Perspective

Tim Christopher Lange(✉) and Ricarda Schlimbach

Heilbronn University of Applied Sciences Faculty MV, Schwäbisch Hall, Germany
timlange@t-online.de

Abstract. The digital transformation in education presents numerous opportunities but also specific challenges, such as the growing skills shortage, the democratization of knowledge, and the increasing demand for personalized learning paths. The use of Artificial Intelligence holds promising potential to make learning processes more effective and sustainable. However, widespread integration of AI is lacking due to uncertainties about its effective application in teaching and learning. Recent research has focused on Conversational AI, which utilizes Natural Language Processing to enable human-machine interactions and is often deployed as Conversational Agents. These systems can evolve from task-oriented chatbots to companionship, offering competency-oriented support to learners. While Bloom's Taxonomy is widely recognized for structuring traditional learning, there is a notable lack of research on how Conversational AI technology can be effectively and sustainably integrated across different competency levels. We identified 56 design features for conversational AI in education through a systematic literature review of 3891 scientific papers. We then mapped these DF to 9 overarching design principles and classified them along Bloom's revised taxonomy. Instantiated mockups were then evaluated within the design research paradigm, contributing to the discourse on effective conversational AI in education.

Keywords: Conversational AI · Bloom's taxonomy · design science research

1 Introduction

The transformation towards competency-based, interactive, and digital teaching in education in recent years [1] has been further accelerated by technological advancements and the forced transition during the global COVID pandemic [2]. Simultaneously, the teaching profession faces increasing demands due to a shortage of qualified personnel, as many educational institutions lack adequately trained staff to meet the evolving requirements of modern education, which is already impacting the quality of numerous educational programs [3]. As learners have to navigate this changing educational environment, the demand for novel tools such as digital learning support to facilitate their learning processes is increasing [1]. A simple digitization of learning content alone cannot replace traditional face-to-face teaching because digital learning processes require new concepts for knowledge transfer [2]. Artificial Intelligence (AI) offers great potential to improve learning processes, with a growing research focus on Conversational AI (CAI), which utilizes Natural Language Processing (NLP) to enable interactions between humans and machines, often implemented as Conversational Agents (CAs) [4]. These systems have the potential to evolve from knowledge transmitters to learning partners who provide competency-based support to learners [5, 6]. However, widespread integration of AI is lacking due to uncertainty about how it can be effectively utilized in the teaching-learning process. In traditional classroom settings, educators deliberately apply learning objective taxonomies such as Bloom's Taxonomy [7, 8] to systematically foster cognitive skills, progressing from lower levels like remembering to higher-order thinking skills like creating new ideas [9]. Bloom's Taxonomy is a hierarchical model that helps learners understand and structure their learning process, gradually advancing from low order to high order thinking skills [10]. In its revised version by Anderson and Krathwohl [9], it comprises six cognitive process dimensions, ranging from basic (remembering, understanding, applying) to complex (analyzing, evaluating, creating) learning objectives. In digital learning environments, the challenge is that existing design knowledge for CAI applications often offers general recommendations without tailoring them to specific learning objectives, which can lead to less targeted support [11]. Therefore, this study examines how CAI applications may be designed to support learning processes along Bloom's Revised Taxonomy. Following the methodology for conducting meta-studies for design knowledge [12] within the Design Science Research paradigm (DSR) [13], we identified design features (DFs) from recent literature and mapped them to the learning objective levels of Bloom's Taxonomy [9]. In doing so, we aim to apply Bloom's Taxonomy to the design knowledge of CAI applications to systematically promote learning processes across the taxonomy levels. This study contributes to the discussion on the meaningful use of CAI in education by providing practical recommendations for creativity-enhancing learning environments aligned with Bloom's Revised Taxonomy, enabling learners to be supported in a competency-based manner in the future.

2 Research Background

Our approach is characterized by its innovative focus on cognitive process dimensions, which transforms the fundamental concept of classroom teaching into digital CAI applications, reusing existing DFs. In their systematic literature review (SLR), Schlimbach et al. [14] identified a research gap in learning goal-adaptive design knowledge for CAI applications. Current CAI design principles in digital learning primarily offer general guidelines instead of addressing specific learning objectives, leading to less effective support [11]. Building on this, we present core theories like Bloom's Revised Taxonomy that form the rigorous knowledge base for mapping our DFs identified in our SLR [15]. The design of CAI applications as socially engaged entities is based on the theory of computers as social actors (CASA) [16, 17]. CASA assumes that users instinctively apply social norms to computers when these systems exhibit human-like characteristics like names or gender-specific personas [16, 17]. The integration of social cues such as emojis, humor or human-like avatars increases social presence, promotes user engagement and improves learning outcomes through the persona effect [18–20]. In order to systematically develop effective AI systems, these social interaction principles are structured along Bloom's Revised Taxonomy [9]. It divides cognitive learning in six hierarchical cognitive process dimensions: **Remembering (1)** involves recalling facts. **Understanding** (2) focuses on explaining concepts. **Applying (3)** uses knowledge in new contexts. **Analyzing (4)** explores relationships. **Evaluating (5)** judges based on criteria. **Creating (6)** generates new ideas. These levels guide the structured learning process and enable the integration of CASA-compatible social features to promote lifelong learning.

3 Methodology

For the consolidation of existing design knowledge for CAI applications in the education sector along Bloom's Revised Taxonomy [9], we adopt the DSR paradigm, a recognized method for creating innovative artifacts that balance practical relevance with scientific rigor [21]. In DSR, the process model of Kuechler & Vaishnavi [22] is an established framework that we apply by conducting several iterative steps during artifact development. Through a SLR [15], we initially consolidated existing design knowledge on CAI applications for the preliminary design. Design principles (DPs) are theoretical abstractions derived from theoretical and empirical research that positively influence the design process, while DFs are specific implementations or functions that realize these principles [23]. Since the learning objective-oriented design of CAI applications depends on the specific implementation of DPs, we emphasize in a SLR, based on Page et al. [15], DFs that have already been derived from DPs and evaluated. Design knowledge is often consolidated and published, but it is rarely reused in the research and practice community [12]. Khosrawi-Rad et al. [12] propose an Meta-Study Process Model to conduct meta-studies for design knowledge that we applied to address the demand for increased reusability of design knowledge in the DSR community.

The proposed methodology involves six steps (see Fig. 1) [12]: The methodology begins by defining the scope (1) of designing CAs for enhanced learning pathways. Next, we conduct a SLR (2) following PRISMA [15] across *Scopus, AIED, ACM Digital Library, IEEE Xplore Digital Library, Taylor & Francis, AIS eLibrary*, and *ERIC*, using the search string: *TITLE-ABS-KEY ("Learning" OR "Education" OR "E-learning" OR "Instruction") AND TITLE-ABS-KEY ("Conversational Agent" OR "Collaborative Agent" OR "Chatbot" OR "Virtual Assistant" OR "Virtual Companion" OR "Interactive Agent")* in German or English language. We excluded studies that lacked an educational context, had no relation to CAs, were in languages other than English or German, were duplicates, focused on language learning or health, or were published before 2016. Only papers that published DPs, implemented the associated DFs, and evaluated them were included. For studies published after 2021, forward citation searching was conducted to include the most recent publications up to 2025 based on the same criteria. During the initial screening and data cleaning (3), we followed Schlimbach et al. [24] and established nine overarching categories (OC) for design principles from 15 fully coded articles: OC1 Human-likeness, OC2 Adaptability, OC3 Proactive/Reactive Behavior, OC4 Relationship Building, OC5 Supportive Content, OC6 Learning Competencies, OC7 Motivational Environment, OC8 Ethical Responsibility, and OC9 Purpose-oriented Functionality. Subsequently, we prioritized the papers (4) based on their alignment with the study's goals, focusing initially on those most relevant to the meta-study's purpose.

The core analysis involves systematically analyzing the DPs and DFs (5), assessing qualitative criteria and establishing a quantitative rating. We followed a 4-step process to evaluate the DPs in terms of reusability, frequency, rationale, and evaluation. Finally, broaden the analysis scope (6) by incorporating additional literature, addressing debatable knowledge, and refining the final set of recognized DFs to improve the reusability of design knowledge within DSR paradigm.

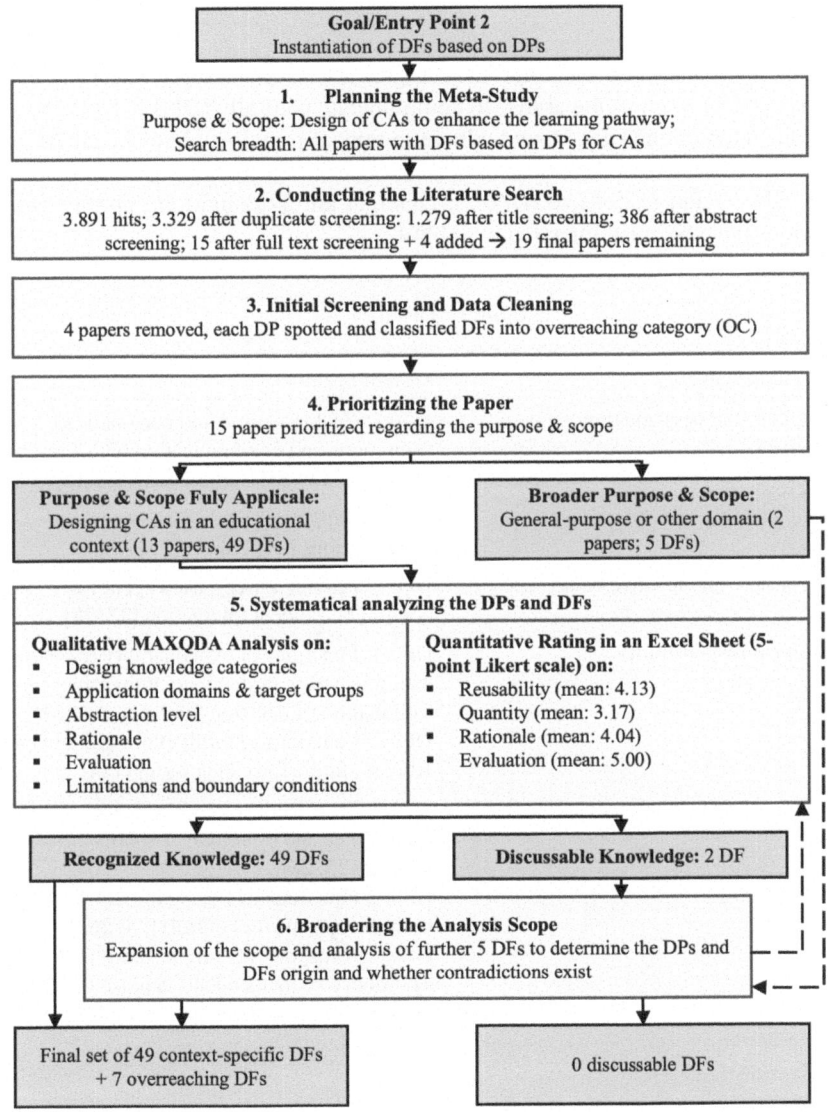

Fig. 1. Meta-Study Process Model based on B. Khosrawi-Rad et al. [12]

After finalizing the set of included 56 DFs and their DPs, we structured the design knowledge according to the stages of Bloom's revised taxonomy. For this, we analyzed the goals of each cognitive process dimension and mapped them to the capabilities of the features to support these goals, ultimately resulting in the theoretical artifact of this work. Finally, had consultants instantiate mock-ups there upon to evaluate the practical usability of our derived framework.

4 Results

Synthesizing the analyzed literature, the design for CAs include essential human characteristics (OC1), such as the ability to communicate naturally (DF0.1; DF0.2), enable continuous interaction (DF0.3), and adhere to ethical principles like ethical AI guidelines (DF0.5) and traceability of actions (DF0.4), while also being easy to understand (DF0.6; DF0.7) and responsive (DF0.7). DFs that are by definition important for CA applications have been summarized in Table 1.

Table 1. DFs for CAs

Overreaching Category	Design Features
OC1: Human-likeness and dialogue management	DF0.1: Enable natural and personalized salutations and communication by e.g. saving the context over the entire conversation [24, 25].
OC2: Adaptability and Adaptivity	DF0.2: Support individual and open-ended conversations [24, 26].
OC3: Proactive and reactive behavior	DF0.3: Provide a web-based agent for continuous student interaction [27, 28].
OC8: Ethical responsibility	DF0.4: Functions of explainability (explaining data processing in dialogue; transparent explanation of decisions and actions) [24]. DF0.5: Functions to fulfill ethics guidelines for AI (e.g., filters for vulgar terms) [24].
OC9: Purpose-oriented functionality and usability	DF0.6: Ensure a persistent overview of chatbot capabilities and optionally display conversation context [25, 28]. DF0.7: Functions of ergonomic design (e.g., multiple options for control) [24–26, 29] DF0.8: A responsive, simple and functional user experience so that students can use the tool intuitively and without distraction for learning tasks [28].

To design CAs that promote remembering, key features include learning-adaptive functions (DF1.1) and reducing cognitive load via multimedia-based information distribution (DF1.2). Limiting usage to the application interface prevents distractions (DF1.3).

Supportive content like learning techniques, strategies, time management materials (DF1.4), and access to tutorials (DF1.5) further enhance the learning process. Design features that also support **remembering (1)** are listed in Table 2.

Table 2. DFs for CAs that promote the learning goal of remembering.

Overreaching Category	Design Features
OC2: Adaptability and Adaptivity	DF1.1: Implement learning-adaptive functions (e.g., according to learning styles) [24]. DF1.2 reduce cognitive load by distributing information across multiple channels, based on the cognitive theory of multimedia learning [30].
OC3: Proactive and reactive behavior	DF1.3 application should be limited to the applications interface as adding links to external websites is not recommended as it leads to distraction [25].
OC5: Provision of supportive content	DF1.4: Teaching content on learning techniques and strategies as well as methods of time management [24]. DF1.5 provide access to learning content, such as tutorials [24].

To design CAs that promote understanding, reactivity and detailed feedback are crucial. Human-like avatars according to the characteristics of a VA (DF2.1) enhance engagement, while context-aware communication (DF2.2) adapts to situations and establishes common goals. Reactive functions address organizational questions and individual challenges (DF2.3). Providing practice exercises, learning materials, and answers to specific questions (DF2.4; DF2.6) supports comprehension. Feedback and diagnostic methods assess progress (DF2.7; DF2.8), while customizable features (DF2.9; DF2.10) ensure usability and inclusivity. Table 3 lists DFs that enhance **understanding (2)**.

To design CAs that promote applying knowledge, the focus is proactivity like learning tips, task planning, and distraction avoidance (DF3.5–DF3.6) to enhance engagement. This brings the focus on companionship, proactivity, and addressing users' psychosocial needs to foster a supportive relationship (DF3.1–DF3.3). Emotional and mental support, shared goals, and addressing psychosocial needs (DF3.7–DF3.9) strengthen the bond. Gamification, motivational communication, and peer networking (DF3.13–DF3.15) further encourage active participation, while adaptive scheduling and time management (DF3.17–DF3.18) ensure usability. Table 4 lists DFs aiding **applying (3)**.

To design CAs that promote analyzing, adaptability and networking are key. Personality-adaptive features (DF4.1) tailor interactions, while proactive redirection to educators (DF4.2) ensures expert guidance. Suggesting related learning topics (DF4.3) fosters independent exploration and connects educational content effectively. Design features that foster **analyzing (4)** are listed in Table 5.

To design CAs that promote evaluating, collaborative and analytical skills are prioritized. Collaborative learning activities and multi-user interaction management

Table 3. DFs for CAs that promote the learning goal of understanding.

Overreaching Category	Design Features
OC1: Human-likeness and dialogue management	DF2.1: Human-like avatar & dynamic evolution of the avatar (e.g. aging) [24, 27].
OC2: Adaptability and Adaptivity	DF2.2: Context-awareness (adapting the communication style to the situation, e.g., friendly vs. admonishing) & establishing a common ground (e.g., joint goals) [24].
OC3: Proactive and reactive behavior	DF2.3: Functions of reactivity (answering organizational questions, mental support for individual challenges) [24].
OC5: Provision of supportive content	DF2.4: Challenges (e.g., providing practice exercises) [24]. DF2.5: Support in collecting learning materials (e.g., encourage exchange between learners or link to relevant literature) [24]. DF2.6: Answers to specific learning questions [24].
OC6: Fostering learning competencies	DF2.7 design agents that provide detailed feedback to learners and support collaboration with assessment processes of learning progress [6] DF2.8 use of appropriate diagnostic methods to assess learners' knowledge level (e.g. pattern comparison) [6]
OC8: Ethical responsibility	DF2.9: Functions of customizability (e.g., of the avatar) to ensure inclusion [24].
OC9: Purpose-oriented functionality and usability	DF2.10: Customizability of the application's functionality (e.g., turning individual features on and off; choosing communication styles, privacy preferences, setting notifications) [24].

(DF5.1–DF5.2) foster teamwork. Multi-agent systems (DF5.3) provide diverse perspectives, while adaptive feedback (DF5.4) evaluates and enhances argumentation levels effectively. Table 6 summarizes DFs supporting the step **evaluating (5)**.

To design CAs that promote creating, creativity-promoting, collaborative features are prioritized. Inspiring and follow-up questions (DF6.1) stimulate learners' thinking. An innovation library (DF6.2) and structured phases (DF6.3) provide guidance. Tools like idea mergers (DF6.4) and image generators (DF6.5) enhance creativity. Facilitating transitions through task completion phases (DF6.6) supports group dynamics, while reminders about inclusivity (DF6.8) ensure equal participation. Table 7 presents the highest cognitive process dimension **(creating, 6)** with appropriate DFs.

4.1 Reflection on its Application

By shifting the focus from the design of CAIs to the design of learning processes enabled by CAIs, a student consultancy developed CAI mockups aligned with the presented DFs and corresponding to the six hierarchically organized cognitive process dimensions outlined in Bloom's revised taxonomy [9]. The focus of this three-week project was the development of CAI mockups to visualize the sequential learning process along bloom's revised taxonomy, culminating in a workshop where a professor of information systems, an AI software developer, and two potential users (students) evaluated the

Table 4. DFs for CAs that promote the learning goal of applying.

Overreaching Category	Design Features
OC1: Human-likeness and dialogue management	DF3.1: Human-like social behavior & communication (e.g. humorous character, emojis, responding to learners' interests) [6, 24–26]. DF3.2: Exposure of a personality [24, 25]. DF3.3: Function of emotional intelligence (e.g., expressing feeling, showing empathy, taking moods into account [24].
OC2: Adaptability and Adaptivity	DF3.4: Functions regarding the adaptability (e.g. the avatar, the personality, the language or the role) [24].
OC3: Proactive and reactive behavior	DF3.5: Functions of proactivity (autonomous suggestions for improvement, learning tips, autonomous assumption for planning tasks, proactive reminding of deadlines) [24, 31]. DF3.6: Functions of active distraction avoidance / support of concentration (e.g. blocking of apps, timer) [24].
OC4: Relationship building	DF 3.7: Functions of emotional and mental support (e.g., empathetic communication) [24]. DF3.8: Functions of promoting common ground and a shared mental model (e.g., setting mutual goals) [24, 27]. DF3.9: Assess the user's psychosocial needs and respond accordingly (e.g. by encouraging breaks or reducing organizational effort) [28, 29]
OC5: Provision of supportive content	DF3.10: Recommendation of suitable practice exercises to the students [32].
OC6: Fostering learning competencies	DF3.11: Learning advice and tips (e.g., individual and context-dependent) [24]. DF3.12: Encouraging communication behavior that stimulates self-reflection through a mentoring role [24].

(continued)

Table 4. (*continued*)

Overreaching Category	Design Features
OC7: Motivational environment	DF3.13: Functions of gamification and digital nudging (e.g., competitive elements, inter-individual performance benchmarking & immersion elements) [24, 33, 34]. DF3.14: Functions of motivational, friendly and supportive communication (e.g., congratulatory messages) [24]. DF3.15: Functions of networking with peers (e.g., community platform, recommendations for learning groups) [24].
OC8: Ethical responsibility	DF3.16 customizable triggering parameters: Learners can adjust the permitted triggering window (e.g. time of day) or suspend the triggers. Learners can manage the types of triggers they receive [31].
OC9: Purpose-oriented functionality and usability	DF3.17: Functions of task scheduling (consideration of travel times in scheduling, reminders and timers for breaks, suggested appointments tailored to the learner's context, personalized learning plans) [24]. DF3.18: Functions of effective time management (to-do lists, overview of appointments and deadlines set by professors, push notifications to remind students of assignments and achievements) [24]. DF3.19: Enabling internal as well as external interfaces (e.g. to Google calendar, to external content such as tutorials on YouTube, and to the university catalog) [24].

Table 5. Required design features for CAs that promote the learning goal of analyzing.

Overreaching Category	Design Features
OC2: Adaptability and Adaptivity	DF4.1: Functions of personality-adaptivity (e.g., according to the big five dimensions) [24].
OC3: Proactive and reactive behavior	DF4.2: Redirection of students to an educator's communication channel when the CA cannot respond [32].
OC5: Provision of supportive content	DF4.3: Proposition of learning topics similar to the current to help students learn on their own [32].

Table 6. Required design features for CAs that promote the learning goal of evaluating.

Overreaching Category	Design Features
OC4: Relationship building	DF5.1: The CA should provide collaborative learning activities [32]. DF5.2: Designed to support collaborative learning environments, addressing challenges such as participation balance and interaction management among multiple users [35].
OC5: Provision of supportive content	DF5.3: Multi-agent systems: Utilizing multiple agents within a system can model ideal behaviors and strategies, offering diverse perspectives and enhancing the learning process [36, 37].
OC6: Fostering learning competencies	DF5.4: Adaptive feedback function for argumentative texts with an analysis of the individual argumentative components and individual feedback that can assess the individual level of argumentation at any time [28].

Table 7. DFs for CAs that promote the learning goal of creating.

Overreaching Category	Design Features
OC3: Proactive and reactive behavior	DF6.1: Inspiring and follow-up questions to stimulate learners' thinking and ability to reiterate the topic when the conversation strays of-topic [38, 39].
OC5: Provision of supportive content	DF6.2: Innovation library with sample cases to showcase best practices [38]. DF6.3: Progressive phases to guide learners through the learning process in a structured way [38].
OC6: Fostering learning competencies	DF6.4: Idea merger to combine learners' ideas [38, 39]. DF6.5: Image generator to visualize concepts [38].
OC7: Motivational environment	DF6.6: Facilitate the transition through phases of task completion, following Tuckman's theory of stages in group discussion [39].
OC8: Ethical responsibility	DF6.7: Remind the group about inclusivity and equal participation, by prompting them to give more opportunities to less-contributing participants [39].

mockups on cognitive process dimensions for implementation. The workshop results reveal user-centric insights across various cognitive dimensions. For **remembering (1)**, the mockups contain various multimedia elements (DF1.2) for a varied mediation of learning content and thus adaptive learning paths (DF1.1), as well as effective time management strategies (DF1.4), which were emphasized by the participants as essential for improving memory performance. In the **understanding (2)** dimension, reactive feedback functions (DF2.6; DF2.7) such as tracking users' progress (DF2.8) and personalized context-aware communication (DF2.2) were presented in the mockups, while the personalized customizability of application functionality (DF2.9; DF2.10) was recognized as a crucial ethical responsibility. The workshops indicated that CAIs facilitate **applying (3)** through proactive features (DF3.5), such as a "Challenge of the Day." Additionally, CAIs can showcase personality (DF3.2) by demonstrating human-like emotional intelligence (DF3.1), including humor (DF3.3), fostering social connections with the user (DF3.7 - DF3.9). Users expressed a desire for motivation (DF3.14) through gamification elements (DF3.13), such as experience points or rewards. The mockups demonstrated that the **analysis (4)** is enhanced by human-in-the-loop strategies (DF4.2). Users expressed a demand for expert support when AI feedback lacks clarity, alongside expectations for personality adaptability (DF4.1) and interdisciplinary topic recommendations (DF4.3). The mockups demonstrated that in the **evaluation (5)** dimension, participants confirmed the advantages of collaborative tools (DF5.1–DF5.3) that enhance students' interaction and utilize multi-agent systems. Furthermore, they highlighted the necessity of adaptive feedback functions for effectively analyzing individual argumentative components (DF5.4). Finally, regarding **creativity (6)**, users noted that time constraints can hinder creative processes in modern educational environments. They recommended inspiration challenges (DF6.1) and innovative library of methods (DF6.2) instead.

5 Discussion

Overall, this study advances the understanding of effective CAI design to foster learners' cognitive processes and lays the foundation for a comprehensive synthesis of the identified findings. The results highlight the need to shift from an application-centered to a learning process-centered perspective, challenging CAI designers in education to integrate an additional cognitive process dimension into future implementations. For example, different roles of CAs, such as tutors, mentors, organizers, or moderators [24], can unfold their potential in different cognitive process dimensions. While time management provided by an organizer is particularly desired when learning to **remember (1)** vocabulary, learners often find time management tools less suitable during the **creating (6)** process. **Remembering (1)** focuses on recalling information, where systems such as ChatGPT[1] can support through targeted prompting but is not designed for more complex cognitive process dimensions [40, 41]. At the **understanding (2)** dimension, the goal shifts to interpreting, explaining, or translating information. Here, CAI applications excel by providing reactive responses to learning inquiries and detailed feedback, making assistance indispensable for fostering deeper comprehension. The **applying (3)** dimension emphasizes the application of acquired knowledge in new contexts, with effective distraction management through a companion tailored to competency-based learning objectives playing a crucial role in maintaining engagement and supporting learners at this stage. Research on CAIs increasingly explores the concept of Learning Companions (LCs), a specific type of CAIs which supports competency-based learning

---

[1] https://chatgpt.com/

objectives, by naturally interacting in their role as digital, humanoid learning facilitators that establish strong relationships with their users [24]. However, the existing literature does not sufficiently consider the learning taxonomy approach [11]. For advanced cognitive process dimensions such as **analyzing (4), evaluating (5), and creating (6)**, a companionship provides an ideal structure by proposing related learning topics that help students independently break down information into its components and recognize their relationships while these Artifacts can also be overstraining for learners to only understand (2) a new topic. Aligning CAIs design with Bloom's Revised Taxonomy is crucial, as low order thinking skills (1–3) require different features than high order thinking skills (4–6). Literature often overlooks this differentiation, risking overcomplexity or misaligned features at lower levels, which may distract learners and negatively impact outcomes, while evaluations remain undifferentiated.

5.1 Implications for Research and Practice

This study contributes to both theoretical and practical advancements in the integration of CAI in education. By aligning 56 DFs with Bloom's Revised Taxonomy, we provide a structured framework for fostering digital learning with CAs across all cognitive process dimensions and thus **contribute to the design knowledge of CAs (R1)**. For Remembering (1), key features include adaptive learning functions (DF1.1), multimedia content (DF1.2), and focused resources like tutorials (DF1.4; DF1.5). Understanding (2) relies on responsive interaction (DF2.3), context-aware communication (DF2.2), and detailed feedback (DF2.7; DF2.8). At Applying (3), proactivity (DF3.5), emotional support (DF3.1–DF3.3), and gamification (DF3.13) enhance engagement. Analyzing (4) emphasizes adaptability (DF4.1), expert redirection (DF4.2), and topic recommendations (DF4.3). Evaluating (5) benefits from collaborative tools (DF5.1–DF5.3) and analytical feedback (DF5.4). Finally, creating (6) is supported by tools like idea generators (DF6.2) and innovation libraries (DF6.1). Considering our deep roots in the established kernel theories such as the CASA [16, 17], which explains human-like behavior towards CAs, it can be summarized, considering the cognitive process dimensions [10], that companionship-driven CAs [42] can be purposefully used to support specific orders of thinking skills (3–6) from Bloom's revised taxonomy [9]. However, we identified a **significant gap in design knowledge for higher cognitive process dimensions (R2)** in Bloom's revised taxonomy [9], emphasizing the need to develop advanced design knowledge that better support learners in higher-order thinking skills. Additionally, we propose a **process-oriented perspective on CAs (R3)**, contrasting with traditional task-oriented approaches [43]. Aligning DFs with Bloom's cognitive dimensions enables goal-specific CA interactions, fostering deeper learning through companionship [44]. This perspective shifts the focus from functionality alone to a holistic view of learning as an interactive and adaptive process. Our research also **adapts Bloom's revised Taxonomy to digital, competency-based learning (R4)**, addressing the growing demand for personalized and competence-oriented tools [1]. This transformation extends beyond conversational agents and is applicable to other digital platforms, offering a scalable framework for competency-driven, adaptive learning environments. This approach ensures that digital tools are not only effective but also aligned with the evolving needs of learners in a digital age. From a practical perspective, our findings emphasize the need for learning solutions that **foster digital learning tools such as CAs (P1)**, particularly in higher-order tasks such as creating. By promoting proactive engagement [24, 31] and collaborative learning activities [35], our approach ensures that learners are empowered to reach the high-level thinking skills. Finally, our study provides **actionable insights for practitioners aiming to design CAs (P2)** that transform traditional educational paradigms [7, 8] into digital paradigms. By doing so, our research highlights that a simple digitization of learning material [2] does not satisfy learners who are already waiting for new digital tools [1].

5.2 Limitations and Future Research Agenda

This study faces three key limitations. First, while aligning DFs with Bloom's Revised Taxonomy [9] offers a novel perspective, the practical implementation and long-term effects remain untested. The assumption of a linear progression through Bloom's cognitive dimensions may oversimplify the complexity of individual learning processes. Second, the study consolidates existing knowledge instead of generating new data, emphasizing the need for novel DFs tailored to learning processes based on Bloom's Revised Taxonomy, as current DFs rely on traditional, application-oriented perspectives [11]. Finally, the reliance on meta-analysis and secondary data introduces potential biases from original studies, and the systematic literature review, despite its breadth, may have excluded relevant studies due to language or database restrictions. Moreover, the proposed DFs have yet to undergo further empirical validation in real-world educational settings, leaving their practical effectiveness uncertain.

Future research should prioritize the empirical validation of the proposed DFs through longitudinal studies, such as semester-long experiments, to evaluate their impact on learning outcomes and their practical applicability in real-world educational settings. Furthermore, in-depth exploration of DFs that specifically foster higher-order thinking skills, such as creativity-enhancing tools, could yield valuable insights and contribute to the further refinement of CAI design. Another critical avenue for future research lies in the development of novel DFs grounded in Bloom's Revised Taxonomy as a kernel theory. A process-oriented perspective on learning may generate fundamentally different DFs compared to the current application-oriented viewpoint.

6 Conclusion

This study presents a comprehensive framework for designing CAI applications in education by systematically aligning 56 DFs with Bloom's Revised Taxonomy [9], aiming to enhance cognitive skill development throughout the traditionally taught learning process. By consolidating existing design knowledge through a systematic literature review, the DFs are clustered according to Bloom's cognitive levels and the results are evaluated through a workshop using mockups. The study highlights the transformative potential of CAIs, which can evolve from simple knowledge transmission to fostering higher-order thinking skills, such as creation, by systematically aligning the design of CAIs with the respective levels of Bloom's Revised Taxonomy [9]. Our framework helps analyze existing CAI applications according to their addressed knowledge level but also provides guidance for purposefully designing novel CAI artifacts in education.

Disclosure of Interests. The authors have no competing interests to declare that are relevant to the content of this article.

References

1. Ngwacho, G.A.: Online teaching competencies for efficacious competency-based implementation in higher education. In: Keengwe, J., Gikandi, J.W. (eds.) Advances in Educational Technologies and Instructional Design, pp. 253–272. IGI Global (2023). https://doi.org/10.4018/978-1-6684-6586-8.ch013
2. Grogorick, L., Robra-Bissantz, S.: Digitales Lernen und Lehren: Führt Corona zu einer zeitgemäßen Bildung? HMD Prax. Wirtsch. **58**, 1296–1312 (2021). https://doi.org/10.1365/s40702-021-00806-z
3. Spieß, C. K.: Fachkräftemangel im Bildungssystem: mehr Druck, weniger Qualität, https://www.bib.bund.de/DE/Aktuelles/2024/2024-10-17-Interview-Spiess-Fachkraeftemangel-im-Bildungssystem-mehr-Druck-weniger-Qualitaet.html (2024).
4. Diederich, S., Brendel, A.B., Morana, S., Kolbe, L.: On the design of and interaction with conversational agents: an organizing and assessing review of human-computer interaction research. J. Assoc. Inf. Syst. **23**, 96–138 (2022). https://doi.org/10.17705/1jais.00724
5. Wambsganss, T., Kueng, T., Soellner, M., Leimeister, J.M.: ArgueTutor: an adaptive dialog-based learning system for argumentation skills. In: Proceedings of the 2021 CHI Conference on Human Factors in Computing Systems, pp. 1–13. Association for Computing Machinery, New York (2021). https://doi.org/10.1145/3411764.3445781
6. Winkler, R., & Roos, J.: Bringing AI into the Classroom: Designing Smart Personal Assistants as Learning Tutors. 10 (2019)
7. Krzyzanowski, A., Nucci, R., & Sevilla, D.: Blooms Taxonomie: Ein umfassender Leitfaden zu Bildungszielen, https://www.getguru.com/de/reference/blooms-taxonomy, last accessed 27 Oct 2024.
8. Universität Zürich: Teaching Tools, https://teachingtools.uzh.ch/de/tools/lernziel-taxonomien, last accessed 27 Oct 2024.
9. Anderson, L. W., & Krathwohl, D. R.: A taxonomy for learning, teaching, and assessing: a revision of Bloom's taxonomy of educational objectives: complete edition. Addison Wesley Longman, Inc. (2001).
10. Bloom, B., Engelhart, M., Furst, E., Hill, W., Krathwohl, D.: Taxonomy of Educational Objectives: The Classification of Educational Objectives. 1, (1956)
11. Meier, E.B.: Designing and using digital platforms for 21st century learning. Educ. Technol. Res. Dev. **69**, 217–220 (2021). https://doi.org/10.1007/s11423-020-09880-4
12. Khosrawi-Rad, B., Grogorick, L., Strohmann, T., Robra-Bissantz, S.: Toward a method for design science research meta-studies to improve the reusability of design principles. In: Mandviwalla, M., Söllner, M., Tuunanen, T. (eds.) Design Science Research for a Resilient Future, pp. 182–196. Springer Nature, Cham (2024). https://doi.org/10.1007/978-3-031-61175-9_13
13. Hevner, A.: A Three Cycle View of Design Science Research. 6 (2007)
14. Schlimbach, R., Rinn, H., Markgraf, D., Robra-Bissantz, S.: A Literature Review on Pedagogical Conversational Agent Adaptation. (2022)
15. Page, M.J., McKenzie, J.E., Bossuyt, P.M., Boutron, I., Hoffmann, T.C., Mulrow, C.D., Shamseer, L., Tetzlaff, J.M., Akl, E.A., Brennan, S.E., Chou, R., Glanville, J., Grimshaw, J.M., Hróbjartsson, A., Lalu, M.M., Li, T., Loder, E.W., Mayo-Wilson, E., McDonald, S., McGuinness, L.A., Stewart, L.A., Thomas, J., Tricco, A.C., Welch, V.A., Whiting, P., Moher, D.: The PRISMA 2020 statement: an updated guideline for reporting systematic reviews. BMJ. **71** (2021). https://doi.org/10.1136/bmj.n71

16. Nass, C., Moon, Y., Fogg, B.J., Reeves, B., Dryer, D.C.: Can computer personalities be human personalities? Int. J. Hum.-Comput. Stud. **43**, 223–239 (1995). https://doi.org/10.1006/ijhc.1995.1042
17. Nass, C., Moon, Y.: Machines and mindlessness: social responses to computers. J. Soc. Issues. **56**, 81–103 (2000). https://doi.org/10.1111/0022-4537.00153
18. Feine, J., Gnewuch, U., Morana, S., Maedche, A.: A taxonomy of social cues for conversational agents. Int. J. Hum.-Comput. Stud. **132**, 138–161 (2019). https://doi.org/10.1016/j.ijhcs.2019.07.009
19. Demeure, V., Niewiadomski, R., Pelachaud, C.: How is believability of a virtual agent related to warmth, competence, personification, and embodiment? Presence. **20**, 431–448 (2011)
20. Lester, J.C., Converse, S.A., Kahler, S.E., Barlow, S.T., Stone, B.A., Bhogal, R.S.: The persona effect: affective impact of animated pedagogical agents. In: Proceedings of the ACM SIGCHI Conference on Human factors in computing systems, pp. 359–366. Association for Computing Machinery, New York (1997). https://doi.org/10.1145/258549.258797
21. Hevner, A., March, S.T., Park, J., Ram, S.: Design science in information systems research. MIS Q. **28**, 75–105 (2004)
22. Vaishnavi, V.K., Kuechler, W.: Design Science Research Methods and Patterns: Innovating Information and Communication Technology, 2nd edn. CRC Press, Boca Raton (2015). https://doi.org/10.1201/b18448
23. Gregor, S., Kruse, L.C., Seidel, S.: Research perspectives: the anatomy of a design principle. J. Assoc. Inf. Syst. **21** (2020). https://doi.org/10.17705/1jais.00649
24. Schlimbach, R., Khosrawi-Rad, B., Lange, T., Strohmann, T., Robra-Bissantz, S.: Design knowledge for virtual learning companions from a value-centered perspective. Commun. Assoc. Inf. Syst. **54**, 293–330 (2024). https://doi.org/10.17705/1CAIS.05411
25. Jain, M., Kumar, P., Kota, R., Patel, S.N.: Evaluating and informing the design of chatbots. Presented at the Proceedings of the 2018 Designing Interactive Systems Conference (2018)
26. Song, D., Oh, E.Y., Rice, M.: Interacting with a conversational agent system for educational purposes in online courses. In: 2017 10th International Conference on Human System Interactions (HSI), pp. 78–82. IEEE, Ulsan (2017). https://doi.org/10.1109/HSI.2017.8005002
27. Elshan, E., Ebel, P.: Let's team up: designing conversational agents as teammates. In: ICIS 2020 Proceedings, Hyderabad (2020)
28. Wambsganß, T., Söllner, M., Leimeister, J.M.: An Adaptive Dialog-Based Tutoring System for Argumentation Skills. 18 (2020)
29. Herrmann-Werner, A., Loda, T., Junne, F., Zipfel, S., Madany Mamlouk, A.: "Hello, my name is Melinda"—students' views on a digital assistant for navigation in digital learning environments; A qualitative interview study. Front. Educ. **5** (2021). https://doi.org/10.3389/feduc.2020.541839
30. Winkler, R., Hobert, S., Salovaara, A., Söllner, M., Leimeister, J.M.: Sara, the Lecturer: improving learning in online education with a scaffolding-based conversational agent. In: Proceedings of the 2020 CHI Conference on Human Factors in Computing Systems, pp. 1–14. Association for Computing Machinery, New York (2020). https://doi.org/10.1145/3313831.3376781
31. Rodriguez, J., Piccoli, G., Bartosiak, M.: Nudging the Classroom: Designing a Socio-Technical Artifact to Reduce Academic Procrastination. (2019). https://doi.org/10.24251/HICSS.2019.533
32. Ramandanis, D., Xinogalos, S.: Designing a Chatbot for contemporary education: a systematic literature review. Information. **14**, 503 (2023). https://doi.org/10.3390/info14090503
33. Halan, S., Rossen, B., Cendan, J., Lok, B.: High Score! - Motivation strategies for user participation in virtual human development. In: Allbeck, J., Badler, N., Bickmore, T., Pelachaud,

C., Safonova, A. (eds.) Intelligent Virtual Agents, pp. 482–488. Springer, Berlin, Heidelberg (2010). https://doi.org/10.1007/978-3-642-15892-6_52
34. Katchapakirin, K., Anutariya, C.: An architectural design of ScratchThAI: a conversational agent for computational thinking development using scratch. In: Proceedings of the 10th International Conference on Advances in Information Technology, pp. 1–7. Association for Computing Machinery, New York (2018). https://doi.org/10.1145/3291280.3291787
35. Kumar, R., Rosé, C.P.: Architecture for building conversational agents that support collaborative learning. IEEE Trans. Learn. Technol. **4**, 21–34 (2011). https://doi.org/10.1109/TLT.2010.41
36. Lippert, A., Shubeck, K., Morgan, B., Hampton, A., Graesser, A.: Multiple agent designs in conversational intelligent tutoring systems. Technol. Knowl. Learn. **25**, 443–463 (2020). https://doi.org/10.1007/s10758-019-09431-8
37. Hayashi, Y.: Multiple pedagogical conversational agents to support learner-learner collaborative learning: effects of splitting suggestion types. Cogn. Syst. Res. **54**, 246–257 (2019). https://doi.org/10.1016/j.cogsys.2018.04.005
38. Schlimbach, R., Lange, T., Wagner, F., Robra-Bissantz, S., Schoormann, T.: An educational business model ideation tool -insights from a design science project. Commun. Assoc. Inf. Syst. **54** (2024). https://doi.org/10.17705/1CAIS.05423
39. Cai, Z., Park, S., Nixon, N., Doroudi, S.: Advancing knowledge together: integrating large language model-based conversational AI in small group collaborative learning. Ext. Abstr. CHI Conf. Hum. Factors Comput. Syst. (2024). https://doi.org/10.1145/3613905.3650868
40. Batista, J., Mesquita, A., Carnaz, G.: Generative AI and higher education: trends, challenges, and future directions from a systematic literature review. Information. **15**, 676 (2024). https://doi.org/10.3390/info15110676
41. Wang, Y., Hanafi Zaid, Y., Li, J., Pan, Y.: Opportunities and challenges of using ChatGPT as a teaching assistant in English language teaching: a systematic literature review. In: Proceedings of the 2024 International Symposium on Artificial Intelligence for Education, pp. 375–382. ACM, Xi'an (2024). https://doi.org/10.1145/3700297.3700362
42. Strohmann, T., Siemon, D., Khosrawi-Rad, B., Robra-Bissantz, S.: Toward a design theory for virtual companionship. Human–Comput. Inter. **38**, 194–234 (2022). https://doi.org/10.1080/07370024.2022.2084620
43. Schlimbach, R., Windolf, C., Robra-Bissantz, S.: A Service Perspective on Designing Learning Companions as Bonding and Mindful Time Managers in Further Education. (2023)
44. Bovill, C.: Co-creation in learning and teaching: the case for a whole-class approach in higher education. High. Educ. **79**, 1023–1037 (2020). https://doi.org/10.1007/s10734-019-00453-w

Designing a Large Language Model Based Conversational Agent for Language Acquisition

Nicolas Neis[1](✉), Philipp Spleth[2], Cecilie Kudlek[2], Rüdiger Zarnekow[2], and Axel Winkelmann[1]

[1] University of Würzburg, 97070 Würzburg, Germany
{nicolas.neis,axel.winkelmann}@uni-wuerzburg.de
[2] Technische Universität Berlin, 10623 Berlin, Germany
{spleth,c.kudlek,ruediger.zarnekow}@tu-berlin.de

Abstract. Language acquisition through tandem learning, where learners practice with native speakers, is widely recognized for its effectiveness in enhancing communication skills and cultural understanding. However, this method faces persistent challenges, including difficulty finding committed partners, scheduling conflicts, inconsistent feedback, and anxiety about making mistakes. While common language exchange apps provide online solutions, these limitations often constrain them. This study explores the potential of a GPT-4o-based conversational agent (CA) as an alternative language exchange partner. CAs offer constant availability, immediate responses, and non-judgmental corrective feedback, presenting a promising solution to the barriers faced in traditional tandem learning. We employ a design science research approach to design, implement, and evaluate a CA specifically for English language learners. The CA's features, including adaptive language levels and contextual conversational abilities, are guided by principles of second language acquisition. Results from user tests and semi-structured interviews reveal its strengths in facilitating consistent practice and reducing learner anxiety while highlighting limitations in emotional connection and cultural depth. This study contributes to understanding how advanced conversational AI can complement traditional language learning methods and offers valuable insights for future educational technology development.

Keywords: Language Learning · Conversational Agent · eTandem

1 Introduction

Language skills are vital for accessing global opportunities in education, business, and social interactions. Practicing with native speakers is considered one of the most effective methods for language acquisition, offering real-life conversational experience. This is not limited to face-to-face exchanges but has been increasingly conducted online [47]. Language exchange apps like HelloTalk [11] and Tandem [45] provide online platforms for connecting learners with native speakers, but these solutions are not without limitations. Challenges such as difficulty in finding committed tandem partners, long response times, and interpersonal barriers like anxiety about mistakes hinder the process [5,13,21].

Conversational agents (CA) have emerged as an alternative to established forms of language practice, offering constant availability, immediate responses, and corrective feedback while potentially reducing learners' anxiety [13]. Unlike traditional language exchange methods, CAs eliminate challenges such as scheduling conflicts and inconsistent feedback from human partners, providing a more accessible and dependable practice tool [54]. Despite these advantages, many CAs fail to maintain coherent and natural conversations, limiting their effectiveness for language learning [5]. The introduction of ChatGPT in November 2022 [30] marked a significant advancement in conversational AI, with features such as contextual understanding, adaptability across diverse topics, and the ability to sustain coherent, multi-turn dialogues, setting it apart from earlier chatbot technologies. Its human-like dialogue capabilities make it a promising tool for language learning, though research on its specific potential for conversational practice remains scarce [18,52].

Hence, we aim to address the following research question: *How should an adaptive GPT-based CA be designed to replace or surpass human language exchange partners for language acquisition?* This question is significant as it examines the potential of cutting-edge AI to address persistent challenges in traditional language learning, such as accessibility and consistent feedback, offering insights into the future of educational technologies. Focusing on English, the most frequently studied second language and the dominant language in GPT training datasets, the study explores how a custom GPT-4o-based CA in the form of a text-based chatbot performs as a conversational partner. A design science research approach guides the study, aiming to design and evaluate a CA that aligns with established success factors in language acquisition.

User tests and semi-structured interviews with English learners familiar with tandem learning provide qualitative data for evaluation. Results highlight the CA's potential to address the limitations of human tandem partners by offering frequent interaction, immediate feedback, and a non-judgmental environment. However, limitations in social communication aspects, such as emotional connection, persist. This research makes three main contributions: (1) It broadens the theory by transferring the social constructivist and interactionist learning theory to designing AI-based CA for language acquisition. (2) It extends the interactionist learning theory by showing that besides human interaction, GPT-4o-based CAs can be used as competent partners for learning but are limited in social contexts. (3) It supports practitioners with guidelines for designing CAs for language learning with DP and evaluating our prototype.

2 Foundation and Related Work

2.1 Principles of Language Exchange

Language exchange, or tandem language learning, pairs speakers of different native languages to mutually learn each other's language through bilingual conversations [47]. The more proficient partner aids in language acquisition by correcting errors and facilitating expression [23]. This method is grounded in social constructivist and interactionist learning theories [29]. The zone of proximal development (ZPD) from social constructivist theory describes the distance between what learners can do independently and what they can do with guidance from a more capable peer [51]. Ohta [29] applies this principle to second language learning and shows a higher level of development when the language is used in collaboration with a more capable dialog partner. In tandem learning, thus, language acquisition takes place within the learner's ZDP by filling this gap through collaborative activities supported by the assistance of the more proficient tandem partner. Interactionist theory shows that learning occurs through conversations, which are not just a medium for practicing [8]. Similarly, Long's [25] interaction hypothesis emphasizes that negotiation for meaning in conversations promotes comprehension and language development.

Tandem learning occurs face-to-face or online (eTandem), including text-based communication [4], on which we focus. Text-based tandem offers unique benefits, such as real-time visibility and achievability, allowing learners to review and reflect on their language use during and after interactions [31]. Modes include asynchronous communication, like emails, and synchronous methods, like online chats [37]. Asynchronous tandem allows learners time to draft responses and detailed corrections, while synchronous tandem resembles oral communication, emphasizing negotiation of meaning but with less detailed feedback [31].

2.2 Conversational Agents for Language Acquisition

Conversational agents (CAs) are systems designed to simulate human dialogue through voice or text interactions [54]. They are broadly categorized into rule-based, retrieval-based, generative-based, and hybrid models [14]. Rule-based CAs rely on manually defined rules, making them suitable for specific tasks but limited in handling complex dialogues and grammatical errors [1,35]. Retrieval-based CAs select responses from a predefined database using similarity measures, offering coherent replies constrained by the quality and breadth of the response repository [16]. Generative-based models, trained on large datasets, dynamically produce responses, leveraging sequence-to-sequence frameworks [42,49]. However, they require extensive filtering to mitigate inappropriate outputs [32].

Developed in the 1960s, ELIZA demonstrated early rule-based CA capabilities in psychotherapy simulations [55]. More advanced retrieval-based systems, such as Cleverbot, utilize large conversational databases for improved response generation [5]. Mitsuku integrates artificial intelligence markup language (AIML) with machine learning techniques to maintain coherent multi-turn interactions

[15]. OpenAI introduced ChatGPT in 2022, marking a significant advancement in CA technology with its foundation on the generative pre-trained transformer (GPT) architecture [30]. This model employs a transformer-based self-attention mechanism [48], enabling nuanced language comprehension and context-aware responses [17]. ChatGPT generates responses autoregressively, predicting tokens sequentially within contextual embeddings [56].

Several related works have investigated CAs for their applicability in language learning. Gallacher et al. [7] examined interactions between Japanese students and Cleverbot, noting the chatbot's effectiveness in vocabulary exposure and its limitations in emotional engagement and contextual appropriateness. Similarly, Shin et al. [40] evaluated Mitsuku for English language learning among Korean students, identifying its lexically rich responses yet noting its tendency for repetitive or irrelevant answers. Belda-Medina and Calvo-Ferrer [3] highlighted ethical concerns, particularly Mitsuku's generation of offensive responses, while recognizing Replika's enhanced user customization features.

Emerging research on ChatGPT's role in language learning suggests promising applications. Studies by Al-Obaydi et al. [2], Kohnke et al. [18], and Liu et al. [24] emphasize its potential for conversation practice, though empirical studies remain limited. Shaikh et al. [39] reported high satisfaction levels, particularly in grammar correction tasks, though the absence of detailed task analysis leaves open questions regarding its educational efficacy. Lorentzen and Bonner [26] explored a personalized ChatGPT chatbot in Japanese university settings, demonstrating increased engagement through persona customization. However, students struggled to maintain natural, detailed interactions, highlighting the need for enhanced conversational depth in AI-driven learning tools. These findings highlight the potential of AI-driven CAs in education and reveal persistent challenges in contextual comprehension, error correction, and user satisfaction, which we address to optimize their pedagogical impact.

3 Research Design

This study adopts the Design Science Research (DSR) methodology to address the research question and develop a chatbot application. DSR focuses on creating innovative artifacts that solve real-world problems, contributing to both practice and the academic knowledge base [12]. The DSR process model by Peffers et al. [34] structures this research into six steps (see Fig. 1).

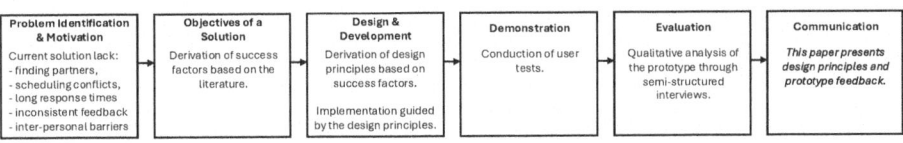

Fig. 1. Research Approach, according to Peffers et al. [34]

The research problem and its motivation were defined in the introduction, supported by a literature review on success factors in tandem language learning and challenges with human tandem partners. Our related work examines the limitations of existing CA solutions for language practice. Based on these insights, design principles were derived to address identified challenges and guide the artifact design and development. We demonstrated the artifact through user tests involving English language learners experienced in human tandem learning. Semi-structured interviews provided qualitative data for the evaluation. Finally, this paper communicates the design knowledge gained in developing a custom conversational agent based on GPT-4o as a language exchange partner. While DSR is often iterative, this research focuses on the initial cycle.

4 Objectives of a Solution

Language acquisition in tandem learning depends on several factors that determine the aims of our solution. Success factors for language acquisition can be derived from existing research using a literature analysis according to [50]. Regular communication provides essential opportunities for language practice. The comprehensible input hypothesis [20] and the output hypothesis [43] highlight the importance of exposure to and production of language for learning. However, asynchronous tandem may be hindered by time zone differences or partner availability [10]. The noticing concept suggests that learners acquire language by consciously identifying errors [38]. Tandem partners, however, often lack professional teaching expertise, leading to inconsistent feedback [22]. Feedback quality depends on partners' commitment and communication focus [31]. Effective tandem learning requires comprehensible input slightly beyond the learner's current level [20]. Disparities in partners' language levels may lead to imbalanced use of languages, limiting opportunities for the less proficient learner [36]. The affective filter hypothesis suggests that high motivation and low anxiety enhance language acquisition [19]. Tandem learning's informal, interest-driven format can increase motivation while reducing anxiety, though mismatched partners or personal complications may hinder progress [46,53]. In summary, tandem learning provides a dynamic platform for language acquisition, blending interactionist principles with the flexibility of modern communication technologies. Learners can maximize their potential in this collaborative learning environment by addressing feedback, frequency, and partner compatibility.

5 Design and Development

5.1 Deriving Design Principles from Theory

We derived five design principles (DP) from our literature review on language acquisition success factors and challenges with human tandem partners and CAs in language learning. Following the format proposed by Gregor et al. [9], we explicated the rationales behind these principles, ensuring a standardized schema

Table 1. Design Principles

DP	Title	Details	Source
1	Natural Communication	*AIM:* Allow human-like communication. *Mechanism:* Produce semantically coherent, natural, and lexically rich responses. *Rationale:* Supports language acquisition (comprehensible input hypothesis) and motivation (affective filter hypothesis).	[6,40]
2	Providing Corrective Feedback	*AIM:* Reflect on language errors. *Mechanism:* Highlight linguistic errors and provide corrections. *Rationale:* Salient feedback aids noticing (noticing hypothesis).	[3,27,31]
3	Adequate Language Level	*AIM:* Adapt input to user level. *Mechanism:* Output messages matching user language level. *Rationale:* Comprehensible input facilitates language acquisition.	[6]
4	Low Affective Filter	*AIM:* Create a stress-free learning environment. *Mechanism:* Use encouraging, non-judgmental language. *Rationale:* Low anxiety promotes acquisition (affective filter hypothesis).	[3,5]
5	Intuitive User Interface	*AIM:* Focus attention on learning. *Mechanism:* Provide an intuitive, easy-to-use interface. *Rationale:* Reduces cognitive load, freeing resources for learning.	[21,44]

that supports reuse and adaptation in similar contexts. The context is set in chatbot-based language learning for all five design principles and is therefore not included in the table to improve clarity (see Table 1).

The primary challenge of CAs used for language learning lies in their limited conversational ability, particularly in maintaining coherent communication over multiple exchanges. Loss of context and irrelevant responses can diminish learner motivation and adherence to language practice [6,40]. To address this, our first design principle emphasizes natural conversational flow. Unlike human tandem partners, most CAs fail to provide consistent corrective feedback [3], so our chatbot will highlight errors after every incorrect user message, leveraging Mayer's [27] signaling principle to focus learners on corrections. While excessive human feedback may discourage [31], its impact on chatbot interactions will be assessed. Additionally, our CA will adapt to users' proficiency levels [6], ensuring supportive and non-offensive interactions [3]. Language learners often feel less anxious with CAs than with humans [5], making emotional safety a key design goal. Lastly, based on Kuhail et al. [21] and Sweller's [44] cognitive load theory, the interface will minimize distractions to support effective communication. These principles, outlined in Table 1, aim to enhance the CA's usability and effectiveness for language learning.

5.2 Chatbot Development

To fulfill the design principles outlined earlier, we developed the chatbot using Python, integrating the OpenAI Application Programming Interface (API) and Streamlit [41] to provide an accessible web application. Upon user input, the system initiates an HTTP call to the OpenAI API, utilizing the GPT-4o model to generate a conversational response and corrective feedback. The system highlights language errors in the user's message with corrections. The chat interface preserves the entire conversation history until the user refreshes or closes the page, ensuring a coherent interaction experience. A sample conversation and the user interface are depicted in Fig. 2.

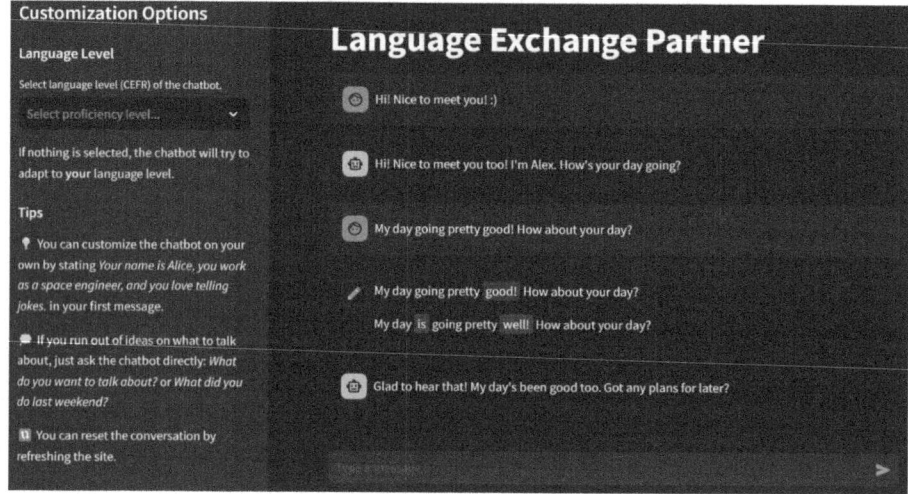

Fig. 2. User Interface of the implemented GPT-based Conversational Agent

We chose GPT-4o due to its capability for structured outputs, aligning with the Response object schema defined using a Pydantic class. The model categorizes input messages into three roles: system, assistant, and user. The system message gives contextual instructions, while the assistant message responds to the user's input and provides corrections. A system prompt instructs the model's behavior by defining tasks such as generating human-like replies and correcting user messages.

The CA emulates human interaction by incorporating a persona with traits such as a name, age, and hobbies into its responses. This ensures alignment with DP1 by enhancing natural communication. To address the verbosity of AI-generated replies and improve language learning efficacy, we instructed the model to provide concise responses, adhering to typical online chat conventions. The CA allows users to select the desired language level based on the Common European Framework of Reference for Languages (CEFR). This functionality supports DP3, ensuring responses match the user's proficiency level. By default, the CA automatically adapts its language level based on user input and provides a manual override for user preference or challenge. To maintain coherence, the CA includes the entire conversation history in its input context. Messages are stored in a list and appended to each new input before being sent to the model. This approach supports DP1 by ensuring contextually relevant responses. Figure 3 illustrates the individual components of the input to and output from the model.

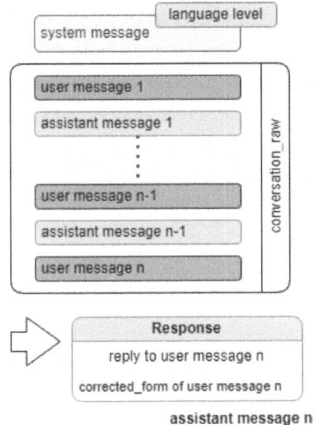

Fig. 3. Input to and Output from the Language Model

The model's context window of 128,000 tokens ($\approx$ 96,000 words) limits the implementation. Although summarization could extend usability, we deemed it unnecessary for the 10–20-minute user tests, as the token limit remained unexceeded. The corrective feedback mechanism addresses DP2. After generating a response, the system compares the user's original message with the corrected form. The correction function highlights errors in red and marks corrections in green when it detects discrepancies. It identifies character or word-level differences. This approach enhances feedback clarity and supports language learning, even for single-word inputs or languages without spaces. We chose GPT-4o, trained to minimize toxic outputs, to create a comfortable learning environment (DP4). Although generally reliable, the model may still generate inappropriate responses under specific conditions. Given the low likelihood of such scenarios, additional mitigation measures, such as explicit prohibitions against generating insults, were deemed unnecessary to avoid increasing input length.

The chatbot's web application, built with Streamlit, features a user-friendly interface optimized for language learning. The design minimizes distractions by organizing supplementary options in a sidebar, such as language level selection. This interface design supports DP5 by promoting user focus on the conversation. Customization options, such as a sample message to define the CA's personality, further enhance engagement. Icons distinguish between user messages, assistant responses, and feedback, maintaining clarity in the conversation history. For further technical details and code, refer to the full implementation at https://github.com/cecik4/chatbot.

6 Demonstration and Evaluation

We adopted a qualitative approach to demonstrate the CA, conducting user tests followed by an evaluation through semi-structured interviews. Participants (n = 9) were recruited via HelloTalk, ensuring familiarity with human tandem learning, and could compare their impressions of our CA with the app. The sample was intentionally diverse, considering language proficiency, age, and the number of corrections made on the HelloTalk correction tool to indicate usage intensity, enabling a broad exploration of user needs [33]. Table 2 summarizes the heterogeneous participant (P1-P9) composition, categorizing participants' occupations as students (S) or employees (E).

Table 2. User Test and Interview Participants

Participant	P1	P2	P3	P4	P5	P6	P7	P8	P9
Age	24	29	51	23	38	48	38	24	58
Gender	F	F	M	M	F	M	M	F	M
Occupation	S	E	E	S	E	E	E	S	E
Language level (CEFR)	C1	B2	A2	B2	A1	C1	B2	A1	C1–C2
HelloTalk corrections	4	1251	49	17	1412	370	109	118	6191

The web-based CA was hosted on Streamlit [41] Community Cloud and accessed via a browser link for the demonstration. Participants interacted with the chatbot in English for 10–20 minutes, treating it as a human tandem partner. Additional message suggestions guided users during interactions, which we logged for interview context. Semi-structured interviews with open-ended questions explored language acquisition, CA design principles, and participants' preferences compared to human tandem partners. An interview guide ensured consistency while allowing new topics to emerge.

We applied Mayring's [28] Qualitative Content Analysis using the Summarization technique to condense the interview data while preserving the core meaning to identify key themes in language acquisition. In the first reduction phase, individual cases were analyzed, with participants' statements about language learning via chatbot/CA or human tandem partners paraphrased. Using explication, we clarified statements with conversation logs and marked ambiguous opinions as positive, neutral, or negative. We generalized these paraphrases to reflect individual perceptions while omitting redundant or insignificant information. In the second phase, we synthesized categories from all cases into overarching themes and counted the frequency of statements to analyze trends. This structured analysis provides the foundation for evaluating the CA [28].

We evaluated the effectiveness of our CA for language learning based on participant feedback. Through the second reduction phase, we identified 39 key themes and organized them into broader topic areas, as presented below.

Conversational Skills and Dialogue Development. Users primarily perceived the chatbot's conversational abilities as positive. Participants highlighted its human-like responses, coherence, and diversity. Follow-up questions encouraged engagement and long-form replies. However, some responses were seen as overly generic or unrealistic compared to human interactions, particularly with emotional topics. The CA's extensive knowledge across topics was appreciated, though a few participants noted this as unnatural in typical conversations. The ability to sustain dialogues and propose new topics was a benefit, especially for language practice. Additionally, participants identified the absence of multimedia functionalities, including image and video exchange, audio calls, and real-time pronunciation feedback, as limitations impeding the CA's ability to replicate human tandem communication.

Corrective Feedback. Participants unanimously found the corrective feedback helpful, emphasizing its immediacy, accuracy, and comprehensiveness. They praised the error highlighting for its visibility, and the CA consistently outperformed human partners in providing unbiased corrections. Specific feedback, such as spelling and grammar corrections, was appreciated, while feedback on minor issues, like punctuation or text formatting, received mixed reactions. Some participants desired automated grammatical explanations and features to track frequent mistakes for future improvement. While the CA could provide explanations upon request, automatic elaboration on errors was preferred.

Language Level and Usage. The CA successfully adapted to participants' language levels, with most finding the default setting appropriate. However, some advanced participants desired more challenging vocabulary and complex responses. The CA's use of accurate and standard English was commended, especially by those with lower proficiency. Simplicity in phrasing enabled ease of understanding, though advanced users expressed interest in incorporating dialects, slang, and idiomatic expressions to enrich their learning experience.

Affective Factors. Participants described the CA as engaging and enjoyable, appreciated its ability to discuss personal interests, and valued its nonjudgmental tone. Unlike human interactions, participants felt less inhibited discussing sensitive or embarrassing topics, which fostered a supportive learning environment. The CA's empathetic responses and positive reinforcement contributed to its perceived user-friendliness. However, participants perceived its emotional depth and expressiveness as limited compared to human interactions.

Usability and Response Speed. The user interface received universal praise for being straightforward, intuitive, and well-organized. Participants valued its customization options, including dark mode and message-type icons. Suggestions for improvement included enabling the personalization of message icons. Users highlighted the chatbot's constant availability and instant responses as key advantages over human tandem partners, often limited by time zones and other commitments. This allowed for independent and flexible language practice.

Social Dimension of Human Communication. Despite its strengths, the CA fell short of replicating human communication's social and emotional dimensions. Participants noted that humans bring cultural experiences, personal anecdotes, and unique writing styles, which enhance language learning. The inability to form emotional connections or develop friendships with the CA was a recurring drawback. Participants emphasized that human interactions remain more engaging and meaningful for long-term language practice.

Intention of Further Use. Four participants expressed strong intentions to continue using the CA, citing its value for practicing low-proficiency languages, receiving immediate feedback, and supplementing human interactions. Others preferred human tandem learning for its emotional richness, cultural insights, and opportunities to build personal connections. The participants witnessed the CA as a valuable tool for specific purposes but not a complete substitute for human interaction in language learning.

7 Discussion

This study's findings highlight both the potential and limitations of GPT-4o-based CAs as language exchange partners. The study confirms that conversational agents can effectively address key challenges associated with human tandem partners, such as availability, consistency, and corrective feedback. The findings align with prior research emphasizing the importance of immediate feedback in language acquisition [27,38]. Unlike human tandem partners, who may provide inconsistent or delayed corrections [22], the CA offered structured and immediate error feedback, supporting Schmidt's noticing hypothesis [38].

Furthermore, the comprehensible input hypothesis [20] and the output hypothesis [43] suggest that language learning is optimized when learners are exposed to slightly challenging but understandable input. The CA successfully adapted to users' proficiency levels, ensuring that interactions remained within their zone of proximal development (ZPD) [51]. However, some advanced users needed more complex language and exposure to informal linguistic features, such as idiomatic expressions and dialectal variations. This suggests that future CAs integrate variable complexity settings to personalize language exposure further. While the CA demonstrated advantages in fostering a low-anxiety learning environment, it was limited in replicating human interactions' social and emotional richness. The affective filter hypothesis [19] suggests that lower anxiety enhances language learning. Participants in this study reported feeling less self-conscious when practicing with the CA compared to human partners, supporting the idea that AI can create a stress-free learning environment [5]. This aligns with findings by Shaikh et al. [39], who observed that AI-driven chatbots reduced language learners' anxiety and increased willingness to engage in conversations. However, the absence of human-like emotional connections was a critical limitation. Participants noted that human interactions offer cultural insights, nuanced personal expression, and opportunities for friendship, which were not replicable by the CA. Prior research highlights that social constructivist learning relies on meaningful interpersonal interactions [29,46], which AI-driven systems struggle to replicate. This underscores the importance of integrating more advanced sentiment analysis and emotional intelligence into CAs to enhance engagement and interpersonal connection.

Users consistently viewed the CA's feedback mechanism as valuable, particularly for grammar and vocabulary corrections. This supports findings from previous studies on AI chatbots in language education, which emphasize the role of automated error detection in language learning [3,24]. However, some participants desired more explicit explanations of errors and a history of their common mistakes, which could enhance metalinguistic awareness. Future CA development should consider integrating explicit grammar explanations and tracking common user errors to promote long-term learning. Additionally, while the CA provided corrective feedback in an unbiased and structured manner, human partners offered more nuanced and contextualized feedback. As O'Rourke [31] suggests, human interactions allow for a more detailed discussion of language nuances, which AI-based systems may struggle to provide. Incorporating contextualized correction explanations and examples within CAs could improve their pedagogical effectiveness. Participants generally praised the CA's usability, interface, and availability, noting that its constant accessibility provided a major advantage over human partners constrained by schedules and time zones. These findings align with research emphasizing the role of usability in AI-driven educational tools [21,44]. Participants suggested integrating multimodal features such as voice interaction, image-based communication, and pronunciation feedback. Given that multimodal learning enhances engagement and comprehension [27], future research should explore features to create a more immersive learning.

While this study demonstrates the potential of GPT-4o-based CAs for language acquisition, several limitations remain. First, the study focused on text-based interactions, limiting the exploration of spoken language practice. Future research should investigate the effectiveness of voice-based conversational agents compared to human interactions. Second, the study's sample size was relatively small (n = 9), restricting the generalizability of findings. A more extensive and diverse participant pool across different proficiency levels and cultural backgrounds would provide a more comprehensive understanding of CA effectiveness. Third, the short duration of the user tests is a limitation, as participants did not explore all customization options, such as adjusting language level or personality settings, which may have influenced the results. Fourth, while participants interacted with the CA over a short-term period, long-term studies are needed to assess sustained engagement and learning outcomes. Longitudinal research could evaluate how users integrate AI-based CAs into their language-learning routines and whether they remain motivated over time. Additionally, future studies should compare CA-driven language learning to traditional classroom settings and human tandem learning to identify optimal use cases.

8 Conclusion

This study contributes to constructivist and interactionist learning theory by demonstrating that AI-driven CAs can serve as effective, consistent, and anxiety-reducing language exchange partners. It extends the interactionist perspective by showing that AI-based dialogue can facilitate language development despite limitations in social interaction. However, human partners remain essential for cultural and emotional engagement. Future research should refine AI's role in adaptive, multimodal, and context-aware communication. By addressing these challenges, AI-based CAs could complement language acquisition, offering learners a scalable and personalized alternative to human tandem partners.

Acknowledgments. This work was carried out as part of the research project KARE, which is funded by the German Federal Ministry of Education and Research (BMBF) (funding number 02L22C206) and managed by the Project Management Agency Karlsruhe (PTKA). The authors are responsible for the content of this publication.

Disclosure of Interests. The authors have no competing interests to declare that are relevant to the content of this article.

References

1. Adamopoulou, E., Moussiades, L.: An overview of chatbot technology. In: Maglogiannis, I., Iliadis, L., Pimenidis, E. (eds.) AIAI 2020. IAICT, vol. 584, pp. 373–383. Springer, Cham (2020). https://doi.org/10.1007/978-3-030-49186-4_31
2. Al-Obaydi, L., Pikhart, M., Klimova, B.: ChatGPT and the general concepts of education: can artificial intelligence-driven chatbots support the process of language learning? Int. J. Emerg. Technol. Learn. (iJET) **18**(21), 39–50 (2023)
3. Belda-Medina, J., Calvo-Ferrer, J.R.: Using chatbots as AI conversational partners in language learning. Appl. Sci. **12**(17), 8427 (2022)
4. Cziko, G.A.: Electronic tandem language learning (eTandem): a third approach to second language learning. CALICO J. **22**(1), 25–39 (2004)
5. Fryer, L.K., Coniam, D., Carpenter, R., Lăpusneanu, D.: Bots for language learning now: current and future directions. Lang. Learn. Technol. **24**(2), 8–22 (2020)
6. Fryer, L.K., Nakao, K., Thompson, A.: Chatbot learning partners: connecting learning experiences, interest and competence. Comput. Hum. Behav. **93**, 279–289 (2019)
7. Gallacher, A., et al.: My robot is an idiot!–Students' perceptions of AI in the L2 classroom. In: Future-proof CALL: Language Learning as Exploration and Encounters–Short Papers from EUROCALL, pp. 70–76 (2018)
8. Gass, S.M.: Input and interaction. In: Doughty, C., Long, M. (eds.) The Handbook of Second Language Acquisition, pp. 224–255. Blackwell (2003)

9. Gregor, S., Kruse, L.C., Seidel, S.: Research perspectives: the anatomy of a design principle. J. Assoc. Inf. Syst. **21**(6), 2 (2020)
10. Gutiérrez, B., O'Dowd, R.: Virtual exchange: connecting language learners in online intercultural collaborative learning. In: Beaven, T., Rosell-Aguilar, F. (eds.) Innovative Language Pedagogy Report, pp. 17–22. Research-publishing.net (2021)
11. Hellotalk: Homepage. https://www.hellotalk.com/. Accessed 20 Jan 2025
12. Hevner, A.R., March, S.T., Park, J., Ram, S.: Design science in information systems research. MIS Q. **28**(1), 75–105 (2004)
13. Huang, W., Hew, K.F., Fryer, L.K.: Chatbots for language learning–are they really useful? A systematic review of chatbot-supported language learning. J. Comput. Assist. Learn. **38**(1), 237–257 (2022)
14. Hussain, S., Ameri Sianaki, O., Ababneh, N.: A survey on conversational agents/chatbots classification and design techniques. In: Barolli, L., Takizawa, M., Xhafa, F., Enokido, T. (eds.) WAINA 2019. AISC, vol. 927, pp. 946–956. Springer, Cham (2019). https://doi.org/10.1007/978-3-030-15035-8_93
15. ICONIQ: Kuki (2024). https://www.kuki.ai/research. Accessed 01 Jan 2025
16. Ji, Z., Lu, Z., Li, H.: An information retrieval approach to short text conversation. arXiv preprint arXiv:1408.6988 (2014)
17. Jurafsky, D., Martin, J.H.: Speech and Language Processing: An Introduction to Natural Language Processing, Computational Linguistics, and Speech Recognition with Language Models. 3rd edn. (2025). https://web.stanford.edu/~jurafsky/slp3/
18. Kohnke, L., Moorhouse, B., Zou, D.: ChatGPT for language teaching and learning. RELC J. **54**(2), 537–550 (2023)
19. Krashen, S.D.: Principles and Practice in Second Language Acquisition. Language Teaching Methodology Series, Pergamon Press, Oxford, reprinted edn. (1984)
20. Krashen, S.D.: Second Language Acquisition and Second Language Learning. Oxford, reprinted edn., Language Teaching Methodology Series, Pergamon (1985)
21. Kuhail, M.A., Alturki, N., Alramlawi, S., Alhejori, K.: Interacting with educational chatbots: a systematic review. Educ. Inf. Technol. **28**(1), 973–1018 (2023)
22. Lewis, T.: From tandem learning to e-tandem learning: how languages are learnt in tandem exchanges. In: Enseigner et apprendre les langues au XXIe siècle: Méthodes alternatives et nouveaux dispositifs d'accompagnement, pp. 107–127 (2020)
23. Little, D., Brammerts, H.: A guide to language learning in tandem via the internet. CLCS Occasional Paper, vol. 46. Trinity College, Dublin, Centre for Language & Communication Studies (1996)
24. Liu, G.L., Darvin, R., Ma, C.: Exploring AI-mediated informal digital learning of English (AI-IDLE): a mixed-method investigation of Chinese EFL learners' AI adoption and experiences. Comput. Assist. Lang. Learn. 1–29 (2024)
25. Long, M.H.: The role of the linguistic environment in second language acquisition. In: Ritchie, W., Bhatia, T. (eds.) Handbook of Research on Language Acquisition, pp. 413–468. Academic Press, New York (1996)
26. Lorentzen, A., Bonner, E.: Customizable ChatGPT AI chatbots for conversation practice. The FLTMAG (2023)
27. Mayer, R.: Using multimedia for e-learning. J. Comput. Assist. Learn. **33**(5), 403–423 (2017)
28. Mayring, P.: Qualitative content analysis: theoretical foundation, basic procedures and software solution. Klagenfurt (2014). https://nbn-resolving.de/urn:nbn:de:0168-ssoar-395173. Accessed 20 Jan 2025. Social Science Open Access Repository (SSOAR)

29. Ohta, A.S.: Applying sociocultural theory to an analysis of learner discourse: learner-learner collaborative interaction in the zone of proximal development. Issues Appl. Linguist. **6**(2), 93–121 (1995)
30. OpenAI: Introducing ChatGPT (2022). https://openai.com/index/chatgpt/. Accessed 20 Jan 2025
31. O'Rourke, B.: Models of Telecollaboration (1): eTandem. In: O'Dowd, R. (ed.) Online Intercultural Exchange, pp. 41–61. Multilingual Matters, Clevedon (2007)
32. Ouyang, L., et al.: Training language models to follow instructions with human feedback. Adv. Neural. Inf. Process. Syst. **35**, 27730–27744 (2022)
33. Patton, M.Q.: Qualitative Research & Evaluation MethodsâĂŕ: Integrating Theory and Practice, 4th edn. SAGE Publications, Thousand Oaks (2015)
34. Peffers, K., Tuunanen, T., Rothenberger, M., Chatterjee, S.: A design science research methodology for information systems research. J. Manage. Inf. Syst. **24**, 45–77 (2007)
35. Peng, Z., Ma, X.: A survey on construction and enhancement methods in service chatbots design. CCF Trans. Pervas. Comput. Interact. **1**(3), 204–223 (2019)
36. Rivera, A.V.: Hellotalk. CALICO J. **34**(3), 384–392 (2017)
37. Rosell-Aguilar, F.: State of the app: a taxonomy and framework for evaluating language learning mobile applications. CALICO J. **34**(2), 243–258 (2017)
38. Schmidt, R.W.: The role of consciousness in second language learning. Appl. Linguist. **11**(2), 129–158 (1990)
39. Shaikh, S., Yayilgan, S.Y., Klimova, B., Pikhart, M.: Assessing the usability of ChatGPT for formal English language learning. Eur. J. Invest. Health Psychol. Educ. **13**(9), 1937–1960 (2023)
40. Shin, D., Kim, H., Lee, J.H., Yang, H.: Exploring the use of an artificial intelligence chatbot as second language conversation partners. Korean J. Engl. Lang. Linguist. **21**(21), 375–391 (2021)
41. Streamlit Inc.: Streamlit Docs. https://docs.streamlit.io/. Accessed 20 Jan 2025
42. Sutskever, I., Vinyals, O., Le, Q.V.: Sequence to sequence learning with neural networks. arXiv preprint arXiv:1409.3215 (2014)
43. Swain, M.: The output hypothesis: just speaking and writing aren't enough. Can. Mod. Lang. Rev. **50**(1), 158–164 (1993)
44. Sweller, J.: Cognitive load during problem solving: effects on learning. Cogn. Sci. **12**(2), 257–285 (1988)
45. Tandem: Tandem Homepage. https://tandem.net/. Accessed 20 Jan 2025
46. Ushioda, E.: Tandem language learning via e-mail: from motivation to autonomy. ReCALL **12**(2), 121–128 (2000)
47. Vassallo, M.L., Telles, J.A.: Foreign language learning in-tandem: theoretical principles and research perspectives. The ESPecialist **27**(1), 83–118 (2006)
48. Vaswani, A., et al.: Attention is all you need. In: Advances in Neural Information Processing Systems, vol. 30. Curran Associates, Inc. (2017)
49. Vinyals, O., Le, Q.: A neural conversational model. arXiv preprint arXiv:1506.05869 (2015)
50. vom Brocke, J., Simons, A., Niehaves, B., Riemer, K., Plattfaut, R., Cleven, A.: Reconstructing the giant: on the importance of Rigour in documenting the literature search process. In: 17th European Conference on Information Systems (2009)
51. Vygotsky, L.S.: Mind in Society: Development of Higher Psychological Processes. Harvard University Press (1978)
52. Wang, F., Cheung, A.C., Neitzel, A.J., Chai, C.S.: Does chatting with chatbots improve language learning performance? A meta-analysis of chatbot-assisted language learning. Rev. Educ. Res. (2024)

53. Wardak, M.: It's tandem, not tinder! Interrogating authenticity and trustworthiness of language exchange applications in adult learners: a Central Asian and Middle Eastern perspective. WJEL **14**(2), 293–303 (2024)
54. Weber, F., Wambsganss, T., Rüttimann, D., Söllner, M.: Pedagogical agents for interactive learning: a taxonomy of conversational agents in education. In: ICIS 2021 Proceedings (2021)
55. Weizenbaum, J.: Eliza–a computer program for the study of natural language communication between man and machine. Commun. ACM **9**(1), 36–45 (1966)
56. Zhou, C., et al.: A comprehensive survey on pretrained foundation models: a history from BERT to ChatGPT. IJMLC, pp. 1–65 (2024)

Designing Digital Infrastructures for Trans-situated Learning

Jonas Sjöström[1,2](✉) and Hannes Göbel[1]

[1] University of Borås, Borås, Sweden
jonas.sjostrom@hb.se
[2] Halmstad University, Halmstad, Sweden

Abstract. This paper investigates how digital infrastructures, guided by growth tactics, can support trans-situated learning within networks of practice, promoting transparency, collaboration, and knowledge sharing across organizational boundaries. Using a design science research (DSR) approach, we developed and evaluated "SISA News," an information infrastructure for the Swedish Information Systems (IS) research community. The system aggregates news from 18 IS departments via RSS feeds, social media, and digital signage, facilitating cross-departmental engagement and vicarious learning.

The evaluation, based on the FEDS framework [22], includes proof-of-concept, proof-of-use, and proof-of-value stages [13], combining technical tests, social network analysis, and user feedback. Results demonstrate the infrastructure's effectiveness in enhancing transparency, enabling legitimate peripheral participation, and fostering knowledge exchange. Key challenges include achieving critical mass and maintaining content relevance across diverse stakeholders.

This study contributes to theory by advancing understanding of trans-situated learning and the role of growth tactics—such as adding services and providing interfaces—in the scalability and adaptability of digital infrastructures. It also highlights the mutual interplay between social learning processes and platform design .

Keywords: Digital infrastructures · Trans-situated learning · CoP · NoP · design science research

1 Introduction

DeSanctis [5] underscores the critical importance of the social life within the information systems (IS) research community, asserting that, "The social life of the IS research community is its future. How we attract and retain members, and the nature of our scholarly discourse with one another, will be the ultimate determinants of the legitimacy of the field" (p. 394). DeSanctis' reflection – a response to the 'IS crisis debate' initiated by Benbasat and Zmud in the early 2000s [4] – emphasizes the need for stronger collaboration, transparency, and connectivity within the field. Building on this vision, this paper explores how improved transparency and stronger inter-departmental relations can foster collaboration, spur ideation, and ultimately enable joint advancements in research and education.

The increasing emphasis on collaboration is further supported by funding agencies and academic institutions, which recognize its critical role in enhancing research quality and educational outcomes. For instance, the 2016 Swedish government's proposition for research funding [8] highlights the significance of collaboration, both nationally and internationally, as well as between academia and practice. Similarly, funding agencies worldwide increasingly prioritize multi-institutional and cross-sector consortia involving universities, industry, and the public sector.

Beyond funding imperatives, IS researchers and educators naturally operate within a community of practice [5], working in concert with colleagues from other universities and institutions. The creation of high-impact research environments often depends on the ability to cultivate meaningful external collaborations [7, 12, 17]. This collaborative spirit is equally evident in the realm of education, as illustrated by the AIS curriculum guideline initiatives [19, 20] and the activities of the AIS special interest group on education, demonstrating a shared enthusiasm for joint efforts to address curricular and pedagogical challenges.

Transparency, however, must extend beyond the academic and research community to engage society at large. In accordance with a recent EJIS publication [18], we assert that IS researchers must improve communication with practitioners, not only through publications but by fostering greater visibility of ongoing research and its societal impact. Efforts such as the EJIS initiative, which transforms research articles into practitioner-oriented summaries, echo similar long-standing practices in outlets like the Harvard Business Review.

This paper positions transparency and collaboration as central to addressing the challenges of inter-organizational learning. Specifically, it focuses on the concept of trans-situated learning (TSL), introduced by Vaast and Walsham [21], as a means to conceptualize and facilitate learning across multiple communities of practice (CoPs). TSL enriches the IS discourse by linking the emergence of networks of practice (NoPs) to the role of digital infrastructures. The design and development of such infrastructures, however, require distinct strategies, often referred to as *growth tactics* [11], to address the complexities of inter-organizational learning.

In this paper, we extend the discourse on TSL by examining the role of digital infrastructures in the Swedish IS research community through a design science research (DSR) initiative. We specifically address the research question:

How can growth tactics be employed to design digital infrastructures for trans-situated learning in networks of practice?

The paper follows Gregor and Hevner's [6] proposed structure for reporting DSR. Section 2 introduces the empirical research setting and outlines the applied research. Section 3 delves into the theoretical foundations underpinning the study. Section 4 describes the design and implementation of the information infrastructure, "SISA News," while Sect. 5 presents evaluation results and theoretical development. Finally, Sect. 6 summarizes the contributions of this research, highlighting its implications for both practice, and planned future inquiry into digital infrastructures for TSL.

2 Research Approach

This section outlines the empirical context of the SISA network of practice, the innovation opportunity that catalyzed this study, and the situated design science research (DSR) approach employed to address it.

2.1 Research Setting

The Swedish IS Academy (SISA) serves as the empirical context for this study. Founded in 2010, SISA is a network of 20 IS departments across Sweden, dedicated to fostering collaboration and building shared interests in research, education, and outreach. Its activities include organizing annual meetings, awarding pedagogical and research achievements, and promoting interaction between academia and external stakeholders, such as students, practitioners, funding organizations, and policymakers.

At the 2017 annual SISA meeting, participants identified the need to enhance collaboration and awareness across member departments. A specific proposal emerged: the development of a shared news outlet to increase transparency and foster connections across the community. This idea provided the basis for designing and deploying the SISA News information infrastructure, which aggregates and disseminates departmental news to support cross-organizational learning and collaboration.

2.2 Situated Design Science Research Approach

Given the aim of deriving actionable design knowledge for digital infrastructures that support TSL, this study follows the three core cycles of DSR [9, 10]: The relevance cycle, the rigor cycle, and the design and evaluation cycle.

Grounded in the SISA network of practice, the *relevance* cycle ensures the design addresses the practical needs of fostering transparency and collaboration within the Swedish IS community. The relevance cycle also includes field testing of the artifact, i.e., implementing it into practice and evaluating its qualities in a naturalistic use environment. The evaluation in this cycle corresponds to the proof-of-use and proof-of-value evaluation in the next section.

The *rigor* cycle consists of drawing from the knowledge base, including design science methodology), trans-situated learning [21], and growth tactics for digital infrastructures [11], the rigor cycle promotes that the system design is theoretically informed and generalizable.

The *design and evaluation* cycle encompasses the iterative design, implementation, and artificial evaluation of the SISA News system. It aims to test the artifact's ability to promote TSL while contributing theoretical insights. The evaluation in this cycle corresponds to the proof-of-concept evaluation presented in the next section.

Within our DSR frame, we adopt a mixed-methods approach [1, 23]. The combination of qualitative and quantitative methods allows for evaluation drawing on both use statistics (i.e., understanding the characteristics of actual use) and an inquiry into people's perceptions about the design. The mixed-methods approach allowed for a comprehensive evaluation of the system.

2.3 Evaluation Approach Using the FEDS Framework

Our evaluation strategy is based on the Framework for Evaluation in Design Science Research (FEDS) proposed by Venable et al. [22]. The evaluation trajectory integrates formative and summative assessments across artificial and naturalistic settings:

1. **Proof-of-Concept** (Formative and artificial evaluation): Early testing focused on the technical feasibility of aggregating and filtering news feeds from diverse sources (e.g., RSS, Twitter). Iterative debugging and keyword filtering ensured the infrastructure's reliability and usability.
2. **Proof-of-Use** (Summative and naturalistic evaluation): Naturalistic evaluations were conducted using system log data to perform social network analysis of news consumption. This revealed patterns of interaction, regional engagement, and the clustering of news readership, offering insights into the infrastructure's role in fostering cross-departmental connections.
3. **Proof-of-Value** (Summative and naturalistic evaluation): A user survey and qualitative feedback highlighted the perceived value of the system in promoting transparency, fostering collaboration, and enabling knowledge exchange. Stakeholders also identified challenges such as achieving critical mass and ensuring content relevance.

By aligning the design and evaluation cycles with the theoretical framework, the study advances our understanding of TSL and the role of digital infrastructures in networks of practice [21]. The iterative process formalizes the learning gained throughout the study – here we subscribe to the ideas of Sein et al [14] of continuous reflection throughout the DSR process, ensuring that insights from evaluation informs both artifact and theory development. Moreover, the integration of growth tactics [11] into the design promotes scalability, adaptability, and long-term sustainability of digital infrastructures, reinforcing their applicability to other professional communities.

3 Theoretical Foundation

In this section, we outline the two kernel theories that informed our design: TSL (Sect. 3.1) and Growth tactics for digital infrastructures (Sect. 3.2). The detailed application of each kernel theory will be summarized in Sect. 3.3 and further demonstrated through the presentation of the artifact in Sect. 4.

3.1 Trans-situated Learning (TSL)

Figure 1 depicts the interrelationships between various components of learning dynamics within communities of practice (CoPs) and networks of practice (NoPs), and how these are supported and conditioned by the underlying information infrastructure.

The model outlines the notion of TSL – a concept referring to learning that happens beyond the immediate context of a single CoP, involving larger networks (NoPs). It implies a transfer and adaptation of practices and knowledge across different CoPs within the broader network.

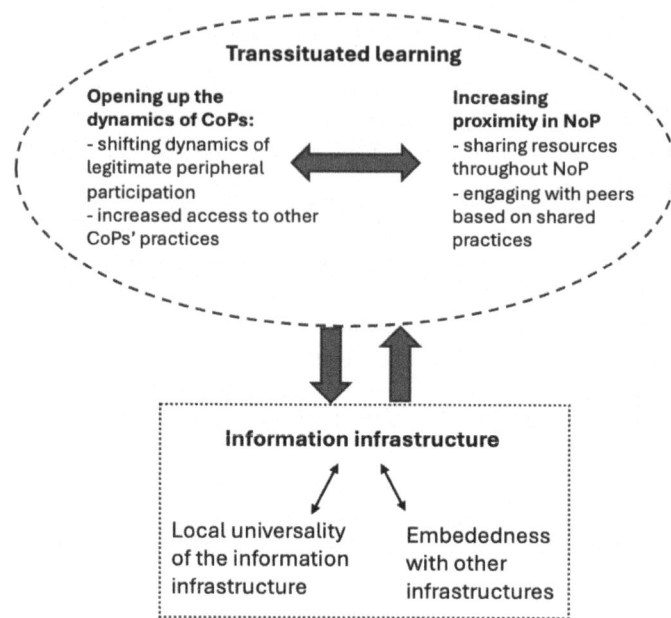

Fig. 1. Trans-situated learning and its relationship with the information infrastructure [after 22]

First, the model shows how the **dynamics of CoPs are opening up**. One factor explaining this process is the dynamics of legitimate peripheral participation (LPP): LPP is a process by which newcomers become integrated into a CoP, moving from peripheral participation to full engagement. In the context of TSL, this dynamic is becoming more fluid, with increased access to practices and knowledge from other CoPs. Another factor is the increased access to other CoPs' practices: The interconnectivity between different CoPs allows practitioners to access a broader range of practices and insights.

Second, the model shows the **Increasing Proximity in NoP**: This aspect of the model refers to the sharing of resources interrelated throughout NoP: Resources, be it knowledge, tools, or practices, are shared across the NoP, transcending the boundaries of individual CoPs. Proximity is also increased through the engagement of peers based on shared practices: Members from different CoPs engage with each other, facilitated by their shared practices and the resources available in the NoP.

The **Information Infrastructure** underpins the entire model, playing critical roles including: (i) Building and supporting conditions for changes in practices: The infrastructure facilitates the sharing of resources and interaction among CoPs and within the NoP. (ii) Local universality of the information infrastructure: It suggests a balance between global standards and local adaptations, enabling the infrastructure to be relevant and useful across diverse local contexts. iii) Embeddedness with other infrastructures: This indicates the integration of the information infrastructure with other systems and structures within the organizations, enhancing its effectiveness and reach.

Vaast and Walsham's view on TSL [21] suggests a co-dependent and mutually constitutive relationship between the social learning dynamics in the NoP and the implementation and use of the information infrastructure. This means that the learning dynamics within the NoP influence and are influenced by the way the information infrastructure is designed and used. The model illustrates how TSL across CoPs and within NoPs is supported by an information infrastructure that facilitates resource sharing, peer engagement, and adaptation of practices. This infrastructure not only responds to the existing practices but also shapes them, contributing to an evolving landscape of learning and knowledge exchange.

3.2 Growth Tactics for Digital Infrastructures

In order to find explicit ideas on how to extend SISA:s infrastructure for TSL, we turn to Henfridsson et al. (2018). They present four growth tactics for digital infrastructures, each with distinct strategies and outcomes: Adding services, providing interfaces, inventing processes, and opening identifiers. Below we introduce these growth tactics and their relevance for our design process:

Adding Services: This tactic involves responding to information service demands by creating a platform that encourages interaction among key stakeholders. For SISA, this could mean developing a shared platform that integrates news from different departments, enabling a more responsive and service-oriented approach to disseminate IS news across the Swedish IS community.

Providing Interfaces: This involves offering external application programming interfaces (APIs) to allow third-party developers to create services that extend the infrastructure's capabilities. In the SISA case, providing APIs could enable external parties to develop applications or services that leverage the SISA news service, potentially leading to innovative ways of presenting and using IS news.

Inventing Processes: This tactic seeks to establish new pathways for distributed service innovation, often through contests or hackathons that stimulate the development of new services. For SISA, we think of the invention of new processes as the guided emergence of the community to find and start using our design, thereby enhancing TSL.

Opening Identifiers: This tactic involves adopting to allow decentralized utilization of data, which encourages new forms of service development beyond the original infrastructure. For SISA, adopting a common standard for news dissemination could facilitate the integration of news services with international platforms, greatly expanding the reach and utility of the IS news service.

In essence, each tactic can contribute to the design of the SISA news service by expanding its functionality, reach, and the innovative potential of the services.

3.3 Summary: Implications for the Design Process

In summary, by building on the concepts outlined above, the SISA news system is envisioned as an information infrastructure to promote TSL, supporting the Swedish IS community in sharing knowledge and fostering a collective identity. Our design process factors in these ideas, effectively making them kernel theories in the DSR process. The notion of growth tactics for digital infrastructures specifically guides the design process through its conceptualization of extension strategies for digital infrastructures.

Before parting from the theoretical starting points, we need to briefly comment on the advent of generative AI (GenAI). Clearly, GenAI relates to several aspects of the SISA news service (e.g., for summarizing and translating news, and for classifying whether or not content is relevant for IS researchers). Given the timeline of the empirical work presented here (2018–2022), GenAI was not factored into the design process. We will, however, reflect about our results in relation to GenAI in the concluding discussion.

4 Artifact Design: The SISA News System

The solution architecture (Fig. 2) illustrates a digital infrastructure designed to support TSL learning within a distributed network of practice, such as the Swedish IS academic community. The model integrates growth tactics for digital infrastructures and theoretical principles of TSL learning with the goal to promote collaboration, transparency, and community engagement across institutional boundaries.

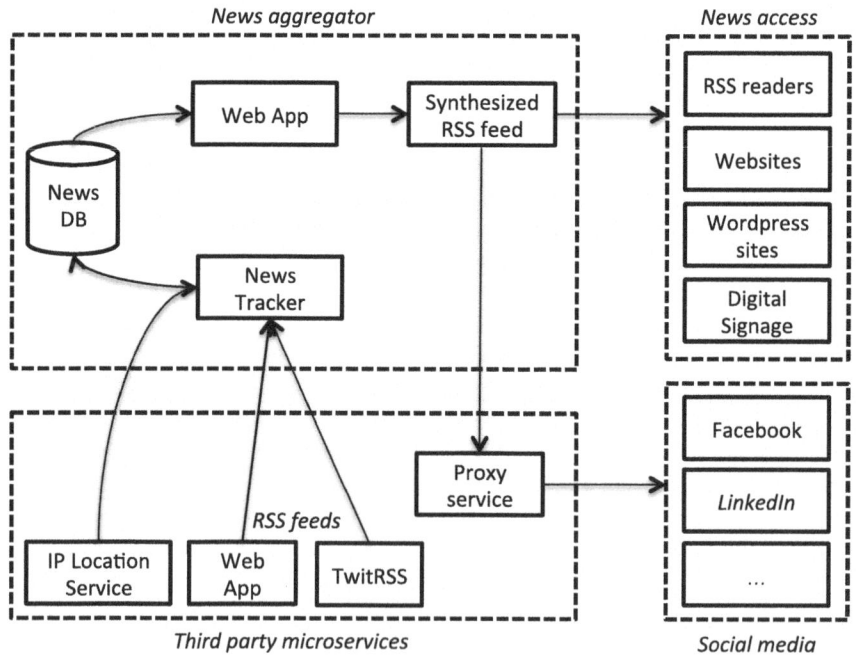

Fig. 2. Solution architecture for the SISA news system

The core of the system is the News Database (News DB), which aggregates news items from a variety of input streams. The News Tracker, a key processing unit, collects content from multiple sources, including RSS feeds from websites and Twitter streams via tools like TwitRSS and a Proxy Service. These sources are processed to ensure relevant, high-quality information is retained, reflecting a growth tactic of adding services—extending the functionality of existing infrastructures by integrating diverse data streams. The IP Location Service enriches the system with geographical metadata, enabling content customization and improving relevance for users across different regions, which is crucial for fostering TSL.

The Web App serves as the user-facing interface, allowing stakeholders to access and manage aggregated news. This component also generates a Synthesized RSS Feed, which acts as a standardized output for automated content distribution. This feed is critical for providing interfaces, another growth tactic, as it ensures compatibility with a wide range of downstream systems, including RSS readers, websites, WordPress sites, and digital signage. By offering a consistent and flexible interface, the system lowers barriers for integration with external tools and facilitates seamless dissemination of knowledge, a vital enabler of TSL.

The infrastructure's design supports dissemination to social media platforms such as Facebook and LinkedIn. This multi-channel strategy reflects the growth tactic of inventing processes, creating new pathways for information to flow within and beyond the immediate academic community. This promotes broader reach and engagement, which are essential for creating leaky knowledge flows that underpin TSL.

A significant feature of the infrastructure is its built-in evaluation and logging capabilities. These enable administrators to monitor user interactions, such as content consumption and engagement patterns. This meta-level functionality supports relevance optimization, allowing iterative improvements based on user feedback and system performance. For instance, usage logs can highlight regional engagement trends or identify underutilized content areas, informing refinements to both the content and the system design. This aligns with the principle of TSL by continuously adapting to the evolving needs of the network of practice.

The system's modular architecture, underpinned by microservices, ensures scalability and adaptability. Each component, from the News Tracker to the Synthesized RSS Feed, operates independently, allowing the infrastructure to evolve incrementally without disrupting existing functionality. This modularity exemplifies the growth tactic of service extension, enabling seamless integration of new features or data sources as the needs of the community change.

From a theoretical perspective, the design explicitly supports TSL by enabling knowledge sharing across diverse communities of practice. The system connects fragmented sources of information and presents them in a unified, accessible format, fostering peripheral awareness and cross-boundary collaboration. Through logging mechanisms following [16]—elaborated in the next section—the design is also intended to facilitate evaluation of these interactions, enabling the network continually learn and refine its practices and the underlying digital infrastructure.

In summary, the architecture reflects a strategic integration of growth tactics for digital infrastructures and the principles of TSL. By combining modular design, seamless integration, and user-centric features, the system enhances collaboration, fosters engagement, and supports the continuous evolution of the network of practice. This approach ensures that the infrastructure not only meets the current needs of its users but also remains adaptable to future challenges and opportunities.

5 Evaluation

From January 1, 2018, the news were available on a Facebook page, integrated into the SISA web site [15], or by subscribing to the RSS feed using a standard RSS reader. 18/20 Swedish IS departments are included in the aggregated news. We are able to conduct a naturalistic evaluation [22] drawing from the actual use of the system in a practical setting. Following Nunamaker and Briggs [13] we structure our evaluation into *proof-of-concept*, *proof-of-use*, and *proof-of-value*.

5.1 Proof-of-Concept

Technically, the artifact was uncomplicated. The transition from concept to functional software was achieved within the span of a week (November 1 to November 8, 2017). The development phase included iterative testing, which was instrumental in identifying and rectifying software bugs. Moreover, the integration of RSS feeds necessitated adjustments to accommodate variances from the standard RSS specifications due to inconsistencies in the RSS flows.

In practice, the incorporation of new RSS feeds into the federated news system was a straightforward process of adding a new entry, comprising the feed's URL and optional filtering keywords, to the database's feed table. However, we acknowledge the potential need to refine the tracker subsystem to address issues stemming from non-standard RSS feeds that may arise with future expansions. Initially, with 14 RSS feeds, the system cataloged 258 IS news items, though it is noteworthy that many RSS feeds present only a recent selection of items, hence older news may not be captured. Of these, 152 items were from the year 2017 (January 1–November 9). The news frequency, thus, averaged approximately one new item every two days, with projections indicating a daily news item if all 20 member entities commence content contributions. Consistent with literature on user engagement, regular updates are crucial in sustaining user interest in web applications (Naaman, Becker, & Gravano, 2011).

The SISA news feed was seamlessly integrated into the organization's website using a WordPress plugin on November 8, 2017. Progression entailed a strategic action plan, including the dissemination of information to SISA members about the news feed and its accessibility, the creation of an informative guide on content provision via RSS or Twitter dated November 30, 2017, and the proposal to discuss enhancements at an upcoming workshop.

The utility of a federated news feed is inherently dependent on the quality of its sources. We identified and communicated specific issues such as faulty links and non-compliance with RSS standard attributes to the respective feed managers. While some improvements have been implemented, challenges persist with direct article links within the feed. Despite these issues, as detailed in Table 1, the software has required minimal maintenance (Table 1) since January 1, 2018. The conceptual architecture has proven effective, aggregating a total of 1169 news items by January 27, 2020, and distributing them via web, social media, and RSS readers. Since then, the news publication and aggregation has proceeded in a similar pace.

Table 1. Issues that required maintenance attention from 2018–2022.

Issue	Description
Twitter integration	A change of policy at Twitter rendered the third-party service in use non-functional. It was replaced by another third-party service, but there is a risk that the new one also breaks down.
IP location lookup	The third-party IP location service has had some downtime. Tweaks were made to the SISA News tracker to minimize the dependency on the location service.
Bad source data	Double posts in a department's news feed renders double posts in the SISA feed.
Bad source data II	A department's news feed was hacked, leading to news of questionable content posted in their Twitter feed. Since the SISA news aggregation algorithm does not discriminate content, the questionable feeds were also integrated into the SISA news feed.
Relevance	Due to the pandemic, the work "digital" occurs frequently in all types of university news, which has increased the number of irrelevant posts from general feeds included through keyword filtering.

5.2 Proof-of-Use

Our second evaluative endeavor consisted of a cross-regional analysis of news engagement, utilizing log data as a substrate. Each interaction with a news item was meticulously recorded, capturing a timestamp, the unique identifier of the news article, as well as the geolocation data of the reader, encompassing both country and region.

The dataset underpinning our analysis spanned from January 1, 2018, to January 27, 2020. On average, users posted one news article daily, with nearly 8000 news articles receiving clicks. Within this context, we define a 'click' as a user's action to open a news item summary to view the full article, which we interpret as indicative of a news read. Nonetheless, it is plausible to surmise that additional users may have perused summaries without registering a click, such as within a Facebook feed. Notably, the Facebook page associated with the news service boasts 100 followers, an audience that equates to roughly one-third of all IS department staff across the 20 Swedish IS departments.

To glean deeper insights into the structural dynamics of network interactions, we leveraged network analysis methodologies facilitated by R. Our analysis incorporated community detection techniques to discern potential clustering patterns among the regions—that is, to identify whether certain groups of regions exhibited a heightened frequency of news reads in contrast to the overall national interaction (see Fig. 2). We selected a multi-level community detection analysis strategy, adhering to Yang et al.'s [24] guidelines, which underscore the suitability of various clustering algorithms contingent upon the analytical context.

Figure 3 delineates the regional network interactions, and the clusters identified therein. Each connection visualized represents a regional interaction within Sweden.

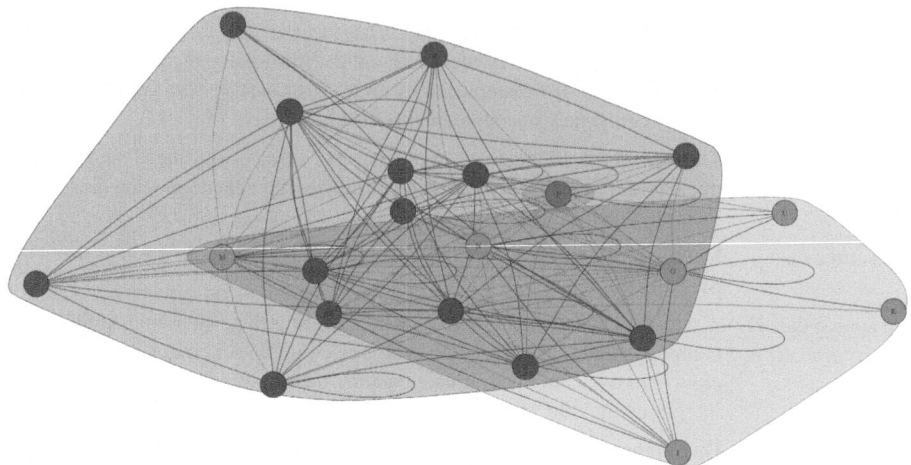

Fig. 3. Regional network interactions and identified clusters. Each edge represents a region in Sweden.

Employing a multi-level algorithm, the analysis proceeded iteratively, determining the optimal node clustering to maximize the modularity score—a metric that intensifies when interactions within clusters (akin to cohesion in software engineering vernacular) proliferate, and diminish when inter-cluster interactions (or coupling) are scant.

Owing to the algorithm's requirement for an undirected graph, we transformed the directed network graph into its undirected counterpart by aggregating the news reads from one region to another and vice versa. Consequently, each vertex embodies the aggregate news reads shared between two regions. This multi-level clustering unveiled three distinct clusters, accompanied by a modularity score of 0.1. A modularity score of 1 would imply exclusive intra-cluster interactions. Here, the modularity score verging on zero suggests that the clusters are not strongly demarcated, revealing an extensive degree of interaction among all regions—a finding that resonates well with SISA's objective to bolster transparency and foster cross-departmental interactions.

5.3 Proof-of-Value

In early 2019, approximately one year after the launch of the SISA news service, an online survey was initiated to gauge user perceptions of the news flow. Advertised within the very news flow it aimed to scrutinize, the survey unfortunately garnered a modest response rate, with 31 participants and 5 of those opting out of research utilization of their feedback. The survey, rich with open-ended queries, yielded qualitative data reflective of the perceived value of the SISA news service. We thematically parsed 58 statements, categorizing them into five distinct themes that encapsulate both the values and concerns associated with the news service. These categories were further classified as "Type I (actual)" or "Type II (potential)," with Type I indicative of actualized learning within local practices, whereas Type II pointed to technological utilization and the latent capacity for augmenting TSL.

In the realm of *Intelligence* (Type I), respondents characterized the news flow as a conduit for business intelligence within the Swedish IS sphere. Engagement with the news varied, with some participants admitting to a cursory glance at headlines, while others immersed themselves in the content, acknowledging the benefits of staying abreast of developments at other universities. This gamut of engagement levels underscores a Type I category: Unspecified learning; where an enhanced awareness is deemed crucial and is to be integrated with theoretical constructs.

Under the theme of *Internal News Production* (Type I), the relevance of news emerged as a reflective point for departments, sparking introspection about the very act of news creation within their realms: "One challenge is to get the internal 'happenings' in the groups to become news in the first place!" Time constraints and the need for staff engagement in external communication were also recurrent themes, alongside a call for greater acknowledgment of student accomplishments. This introspection is a direct result of interaction with the information infrastructure, leading to contemplation about the attributes of internal news production.

When considering *Contributions to the Discipline* (Type I), the feedback suggested that the news feed bolstered the discipline's visibility, reinforcing the collective knowledge at the national scale and fostering a deeper connection within the Swedish IS community. Even though some remarks were broad, like "It works" and "Great value for the development of the information systems discipline," they collectively signal the integral role of the field for the flourishing of local practices, congruent with the very existence of SISA.

The theme of *Critical Mass* (Type II) surfaced from expressions of necessity to engage the entirety of the IS research community. The prevalence of unawareness about the news service among IS scholars was highlighted, prompting suggestions for more robust internal marketing efforts. Concerns regarding the attainability of a critical mass were raised, attributed to the perceived abstraction and complexity of the discipline, suggesting that reaching beyond the already committed individuals might necessitate enhanced personal interactions across various media. This represents an opportunity for improvement, where increased utilization of the information infrastructure could amplify its value.

Lastly, *Relevance* (Type II) was a theme rife with discussions on the news filtering process and divergent views on what constitutes relevant content, reflecting the eclectic interests within the IS research community. Calls for a broader scope and a more inclusive disciplinary identity were evident, suggesting a pressing need for improvement in how the information infrastructure aligns with the varied scholarly preferences.

6 Concluding Discussion

This study contributes to the IS and DSR literature through a research process that spans problem identification, artifact design, evaluation, and knowledge contribution. Here we reflect on the contributions from this study, drawing on the idea of various type of contribution from IS research: Empirical contributions [2], artefactual/technological contributions [2, 3], and theoretical contributions [2, 3].

The empirical contribution consists of an account of how digital infrastructures can enable TSL within networks of practice. Using the SISA News platform as an instantiation, we have shown a detailed example of how digital infrastructures play a crucial role in fostering leaky knowledge flows. These flows facilitate peripheral awareness and engagement across distributed academic communities, enhancing transparency and interaction by consolidating information from various institutions into a unified platform. These insights offer empirical support for the critical role of digital infrastructures in bridging organizational boundaries and enabling TSL.

The design of the SISA News platform itself represents a significant artifactual contribution. The platform introduces a novel conceptual software design that integrates seamlessly with existing digital infrastructures, such as RSS feeds and social media aggregation tools. This modular and scalable approach minimizes costs for stakeholders while enabling targeted growth and adaptability. The artifact exemplifies how digital tools can be designed to extend existing infrastructures, thereby enhancing their relevance and utility.

From a theoretical standpoint, this study extends Henfridsson et al.'s framework on growth tactics for digital infrastructures by proposing a new tactic: *Community Engagement and Relevance Optimization*. This growth tactic emphasizes active participation, encouraging users to contribute content and feedback to foster ownership and engagement. It also highlights the importance of tailored content delivery, leveraging algorithms and user preferences to ensure the platform remains relevant to diverse stakeholders. This addition enriches the theoretical understanding of how digital infrastructures can evolve dynamically in response to user needs.

The study also advances the theoretical discourse on the functions of digital infrastructures for TSL. It demonstrates how such infrastructures can operate as meta-level platforms, not only facilitating content aggregation but also monitoring and evaluating user interactions. This functionality provides valuable insights into both technological matters and underlying social processes, enabling iterative improvements by identifying engagement gaps and optimizing design features. By emphasizing this meta-level capability, the research contributes to a deeper understanding of how information infrastructures can support continuous refinement in collaborative processes within NoPs.

Overall, the study bridges a gap between theory and practice by positioning digital infrastructures as dynamic systems that not only enable knowledge sharing but also serve as tools for studying and tuning TSL processes.

Future research will include a new design cycle, building on how to expand the artifact by adding generative AI into the infrastructure mix. We believe that such a development has great potential to add value to the artifact, and it would allow for further evaluation and theorizing about growth tactics for digital infrastructures.

Regarding future research, integrating generative AI services into the SISA news service offers significant potential to enhance both Type I (actual) and Type II (potential) learning capabilities. AI could dynamically create tailored content and personalized news feeds, addressing user concerns about relevance and engagement. For instance, AI-generated summaries and adaptive filtering could save time, increase awareness, and ensure the content aligns with diverse scholarly preferences. Additionally, automating the identification of internal newsworthy events would reduce staff effort and encourage broader participation. Future research should explore these possibilities while addressing ethical concerns around data privacy and algorithmic bias to ensure transparent and equitable use of AI in enhancing TSL infrastructures.

References

1. Ågerfalk, P.J.: Embracing diversity through mixed methods research. Eur. J. Inf. Syst. **22**(3), 251–256 (2013). https://doi.org/10.1057/ejis.2013.6
2. Ågerfalk, P.J., Karlsson, F.: Artefactual and empirical contributions in information systems research. Eur. J. Inf. Syst. **29**(2), 109–113 (2020). https://doi.org/10.1080/0960085X.2020.1743051
3. Baskerville, R., et al.: Design science research contributions: finding a balance between artifact and theory. J. Assoc. Inf. Syst. **19**(5), 3 (2018)
4. Benbasat, I., Zmud, R.W.: The identity crisis within the IS discipline: defining and communicating the discipline's core properties. MIS Q., 183–194 (2003)
5. DeSanctis, G.: The social life of information systems research: a response to Benbasat and Zmud's call for returning to the IT artifact. J. Assoc. Inf. Syst. **4**(1), 16 (2003)
6. Gregor, S., Hevner, A.R.: Positioning and presenting design science research for maximum impact. MIS Q. **37**(2), 337–355 (2013)
7. Grönqvist, H., et al.: Fifteen challenges in establishing a multidisciplinary research program on ehealth research in a university setting: a case study. J. Med. Internet Res. **19**(5), e173 (2017)
8. Hellmark Knutsson, H.: Kunskap i samverkan-för samhällets utmaningar och stärkt konkurrenskraft. (2016)
9. Hevner, A.R.: A three cycle view of design science research. Scand. J. Inf. Syst. **19**(2), 87–92 (2007)
10. Hevner, A.R., et al.: Design science in information systems research. MIS Q. **28**(1), 75–105 (2004)
11. Koutsikouri, D., et al.: Extending digital infrastructures: a typology of growth tactics. J. Assoc. Inf. Syst. **19**(10), 2 (2018)
12. Nunamaker, J.F., et al.: Creating high-value real-World impact through systematic programs of research. MIS Q. **41**, 2–351 (2017)
13. Nunamaker Jr., J.F., Briggs, R.O.: Toward a broader vision for information systems. ACM Trans. Manag. Inf. Syst. TMIS. **2**, 20 (2011)
14. Sein et al.: Action design research. MIS Q. 35, 1, 37 (2011). https://doi.org/10.2307/23043488
15. SISA: Svenska Informationssystemakademin, http://sisa-org.se
16. Sjöström, J., et al.: Software-embedded evaluation support in design science research. In: Chatterjee, S., et al. (eds.) Designing for a Digital and Globalized World - 13th International Conference, DESRIST 2018, Chennai, India, June 3–6, 2018, Proceedings, pp. 348–362. Springer (2018). https://doi.org/10.1007/978-3-319-91800-6_23
17. Sjöström, J., et al.: The origin and impact of ideals in ehealth research: experiences from the U-CARE research environment. JMIR Res. Protoc. **3**(2), e28–e28 (2014)

18. Te'eni, D., et al.: Stimulating dialog between information systems research and practice. Eur. J. Inf. Syst. **26**(6), 541–545 (2017). https://doi.org/10.1057/s41303-017-0067-9
19. Topi, H., et al.: IS 2010: curriculum guidelines for undergraduate degree programs in information systems. Commun. Assoc. Inf. Syst. **26, 1**, 18 (2010)
20. Topi, H., et al.: MSIS 2016 global competency model for graduate degree programs in information systems. Commun. Assoc. Inf. Syst. **40**, 18 (2017)
21. Vaast, E., Walsham, G.: Trans-situated learning: supporting a network of practice with an information infrastructure. Inf. Syst. Res. **20**(4), 547–564 (2009)
22. Venable, J., et al.: FEDS: a framework for evaluation in design science research. Eur. J. Inf. Syst. **25**(1), 77–89 (2016)
23. Venkatesh, V., et al.: Bridging the qualitative-quantitative divide: guidelines for conducting mixed methods research in information systems. MIS Q. **37**(1), 21–54 (2013)
24. Yang, Z., et al.: A comparative analysis of community detection algorithms on artificial networks. Sci. Rep. **6**, 30750 (2016)

Healthcare Systems, Ageing and Wellbeing

Towards Digital Pause: A Framework for Promoting Well-Being in Adults Through Conscious Unplugging

Tahereh Miari[✉], Zelal Kutby, Javier Aguilar, and Samir Chatterjee

Claremont Graduate University, Claremont, CA 91711, USA
tahereh.miari@cgu.edu

Abstract. The pervasive integration of digital devices has fundamentally reshaped daily life, delivering numerous benefits while simultaneously posing challenges, including increased digital dependency and diminished well-being. Motivated by the principles of cyberpsychology, this study reframes the traditional view of digital detox by exploring "unplugging" as an emerging phenomenon aimed at mitigating the harmful effects of constant digital engagement. Despite its growing relevance, limited research exists on how unplugging can be intentionally practiced and what conditions foster its success. Using a two-phase methodology, we first apply Grounded Theory coding techniques to explore the problem space, analyzing 15 in-depth interviews to uncover underlying triggers, contextual factors, and behavioral patterns that motivate or act as barriers to digital disengagement. These findings inform a redefinition of unplugging as a purposeful, sustainable practice embedded in daily life and oriented toward long-term well-being. In the second phase, we employ Design Science Research (DSR) to develop and iteratively refine a conceptual framework intended to support strategies that reduce digital dependency and promote well-being among adults. This framework lays the groundwork for future research and the development of intervention artifacts that promote sustainable digital well-being.

Keywords: Digital Addiction · Unplugging · Sustainable Digital Well-being · Cyberpsychology · Design Science Research · Grounded Theory Coding

1 Introduction

The rapid evolution of digital technology has profoundly transformed modern life, embedding digital devices into nearly every aspect of human interactions. In the United States, the average internet-connected household now owns 17 devices [11], reflecting a growing trend of digital integration. Globally, this trend persists, with the average number of devices and connections per person increasing from 2.4 in 2018 to 3.6 in 2023, highlighting the pervasive nature of digital overconsumption [15]. Parallel to this increase in device proliferation is the dramatic rise in global internet users, which has surged from approximately 1 billion in 2005 to an estimated 5.5 billion in 2024 [40]. Notably, the largest growth occurred between 2019 and 2020, with an increase of 466 million users, driven largely by the COVID-19 pandemic and the subsequent reliance on digital platforms for communication, work, and education. This technological intimacy creates a growing challenge: maintaining a balance between digital engagement and personal well-being.

Research suggests that digital dependency is influenced by various factors, primarily arising from both short and long-term reliance on technology [31]. However, the extent and nature of this dependency vary across demographics and contexts. For instance, adults tend to exhibit lower levels of technology dependency compared to digital natives, who have grown up immersed in a technology-rich environment [29]. Gender-specific trends are also evident in which males are more likely to develop addictive behaviors related to video games, while females are more prone to excessive social media use [4]. Cross-national comparisons further reveal that countries with differing levels of digital infrastructure, as well as regional and socio-economic factors, shape the ways individuals manage the abundance of information in their daily lives [24, 30].

Excessive digital dependency on social media and apps can lead to mental health issues, decreased productivity, and social disconnection. Constant notifications and algorithm-driven content create dopamine-driven feedback loops, making users crave continuous engagement, often leading to addiction and anxiety. Beyond personal well-being, digital overuse also raises ethical and safety concerns. For instance, a recent lawsuit in Texas against Character.ai revealed that a 17-year-old engaged with a chatbot that appeared to normalize extreme behavior, including offering alarming suggestions that rationalized familial violence as a response to screen time restrictions [12]. Such cases highlight the potential dangers of unregulated, excessive digital engagement.

The emergence of cyberpsychology as a discipline underscores the growing urgency to address the behavioral and social implications of digital dependency [39]. As digital technologies continue to permeate every aspect of life, the need for strategies that prioritize well-being and intentional technology use becomes increasingly evident [3].

2 Problem Space: Research Goals and Questions

While digital technology offers significant benefits, the unregulated surge in digital engagement poses substantial risks to well-being, productivity, and social connection. Excessive and habitual interaction with technology has been associated with a wide array of psychological, physiological, and social harms, including reduced productivity, heightened stress, and disruptions to social and emotional health [38]. Internet Addiction Disorder (IAD), for instance, has been shown to contribute to neurological complications, psychological disturbances, and social challenges, emphasizing the urgency of addressing digital dependency [8].

Recent research highlights the detrimental effects of prolonged engagement with digital devices. Nakshine et al. [28] demonstrate correlations between high screen time and adverse outcomes such as poor sleep quality, heightened anxiety, depression, self-esteem issues, and physical health concerns. Among various forms of IAD, Social Media Addiction (SMA) has become a significant concern, particularly among adolescents, contributing to psychological distress and increased mental health risks such as anxiety and depression [14, 20, 37, 45]. Although not yet classified as a formal clinical disorder, studies reveal an increasing trend of digital addiction over the past two decades [24].

The situation is approaching a critical point with the emergence of new social media platforms and the widespread use of persuasive design techniques that intentionally manipulate user behavior [5]. Despite growing societal awareness and the emergence of initiatives like the Global Day of Unplugging and various digital detox interventions, there remains a lack of effective, evidence-based strategies for fostering sustainable digital habits, particularly among adults. Many of these approaches frame disconnection as a temporary, reactive response to digital overload, rather than as part of a proactive, long-term strategy to improve well-being [2]. As noted by Radtke et al. [35], digital detox is typically defined as a short-term timeout from device usage, yet its effectiveness in promoting healthier digital lifestyles remains inconclusive. Several studies suggest that digital detox interventions can improve mental health and attention [1, 9]. However, other research presents more mixed outcomes, for example, Wadsley and [43] found that reduced social media use led to decreased negative effects but also lowered positive impact, suggesting complex emotional responses. These inconsistencies indicate that temporary breaks from technology alone may not address deeper behavioral patterns and contextual demands adults face in managing digital life.

In addition, much of the existing literature on digital disconnection focuses on younger generations, particularly social media detox among adolescents and young adults. For example, the work in [13] demonstrated that limiting social media usage to 30 minutes per day can improve addiction levels and well-being, but their findings are primarily youth-centered and do not address broader life and work-related digital dependencies. Similarly, the research in [25] explored motivations for digital detox in young adults, emphasizing self-control and relational maintenance, yet their work does not extend to adults navigating digital overuse in professional and personal settings.

To address this gap, *this study introduces the Conscious Digital Unplugging Framework, a five-phase model grounded in insights from in-depth interviews with adult participants and designed to promote the development of healthy digital habits over time.* Rather than relying on short-term digital detoxes or abrupt disconnection from devices, the proposed conceptual framework guides individuals to gradually build awareness, clarify personal motivations, recognize barriers, and adopt actionable strategies that support sustainable digital well-being. This study is structured around the following research questions, each aligned with our specific objectives:

RQ1: What are the perceived benefits, challenges, and impacts of unplugging for adults, and in which contexts is digital disengagement considered appropriate or impactful?
RQ2: How can we design an artifact to support digital unplugging by overcoming barriers to screen time reduction and promoting healthier habits to enhance well-being and productivity?

3 Research Approach

This study employs a multi-phase research approach, integrating Grounded Theory coding techniques to explore the problem space with Design Science Research (DSR) for the design and evaluation of the artifact. This combination ensures a robust foundation for understanding the complexities of digital disengagement and guiding the creation of a practical, user-centered solution. As highlighted by [26], there is a growing emphasis on the need for a comprehensive exploration of the problem space to ensure research relevance and meaningful impact within the DSR community.

This exploration is crucial, as effective and impactful DSR requires not only appropriate research conduct but also a well-defined research problem [34]. By combining GT coding techniques for problem discovery and DSR for solution design, this study addresses the dual imperatives of advancing theoretical understanding and delivering actionable outcomes.

3.1 Grounded Theory Coding: Problem Space Exploration

The initial phase of this study focuses on problem exploration using Grounded Theory coding techniques to understand the dynamics of digital unplugging, an emerging and context-dependent phenomenon. Rather than pursuing full theory development as prescribed by Grounded Theory Methodology (GTM), we adopt its structured coding techniques as a qualitative lens to systematically surface patterns, categories, and relationships grounded in participants' lived experiences related to digital disengagement [16]. This approach aligns with the interpretivist paradigm, which emphasizes understanding phenomena through the meanings individuals assign to their actions and contexts [6, 21, 32].

Our study employs the three stages of GTM coding [27] to explore participants' motivations, challenges, and strategies for digital unplugging. The process involves: (1) *Open Coding* to categorize concepts, (2) *Axial Coding* to refine and connect categories, and (3) *Theoretical Coding* to establish connections between constructs and participants' insights [44].

3.1.1 Data Collection and Tool Setup

This study draws on 15 one-on-one interviews with adults from diverse backgrounds, conducted both in person and virtually, each lasting up to 35 minutes. Participants ranged in age from 20 to 52 and were purposefully selected to capture a broad range of perspectives on digital habits and unplugging behaviors. Informed consent was obtained, ensuring that all participants were fully informed about the study's purpose, data confidentiality, and future use of their responses before participation. We employed a semi-structured interview format, consisting of ten pre-formulated questions designed to explore participants' digital usage, motivation for unplugging, perceived barriers, and experiences with intentional disconnection. Interviews were transcribed using Otter.AI and later analyzed in Atlas.ti.

The data analysis process began with an open coding phase in Atlas.ti, during which over 52 initial codes were generated, capturing a broad spectrum of ideas and perspectives shared by participants. These codes were iteratively refined, consolidated, and merged into a final set of 38 codes. This process enabled the identification of primary themes and patterns, laying a strong foundation for subsequent axial and theoretical coding. The iterative coding process, illustrated in Table 1, demonstrates how raw qualitative data were systematically transformed into meaningful insights, serving as a foundational exploratory phase within our DSR methodology to guide artifact development and theoretical refinement.

Table 1. A Thematic Analysis Using Atlas.ti with Key Insights and Frequencies

Theme/Code Group	Key Codes (Subthemes)	Frequency	Key Insights
Beliefs and perceptions	Belief in excessive digital device usage	44	Participants recognized their excessive usage and emphasized the value of unplugging for improving work-life balance, interpersonal relationships, and well-being.
	Recognition and value of unplugging	34	
	Value of unplugging related to work-life balance	59	
Challenges in unplugging	Challenges of unplugging from digital devices	45	Barriers included work dependency, ingrained habits, and hesitation to adopt unplugging strategies, driven by professional and social obligations.
	Digital device usage based on nature of work	41	
	Resistance to reducing device usage	28	
Effective strategies	Effective strategies taken or planned for unplugging	58	Participants emphasized setting boundaries, scheduling unplugging times, reducing social media use, and engaging in outdoor or social activities to unplug.
	Preferred times for unplugging	30	
	Unplugging from social media	30	
	Engagement in outdoor activities	31	
Impact of digital use	Impact of unplugging on well-being and productivity	73	Unplugging was linked to reduced stress, improved productivity, and better mental health. Younger generations were highlighted as particularly vulnerable.
	Negative impact of social media and digital devices	41	
	Vulnerability of younger generations	26	
Awareness and education	Lack of awareness about unplugging day	22	Participants noted limited awareness of digital detox initiatives, underscoring the need for campaigns and education to encourage unplugging practices.
	Perceived need for education on unplugging	23	
	Importance of education regarding unplugging	19	

3.2 Insights from Problem Space Exploration

Phase 1 of this research provided critical insights into the phenomenon of intentional digital unplugging, uncovering its underlying challenges and opportunities. These thematic findings defined the problem space and informed the design and development of the proposed artifact. Below are the key insights that emerged from this phase:

Awareness of Excessive Usage: Participants expressed a growing awareness of their excessive reliance on digital devices. Many acknowledged that their usage often surpassed healthy limits, contributing to feelings of dependency and diminished personal well-being.

Motivation to Reduce Screen Time: There was a notable motivation among participants to reduce screen time, particularly concerning non-essential digital activities such as prolonged use of social media platforms. This motivation was often driven by a desire to regain control over time management, improve mental health, and establish a sense of balance.

Key Barriers to Unplugging: Participants faced several barriers that made it challenging to unplug from digital devices, driven by a mix of personal habits, external demands, and environmental factors.

- Work Dependency: The integration of technology into professional life made disconnecting difficult, as digital devices were essential for work-related tasks.
- Lack of Unplugging Strategies: Many participants (nearly 90%) lacked practical methods or strategies to effectively reduce screen time, leading to unintentional and habitual device usage.
- Habitual Reliance: Across almost all participants, it was observed that ingrained behaviors, such as reflexively checking notifications or endlessly scrolling through social media, reinforced digital dependency, making it an unavoidable digital habit.

Positive Outcomes of Unplugging: Despite the barriers, participants who successfully unplugged reported significant benefits, particularly in their mental and professional lives. Improved well-being emerged as a key outcome, with many experiencing enhanced mental health and reduced stress. Additionally, participants highlighted increased productivity, as limiting distractions allowed them to focus better and complete tasks more effectively. These positive changes underscore the potential of unplugging to promote healthier habits and support overall life satisfaction.

These findings provided a strong foundation for the design of the Conscious Digital Unplugging Framework, which serves as the central artifact in this study. Given the complexity of digital disengagement, our conceptual framework offers a flexible yet structured approach to guide intentional behavior change. To move from insight to impact, we adopted the DSR methodology, which enables the design and iterative refinement of IT-related artifacts grounded in real-world contexts.

3.3 Using DSR Methodology to Develop Conscious Unplugging Framework

Recognizing the importance of thoroughly exploring the problem space, this study transitions to the Design Science Research methodology to guide the development of the

Conscious Digital Unplugging Framework. DSR is particularly effective for addressing complex, real-world problems by enabling the iterative design and refinement of IT-enabled artifacts [18, 19]. Compared to traditional approaches, DSR's emphasis on practical relevance, theoretical grounding, and continuous improvement ensures that the resulting framework is both scientifically rigorous and deeply informed by user experience. As illustrated in Fig. 1, DSR operates through three interrelated cycles, Relevance, Rigor, and Design, each playing a critical role in ensuring the artifact's contextual applicability, scientific grounding, and continuous improvement.

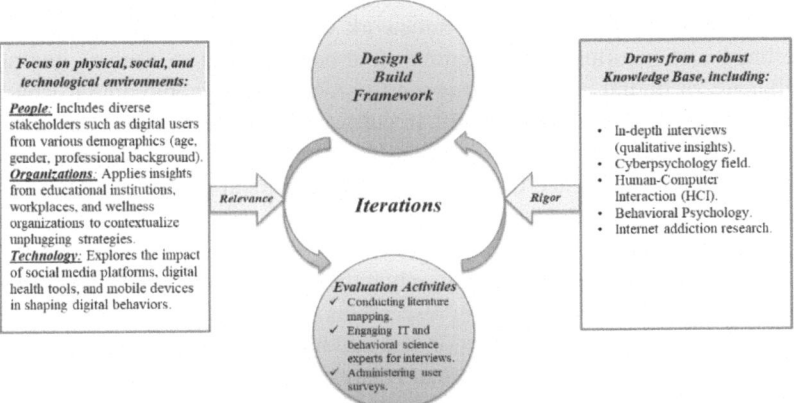

Fig. 1. Adapted DSR Iterative Cycle

Relevance Cycle. This cycle connects the design of the framework to the real-world problem of digital overuse. Insights from the previous phase were used to define the framework's requirements and user-centered design criteria. This ensured that the framework responds to the diverse contexts in which digital overuse occurs, including varying professional, personal, and social demands.

Rigor Cycle. The rigor cycle ensures scientific validity by grounding the framework in established theories and empirical findings. Behavioral change models, habit-formation literature, and user experience principles informed the structure of the framework, supporting both effectiveness and theoretical soundness. Domain-specific literature in digital wellness and unplugging strategies further guided the design.

Design Cycle. This cycle focuses on the iterative creation, evaluation, and refinement of the Conscious Digital Unplugging Framework as a purposeful artifact. Feedback was incorporated through multiple evaluation mechanisms including literature mapping, expert interviews, and user surveys to ensure that the framework remains relevant, adaptable, and aligned with the contextual needs and lived experiences of adult users.

By aligning with the three DSR cycles, this study bridges the gap between problem exploration and solution development, resulting in a robust, user-centered conceptual framework. As noted by [33], a framework within a scientific domain serves to organize and structure knowledge, defining the scope, key conceptual elements, and relationships within that space. The Conscious Digital Unplugging Framework functions as both a diagnostic and guiding tool, helping individuals reflect on their digital habits and develop healthier relationships with technology. At the same time, it provides a conceptual foundation for future research and interventions aimed at promoting sustainable digital well-being. The next section elaborates on the framework's design and refinement process.

3.4 Conscious Digital Unplugging Framework Design Cycle

The Conscious Digital Unplugging Framework builds upon the foundational principles outlined earlier, offering a structured, five-phase model to analyze and address the challenges of digital overuse. Designed to promote sustainable digital well-being, the proposed framework supports adults in cultivating healthier digital habits and fostering a more intentional, mindful relationship with technology. Grounded in qualitative insights, this experience-driven artifact fills a critical gap in literature by moving beyond conceptual models to provide practical guidance for facilitating sustainable digital disengagement.

Our proposed framework serves not only individual end-users but also offers value to system designers, digital well-being researchers, health IT practitioners, and organizational leaders seeking to implement or evaluate interventions aimed at mindful technology use. By supporting both individual behavioral change and broader intervention design, this framework contributes to the advancement of user-centered digital well-being strategies in both research and applied contexts. Figure 2 provides an overview of the framework's five key phases and their corresponding objectives, which collectively promote intentional and sustainable digital disengagement.

Self-awareness. This foundational phase centers on developing a deeper understanding of one's digital habits. It encourages individuals to evaluate their current technology use, recognize how it impacts their well-being, productivity, and relationships, and identify specific emotional or situational triggers that contribute to overuse. Through this reflective process, users establish a critical baseline for intentional unplugging. By acknowledging the varying effects of digital disconnection across personal, professional, and demographic contexts (e.g., age, gender, occupation), this phase empowers individuals to begin their journey toward healthier digital engagement.

Motivation Exploration. This phase focuses on helping individuals clarify their personal motivations for unplugging by reflecting on how high digital engagement affects their mental and physical well-being, focus, and overall life balance. Recognizing what matters most, whether it is reducing mental fatigue from constant digital input or restoring emotional connection, enables individuals to align their unplugging goals with their broader values and needs.

Identifying Barriers. This phase focuses on helping individuals pinpoint the specific challenges that prevent them from unplugging, such as habitual dependence, fear of missing out (FOMO), work obligations, or lack of guidance. By raising awareness of these disruptions and their impact on physical health, mental well-being, productivity,

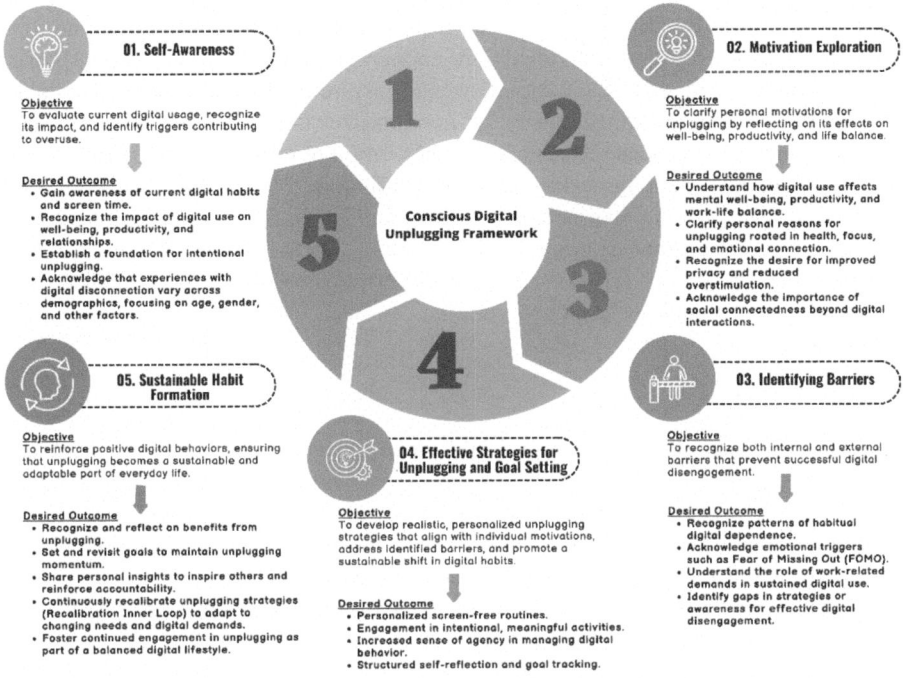

Fig. 2. Proposed Conscious Digital Unplugging Framework

and relationships, individuals can gain a clear understanding of their barriers. This clarity builds a foundation for developing tailored strategies in the next phase to address these challenges effectively and promote healthier digital habits.

Effective Strategies for Unplugging and Goal Setting. This phase centers around practical methods to reduce screen time while setting realistic, personalized goals to foster healthier digital habits. Key strategies include creating device-free zones in the home (e.g., bedrooms and dining areas), scheduling regular unplugging periods, and identifying meaningful alternative activities to replace excessive technology use. Examples of such activities range from hobbies like painting, gardening, or cooking [7], to physical exercises such as jogging, yoga, or group sports [23], and mindfulness practices like meditation or deep breathing. Also, spending time outdoors, engaging in community service, or enjoying face-to-face interactions with friends and family are effective ways to create a sense of balance and connection. This phase emphasizes the importance of a clear action plan such as tracking screen time through apps or journals, regularly measuring progress, and celebrating milestones to sustain motivation. By combining intentional strategies with structured goal setting, individuals are empowered to build a more fulfilling and mindful relationship with technology.

Sustainable Habit Formation. This final phase focuses on reinforcing positive digital behaviors and supporting long-term well-being through consistent unplugging practices. It encourages individuals to reflect on the benefits of unplugging and integrate those practices into their daily routines. This phase is grounded in behavioral research on habit formation. As noted by [10], success stems from consistent, daily habits, not one-time efforts. To sustain progress, individuals are encouraged to set ongoing goals, pursue them consistently, and share their experiences to inspire others and build accountability within their communities. Similarly, [22] emphasizes that habit formation relies on repeated behavior in response to contextual cues, often requiring sustained effort over time to achieve automaticity. A key concept in this phase is the Recalibration Inner Loop, which allows users to periodically reassess and adjust their strategies in response to evolving life circumstances, goals, and digital demands [41]. This built-in adaptability ensures the framework remains relevant and responsive, fostering a balanced and mindful relationship with technology over time.

4 Evaluation

This section outlines the evaluation methods used to iteratively refine the Conscious Digital Unplugging Framework into a user-centered and impactful solution. In DSR, evaluation is a critical component that provides proof-of-use, demonstrating how well the artifact performs in addressing the stated research question(s). Our evaluation employs a structured mixed methods approach to assess the utility, efficacy, and quality of the proposed framework, ensuring it is both theoretically grounded and practically effective. To achieve this, we triangulated data from three key sources:

1. **Literature Mapping:** To position the framework within current academic discourse and identify gaps it addresses.
2. **Expert Validation Interviews:** To gather insights from domain experts regarding the framework's design, theoretical grounding, and practical relevance.
3. **Participant Surveys:** To assess usability and effectiveness based on real-world experiences and perceptions of adult users.

These methods are operationalized and tested using the Framework Evaluation in Design Science (FEDS) methodology, which provides a structured strategy for assessing the utility and effectiveness of artifacts in real-world settings [42]. Our research adopts a formative, naturalistic approach aimed at improving outcomes and guiding effective action, aligning with the Human Risk and Effective Strategy category. It focuses on rigorously evaluating the artifact's effectiveness, ensuring its utility and benefits are sustained even when implemented in real-world environments, despite the complexities of human and social adoption challenges. The key contributions of our evaluation include:

- **Filling a critical gap**: Unlike existing approaches, the framework captures unique insights from user experiences, addressing disruptions caused by excessive digital engagement. It offers actionable strategies that are grounded in real-world challenges and practical needs.
- **Real-world impact**: By adopting a formative and naturalistic evaluation approach, the framework emphasizes usability and relevance, ensuring its sustained effectiveness in promoting conscious digital unplugging.

The following outlines our triangulation evaluation approach, designed to ensure a comprehensive and systematic refinement of the Conscious Digital Unplugging Framework. This approach comprises three stages:

Literature Mapping: The literature mapping involved a structured review of over 25 closely related studies from 2018 to 2024, using key terms such as "digital detox", "screen time reduction", "technology addiction", "digital well-being", and "mindful technology use". This comprehensive review aimed to identify research gaps, validate the framework's foundation, and assess its constructs against thematic elements from existing studies on digital detox and excessive digital usage. Mapping against established knowledge demonstrates the proposed framework's novelty and contribution to the problem space. Further details on the literature mapping findings and their role in refining our framework are summarized in Table 2.

Expert Validation: To ensure theoretical robustness and practical relevance of the framework, feedback was gathered through open-ended interviews with two domain experts. Their insights helped validate the proposed solution and provided constructive suggestions for improvement:

- *Subject #1: [Organizational Information Security Management Professor]* "The framework reflects best practices in fostering healthier digital habits. The framework aligns well with research in digital wellness...It effectively covers key stages of behavior changes. Additionally, it could benefit from deeper integration of behavioral theories, such as incorporating habit tools theory (cue, routine, reward)."
- *Subject #2: [Management Professor]* "...it could improve by incorporating strategies to make it more comprehensive and effective in overcoming the common barriers to digital unplugging in a few areas: work dependency, community and peer support, social and environmental influence and pressure, habit entrenchment and balancing digital and offline engagement."

Survey-Based Evaluation: Feedback from 15 participants with varying technology use levels was gathered to assess the framework's relevance and applicability. Using a validated questionnaire, which achieved Cronbach's alpha coefficient of 0.801, the survey confirmed internal consistency and reliability. Participant demographics included ages 25–34 (27%), 35–44 (45%), 45–54 (9%), and 55 and over (18%), with primary technology use focusing on work-related activities (46%), education/learning (27%), and socializing/connecting (27%). Regarding the framework's usefulness, 90% of participants rated it as either Excellent (45%) or Good (45%), while the framework's relevance was rated as Extremely Well (55%), Very Well (36%), and Moderately Well (9%). The survey also captured perspectives on its alignment with participants' experiences and challenges, offering a preliminary assessment of usability and effectiveness. These findings underscore the framework's strong relevance and effectiveness in promoting conscious digital unplugging.

4.1 Iterative Refinement and Evidence of Utility

The evaluation process played a crucial role in identifying opportunities for improvement within our proposed Conscious Digital Unplugging Framework. Phases 3 (Identifying Barriers) and 4 (Effective Strategies for Unplugging and Goal Setting) were particularly

Table 2. Iterative Refinement of the Conscious Digital Unplugging Framework

Area of Improvement	Key Enhancements	Expected Benefits
Sustainable Habit Formation (Phase 5): • Recalibration Inner Loop • Theoretical Integration	We identified the need for a *Recalibration Inner Loop* through literature mapping, emphasizing its alignment with Person-Fit and Environment-Fit (Vanden Abeele et al., 2024). This Inner Loop complements the framework's existing structure by adding: ✓ Adaptability: Responding to life changes and shifting priorities. ✓ Iteration: Continuous improvement over time. ✓ Sustainability: Reinforcing long-term adherence to healthier digital habits. ✓ Strengthen the theoretical foundation of the framework by incorporating behavioral theories, such as the habit loop (cue, routine, reward).	By embedding this feature into the Sustainable Habit Formation phase, our proposed framework becomes a dynamic, iterative tool for fostering long-term digital well-being.
Motivation Exploration (Phase 2): • Categorizing Motivations	We expanded Phase 2 by incorporating additional categories of motivation identified through literature mapping. Specifically, we added "Privacy Concerns" (Nguyen et al., 2024) and "Physical Health" to complement existing motivations such as Mental Well-being, Productivity, Work-Life Balance, and Social Connectedness. These additions ensure a more comprehensive understanding of user motivations for unplugging.	By adding more motivation categories based on studies and real-world experiences, our proposed framework becomes a more comprehensive and personalized tool for fostering deeper understanding of diverse user motivations, enhancing relevance and engagement, and improving the overall effectiveness of strategies.
Goal Setting and Action Plan (Phase 4): • Rule-Based and Feature-Based Strategies	We acknowledged that experiences with digital disconnection vary across demographics, including age, gender, and life context. To enhance inclusivity and practical relevance, we integrated examples of actionable activities, such as engaging in hobbies and mindfulness practices, that have been shown to effectively support digital well-being.	By embedding this feature into the goal setting and action plan phase, our proposed framework becomes a more inclusive and equitable tool for fostering digital well-being, improving usability for diverse user groups, and driving increased adoption and satisfaction.

impacted by user feedback, prompting refinements that enhanced their user-centricity, clarity, and practical applicability. Figure 3 illustrates the mean and standard deviation of participant ratings, showing how targeted refinements were informed by empirical data and directly contributed to improving the framework's effectiveness. As summarized in Table 2, insights drawn from literature mapping, expert interviews, and participant surveys were instrumental in guiding these iterative enhancements. These triangulated data sources validated the framework's design while strengthening its functional relevance and usability. By systematically integrating qualitative and quantitative feedback, the evaluation process supported the development of a more robust, adaptable, and user-responsive artifact. This aligns with DSR's emphasis on rigorous yet iterative artifact evaluation, positioning the framework as a viable and relevant solution to the digital disengagement challenges identified earlier in the study.

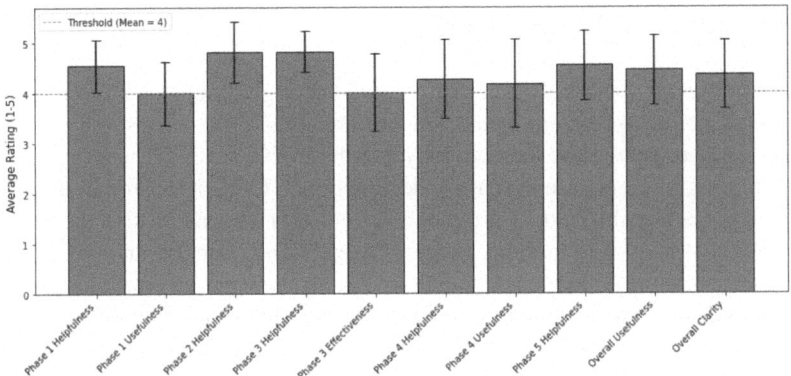

Fig. 3. Mean and Standard Deviation of Ratings

5 Design and Theoretical Contributions

The Conscious Digital Unplugging Framework offers a novel contribution to the growing domain of digital well-being by reimagining digital disengagement as a structured, sustainable practice rather than a short-term detox. It provides actionable, context-aware insights and strategies that help individuals improve focus, productivity, and interpersonal connection across multiple life domains (home, school, work, and social settings). Grounded in empirical user experiences and refined through iterative evaluation, the framework demonstrates how DSR can support mindful technology use in real-world settings [17].

From a theoretical standpoint, the integration of Grounded Theory coding techniques during the problem exploration phase contributes to conceptual constructions that can inform future design theory-building in digital well-being and behavioral design. As can be seen in Table 3, in terms of design knowledge contribution, the framework falls within the "Good Design Practice" quadrant of Design Knowledge Contribution Matrix [36]. This represents a novel applied knowledge contribution at the process level. By translating user-informed insights into a repeatable, evidence-based methodology, the framework offers valuable guidance for future digital intervention design, organizational well-being initiatives, and sustainable behavior change efforts.

Table 3: A Typology of Design Knowledge Creation

Types of Design Knowledge created	Design Process	Design Product
Applied Knowledge (Pragmatic)	Good design practice (novel - applied knowledge and design process)	Design principles (applied knowledge and design product)
Fundamental Knowledge (Fundamental)	Design theories (fundamental knowledge and design process)	Design attributes postulates (novel - fundamental knowledge and design product)

Locus of Knowledge Contribution

6 Conclusion and Future Work

This study addresses the timely and critical issue of digital dependency by reframing unplugging as a proactive, intentional behavior rather than a passive response to overuse. Through a rigorous two-phase methodology, combining Grounded Theory coding techniques and Design Science Research, we developed the Conscious Digital Unplugging Framework, an actionable model grounded in real user experiences. This framework offers practical strategies to mitigate excessive digital engagement, improve productivity, and foster meaningful human connections. The framework's contribution lies in its user-centered design and its potential to guide the creation of intervention artifacts that promote sustainable digital well-being. By synthesizing firsthand insights into a structured model, the study bridges a key gap in the literature, delivering a framework that is both theoretically grounded and practically applicable. Furthermore, it advances the discourse on balancing digital engagement with intentional disengagement, supporting a healthier relationship with technology.

Future research will aim to expand the sample size and demographic scope to include a wider range of age groups and contexts. Incorporating perspectives from behavioral health and social sciences will strengthen the framework's interdisciplinary robustness. Additionally, building on the insights of this study, future efforts will focus on refining the framework and developing tools for assessing problematic digital usage. These tools will enable the implementation of informed interventions, fostering healthier digital habits and advancing the goal of sustainable digital well-being.

References

1. Alanzi, T.M., Arif, W., Aqeeli, R., Alnafisi, A., Qumosani, T., Alreshidi, A., Alhawsawi, S., Alnakli, R., Alotaibi, A., AlOthman, M., Khamisi, M., Alanzi, N.: Examining the impact of digital detox interventions on anxiety and depression levels among young adults. Cureus. **16**, e75625 (2024). https://doi.org/10.7759/cureus.75625
2. Anandpara, G., Kharadi, A., Vidja, P., Chauhan, Y., Mahajan, S., Patel, J.: A comprehensive review on digital detox: a newer health and wellness trend in the current era. Cureus. **16**, e58719 (2024). https://doi.org/10.7759/cureus.58719
3. Ancis, J.R.: The age of cyberpsychology: an overview. Technol. Mind Behav. **1**(1) (2020). https://doi.org/10.1037/tmb0000009
4. Andreassen, C.S., Billieux, J., Griffiths, M.D., Kuss, D.J., Demetrovics, Z., Mazzoni, E., Pallesen, S.: The relationship between addictive use of social media and video games and symptoms of psychiatric disorders: a large-scale cross-sectional study. Psychol. Addict. Behav. **30**(2), 252–262 (2016)
5. Bhargava, V.R., Velasquez, M.: Ethics of the attention economy: the problem of social media addiction. Bus. Ethics Q. **31**(3), 321–359 (2019)
6. Boland, R.J.: Information system use as hermeneutic process. In: Nissen, H.-E., Klein, H.K., Hirschheim, R.A. (eds.) Information Systems Research: Contemporary Approaches and Emergent Traditions, pp. 439–464. North-Holland, Amsterdam (1991)
7. Bone, J.K., Fancourt, D., Sonke, J.K., Fluharty, M.E., Cohen, R., Lee, J.B., Kolenic, A.J., Radunovich, H., Bu, F.: Creative leisure activities, mental health and well-being during 5 months of the COVID-19 pandemic: a fixed effects analysis of data from 3725 US adults. J. Epidemiol. Community Health. **77**(5), 293–297 (2023)

8. Brand, M., Laier, C., Young, K.S.: Internet addiction: coping styles, expectancies, and treatment implications. Front. Psychol. **5**, Article 1256 (2014)
9. Castelo, N., Kushlev, K., Ward, A.F., Esterman, M., Reiner, P.B.: Blocking mobile internet on smartphones improves sustained attention, mental health, and subjective well-being. PNAS Nexus. **4**(2) (2025). https://doi.org/10.1093/pnasnexus/pgaf017
10. Clear, J.: Atomic Habits: an easy & proven way to build good habits & break bad ones. Penguin, New York (2018)
11. Clover, J.: Average number of connected devices in US. Broadband TV News (2024). https://broadbandtvnews.com/2024/01/12/average-number-of-connected-devices-in-us/
12. The Washington Post: Texas lawsuit highlights chatbot dangers after teen accused of attempted parental homicide. https://www.washingtonpost.com/technology/2024/12/10/character-ai-lawsuit-teen-kill-parents-texas/ (2024)
13. Coyne, P., Woodruff, S.J.: Taking a break: the effects of partaking in a two-week social media digital detox on problematic smartphone and social media use, and other health-related outcomes among young adults. Behav. Sci. **13**(12), 1004 (2023)
14. Ergün, N., Özkan, Z., Griffiths, M.D.: Social Media Addiction and Poor Mental Health: Examining the mediating roles of internet addiction and phubbing. (2023) (Note: Add journal name and volume/issue if available)
15. Fleck, A.: Overconsumption: the growing desire for ever more devices. Statista Daily Data (2024). https://www.statista.com
16. Glaser, B.G., Strauss, A.L.: The Discovery of Grounded Theory: Strategies for Qualitative Research. Routledge, London (1967)
17. Gregor, S., Hevner, A.: Positioning and presenting design science research for maximum impact. MIS Q. **37**(2), 337–355 (2013)
18. Gregor, S., Kruse, L.C., Seidel, S.: Research perspectives: the anatomy of a design principle. J. Assoc. Inf. Syst. **21**(6) (2020)
19. Hevner, A., Chatterjee, S.: Design Research in Information Systems, vol. 22. Springer, Boston, MA (2010)
20. Hou, Y., Xiong, D., Jiang, T., Song, L., Wang, Q.: Social media addiction: its impact, mediation, and intervention. Cyberpsychol. J. Psychosoc. Res. Cyberspace. **13**(1) (2019). https://doi.org/10.5817/cp2019-1-4
21. Kaplan, B., Maxwell, J.A.: Qualitative research methods for evaluating computer information systems. In: Anderson, J.G., Aydin, C.E., Jay, S.J. (eds.) Evaluating Health Care Information Systems: Methods and Applications, pp. 45–68. Sage, Thousand Oaks, CA (1994)
22. Lally, P., Van Jaarsveld, C.H.M., Potts, H.W.W., Wardle, J.: How are habits formed: modelling habit formation in the real world. Eur. J. Soc. Psychol. **40**(6), 998–1009 (2010)
23. Liu, H., Soh, K.G., Samsudin, S., Rattanakoses, W., Qi, F.: Effects of exercise and psychological interventions on smartphone addiction among university students: a systematic review. Front. Psychol. **13**, 1021285 (2022)
24. Meng, S.-Q., et al.: Global prevalence of digital addiction in general population: a systematic review and meta-analysis. Clin. Psychol. Rev. **92**, 102128 (2022)
25. Miksch, L., & Schulz, C.: Disconnect to reconnect: The phenomenon of digital detox as a reaction to technology overload. Master's thesis, Lund University, Sweden (2018)
26. Mulgund, P., Purao, S., Agrawal, L.: Fathers with postpartum depression: a problem space exploration. In: The Transdisciplinary Reach of Design Science Research. DESRIST 2022 Lecture Notes in Computer Science, pp. 208–220. Springer, Cham (2022)
27. Myers, M.D.: Qualitative Research in Business and Management. Sage, London (2008)
28. Nakshine, V.S., Thute, P., Khatib, M.N., Sarkar, B.: Increased screen time as a cause of declining physical, psychological health, and sleep patterns: a literary review. Cureus. **14**(10), e30051 (2022). https://doi.org/10.7759/cureus.30051

29. Nguyen, M.H.: Managing social media use in an "always-on" society: exploring digital well-being strategies that people use to disconnect. Mass Commun. Soc. **24**(6), 795–817 (2021). https://doi.org/10.1080/15205436.2021.1979045
30. Nguyen, M.H., Büchi, M., Geber, S.: Everyday disconnection experiences: exploring people's understanding of digital well-being and management of digital media use. New Media Soc. **26**, 3657–3678 (2024). https://doi.org/10.1177/14614448221105428
31. Norman, A.A., Marzuki, A.H., Faith, F., Hamid, S., Ghani, N.A., Ravana, S.D., Arshad, N.I.: Technology dependency and impact during COVID-19: a systematic literature review and open challenges. IEEE Access. **11**, 40741–40760 (2023). https://doi.org/10.1109/ACCESS.2023.3250770
32. Orlikowski, W.J., Baroudi, J.J.: Studying information technology in organizations: research approaches and assumptions. Inf. Syst. Res. **2**(1), 1–28 (1991)
33. Partelow, S.: What is a framework? Understanding their purpose, value, development and use. J. Environ. Stud. Sci. **13**(3), 510–519 (2023). https://doi.org/10.1007/s13412-023-00833-w
34. Purao, S.: Design science research problems … where do they come from? In: The Next Wave of Sociotechnical Design. DESRIST 2021 Lecture Notes in Computer Science, pp. 99–111. Springer, Cham (2021). https://doi.org/10.1007/978-3-030-82405-1_12
35. Radtke, T., Apel, T., Schenkel, K., Keller, J., Von Lindern, E.: Digital detox: an effective solution in the smartphone era? A systematic literature review. Mob. Media Commun. **10**(2), 190–215 (2022). https://doi.org/10.1177/20501579211028647
36. Chatterjee, S., Bhattacherjee, A., Gilb, T.: A typology of knowledge creation in design science research projects. In: DESRIST 2024 LNCS, vol. 14621, pp. 141–154. Springer, Cham (2024)
37. Santhosh, J., Chatterjee, S.: Towards a taxonomy to understand social media addictions of adolescents. In: AMCIS 2024 Proceedings, Paper 22. Association for Information Systems (2024) https://aisel.aisnet.org/amcis2024/social_comp/social_comput/22
38. Scott, D.A., Valley, B., Simecka, B.A.: Mental health concerns in the digital age. Heal. Addict. **15**(3), 604–613 (2016). https://doi.org/10.1007/s11469-016-9684-0
39. Singh, A.K., Singh, P.K.: Digital addiction: a conceptual overview. Libr. Philos. Pract. (2019)
40. Statista: Global number of internet users 2005–2024. https://www.statista.com/statistics/273018/number-of-internet-users-worldwide/ (last accessed 29 Mar 2025)
41. Vanden Abeele, M.M.P., et al.: Why, how, when, and for whom does digital disconnection work? A process-based framework of digital disconnection. Preprint (2024)
42. Venable, J., Pries-Heje, J., Baskerville, R.: FEDS: a framework for evaluation in design science research. Eur. J. Inf. Syst. **25**(1), 77–89 (2016). https://doi.org/10.1057/ejis.2014.36
43. Wadsley, M., Ihssen, N.: Restricting social networking site use for one week produces varied effects on mood but does not increase explicit or implicit desires to use SNSs. PLoS One. **18**(11), e0293467 (2023). https://doi.org/10.1371/journal.pone.0293467
44. Williams, M., Moser, T.: The art of coding and thematic exploration in qualitative research. Int. Manag. Rev. **15**(1), 45 (2019)
45. Xuan, Y.J., Amat, M.A.C.: Social media addiction and young people: a systematic review of literature. J. Crit. Rev. **7**(13), 537–541 (2020)

From Stress to Success: Designing a Diagnosis and Intervention Platform for Knowledge Workers

Falco Korn(✉) [iD], Erik Karger [iD], Frederik Ahlemann [iD], and Alexandar Schkolski [iD]

University of Duisburg-Essen, Universitätsstraße 9, 45141 Essen, Germany
{falco.korn,erik.karger,frederik.ahlemann,
alexandar.schkolski}@uni-due.de

Abstract. The increasing prevalence of mental illnesses, including stress-related disorders, has made workplace strain a growing concern, particularly for knowledge workers who face high cognitive demands, non-linear workflows and tight deadlines. The complex interplay between workplace conditions, self-management strategies, and individual health remains largely under-studied, especially in real-world settings, and help-seeking behavior to mitigate health and well-being challenges remains low. Although advances in digitalization facilitate the capture and analysis of workplace-specific contexts, they have not yet been fully leveraged in multimodal diagnosis and intervention systems for pattern recognition that may enable targeted interventions, leaving a gap for a comprehensive solution. To address this gap, we applied the Design Science Research approach to develop an architecture for a multimodal diagnosis and intervention platform. Using a mixed-methods study, we derived requirements from a comprehensive literature review, semi-structured interviews (n = 12), and a survey (n = 32) with knowledge workers. The derived design principles guided the development of a process-oriented architecture, which was evaluated and refined based on expert feedback (n = 6). Our work provides a basis for future research and practical implementations to advance workplace well-being technologies.

Keywords: Knowledge work · Well-being · Stress · Architecture

1 Introduction

Recent statistics on psychological illnesses highlight a concerning trend, with conditions such as anxiety, depression, and stress-related disorders reaching unprecedented levels globally. Data from the WHO [1] revealed that 301 million people globally were living with anxiety disorders in 2019, alongside 280 million individuals affected by depression. Stress stands out as a universal correlating factor of psychological and physiological strain [2]. Despite the significant burden posed by these issues, help-seeking behaviors remain consistently low, further highlighting the gap in addressing these pervasive challenges [3].

The workplace presents unique challenges that contribute to health concerns. Psychosocial working conditions are significant protective and risk factors for mental well-being [4], and employee motivation and performance [5]. In particular, knowledge workers, who face high cognitive demands, time pressure, and multitasking, experience unique stressors that require targeted investigation and intervention [6]. With their work heavily reliant on digital devices, balancing productivity and self-care is essential to address these stressors and associated health risks [7]. While substantial knowledge exists regarding the impact of individual occupational stressors, the complex interplay between workplace conditions, self-management, and individual health remains largely unexplored, especially in real-world settings [8]. Understanding the relationships in-between these dimensions is crucial for designing more individualized and thus more effective interventions. Advances in digitalization provide new opportunities to capture and analyze specific workplace-related contexts, enabling the identification of problematic contexts and more tailored interventions when integrated with objective stress and subjective strain data [7].

Previous studies, such as the work by Alberdi et al. [9], demonstrated the potential of multimodal approaches, combining physiological, psychological, and contextual data for accurate stress detection. However, these efforts primarily focused on identifying stress, without progressing toward personalized interventions or comprehensive stress management solutions. To address this gap, our research aims to design a sociotechnical system integrating diagnostic precision with effective intervention capabilities. Drawing on the echelon-oriented Design Science Research (DSR) approach by Tuunanen et al. [10], we break down the larger problem into modular components, focusing on designing a comprehensive architecture as a vital step towards future instantiations. The system aims to (1) discreetly collect multimodal data in every-day settings, (2) merge and centrally store the data, and (3) apply advanced analytics to provide a holistic understanding of knowledge workers' strain levels and well-being. While the long-term vision involves delivering personalized interventions to advance workplace health, the current focus lies on diagnostic and analytical capabilities to progress empirical research opportunities with stress management as a key example.

This leads to two research questions (RQs) - **RQ1**: *How can a multimodal platform be designed to capture and integrate physiological, psychological, behavioral, and contextual data for well-being assessment among knowledge workers?* and **RQ2**: *What design principles ensure the efficacy of both user well-being and rigorous empirical workplace research?*

To address our RQs, we employed the DSR approach by Peffers et al. [11], deriving design principles through a mixed-methods approach by combining a literature review with qualitative insights from interviews (n = 12) and quantitative data from a survey (n = 32) of knowledge workers. These principles were implemented in a process-oriented architecture and evaluated by domain experts (n = 6). Both principles and architecture were finally refined based on their feedback.

The remainder of the paper is organized as follows: Section 2 examines related work on knowledge work, stress and well-being. In Sect. 3, we articulate the DSR-based methodological approach to reach our objective. In Sect. 4, we present our developed requirements, design principles and the system architecture. Section 5 includes the results' discussion, directions for future research and the study's limitations. The paper concludes with a summary of theoretical and practical contributions and outlook.

2 Foundations

2.1 Knowledge Work

Since the early twenty-first century, technological advancements have accelerated the automation of manual labor, shifting societies toward a knowledge- and service-oriented economy. This transformation has elevated the importance of knowledge work, described by Kelloway and Barling [12] as discretionary behavior focused on creating, applying, and transmitting knowledge. Unlike traditional labor, knowledge work relies on advanced cognitive skills, high task complexity and effective management strategies. Knowledge workers use information as input of their work, utilize existing knowledge, and create new knowledge as output [13].

The cognitive demands of knowledge work are significant, often requiring sustained mental engagement, adaptability, and precision [14]. For instance, a financial analyst synthesizing market data must balance competing priorities, manage time constraints, and make critical decisions under pressure. Knowledge work also involves nonlinear workflows and dynamic problem-solving [15]. For example, software developers frequently shift between coding, debugging, and collaborative meetings, adapting to changing project requirements [15]. These characteristics make knowledge workers particularly vulnerable to stress, as they must continually balance high cognitive demands with the need to deliver consistent performance [16].

Knowledge workers routinely use and increasingly rely on digital tools for communication, data storage, task and time management, note taking and several others. In this context, technology plays a dual role: while it serves as an essential enabler of modern knowledge work by boosting efficiency, their ubiquity has introduced new challenges like technostress [17]. This phenomenon manifests in various forms, such as information overload, constant connectivity, and the need to adapt to ever-changing digital tools. The blurring of work-life boundaries and frequent updates or the complexity of software tools may foster frustration and anxiety. Research demonstrates that technostress not only impairs productivity but also diminishes job satisfaction and mental well-being [18].

2.2 Well-being and stress

Well-being is a multifaceted concept that encompasses physical, emotional, and psychological health and often includes factors such as happiness, satisfaction, and a sense of fulfillment, alongside the absence of negative conditions like stress or illness [19]. In the context of knowledge workers, well-being extends beyond traditional health metrics, incorporating factors such as job satisfaction, work-life balance, cognitive engagement, and a sense of purpose within one's role [20]. Positive workplace conditions, including supportive leadership and adequate resources, enhance well-being, which in turn can boost productivity and innovation [21]. Conversely, poor well-being can lead to burnout, disengagement, and decreased performance, with adverse outcomes for both individuals and organizations [21].

Given stress's significant influence on well-being, its impact on employees and organizations is a critical concern. Work-related stress can stem from high job demands, personal expectations, and other workplace challenges. When prolonged, it may lead to significant physical and mental health issues, as well as economic losses for organizations [22]. Stress, as defined by Koolhaas et al. [23], is the perceived or expected inability to effectively manage situations exceeding one's adaptive capacity. It can be classified as *eustress* (positive, performance-enhancing) and *distress* (negative, harmful) [24]. Also, it falls into *acute* (short-term, linked to "fight-or-flight") and *chronic* (long-term, caused by persistent stressors) categories [25]. Accurate stress measurement is crucial for understanding its effects on well-being, cognitive demands, and workload [26]. Different forms of stress can be observed through various performance, psychological, physiological, and behavioral symptoms [27].

Despite advancements in stress and well-being diagnostics, existing methods remain limited. Subjective self-reported questionnaires (self-reports) and clinical interviews, while simple and cost-effective, are prone to biases like social desirability and recall inaccuracies, compromising their reliability [28]. Objective biological measures often rely on invasive or resource-intensive procedures, making them impractical for continuous real-world monitoring [29]. Furthermore, current tools often fail to integrate crucial contextual information, such as task-specific or environmental stressors, leading to fragmented insights that hinder holistic intervention strategies. These interventions may include behavioral nudges, such as reminders for breaks, guided breathing exercises, or mindfulness techniques [30]. Beyond immediate stress relief, they may also foster tailored self-management techniques [31]. This underscores the need for multimodal, real-time, and non-invasive diagnostic systems capable of capturing the complex interplay between knowledge worker strain and well-being across diverse contexts [32].

3 Research Method

In this study, we adopt the DSR approach by Peffers et al. [11] to derive requirements and formulate design principles (DPs) for an experimental platform that supports knowledge workers' well-being and enables researchers to gain empirical insights. Using a problem-centered approach (see Fig. 1), we ensure the design directly addresses needs and challenges of this user group.

The first two DSR steps - problem identification and solution objectives - are covered in the introduction. For the third step, we conducted a literature review and an exploratory mixed-methods study to derive requirements and formulate DPs. In the literature review to identify literature requirements (LRs) we followed vom Brocke et al. [33] and focused on stress detection and intervention systems, multimodal data integration and workplace well-being. To capture user requirements (URs), we conducted 12 semi-structured interviews and a survey with 32 potential users – knowledge workers facing common knowledge work challenges, including IT consultants, researchers, and students. Interviews averaged 31:54 minutes and were guided by 21 questions exploring work environments, expectations regarding platform usefulness, and potential concerns

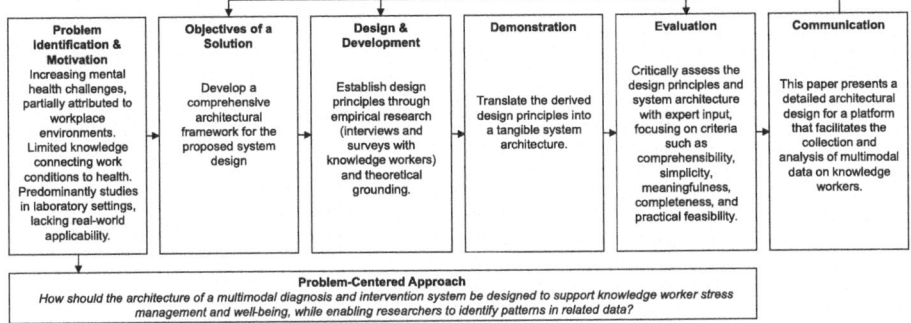

Fig. 1. Design Science Research Method. Adapted from *Peffers et al.* [11].

related to its adoption. Participants had a mean age of 28.2 years, with an equal gender distribution. The survey, consisting of 18 Likert scale and multiple-choice questions, complemented the interviews by providing quantitative insights into the same thematic areas.

Drawing from the LRs and URs, we derived DPs in accordance with Gregor et al. [34] which guided the development of the system architecture. Subsequently, we evaluated both DPs and architecture through six expert interviews with four professors and two postdoctoral researchers specializing in related fields such as occupational medicine, e-health, and NeuroIS. The evaluation followed Sonnenberg and vom Brocke's [35] criteria, specifically focusing on completeness, ease of use, meaningfulness, simplicity, and understandability. The expert interviews, averaging 39:33 minutes, provided valuable feedback that led to iterative improvements. In both rounds of interviews, we followed Mayring [36] for qualitative content analysis.

4 Results

4.1 Literature and User Requirements

To illustrate the interrelationship of LRs and URs, we present both types of requirements side by side in this subsection. **Fig. 2** highlights the six LRs and eleven URs identified in our study, as well as the ten resulting DPs.

The acquisition of data has generated several requirements from both the literature and users. Research on multimodal data integration suggests that combining digital biomarkers with subjective self-reports provides a comprehensive and accurate triangulated approach to stress detection [37], forming **LR1**. Subjective self-reports are particularly emphasized as they capture personal experiences and perception of stress that cannot be understood through physiological data alone [37]. While numerous self-report instruments exist, some, like the Trier Inventory for Chronic Stress (TICS) [38] with 57 items, are time-intensive and susceptible to recall bias due to their retrospective nature [28]. To address these limitations, ecological momentary assessment (EMA) [39] is commonly employed, often using single-item measures like a direct question on stress perception. These short-form assessments minimize user burden and prevent overload [39] (**LR4**),

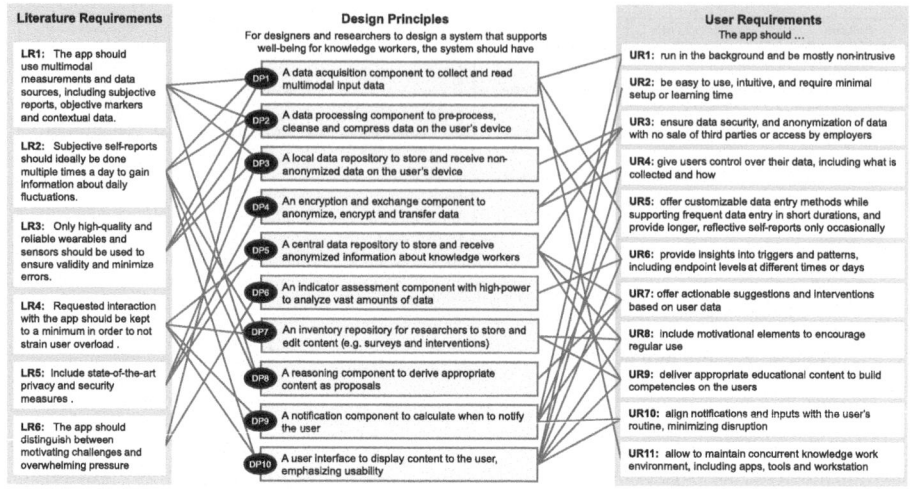

Fig. 2. Literature and User Requirements with derived Design Principles.

which aligns with the preference of participants for non-intrusive systems (**UR1**). For instance, participant 1 (P1) emphasized, the app should "run in the background as much as possible", further underpinned by P4's comment needing it to be "unobtrusive, not disruptive" and P5 suggested it should ideally be "purely passive". Additionally, notifications must be carefully aligned with user routines to avoid interruptions (**UR10**). As P4 stated, "If a pop-up comes up and annoys me and my concentration, it would be very detrimental" and P2 added that notification should not appear in "phases of high concentration, or other unsuitable moments".

Despite the preference for non-intrusiveness, some participants questioned whether short EMA responses alone could provide sufficient value. For instance, P7 observed that "it may simplify many topics too much, which means that it may not be possible to provide enough valuable input". These participants requested additional features such as a "journaling function" (P10) or "speech-to-text for its potential therapeutic benefits" (P8). For long-term monitoring, frequent self-reports - triggered by events or at fixed intervals - are deemed necessary, potentially requiring multiple entries per day [39] (**LR2**). Participants generally accepted frequent short interactions but preferred longer self-reports to be occasional (**UR5**). While some participants, like P1 and P10, were willing to complete entries up to five times per day, others preferred schedules tied to specific times, such as "before and after working hours" (P2) or "twice a day in breaks" (P4).

In addition to self-reports, the literature supports the integration of objective biomarkers such as heartrate and heart rate variability, which can be measured using technologies like electrocardiogram (ECG) [40], photoplethysmography (PPG) or electrodermal activity (EDA) [41]. ECG is widely regarded as the most reliable digital technique for stress detection. However, ensuring the reliability of wearable devices is critical, as only certain consumer and specialized devices are capable of accurately capturing these biomarkers [42] (**LR3**). While multimodal data integration holds significant potential, it introduces challenges related to data compatibility, synchronization, and analytical complexity, all of which require careful consideration [43]. Since challenges can have both positive and negative effects, the system should be capable of distinguishing between stress that is positively associated with performance (eustress) and overwhelming pressure (distress) to ensure that interventions support productivity without disrupting beneficial working states [44] (**LR6**).

Long-term user engagement is a key challenge, necessitating incentivization strategies, forming **UR8**. Participants suggested motivational features like "motivational slogans" (P3), "a virtual avatar or mascot" (P4), or "shared challenges with friends" (P11). P4 added "if it is approached in a playful way and not in the sense of 'we are going to make for the best efficiency' but rather improving well-being". While five interview participants expressed altruistic motivation to support research, further amplified by a Likert scale mean score of 3.28 in the survey, the most frequently requested feature was actionable suggestions and interventions to help manage strain effectively (**UR7**). All participants expressed willingness to experiment with interventions and P12 added "if they can be integrated into daily events". Survey results showed a preference for short-duration interventions (3–5 minutes: 40.6%), with diminishing willingness for longer interventions (>10 minutes: 6.3%). Additionally, nine participants emphasized the importance of providing insights into stress patterns and triggers (**UR6**), suggesting features like "trend lines/diagrams" (P2, P5, P7), "stress scores" (P3), or "a dashboard with metrics" (P8). Four participants also expressed a need for educational content (**UR9**). For instance, P3 requested materials to help "prevent rather than extinguish (strain)" and P8 drew a parallel to understanding health consequences of smoking.

Data security and privacy emerged as critical concerns. All participants stressed the importance of secure data handling and prohibiting third-party data sales (**UR3**). Specifically, participants expressed concerns about potential misuse of data, such as efficiency tracking by employers (P2, P4, P6, P8, P10). Survey results revealed high acceptance of anonymized and aggregated data transmission (Likert 3.41-3.78) compared to non-anonymized data (1.94-2.25). Acceptance levels also varied by data type, with context data from digital devices and software usage receiving the highest scores (up to 3.78), followed by self-reported data (up to 3.63), and physiological data being the least accepted (up to 3.41). The literature reinforces the importance of robust data security for user trust and regulatory compliance, especially when working with sensitive data [45] (**LR5**). Participants also expressed a strong preference for retaining control over their data (**UR4**). Several participants requested features like viewing, editing, or deleting data (P6, P8, P10, P11), while others preferred one-time permissions (P12). Consequently, anonymization and aggregation before storage are essential to address these privacy concerns.

Finally, the application must adhere to general usability standards, ensuring ease of use, intuitiveness, and minimal setup time (**UR2**). Participants also emphasized the importance of compatibility with the existing work environment, such as integration with commonly used apps and workspace configurations (**UR11**).

4.2 Design Principles and Architecture

By combining both theoretical and practical requirements, we derived ten DPs, as shown in Fig. 2. These principles are intrinsically aligned with the system architecture. To enhance clarity, the sequence of DPs was structured process-logically. While the principles outline what the system must achieve, the architecture demonstrates how these objectives can be operationalized. Although the system should also meet general software requirements, such as learnability, efficiency, memorability, error management, and satisfaction [46], we focus on the theme-specific DPs and their realization in the architecture.

The proposed architecture (Fig. 3) consists of two key data flows: (1) data provision for research, which flows from the knowledge worker to the researcher (top layer), and (2) user-facing features, which flow in the opposite direction (bottom layer). These dual flows reflect the system's objectives by supporting both empirical diagnostic research and user engagement.

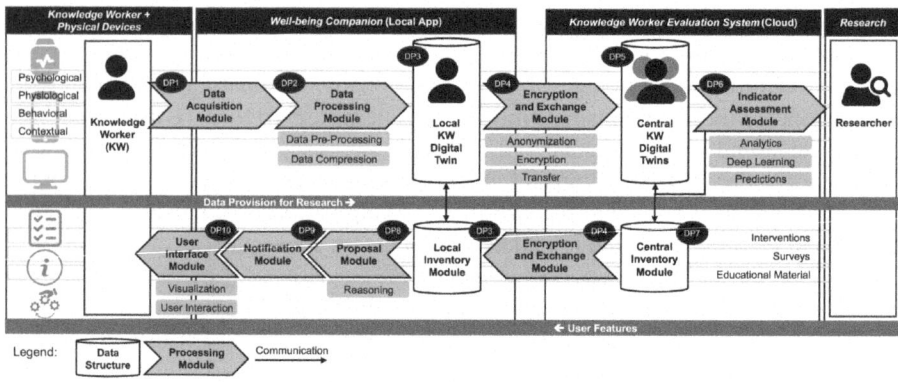

Fig. 3. Architecture based on Design Principles.

The first data flow begins with multimodal data collection (**DP1**) through **the Data Acquisition Module**. This module gathers four primary data types: (1) psychological data obtained through subjective self-reports to capture users' emotional and mental states, (2) physiological data, measured by wearables, such as heart rate or heart rate variability, (3) behavioral data, collected from user devices, like task completion, screen time, and prioritization, and (4) contextual data representing external factors, like location, time of day, or environmental conditions. Notably, the distinction between behavioral and contextual data is often blurred; for example, email response time could reflect behavioral efficiency or be influenced by contextual factors such as workload.

After acquisition, data is pre-processed and stored locally on the user's device within the Well-being Companion app to ensure data privacy. Given the vast amounts of data that is collected, it is impractical to perform both the analyses and the storage solely on the user's device. Therefore, the **Data Processing Module** performs only essential pre-processing (**DP2**) tasks, such as noise removal and data compression, to reduce storage and optimize network efficiency. Locally processed data is then stored (**DP3**) in the **Local**

Knowledge Worker Digital Twin (Local KWDT) which temporarily stores processed data and indicators collected. The visionary concept of a human digital twin (e.g. [47]) serves as more than just a static data repository; it functions as a dynamic representation – here: of the knowledge worker - enabling in-depth analyses and predictions about their state. The Local KWDT ensures data continuity, even without network connectivity, by storing processed indicators until they are transmitted to the cloud for advanced analysis.

The **Knowledge Worker Evaluation System** (KWES) serves as the central cloud-based infrastructure for advanced processing and research. We argue for a cloud infrastructure for reasons including scalability and elasticity [48]. The **Encryption and Exchange Module** (DP4) ensures secure data transfer by anonymizing identifiers, encrypting data at rest and in transit, and facilitating its transmission to the **Central KWDT** (DP5). This dynamic data pool serves as a central storage solution to handle the vast amounts of data generated over time by various individuals. Advanced analytics are performed in the **Indicator Assessment Module** (DP6) leveraging high-performance computing and AI to derive patterns, insights, and predictions (e.g. [49]). These refined indicators enhance the Central KWDT, providing researchers with comprehensive datasets for multi-individual analyses.

The second data flow focuses on delivering user-facing features. The **Central Inventory Module** (DP7) within the KWES stores dynamic content, such as surveys, interventions, and educational materials, curated and updated by researchers to maintain scientific relevance. When the Indicator Assessment Module detects significant signals in user data, relevant content is securely transmitted to the Well-being Companion via the Encryption and Exchange Module.

The **Local Inventory Module** (DP3) manages and stores this content, allowing users to interact with previously processed data. Three additional modules operationalize the user-facing aspects: The **Proposal Module** (DP8) determines appropriate content, such as interventions or surveys, tailored to the user's state through logical and heuristic methods; the **Notification Module** (DP9) calculates optimal timing for delivering content to minimize disruption and maximize engagement; and finally the **User Interface Module** (DP10) provides an interface for users to interact with the system. This module also visualizes key metrics, interventions, and educational materials while enabling users to edit or update their data, providing them with the tools to make informed decisions about their well-being.

4.3 Evaluation

To validate our DSR process, we evaluated the LRs, URs, and DPs as well as the architecture through six expert interviews, applying the criteria of completeness, ease of use, meaningfulness, simplicity, and understandability, as outlined by Sonnenberg and vom Brocke [35].

Experts viewed the LRs, URs, and DPs easy to understand and appropriately detailed. Expert 2 (E2) remarked that the requirements "coincide in very, very many cases with the impressions that (they) were able to gain (them)self", supporting their validity. Nonetheless, the experts made suggestions for improvements. E3 noted adding usability into DP10, and feedback by them led to revising DP5 to specify a "central storage location" instead of a cloud-based approach in general. While most experts found the DPs to be "target-oriented and abstract enough" (E3), E4 expressed concerns that they might be too abstract for implementation purposes. E5 praised their "good inner logic". E6 stressed that "everything hinges on LR1", recommending further elaboration without overcomplicating the requirements. Suggestions by E6 also included differentiating between eustress and distress (leading to LR6) and enhancing self-reports with interactive methods like audiovisual exchanges. E1 clarified that the focus remains on fundamental research, with personalized interventions being a long-term goal. E5 highlighted the need to address both individual feedback and broader working conditions.

All experts agreed that the DPs were appropriately applied in the architecture, clearly aligning components with their intended purpose. For the two experts who were unfamiliar with the concept of the digital twin, it became clear after explanation. Feedback also prompted changes to the data flow, adding a second flow for clarity and functionality, and explicitly integrating the researcher into the diagram. E1 described the architecture as having a "good, very clear layout". However, opinions on feasibility highlighted critical challenges. E2 highlighted difficulties with acquiring non-sensor-driven data, E6 questioned the ability to determine contextual phenomena accurately, and E4 cited concerns with data security and data fusion. E5 noted the system would require significant time to analyze patterns before enabling personalized interventions. Two experts refrained from providing specific comments on feasibility due to their lack of a technical background.

5 Discussion and Future Research

In this study we designed an architecture for a multimodal diagnosis and intervention platform aimed to support knowledge worker well-being. Using the DSR approach by Peffers et al. [11], we developed ten DPs based on a comprehensive literature review and empirical data collection, including semi-structured interviews (n = 12) and surveys (n = 32) with potential users, which were then evaluated by experts (n = 6) and refined.

The findings underscore the need to balance literature- and user-derived requirements, emphasizing system interaction and data security. First, while existing research highlights the value of multimodal data integration, potential users strongly emphasized the need for minimally intrusive and contextually aware systems, reinforcing the challenge of missing self-reported data [50]. However, the integration of different data modalities creates a symbiotic relationship, where each type of data enhances the interpretation of the others [37]. Subjective self-reports provide essential context for understanding physiological biomarkers, while behavioral and contextual data frame these signals within the broader work environment. Additionally, contextual data presents opportunities to optimize user interaction, for example, by identifying ideal time windows - such as calendar breaks between meetings - to prompt user input with minimal disruption. Second, data security and privacy also emerged as key concerns by users, a finding reinforced by the literature [45]. While collecting extensive data and utilizing cloud-based storage offers opportunities for advanced analysis, they also raise concerns. To address this, the architecture showcases two parallel execution layers: local device storage with initial processing capabilities, and anonymized cloud storage for advanced analysis. A similar approach is used by Apple's Private Cloud Compute [51].

We figured out that a dual-purpose system is essential for success. Without regular user input, data collection may fall short, compromising both its diagnostic and research functions. Thus, providing meaningful incentives to maintain user engagement is crucial for the system's effectiveness. The proposed architecture features two data flows to support these two objectives: one for research-oriented data collection and another for user-facing features, such as interventions or educational content, to sustain engagement and motivation. Experts emphasized an initial focus on diagnostics to establish a reliable foundation for future developments. While causal relationships remain complex, future iterations may offer tailored interventions to enhance resilience, well-being, and productivity. Meanwhile, generic interventions may maintain engagement and serve as a foundation for empirical research.

This research objective is part of a broader agenda. The proposed system is designed to be highly adaptable and customizable, allowing it to evolve to meet future needs in enhancing the well-being and performance of knowledge workers. Although the current version focuses on stress, the flexible architecture supports the integration of additional dimensions of health, including aspects like chronobiology, cognitive load, job satisfaction, motivation, multitasking, and work-life balance, thereby enriching the KWDT. For instance, leveraging chronobiology allows for time-of-day-specific interventions - such as scheduling high-focus tasks during peak performance periods or suggesting relaxation techniques when fatigue is imminent - tailored to individual circadian rhythms [52]. This could be further enhanced by incorporating sleep patterns and activity levels. Furthermore, incorporating motivational elements through gamification, like progress tracking, badges, or goal-setting challenges, can foster sustained user engagement [53]. Additionally, the system could be enriched with other context-specific features, such as cultural and demographic adaptations, ensuring that the platform remains relevant and effective across diverse user groups [54].

The next step of future research should refine the proposed architecture and develop a functional prototype for pilot testing, with stress management serving as an optional entry point for exploration. Special attention is needed to analyze the statistical relationships between stress predictors (e.g. workload, time pressure, and environmental factors) and actual strain (e.g. physiological, emotional, and cognitive responses). This will ensure accurate measurement and guide the development of targeted interventions to mitigate workplace strain.

Despite the contributions of this study, several limitations should be acknowledged. First, the relatively small sample and the predominantly young age of participants may have introduced selection bias and could limit generalizability. Future studies should include more diverse age groups, industries, and cultural contexts. Second, while the architecture was conceptually validated, implementation may reveal unforeseen technical or usability challenges. Finally, the current focus on stress does not fully capture the multifaceted nature of well-being. Future iterations should expand to broader well-being dimensions.

6 Contribution

Our work offers several important contributions to both theory and practice. First, we provide empirical insights into user requirements through a combination of qualitative and quantitative analyses. Second, we derived a set of user- and literature-centered design principles that can guide future researchers and practitioners in the development of similar platforms, ensuring that they are both scientifically grounded and user-focused. Third, we designed and evaluated a comprehensive architecture that serves as a practical blueprint for developers in the field of digital health and well-being applications. This architecture not only addresses technical challenges such as data integration, processing, and privacy but also aligns with user-centric considerations, making it a valuable resource for advancing the development of effective and secure digital health solutions.

Disclosure of Interests. The authors have no competing interests to declare that are relevant to the content of this article.

References

1. World Health Organization: Mental disorders, https://www.who.int/news-room/fact-sheets/detail/mental-disorders, last accessed 2025/01/28
2. Schneiderman, N., Ironson, G., Siegel, S.D.: STRESS AND HEALTH: psychological, behavioral, and biological determinants. Annu. Rev. Clin. Psychol. **1**, 607–628 (2005). https://doi.org/10.1146/annurev.clinpsy.1.102803.144141
3. Goodwin, R.D., Dierker, L.C., Wu, M., Galea, S., Hoven, C.W., Weinberger, A.H.: Trends in U.S. depression prevalence from 2015 to 2020: the widening treatment gap. Am. J. Prev. Med. **63**, 726–733 (2022). https://doi.org/10.1016/j.amepre.2022.05.014
4. Niedhammer, I., Bertrais, S., Witt, K.: Psychosocial work exposures and health outcomes: a meta-review of 72 literature reviews with meta-analysis. Scand. J. Work Environ. Health. **47**, 489–508 (2021). https://doi.org/10.5271/sjweh.3968
5. Humphrey, S.E., Nahrgang, J.D., Morgeson, F.P.: Integrating motivational, social, and contextual work design features: a meta-analytic summary and theoretical extension of the work design literature. J. Appl. Psychol. **92**, 1332–1356 (2007). https://doi.org/10.1037/0021-9010.92.5.1332
6. Thite, M.: Managing people in the new economy. Int. J. Knowled. Cult. Change Manag. Ann. Rev. **4** (2005). https://doi.org/10.18848/1447-9524/CGP/v04/59188
7. Chow, K., Fritz, T., Holsti, L., Barbic, S., McGrenere, J.: Feeling stressed and unproductive? A field evaluation of a therapy-inspired digital intervention for knowledge workers. ACM Trans. Comput.-Hum. Interact. **31**, 1–33 (2024). https://doi.org/10.1145/3609330
8. González Ramírez, M.L., García Vázquez, J.P., Rodríguez, M.D., Padilla-López, L.A., Galindo-Aldana, G.M., Cuevas-González, D.: Wearables for stress management: a scoping review. Healthcare. **11**, 2369 (2023). https://doi.org/10.3390/healthcare11172369
9. Alberdi, A., Aztiria, A., Basarab, A.: Towards an automatic early stress recognition system for office environments based on multimodal measurements: a review. J. Biomed. Inform. **59**, 49–75 (2016). https://doi.org/10.1016/j.jbi.2015.11.007
10. Tuunanen, T., Winter, R., Vom Brocke, J.: Dealing with complexity in design science research: a methodology using design echelons. MISQ. **48**, 427–458 (2024). https://doi.org/10.25300/MISQ/2023/16700
11. Peffers, K., Tuunanen, T., Rothenberger, M.A., Chatterjee, S.: A design science research methodology for information systems research. J. Manag. Inf. Syst. **24**, 45–77 (2007). https://doi.org/10.2753/MIS0742-1222240302
12. Kelloway, E.K., Barling, J.: Knowledge work as organizational behavior. Int. J. Manag. Rev. **2**, 287–304 (2000). https://doi.org/10.1111/1468-2370.00042

13. Drucker, P.F.: Knowledge-worker productivity: the biggest challenge. Calif. Manag. Rev. **41**, 79–94 (1999). https://doi.org/10.2307/41165987
14. Olshannikova, E., Ometov, A., Anagnostaki, T., Hasan, N., Kuketaeva, A., Ahtinen, A., Olsson, T., Koucheryavy, Y.: Towards better knowledge work experiences with new Ambient workspace: Concept and prototype. In: 2016 19th Conference of Open Innovations Association (FRUCT), pp. 173–181 (2016). https://doi.org/10.23919/FRUCT.2016.7892198
15. Meyer, A.N., Barr, E.T., Bird, C., Zimmermann, T.: Today was a good day: the daily life of software developers. IIEEE Trans. Software Eng. **47**, 863–880 (2021). https://doi.org/10.1109/TSE.2019.2904957
16. Pravettoni, G., Cropley, M., Leotta, S.N., Bagnara, S.: The differential role of mental rumination among industrial and knowledge workers. Ergonomics. **50**, 1931–1940 (2007). https://doi.org/10.1080/00140130701676088
17. D'Arcy, J., Gupta, A., Tarafdar, M., Turel, O.: Reflecting on the "dark side" of information technology use. Commun. Assoc. Inf. Syst. **35**, 109–118 (2014). https://doi.org/10.17705/1CAIS.03505
18. Sanjeeva Kumar, P.: TECHNOSTRESS: a comprehensive literature review on dimensions, impacts, and management strategies. Comput. Human Behav. Report. **16**, 100475 (2024). https://doi.org/10.1016/j.chbr.2024.100475
19. Diener, E., Oishi, S., Lucas, R.E.: Subjective well-being: the science of happiness and life satisfaction. In: Lopez, S.J., Snyder, C.R. (eds.) The Oxford Handbook of Positive Psychology. Oxford University Press (2009). https://doi.org/10.1093/oxfordhb/9780195187243.013.0017
20. Judge, T.A., Bono, J.E.: Relationship of core self-evaluations traits—self-esteem, generalized self-efficacy, locus of control, and emotional stability—with job satisfaction and job performance: a meta-analysis. J. Appl. Psychol. **86**, 80–92 (2001). https://doi.org/10.1037/0021-9010.86.1.80
21. Warr, P.: Work, Happiness, and Unhappiness. Psychology Press, New York (2011). https://doi.org/10.4324/9780203936856
22. Michie, S.: Causes and management of stress at work. Occup. Environ. Med. **59**, 67–72 (2002). https://doi.org/10.1136/oem.59.1.67
23. Koolhaas, J.M., Bartolomucci, A., Buwalda, B., De Boer, S.F., Flügge, G., Korte, S.M., Meerlo, P., Murison, R., Olivier, B., Palanza, P., Richter-Levin, G., Sgoifo, A., Steimer, T., Stiedl, O., Van Dijk, G., Wöhr, M., Fuchs, E.: Stress revisited: a critical evaluation of the stress concept. Neurosci. Biobehav. Rev. **35**, 1291–1301 (2011). https://doi.org/10.1016/j.neubiorev.2011.02.003
24. Selye, H.: The Stress of Life. Mcgraw Hill, Oxford (1978)
25. McGonagle, K.A., Kessler, R.C.: Chronic stress, acute stress, and depressive symptoms. Am. J. Comm. Psychol. **18**, 681–706 (1990). https://doi.org/10.1007/BF00931237
26. Sanches, P., Höök, K., Vaara, E., Weymann, C., Bylund, M., Ferreira, P., Peira, N., Sjölinder, M.: Mind the body!: designing a mobile stress management application encouraging personal reflection. In: Proceedings of the 8th ACM Conference on Designing Interactive Systems, pp. 47–56. ACM, Aarhus (2010). https://doi.org/10.1145/1858171.1858182
27. Carneiro, D., Castillo, J.C., Novais, P., Fernández-Caballero, A., Neves, J.: Multimodal behavioral analysis for non-invasive stress detection. Expert Syst. Appl. **39**, 13376–13389 (2012). https://doi.org/10.1016/j.eswa.2012.05.065
28. Betts Razavi, T.: Self-report measures: An overview of concerns and limitations of questionnaire use in occupational stress research. University of Southampton - Department of Accounting and Management Science, Papers. (2001)
29. Taskasaplidis, G., Fotiadis, D.A., Bamidis, P.D.: Review of stress detection methods using wearable sensors. IEEE Access. **12**, 38219–38246 (2024). https://doi.org/10.1109/ACCESS.2024.3373010

30. Regehr, C., Glancy, D., Pitts, A.: Interventions to reduce stress in university students: a review and meta-analysis. J. Affect. Disord. **148**, 1–11 (2013). https://doi.org/10.1016/j.jad.2012.11.026
31. Palvalin, M., Van Der Voordt, T., Jylhä, T.: The impact of workplaces and self-management practices on the productivity of knowledge workers. JFM. **15**, 423–438 (2017). https://doi.org/10.1108/JFM-03-2017-0010
32. Dorsey, A., Scherer, E., Eckhoff, R., Furberg, R.: Measurement of Human Stress: A Multidimensional Approach. RTI Press (2022). https://doi.org/10.3768/rtipress.2022.op.0073.2206
33. Vom Brocke, J., Simons, A., Riemer, K., Niehaves, B., Plattfaut, R., Cleven, A.: Standing on the shoulders of giants: challenges and recommendations of literature search in information systems research. CAIS. **37** (2015). https://doi.org/10.17705/1CAIS.03709
34. Gregor, S., Kruse, L.C., Seidel, S.: Research perspectives: the anatomy of a design principle. J. Assoc. Inf. Syst. **21**, 10.17705/1jais.00649 (2020)
35. Sonnenberg, C., vom Brocke, J.: Evaluation patterns for design science research artefacts. In: Helfert, M., Donnellan, B. (eds.) Practical Aspects of Design Science, pp. 71–83. Springer, Berlin, Heidelberg (2012). https://doi.org/10.1007/978-3-642-33681-2_7
36. Mayring, P.: Qualitative content analysis: theoretical foundation, basic procedures and software solution. (2014)
37. Weckesser, L.J., Dietz, F., Schmidt, K., Grass, J., Kirschbaum, C., Miller, R.: The psychometric properties and temporal dynamics of subjective stress, retrospectively assessed by different informants and questionnaires, and hair cortisol concentrations. Sci. Rep. **9**, 1098 (2019). https://doi.org/10.1038/s41598-018-37526-2
38. Schulz, P., Schlotz, W., Becker, P.: Trierer Inventar zum chronischen stress (TICS) [Trier inventory for chronic stress (TICS)] (2004)
39. Shiffman, S., Stone, A., Hufford, M.: Ecolocial momentary assessment. Annu. Rev. Clin. Psychol. **4**, 1–32 (2008). https://doi.org/10.1146/annurev.clinpsy.3.022806.091415
40. Naeem, M., Fawzi, S.A., Anwar, H., Malek, A.S.: Wearable ECG systems for accurate mental stress detection: a scoping review. J. Publ. Heal. (Berl.). (2023). https://doi.org/10.1007/s10389-023-02099-6
41. Klimek, A., Mannheim, I., Schouten, G., Wouters, E.J.M., Peeters, M.W.H.: Wearables measuring electrodermal activity to assess perceived stress in care: a scoping review. Acta Neuropsychiatr., 1–11 (2023). https://doi.org/10.1017/neu.2023.19
42. Gradl, S., Wirth, M., Richer, R., Rohleder, N., Eskofier, B.M.: An overview of the feasibility of permanent, real-time, unobtrusive stress measurement with current wearables. In: Proceedings of the 13th EAI International Conference on Pervasive Computing Technologies for Healthcare, pp. 360–365. ACM, Trento (2019). https://doi.org/10.1145/3329189.3329233
43. Lahat, D., Adali, T., Jutten, C.: Multimodal data fusion: an overview of methods, challenges, and prospects. Proc. IEEE. **103**, 1449–1477 (2015). https://doi.org/10.1109/JPROC.2015.2460697
44. Awada, M., Becerik-Gerber, B., Lucas, G., Roll, S., Liu, R.: A new perspective on stress detection: an automated approach for detecting eustress and distress. IEEE Trans. Affect. Comput. **15**, 1153–1165 (2024). https://doi.org/10.1109/TAFFC.2023.3324910
45. Thapa, C., Camtepe, S.: Precision health data: requirements, challenges and existing techniques for data security and privacy. Comput. Biol. Med. **129**, 104130 (2021). https://doi.org/10.1016/j.compbiomed.2020.104130
46. Nielsen, J.: Usability Engineering. Academic Press, Boston (1993)
47. Lin, Y., Chen, L., Ali, A., Nugent, C., Cleland, I., Li, R., Ding, J., Ning, H.: Human digital twin: a survey. J. Cloud. Comp. **13**, 131 (2024). https://doi.org/10.1186/s13677-024-00691-z
48. Iyer, B., Henderson, J.C.: Preparing for the future: understanding the seven capabilities cloud computing. MIS Q. Exec. **9** (2010)

49. Zhang, J., Yin, H., Zhang, J., Yang, G., Qin, J., He, L.: Real-time mental stress detection using multimodality expressions with a deep learning framework. Front. Neurosci. **16**, 947168 (2022). https://doi.org/10.3389/fnins.2022.947168
50. Fox-Wasylyshyn, S.M., El-Masri, M.M.: Handling missing data in self-report measures. Res. Nurs. Health. **28**, 488–495 (2005). https://doi.org/10.1002/nur.20100
51. Apple: Private Cloud Compute: A new frontier for AI privacy in the cloud, https://security.apple.com/blog/private-cloud-compute/, last accessed 27 Jan 2025
52. Kühnel, J., Bledow, R., Kiefer, M.: There is a time to be creative: the alignment between Chronotype and time of day. AMJ. **65**, 218–247 (2022). https://doi.org/10.5465/amj.2019.0020
53. Spanellis, A., Dörfler, V., MacBryde, J.: Investigating the potential for using gamification to empower knowledge workers. Expert Syst. Appl. **160**, 113694 (2020). https://doi.org/10.1016/j.eswa.2020.113694
54. Leon, R.: The future knowledge worker: an intercultural perspective. Manag. Dynam. Knowled. Econ. **3**, 675–691 (2015)

Designing for Trust: Integrating Self-referencing in Large Language Model-Based Health Coaching

Sophia Meywirth[1](✉), Andreas Janson[2], and Matthias Söllner[1]

[1] University of Kassel, Kassel, Germany
{sophia.meywirth,soellner}@uni-kassel.de
[2] University of St. Gallen, St. Gallen, Switzerland
andreas.janson@unisg.ch

Abstract. This research applies the Design Science Research (DSR) methodology to investigate how self-referencing in Large Language Model (LLM)-based health coaching influences user trust and perceptions of anthropomorphism. We synthesized theory-driven design principles to guide the integration of self-referencing and demonstrated them in a vignette-based prototype. Through a single-factorial between-subjects experiment, analyzed using Partial Least Squares Structural Equation Modeling (PLS-SEM) and qualitative feedback, we identified a dual effect of self-referencing: while professional self-referencing enhances trust via increased anthropomorphism, overly personal references can directly undermine trust. Based on these findings, we refined our design principles to optimize trust-building in LLM-based coaching. Our contributions provide actionable design guidelines for creating more effective and trustworthy AI-driven health interventions, advancing the understanding of anthropomorphic design in digital coaching contexts.

Keywords: Health behavior change · Coaching · Large language models · Trust · Anthropomorphism

1 Introduction

The health and wellness industry has experienced significant growth in recent years, driven by a rising demand [1] from consumers who prioritize health, fitness, nutrition, and overall well-being. This trend is particularly influenced by a cultural shift towards preventive healthcare, largely advocated by younger generations like Gen Z. They favor proactive health management strategies, emphasizing dietary and fitness modifications to prevent chronic diseases [2, 3]. While the intent to adopt healthier lifestyles is evident, actual behavioral change remains challenging.

Digital interventions, particularly health coaching, have emerged as effective means to support individuals in achieving lifestyle changes through collaborative conversations and personalized guidance [4]. However, the scalability of such interventions is often limited by the availability of human practitioners and and the delayed interactions typical of traditional digital formats, which can diminish engagement [5–7].

With the recent advancements in large language models (LLMs), new possibilities have emerged. These technologies offer the potential for real-time, scalable, and highly personalized coaching interactions, mimicking human conversational capabilities and adapting responses to individual user needs. [6, 8] Preliminary applications of LLMs in fields like nutrition and physical activity coaching have demonstrated promising outcomes by providing dynamic, customized advice [9–12].

To fully leverage the benefits of LLMs in behavioral healthcare, their proper utilization is crucial [13]. Central to successful coaching is the establishment of user trust [8, 14]. A trusting relationship between the coach and coachee is essential, as it encourages users to disclose necessary health information [8] and adhere to the coach's advice [15]. In LLM-based health coaching, anthropomorphism – the extent to which users perceive human-like qualities in the system – can significantly influence trust. Studies suggest that incorporating human-like features in conversational agents makes interactions more natural and relatable, thereby fostering trust [16]. Precisely, anthropomorphic design elements, such as human-like behaviors and verbal social cues, can shape how trustworthy users perceive the system to be.

While prior research on anthropomorphic chatbot design has primarily focused on visual cues, such as the use of avatars and names, and stylistic elements of communication, such as tone and formality [17, 18], there has been limited exploration on how to design content-specific verbal cues in chatbot interactions. Content-specific cues – what is said rather than just how it is said – are particularly impactful in contexts that require ongoing engagement and rapport, such as health coaching [19]. In these settings, meaningful conversation beyond task-oriented dialogue can foster a supportive and trusted relationship between the user and the system [20]. One such underexplored content-specific cue is self-referencing, where the agent refers to itself to appear more human-like [21].

Given the complex role self-referencing plays in user perceptions of AI coaches, this paper investigates the nuanced design impacts of this anthropomorphic trait. We aim to explore the following design-based research question:

RQ: How should an LLM-based coaching intervention be designed to integrate self-referencing to foster trust?

To address our research question, we adopted a design science research methodology as outlined by Peffers et al. [22]. Our study aimed to establish initial design principles using a theory-driven and exploratory approach. We assessed these principles through a single-factorial between-subjects experiment, specifically examining the impact of self-referencing on perceptions of anthropomorphism and trust within LLM-based health coaching contexts. We employed partial least squares structural equation modeling (PLS-SEM) to analyze the contributions and effects of these human-like cues. Additionally, we integrated qualitative data from the experiments to further refine our findings and the evolving design principles. This comprehensive approach allowed us to explore both the positive and negative implications of self-referencing in enhancing the efficacy of digital health interventions.

2 Theoretical Background

2.1 Anthropomorphic Design

Anthropomorphism involves attributing human traits and characteristics to non-human entities like computers or systems [23–25]. Nass and Moon [25] introduced the "Computers are Social Actors" (CASA) paradigm, explaining that despite their lack of emotions, self-reference, and physical presence, people still apply social roles and expectations to computers, treating them as social beings. This tendency has been examined through two main theoretical lenses: one suggests humans automatically respond to lifelike or social cues without conscious thought, while the other proposes that people form mental models based on how systems mimic human behavior, influencing their interactions with these systems [24, 26].

Advances in AI since 2000 have significantly enhanced the capabilities of computers, enabling them to simulate emotions, use personal pronouns, and exhibit human-like behaviors [25]. This has transformed user interactions, particularly in the development of conversational agents that now incorporate a broad range of social cues, enhancing user engagement through more natural interactions [26, 27]. Feine et al. [21] detailed this in their taxonomy of social cues for conversational agents, highlighting differences in verbal, visual, auditory, and invisible cues.

Previous research has predominantly focused on the visual and stylistic aspects of anthropomorphic chatbot design, such as avatars, names, tone, and formality [17, 18]. However, there has been limited exploration of content-specific verbal cues, which are crucial in settings requiring sustained engagement and rapport, like health coaching [19]. These cues, focusing on what is communicated rather than just how it is communicated, can significantly foster a supportive and trusted relationship between users and systems [20].

2.2 Trust

In IS research, trust is often studied in two contexts: interpersonal trust, applicable to both individuals and organizations and trust in IT systems or artifacts [28–30]. Trust formation relies on perceived characteristics such as ability, benevolence, and integrity for individuals, and functionality, helpfulness, and reliability for technology [31–33]. In health coaching, trust hinges on the coach's perceived competence, goodwill, and reliability, which are crucial for client engagement [8].

We adopt the definition of trust proposed by Mayer et al. ([35], page 712): "Trust is the willingness of a party to be vulnerable to the actions of another party based on the expectation that the other will perform a particular action important to the trustor, irrespective of the ability to monitor or control that other party." This definition emphasizes the critical role of vulnerability in trust dynamics, where individuals willingly expose themselves to risk in relationships [35, 36]. Designing IT artifacts that foster trust requires a systematic approach grounded in trust theory [37], ensuring that key trust-building factors are embedded the system's functionality. In LLM-based health coaching, one such approach is anthropomorphic design, which can enhance user perceptions of the system's trust antecedents [16].

In LLM-based health coaching, the extent to which users perceive human-like qualities in the system, or anthropomorphism, significantly influences trust. Studies indicate that incorporating human-like features into conversational agents makes interactions more natural and relatable, enhancing trust [16]. Specifically, anthropomorphic design elements like human-like behaviors and verbal social cues shape user perceptions of trustworthiness. Supporting research shows that users form richer mental models of anthropomorphic systems than of mechanical ones, suggesting that these effects also apply to digital systems [24]. Moreover, trust in conversational agents is notably improved by anthropomorphic features, including visual and auditory cues [38].

3 Methodology

This research follows the Design Science Research (DSR) methodology as described by Peffers et al. [22], which is structured into six distinct phases depicted in Fig. 1. We followed the problem-centered approach, where the initial step involves identifying the problem and establishing motivation – details of which are presented in the introduction of this paper.

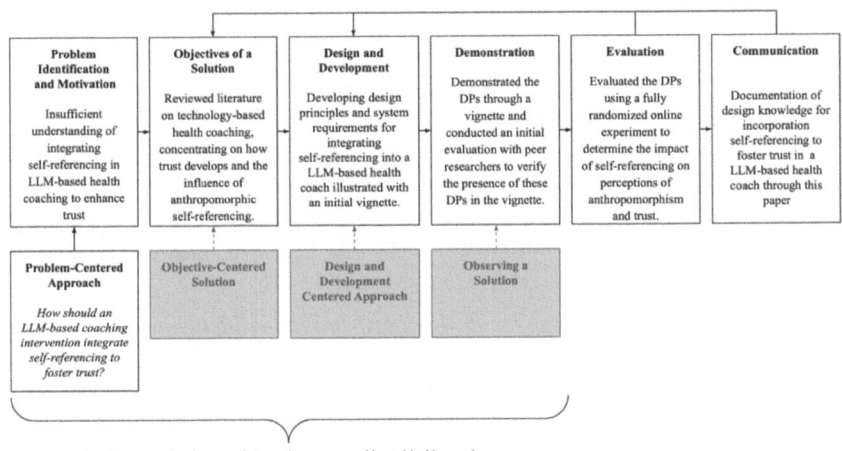

Fig. 1. Design Science Research Process adapted from Peffers et al. [22]

The second phase focuses on specifying the objectives of the solution. The primary goal of our solution is to integrate the content-specific verbal social cue of self-referencing into an LLM-based health coaching intervention to enhance users' perception of anthropomorphism and trust. More broadly, self-referencing contributes to anthropomorphic design by making the conversational agent appear more human-like. Sharing personal experiences and demonstrating behaviors are inherently human traits that foster personalization, build rapport, and strengthen trust. Feine et al. highlight content-specific social cues, such as self-disclosure and references to past events, as key factors in enhancing user engagement [21]. By incorporating relevant self-references, the LLM-based coach can create more relatable and engaging interactions, ultimately improving the overall coaching experience.

In the third phase, Design and Development, we adopt a theory-driven approach, deriving design principles from the literature on anthropomorphic chatbot design and health coaching. After establishing initial design principles based on the guidelines of Gregor et al. [39], we developed a vignette-based prototype. This prototype serves to demonstrate and evaluate our design principles in phases five and six, respectively, through a fully randomized online experiment.

The research cycle concludes with the refinement of our design principles, incorporating insights gained from the experimental results and additional qualitative user feedback. This iterative process ensures that our findings are both robust and relevant to the field of digital health coaching.

4 Design and Development

4.1 Deriving Initial Design Principles from Theory

Self-referencing is a content-specific social cue with multiple potential benefits in LLM-based health coaching. Coaching inherently involves clients disclosing personal information about their goals and habits, often on intimate topics, particularly in health-related discussions [8]. However, individuals are generally hesitant to share such information unless reciprocity is present. Research has demonstrated that users are more willing to disclose personal details when their conversational partner also shares intimate information [40]. Moon's study [40], grounded in the CASA paradigm, shows that this reciprocity effect extends to human-computer interactions. Similarly, Lee et al. found that greater self-disclosure by a chatbot led to increased self-disclosure from users, as well as higher enjoyment and intimacy in the interaction [41]. We therefore propose the following design principle:

DP1: For designers and researchers to design LLM-based health behavior change interventions effectively for individuals desiring to change their health behaviors, ensure that the LLM-based coach engages in self-referencing by sharing relevant information about itself in a way that fosters reciprocity, so that user openness is encouraged, thereby strengthening trust and engagement.

Beyond fostering openness, self-referencing aligns with established behavior change techniques (BCTs). The taxonomy by Michie et al. [42] identifies 93 distinct BCTs, including the "comparison of behavior" cluster, which highlights the role of demonstrating behaviors and fostering social comparison. Self-referencing allows the LLM-based coach to position itself as a role model, verbally demonstrating behaviors that clients might adopt. For example, the coach could reference its own strategies for maintaining habits or overcoming challenges, encouraging clients to reflect on their own behaviors and implement changes accordingly. We therefore propose the following design principle:

DP2: For designers and researchers to design LLM-based health behavior change interventions effectively for individuals desiring to change their health behaviors, ensure that the LLM-based coach verbally demonstrates desirable behaviors, so that social comparison is facilitated and users are encouraged to adopt healthier habits.

Furthermore, self-referencing plays a crucial role in fostering trust. When assessing trustworthiness, people evaluate key characteristics such as ability, benevolence, and integrity [34]. By referencing its own coaching-relevant experiences, the LLM-based coach can establish its ability and credibility, demonstrating expertise in guiding users toward their health goals. We therefore propose the following design principle:

Table 1. Exemplary Dialogue Elements Based on Initial Design Principles

Design Principles		Implementation in Vignette
For designers and researchers to design LLM-based health behavior change interventions effectively for individuals desiring to change their health behaviors, ...		Embedded within conversation between LLM-based coach and client aimed at fostering healthy nutrition and fitness.
DP1	ensure that the LLM-based coach engages in self-referencing by sharing information about itself in a way that fosters reciprocity, so that the user's openness is encouraged thereby enhancing trust and engagement.	"A bit about me — I've always been passionate about helping others live their healthiest lives, inspired by my own wellness journey."
		"I used to do homemade pizza nights with friends to see who could make the healthiest, tastiest toppings."
		"Wednesday: Rest day — I usually use this to catch up on reading or plan the week."
DP2	ensure that the LLM-based coach verbally demonstrates desirable behaviors, so that social comparison is reinforced and users are encouraged to adopt healthier habits.	"For lunch, how about switching to wraps with lean meats and veggies instead of the usual sandwiches? It's an easy, tasty swap I love for eating better on the go."
		"Here's a plan for the week that includes some of my personal favorites for inspiration: **Monday & Thursday:** 15-minute morning walk. — starting the day with a walk really energizes me, and it might do the same for you."
DP3	ensure that the LLM-based coach utilizes self-referencing to demonstrate its expertise and reliability, so that the user feels confident in the coach's abilities and trusts the guidance provided, thereby fostering a committed and effective coaching relation-ship.	„I have other clients who are vegan, so I'm quite familiar with a variety of dishes that could work well for you."
		„For example, a client of mine also had a desk job and found success by scheduling short, 10 minute walks during her lunch break."

DP3: For designers and researchers to design LLM-based health behavior change interventions effectively for individuals desiring to change their health behaviors, ensure that the LLM-based coach utilizes self-referencing to demonstrate its expertise and reliability, so that the user feels confident in the coach's abilities and trusts the guidance provided, thereby fostering a committed and effective coaching relationship.

4.2 Development of Vignettes and Demonstration

We developed a vignette-based LLM health coaching intervention designed to simulate trust-building interactions in a realistic setting [43] and to demonstrate our initial design principles. The vignette represents an initial chat-based session with a lifestyle coach focused on goal-setting – an essential component of health coaching [6]. To reinforce this, we incorporated techniques from the "goals and planning" cluster of the behavior change technique taxonomy [42] and integrated dietary advice and strategic recommendations. These elements address key trust factors, such as sharing personal goals [8] and following expert advice [44].

Building on design principles derived from theory, we crafted a prototype dialogue demonstrating DP1, DP2, and DP3. Table 1 outlines these principles alongside the corresponding self-reference phrases embedded in the vignettes. The dialogue includes self-references aligned with our initial design knowledge, while a control vignette, omitting these self-references, was developed for baseline comparison. Each interaction began with an introductory message clarifying that the coach was powered by an LLM.

These messages were implemented in a Figma prototype designed to replicate the mobile version of ChatGPT, ensuring a familiar user experience while avoiding additional social cues beyond those typical of LLM-based interactions.

We conducted a preliminary evaluation of the vignettes with five peer researchers to ensure they effectively demonstrated our design principles. Based on their feedback, we made slight adjustments to refine clarity and alignment with the intended design elements.

5 Evaluation

5.1 Experimental Procedure

We conducted a fully randomized online experiment to assess the impact of our design principles on user trust and perceptions of anthropomorphism. Our evaluation followed the DSR evaluation framework proposed by Venable [45], adopting a formative intermediate approach situated between ex-ante and ex-post evaluation. The experiment was well suited for this purpose, as it focused on relational mechanisms – such as trust, anthropomorphism, and reliance – that are central to the intended effects of the proposed design principles.

A total of 149 participants were recruited via Prolific [46] in accordance with guidelines for online studies [47]. After excluding six responses for failing attention checks and three responses due to excessively rapid survey completion (under five minutes), the final sample comprised 140 valid responses, with 74 participants in the control group and 66 in the treatment group.

The sample consisted of slightly more males (49.3%) than females (47.9%), with a small percentage of non-binary participants (2.9%). Participants had a mean age of 38 years (ranging from 18 to 74 years). In terms of education, 43.6% held a bachelor's degree as their highest qualification, while 29.3% had completed a high school diploma. Moreover, 63.6% reported no prior experience with health or lifestyle coaching, and 80% aimed to improve their fitness and nutrition.

The experiment unfolded in three steps. First, participants received a brief overview of the study's objectives and context. Second, they were introduced to a vignette scenario in which they assumed the role of an individual receiving LLM-based coaching for healthy nutrition and physical activity – initiating goal-setting via an online chat. Finally, participants were presented with the prototype vignette depicting the initial coaching session and were asked to evaluate its content through an online survey.

Perceived anthropomorphism was measured using seven indicators adapted from Seymour et al. [48], reliance was assessed with three indicators adopted from Chua et al. [49] and Gursoy et al. [50], and trust was evaluated using three indicators adapted from Gefen [51]. Additionally, open-ended questions were included to capture exploratory insights during this initial iteration.

Afterward, we used structural equation modeling (SEM) with the variance-based partial least squares (PLS) [52, 53] approach to analyze our data. PLS-SEM is a multivariate analysis technique widely used to investigate causal-predictive relationships in information systems. It does this by employing weighted composites of variables as proxies for latent variables, which allows for the estimation of their relationship. [54]

5.2 Results

We started by evaluating our measurement model. We checked the univariate normality of the measurements and found that none of our measures exceeded the threshold of 2 or −2 for skewness or kurtosis values of 2 or −2 [55]. Subsequently, we assessed the construct's reliability and convergent validity. We employed Cronbach's Alpha, composite reliability (rho_c and rho_a), and average variance extracted (AVE) as indicators. Our findings indicated that all indicators met the thresholds of 0.7 or above for Cronbach's alpha, rho_c, and rho_a, and 0.5 or above for AVE [55]. Furthermore, we evaluated the discriminant validity by measuring the heterotrait-monotrait (HTMT) ratios of correlations. The discriminant validity measures to what extent the latent constructs are truly distinct from each other [56]. None of our latent constructs exhibited a value above the suggested threshold of 0.9 [55].

The results of the structural model are presented in detail using path coefficients (β), significance levels (p-values), and effect sizes (f^2). A 5,000-sample bootstrapping algorithm was used to determine the statistical significance of the path coefficients. The results are summarized in Fig. 2.

Our results show a significant relationship with a p-value less than 0.01 between anthropomorphism and trust (p-value = 0.000). Additionally, we found a significant relationship between self-referencing and anthropomorphism with a p-value of 0.003. Furthermore, we identified a marginally significant relationship between self-referencing and trust with a p-value of 0.086. Moreover, we revealed a significant relationship between trust and reliance.

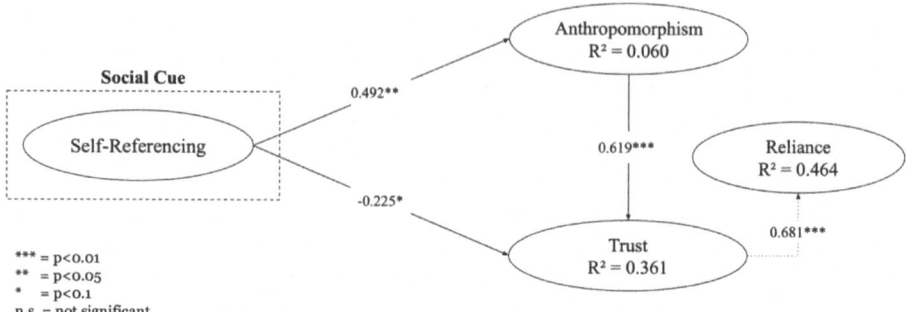

Fig. 2. Structural Model

In terms of effect size, values above 0.020, 0.150, and 0.350 indicate a low, moderate, and high effect at the structural level, respectively [57]. The analysis confirmed a significant and positive relationship between anthropomorphism and trust, as indicated by a strong path coefficient ($\beta = 0.619$, $p \leq 0.01$) and a high effect size ($f^2 = 0.563$). Similarly, the relationship between self-referencing and anthropomorphism was significant and positive, with a moderate path coefficient ($\beta = 0.492$, $p \leq 0.05$) and a low effect size ($f^2 = 0.064$). In contrast, the relationship between self-referencing and trust was significant but negative, with a path coefficient ($\beta = -0.225$, $p \leq 0.1$) and a marginal effect size ($f^2 = 0.019$). Moreover, the analysis identified a significant relationship between trust and reliance with a strong path coefficient ($\beta = 0.681$, $p = 0.000$) and a substantial explained effect size ($f^2 = 0.866$). The R^2 values for trust ($R^2 = 0.361$) and reliance ($R^2 = 0.464$) are considered substantial based on Chin's [52] guidelines.

6 Discussion and Revision of Design Principles

Our results reveal a dual effect of self-referencing in digital coaching applications. While it enhances anthropomorphism and can foster trust, it may also undermine trust if not carefully calibrated. Participants responded negatively to experiential self-references – such as anecdotes about pizza nights or personal routines – often perceiving them as unsettling or inauthentic. One participant noted, "It also wrote as though it was alive and had friends and ate things, which is weird." Another remarked, "I did NOT like the LLM coach pretending to be human. An LLM doesn't have pizza nights, take morning walks, and spend Wednesday breaks reading."

These reactions highlight a key insight: overly human-like self-references can compromise the system's perceived integrity – a cornerstone of trust [34]. In contrast, professional self-referencing, such as references to experiences with other clients, was perceived as helpful and credible. Since self-referencing increases anthropomorphism – positively affecting trust –, we recommend incorporating it at a professional level while integrating emotions and empathy. These elements were not perceived as uncanny and contributed to a more human-like yet credible interaction.

In light of these findings, we revised our original design principles to reflect the nuanced role of self-referencing in building trust. Specifically, we recommend avoiding fabricated personal anecdotes and instead suggest referencing generalized client experiences and providing empathetic responses that mirror user emotions without implying human-like experiences.

DP1, which originally focused on fostering openness through self-referencing, is now refined to emphasize professional reciprocity rather than fabricated personal stories. Empathy remains important but should be conveyed in ways that do not imply human identity.

DP2 emphasized self-referencing as a role-modeling strategy, aligning with behavior change techniques such as social comparison. However, user feedback suggests this should not include personal anecdotes or imply human-like experiences. Instead, LLM-based coaches should reference other clients' experiences to encourage reflection while maintaining an AI-appropriate persona.

Based on our evaluation, we find no need to revise DP3, which focuses on establishing the coach's ability through references to professional experiences. However, we propose adding DP4, which underscores the importance of avoiding experiential self-references in LLM-based coaching. Table 2 provides an overview of the revised design principles.

Table 2. Revised Design Principles

Revised Design Principles	
For designers and researchers to design LLM-based health behavior change interventions effectively for individuals desiring to change their health behaviors, …	
DP1	…ensure that the LLM-based coach engages in self-referencing by sharing generalized insights and experiences from other clients in a professional manner and providing empathetic responses that mirror users' emotions without implying personal experiences, so that users feel a sense of commonality and reciprocity, encouraging openness and fostering trust and engagement.
DP2	…ensure that the LLM-based coach verbally demonstrates desirable behaviors by referencing other clients' strategies, so that social comparison is reinforced and users are encouraged to adopt healthier habits.
DP3	…ensure that the LLM-based coach utilizes self-referencing to demonstrate its expertise and reliability, so that the user feels confident in the coach's abilities and trusts the guidance provided, thereby fostering a committed and effective coaching relation-ship.
DP4	…ensure that the LLM-based coach avoids experiential self-references, such as sharing human-like personal experiences, so that users accept the system and do not experience feelings of eeriness.

7 Conclusion

In our study, we synthesized three theory-driven design principles for integrating self-referencing in LLM-based health coaching to foster trust. We demonstrated these principles through a vignette-based prototype, which we evaluated in a single-factorial between-subjects experiment. Using PLS-SEM analysis and additional qualitative data, we identified a dual effect of self-referencing on trust and reliance in digital coaching applications: while self-referencing can enhance trust by increasing perceived anthropomorphism, it can also directly undermine trust when not carefully calibrated. Based on these findings, we refined our design principles to optimize the use of self-referencing in LLM-based health coaching for trust-building.

While our study provides valuable insights, it is important to acknowledge the limitations inherent in the iterative nature of the Design Science Research methodology. This study represents the first iteration, where evaluation results informed the revision of our design principles, which should be further tested in subsequent iterations. Future research should extend beyond vignette-based prototypes to implement and evaluate the revised design principles in real-world settings. Additionally, further studies should assess the intervention's effectiveness in collaboration with behavioral healthcare experts, such as therapists, certified dietitians, and researchers, to validate its practical applicability. Finally, future research must also address potential biases inherent in the natural training data of LLMs to ensure ethical and unbiased coaching interactions.

References

1. Statista: Digital Health - Worldwide, https://www.statista.com/outlook/hmo/digital-health/worldwide, last accessed 16 Apr 2024
2. Park, M.J., Kim, D.J., Lee, U., Na, E.J., Jeon, H.J.: A literature overview of virtual reality (VR) in treatment of psychiatric disorders: recent advances and limitations. Front. Psych. 10 (2019). https://doi.org/10.3389/fpsyt.2019.00505
3. OECD/European Union: Health at a glance: Europe 2022: state of health in the EU cycle. OECD (2022). https://doi.org/10.1787/507433b0-en
4. Huffman, M.: Health coaching: a new and exciting technique to enhance patient self-management and improve outcomes. Home Healthc. Now. 25, 271 (2007). https://doi.org/10.1097/01.NHH.0000267287.84952.8f
5. Mitchell, E.G., Elhadad, N., Mamykina, L.: Examining AI methods for micro-coaching dialogs. In: CHI Conference on Human Factors in Computing Systems, pp. 1–24. ACM, New Orleans, LA (2022). https://doi.org/10.1145/3491102.3501886
6. Mitchell, E.G., Maimone, R., Cassells, A., Tobin, J.N., Davidson, P., Smaldone, A.M., Mamykina, L.: Automated vs.: Human health coaching: exploring participant and practitioner experiences. Proc. ACM Hum.-Comput. Interact. 5, 99 (2021). https://doi.org/10.1145/3449173
7. Brandt, C.J., Søgaard, G.I., Clemensen, J., Søndergaard, J., Nielsen, J.B.: Determinants of successful eHealth coaching for consumer lifestyle changes: qualitative interview study among health care professionals. J. Med. Internet Res. 20, e237 (2018). https://doi.org/10.2196/jmir.9791
8. Schiemann, S.J., Mühlberger, C., Schoorman, F.D., Jonas, E.: Trust me, I am a caring coach: the benefits of establishing trustworthiness during coaching by communicating benevolence. J. Trust Res. 9, 164–184 (2019). https://doi.org/10.1080/21515581.2019.1650751
9. Alanezi, F.: Examining the role of ChatGPT in promoting health behaviors and lifestyle changes among cancer patients. Nutr. Health, 02601060241244563 (2024). https://doi.org/10.1177/02601060241244563
10. Arslan, S.: Exploring the potential of chat GPT in personalized obesity treatment. Ann. Biomed. Eng. 51, 1887–1888 (2023). https://doi.org/10.1007/s10439-023-03227-9

11. Kirk, D., van Eijnatten, E., Camps, G.: Comparison of answers between ChatGPT and human dieticians to common nutrition questions. J. Nutrit. Metabol. **2023**, e5548684 (2023). https://doi.org/10.1155/2023/5548684
12. Willms, A., Liu, S.: Exploring the feasibility of using ChatGPT to create just-in-time adaptive physical activity mHealth intervention content: case study. JMIR Med. Educ. **10**, e51426 (2024). https://doi.org/10.2196/51426
13. Demszky, D., Yang, D., Yeager, D.S., Bryan, C.J., Clapper, M., Chandhok, S., Eichstaedt, J.C., Hecht, C., Jamieson, J., Johnson, M., Jones, M., Krettek-Cobb, D., Lai, L., JonesMitchell, N., Ong, D.C., Dweck, C.S., Gross, J.J., Pennebaker, J.W.: Using large language models in psychology. Nat Rev Psychol., 1–14 (2023). https://doi.org/10.1038/s44159-023-00241-5
14. Terblanche, N.H.D., Heyns, M.: The impact of coachee personality traits, propensity to trust and perceived trustworthiness of a coach, on a coachee's trust behaviour in a coaching relationship. SA J. Ind. Psychol. **46**, 1–11 (2020). https://doi.org/10.4102/sajip.v46i0.1707
15. Wu, Z., Helaoui, R., Reforgiato Recupero, D., Riboni, D.: Towards effective automatic evaluation of generated reflections for motivational interviewing. In: Companion Publication of the 25th International Conference on Multimodal Interaction, pp. 368–373. Association for Computing Machinery, New York, NY (2023). https://doi.org/10.1145/3610661.3616127
16. de Visser, E., Monfort, S., Mckendrick, R., Smith, M., Mcknight, P., Krueger, F., Parasuraman, R.: Almost human: anthropomorphism increases trust resilience in cognitive agents. J. Exp. Psychol. Appl. **22** (2016). https://doi.org/10.1037/xap0000092
17. Janson, A.: How to leverage anthropomorphism for chatbot service interfaces: the interplay of communication style and personification. Comput. Hum. Behav. **149**, 107954 (2023). https://doi.org/10.1016/j.chb.2023.107954
18. Fadhil, A., Schiavo, G., Wang, Y., Yilma, B.A.: The Effect of emojis when interacting with conversational interface assisted health coaching system. In: Proceedings of the 12th EAI International Conference on Pervasive Computing Technologies for Healthcare, pp. 378–383. Association for Computing Machinery, New York (2018). https://doi.org/10.1145/3240925.3240965
19. Jörke, M., Sapkota, S., Warkenthien, L., Vainio, N., Schmiedmayer, P., Brunskill, E., Landay, J.: Supporting Physical Activity Behavior Change with LLM-Based Conversational Agents, http://arxiv.org/abs/2405.06061 (2024). https://doi.org/10.48550/arXiv.2405.06061
20. Ryan, K., Dockray, S., Linehan, C.: Understanding how eHealth coaches tailor support for weight loss: towards the design of Person-centered coaching systems. In: CHI Conference on Human Factors in Computing Systems, pp. 1–16. ACM, New Orleans, LA (2022). https://doi.org/10.1145/3491102.3501864
21. Feine, J., Gnewuch, U., Morana, S., Maedche, A.: A taxonomy of social cues for conversational agents. Int. J. Human-Comput. Stud. **132**, 138–161 (2019). https://doi.org/10.1016/j.ijhcs.2019.07.009
22. Peffers, K., Tuunanen, T., Rothenberger, M., Chatterjee, S.: A design science research methodology for information systems research. J. Manag. Inf. Syst. **24**, 45–77 (2007)
23. Epley, N., Waytz, A., Cacioppo, J.T.: On seeing human: a three-factor theory of anthropomorphism. Psychol. Rev. **114**, 864–886 (2007). https://doi.org/10.1037/0033-295X.114.4.864
24. Fink, J.: Anthropomorphism and human likeness in the design of robots and human-robot interaction. In: Ge, S.S., Khatib, O., Cabibihan, J.-J., Simmons, R., Williams, M.-A. (eds.) Social Robotics, pp. 199–208. Springer, Berlin, Heidelberg (2012). https://doi.org/10.1007/978-3-642-34103-8_20
25. Nass, C., Moon, Y.: Machines and mindlessness: social responses to computers. J. Soc. Issues. **56**, 81–103 (2000). https://doi.org/10.1111/0022-4537.00153

26. Lee, S.-L., Lau, I., Kiesler, S., Chiu, C.Y.: Human Mental Models of Humanoid Robots. (2005). https://doi.org/10.1109/ROBOT.2005.1570532
27. Stein, J.-P., MacDorman, K.F.: After confronting one uncanny valley, another awaits. Nat. Rev. Electr. Eng. **1**, 276–277 (2024). https://doi.org/10.1038/s44287-024-00041-w
28. Söllner, M., Hoffmann, A., Hoffmann, H., Wacker, A., Leimeister, J.M.: Understanding the formation of trust in IT artifacts. In: International Conference on Information Systems (ICIS) 2012, Orlando, FL (2012)
29. Söllner, M., Hoffmann, A., Leimeister, J.M.: Why different trust relationships matter for information systems users. Eur. J. Inf. Syst. **25**, 274–287 (2016). https://doi.org/10.1057/ejis.2015.17
30. Thiebes, S., Lins, S., Sunyaev, A.: Trustworthy artificial intelligence. Electron Markets. **31**, 447–464 (2021). https://doi.org/10.1007/s12525-020-00441-4
31. Mcknight, D.H., Carter, M., Thatcher, J.B., Clay, P.F.: Trust in a specific technology: an investigation of its components and measures. ACM Trans. Manag. Inf. Syst. **2**, 1–25 (2011). https://doi.org/10.1145/1985347.1985353
32. Söllner, M., Pavlou, P.A., Leimeister, J.M.: Understanding Trust in IT Artifacts – A New Conceptual Approach, https://papers.ssrn.com/abstract=2475382 (2013). https://doi.org/10.2139/ssrn.2475382
33. Thatcher, J.B., McKnight, D.H., Baker, E.W., Arsal, R.E., Roberts, N.H.: The role of trust in Postadoption IT exploration: an empirical examination of knowledge management systems. IEEE Trans. Eng. Manag. **58**, 56–70 (2011). https://doi.org/10.1109/TEM.2009.2028320
34. Mayer, R.C., Davis, J.H., Schoorman, F.D.: An integrative model of organizational trust. Acad. Manag. Rev. **20**, 709–734 (1995). https://doi.org/10.2307/258792
35. Rousseau, D., Sitkin, S., Burt, R., Camerer, C.: Not so different after all: a cross-discipline view of trust. Acad. Manag. Rev. **23** (1998). https://doi.org/10.5465/AMR.1998.926617
36. Lee, J.D., See, K.A.: Trust in Automation: designing for appropriate reliance. Hum. Factors. (2004)
37. Hoffmann, H., Söllner, M.: Incorporating behavioral trust theory into system development for ubiquitous applications. Pers. Ubiquit. Comput. **18**, 117–128 (2014). https://doi.org/10.1007/s00779-012-0631-1
38. Rheu, M., Shin, J.Y., Peng, W., Huh-Yoo, J.: Systematic review: trust-building factors and implications for conversational agent design. Int. J. Human-Comp. Interact. **37**, 1–16 (2020). https://doi.org/10.1080/10447318.2020.1807710
39. Gregor, S., Chandra Kruse, L., Seidel, S.: The anatomy of a design principle. J. Assoc. Inf. Syst. **21**, 1622–1652 (2020). https://doi.org/10.17705/1jais.00649
40. Moon, Y.: Intimate exchanges: using computers to elicit self-disclosure from consumers. J. Consum. Res. **26**, 323–339 (2000). https://doi.org/10.1086/209566
41. Lee, Y.-C., Yamashita, N., Huang, Y., Fu, W.: "I Hear You, I Feel You": encouraging deep self-disclosure through a Chatbot. In: Proceedings of the 2020 CHI Conference on Human Factors in Computing Systems, pp. 1–12. Association for Computing Machinery, New York (2020). https://doi.org/10.1145/3313831.3376175
42. Michie, S., Richardson, M., Johnston, M., Abraham, C., Francis, J., Hardeman, W., Eccles, M., Cane, J., Wood, C.: The behavior change technique taxonomy (v1) of 93 hierarchically clustered techniques: building an international consensus for the reporting of behavior change interventions. Ann. Behav. Med. Publ. Soc. Behav. Med. **46** (2013). https://doi.org/10.1007/s12160-013-9486-6
43. Aguinis, H., Bradley, K.J.: Best practice recommendations for designing and implementing experimental vignette methodology studies. Organ. Res. Methods. **17**, 351–371 (2014). https://doi.org/10.1177/1094428114547952

44. Wu, D., Lowry, P.B., Zhang, D., Tao, Y.: Patient Trust in Physicians Matters—Understanding the role of a Mobile patient education system and patient-physician communication in improving patient adherence behavior: field study. J. Med. Internet Res. **24**, e42941 (2022). https://doi.org/10.2196/42941
45. Venable, J., Pries-Heje, J., Baskerville, R.: FEDS: a framework for evaluation in design science research. Eur. J. Inf. Syst. **25**, 77–89 (2016). https://doi.org/10.1057/ejis.2014.36
46. Palan, S., Schitter, C.: Prolific.ac—a subject pool for online experiments. J. Behav. Experi. Finan. **17**, 22–27 (2018). https://doi.org/10.1016/j.jbef.2017.12.004
47. Lowry, P.B., D'Arcy, J., Hammer, B., Moody, G.D.: "Cargo cult" science in traditional organization and information systems survey research: a case for using nontraditional methods of data collection, including mechanical Turk and online panels. J. Strateg. Inf. Syst. **25**, 232–240 (2016). https://doi.org/10.1016/j.jsis.2016.06.002
48. Seymour, M., Yuan, L., Dennis, A.R., Riemer, K.: Have we crossed the uncanny valley? understanding affinity, trustworthiness, and preference for realistic digital humans in immersive environments. JAIS. **22**, 591–617 (2021). https://doi.org/10.17705/1jais.00674
49. Chua, A.Y.K., Pal, A., Banerjee, S.: AI-enabled investment advice: will users buy it? Comput. Hum. Behav. **138**, 107481 (2023). https://doi.org/10.1016/j.chb.2022.107481
50. Gursoy, D., Chi, O.H., Lu, L., Nunkoo, R.: Consumers acceptance of artificially intelligent (AI) device use in service delivery. Int. J. Inf. Manag. **49**, 157–169 (2019). https://doi.org/10.1016/j.ijinfomgt.2019.03.008
51. Gefen, D.: Customer loyalty in E-commerce. J. Assoc. Inf. Syst. **3** (2002). https://doi.org/10.17705/1jais.00022
52. Chin, W.W.: The partial least squares approach to structural equation modeling. In: Marcoulides, G.A. (ed.) Modern Methods for Business Research. LEA, London (1998)
53. Wold, H.O.A.: Soft modeling: the basic design and some extensions. In: Jöreskog, K.G., Wold, H.O.A. (eds.) Systems Under Indirect Observation, pp. 1–54. North-Holland, Amsterdam (1982)
54. Richter, N.F., Schubring, S., Hauff, S., Ringle, C.M., Sarstedt, M.: When predictors of outcomes are necessary: guidelines for the combined use of PLS-SEM and NCA. IMDS. **120**, 2243–2267 (2020). https://doi.org/10.1108/IMDS-11-2019-0638
55. Hair, J., Hult, G.T.M., Ringle, C., Sarstedt, M.: A Primer on Partial Least Squares Structural Equation Modeling (PLS-SEM) (2022)
56. Ab Hamid, M.R., Sami, W., Mohmad Sidek, M.H.: Discriminant validity assessment: use of Fornell & Larcker criterion versus HTMT criterion. J. Phys. Conf. Ser. **890**, 012163 (2017). https://doi.org/10.1088/1742-6596/890/1/012163
57. Henseler, J., Ringle, C.M., Sinkovics, R.R.: The use of partial least squares path modeling in international marketing. In: Sinkovics, R., Ghauri, P. (eds.) New Challenges to International Marketing, pp. 277–319. Emerald Group Publishing Limited (2009). https://doi.org/10.1108/S1474-7979(2009)0000020014

Author Index

A

Abbasi, Ahmed   I-83
Aguilar, Javier   I-265
Ahlemann, Frederik   I-281, II-256
Aldenhoff, Timon T.   I-178, II-3
Arz von Straussenburg, Arnold F.   I-178, II-3
Assumpta-Komugabe, Maria   I-137

B

Biller, Martin   II-80
Bittner, Eva   II-241
Bode, Alexander   II-241
Borchers, Marten   II-241
Böttcher, Timo Phillip   II-80, II-178, II-271
Brée, Tim   II-256
Bretschneider, Ulrich   II-21
Burcheri, Lorenzo Matthias   II-286
Buyssens, Hanna   I-3, I-32

C

Chatterjee, Samir   I-137, I-265
Crusius, Katja   I-137

D

Dawson, Juanita   II-97
Dickhaut, Ernestine   II-223

F

Fielt, Erwin   II-178
Fischer, Raphael   II-65
Fridgen, Gilbert   II-286

G

Gau, Michael   I-18, I-99
Gebhardt, Leonhard   II-115
Göbel, Hannes   I-248
Gordetzki, Philipp   I-151
Greiner, Maximilian   II-193
Gunasekara, Sachini   II-36

H

Haj-Bolouri, Amir   I-32
Hein, Andreas   II-80
Herrera, Paniz   I-137
Hevner, Alan   I-164
Hönemann, Kay   II-131

J

Janiesch, Christian   II-50, II-65
Janson, Andreas   I-296

K

Kamlage, Jan-Hendrik   II-256
Karger, Erik   I-281, II-256
Karimov, Ayaz   II-36
Khosrawi-Rad, Bijan   I-57, I-116
Kipping, Gregor   I-99
Konopka, Björn   II-131
Korn, Falco   I-281
Kowalkiewicz, Marek   II-178
Kratz, Marc E.   I-68
Krcmar, Helmut   II-80, II-178, II-271
Kretzer, Felix   I-18
Kroop, Sylvana   I-199
Krüger, Kim   II-271
Krumme, Klaus   II-256
Kudlek, Cecilie   I-232
Kumari, Jyoti   II-286
Kutby, Zelal   I-265

L

Lalor, John P.   I-83
Lange, Tim Christopher   I-216
Lechner, Ulrike   II-193
Li, Mahei Manhai   II-21
Li, Wenxuan   II-271
Lohmar, Fabian   II-256

M

Ma, Tengteng I-164
Maedche, Alexander I-18
Magdych, Valeria II-241
Magnusson, Johan II-146
Marxen, Hanna II-286
Mauer, René II-208
Meywirth, Sophia I-296
Miari, Tahereh I-265
Milutzki, Enrico II-241

N

Nadj, Mario II-50
Neis, Nicolas I-232
Nielsen, Ann-Dorte F. II-162
Nilsson, Andreas II-146

O

Oeste-Reiß, Sarah II-21

P

Päivärinta, Tero II-146
Poitz, Katharina II-65
Prat, Nicolas I-83
Pries-Heje, Jan II-162

R

Reiners, Sebastian I-99
Reinhard, Philipp II-21
Remke, Konstantin II-115
Ren, Yanjing I-164
Riehle, Dennis M. I-178, II-3
Robra-Bissantz, Susanne I-57
Rogall, Marius II-256

S

Saarela, Mirka II-36
Scheiber, Christoph II-178
Schkolski, Alexander I-281
Schlimbach, Ricarda I-216
Seckler, Christoph I-68, II-208
Semmann, Martin II-241
Shivendu, Shivendu I-164
Sjöström, Jonas I-248
Söllner, Matthias I-296, II-223
Speckmann, Pauline II-50
Spleth, Philipp I-232
Straub, Lisa II-193
Strohmann, Timo I-57, I-116

T

Tingelhoff, Fabian I-99

U

Uwaoma, Chinazunwa II-97

V

van der Staay, Alexander II-65
Vandaele, Joachim II-208
Viaene, Stijn I-3, I-32
vom Brocke, Jan I-18, I-57, I-68

W

Weber, Michael II-80, II-178
Wiesche, Manuel II-131
Winkelmann, Axel I-232, II-193
Wischnewski, Magdalena II-65
Wolters, Anna II-3

Z

Zahn, Eva-Maria II-223
Zarnekow, Rüdiger I-232
Zeiß, Christian II-193

The manufacturer's authorised representative in the EU is Springer Nature Customer Service Centre GmbH, Europaplatz 3, 69115 Heidelberg, Germany. If you have any concerns regarding our products, please contact ProductSafety@springernature.com

Printed and bound by CPI Group (UK) Ltd, Croydon, CR0 4YY
26/03/2026
02078961-0002